People in Organizations

PEOPLE IN ORGANIZATIONS

Norman Smith
Hilary Vigor

General Editors
John Eve
North Staffordshire Polytechnic
Allister Langlois
Guernsey College of Further Education

Oxford University Press 1991

Oxford University Press,
Walton Street, Oxford OX2 6DP

Oxford New York Toronto
Delhi Bombay Calcutta Madras Karachi
Petaling Jaya Singapore Hong Kong Tokyo
Nairobi Dar es Salaam Cape Town
Melbourne Auckland

and associated companies in
Berlin Ibadan

ISBN 0 19 832752 8

Typeset by Times Graphics, Singapore
Printed in Great Britain by Butler & Tanner Ltd., Frome

Contents

Acknowledgements

The authors and publishers would like to thank the following for permission to reproduce copyright material:

C K Brunstrom of PE-International for his article "Why it pays to make the customer king"; Clive Memmott, Ken Beardsell and ICI for the extract "Research programme and the new British Standard" from "The Hidden Giant" in *Plastics Today*, No. 23. The cartoon on page 233 is reproduced by permission of *Punch*.

Every effort has been made to contact copyright holders. If any omissions are notified, the publishers will be pleased to make proper acknowledgement in subsequent printings.

Coverage of General Objectives and Indicative Content of BTEC Unit

A Understand the principle features of organizational structures and operations and how these affect the communication system in an organization.

Large and small organization in the public and private sectors.	Block 1
Information resources.	Block 4
Information Storage. Manual and electronic.	Block 2,4,5,6,7,8
Levels of authority and responsibility.	Block 2,4,8
Functional areas of sample organizations.	Block 1,9
Relationship between organizational structure and communication system.	Block 1,2,3,4,5
Physical and psychological barriers to communication within the organization.	Block 3,4,8
Organization factors facilitating or inhibiting change.	Block 1,2,3,4,8
Support systems. Administration, technical and clerical.	Block 2,4,6,9

B Give and exchange information.

Oral and written information, personal exchanges, telephone techniques.	Block 1,2,3,5,6,7,8,9
Types and format of main business documents.	Block 1,2,5,6,7,8,9
Understanding information systems and information flows.	Block 1,2,3,4,5,6,7,8,9
Internal communication systems – memos notices, personal exchanges.	Block 1,2,3,5,7,8
Information co-ordination and control of organizations.	Block 1,2,3,6,9
External communications, letter, telephone, telex.	Block 1,4,5,7
Interpretation of statistical, financial and graphical information.	Block 2,5,6,8,9

C Examine information systems and their impact on an organization's operations in terms of the end use of a range of formats for information handling.

Relevance of format to content purpose and intended recipient.	Block 1,2,3,4,5,7,8,9
Design structure and use of appropriate formats for a variety of uses – invoices, records, applications etc.	Block 2
Grammatical conventions, sentence structure, layout of formal communications.	Block 2,5,7
Reports for specific purposes.	Block 2,7,8,9

D Assess the uses of Electronic Technology as a means of communication.

Main commercial applications for routine D.P.	Block 4
Methods of data storage and retrieval.	Block 4
Application of basic W.P. and accounting packages.	Block 4,9
Economic and personal problems associated with the introduction of electronic technology.	Block 4
Impact of computers on the nature and method of information storage and retrieval.	Block 4,8

E Present and disseminate information using appropriate means.

Use of basic documentation systems and procedures.	Block 2,6,7,9
Application of business equipment associated with sales, purchasing, transmission and reprography.	Block 4
Diagrammatic representation of business information.	Block 2,4
Presentation of organization charts and communication systems in diagrammatic form.	Block 1,2,6,9
Verbal and visual presentation of information.	Block 1,2,3,5,7,9

F Appreciate the importance of personal relationships and the social environment.

Verbal and non-verbal communication.	Block 3,8
Social skills in work content.	Block 3,8
Interviewing and counselling skills.	Block 3,8
Adapting messages to the need of the recipient.	Block 2,3,8
Factors that influence the process and effectiveness of groups.	Block 3,8
Effective presentation of ideas.	Block 3,5,8

G Recognize factors which contribute to efficient working within an organization, and ways in which this can be assessed and influenced.

Selection interviewing techniques, both as interviewee and interviewer.	Block 8
Identification of levels of authority and authority.	Block 1,3
Management style in different situations.	Block 1,3,8
Ways of assessing efficiency in organizations e.g. work study, appraisal techniques etc.	Block 3,8
Formulation of persuasive and rational arguments, taking into account needs and attitudes of others.	Block 3,7
Preparation and structure of presentation or response.	
Evaluation of conclusions drawn from information e.g. false argument etc.	

H Assess relationship between the working environment and the employees performance.

Comparison of different office/workplace layouts and their effect on employee satisfaction.	Block 6,8
Organization of work.	Block 8
Organization and Methods.	Block 6
Job Design.	Block 8
Job Enrichment and Job Satisfaction.	Block 8
Health and Safety at Work.	Block 8

I Identify the constraints and opportunities of group working, sources of conflict and methods of conflict management.

Participation in decision making.	Block 7,8
Group processes, norms, roles.	Block 3
Sources of conflict within and between groups.	Block 3,8
Relation between motivation (intrinsic/extrinsic) and effective performance.	Block 3
Effect of social and work organizations on the individual attitude to work and colleagues.	Block 3

J Analyse changes which affect the work of individuals and groups within organizations.

Skills and attitudes associated with new working methods.	Block 4
Patterns of employment.	
Changing legislation.	

Introduction

Approach and method

It is important to study this introduction before making use of the book

This book has been written with several kinds of student in mind: those doing the BTEC National Awards, others who aim at a supervisory qualification, and yet others interested in the Institute of Management at a more advanced level – anyone in fact who needs to understand how to manage, motivate and reward people working in business organizations.

The book is divided into nine blocks. Each block takes an area of activity or a section of an organization, such as personnel or finance, and looks at how an organization and its employees are affected by the work of that section.

You need not necessarily follow our sequence of presentation; each block stands alone. The activities provided are various. Some are designed to explore a subject and others to test how well you can apply what you learn. Others are revision exercises that will take you back to topics already studied. A case study based on a manufacturing company, Extruded Plastic Tube Ltd, runs throughout the book. At the end of the course you can use 'The country club' as an extended revision exercise.

Be skilful

Following the various activities will help you to stand in the shoes of the people who make up an organization and to develop skills in communicating at all levels, seeing what makes an organization tick, foreseeing difficulties, collecting information and solving problems.

People are the most interesting, as well as the most maddening, part of our lives. If you can handle them successfully, both you and your organization will be well rewarded. This book will help you to do it.

Block 1
Organization Structure

Introduction

This block introduces the basic principles of organization structure design and considers the way the behaviour of the individual is modified and controlled by both formal and informal groupings. The conflicts that can arise from having membership in more than one group are explored.

Many forms of human activity are essential to maintain the fabric of society, eg to provide necessary goods and services, entertainment and relaxation. These activities involve a number of people co-operating in an organized group to achieve objectives which can range from running a cake stall at the local garden fête to governing the country. The way in which a project is organized will depend upon its aim, the number of people involved and the skills they require.

What makes the organization work?

Rules and guidelines have to be laid down for every organization, but they should be seen as 'tools' used by people. It is people within an organization who must co-operate in a predetermined way, which allows the objectives to be achieved. People design the systems used. Organizations work when the right balance between systems and people is achieved.
For example, a football team taking the field with each player unaware of the position he was expected to play would not stand a chance against an organized team. Passengers in an aircraft would be rightly concerned if they overheard the crew arguing about whose turn it was to be the pilot for the trip. A well-designed structure is one in which each employee knows what their job entails, its relationship to other jobs and its contribution to the overall objective.

Activity 1

Split into small groups of three of four and divide the tasks involved in planning a surprise party for a friend based on a buffet meal and a disco. Decide how you will make the arrangements that you are responsible for, so that the whole party is a success.

Constructing the organization

Organizations are structured around various levels of authority and management, each having different defined responsibilities. At each level, activities are divided into the different areas of specialization which have to be co-ordinated.
Co-ordination is achieved by applying rules and procedures which determine what each person is authorized to do.

What is an organization structure?

Reading a dozen books on this subject will give you as many definitions of organization structure. For the purpose of this book, which is concerned with looking at people in organizations, the following will serve:

> 'The structure of an organization provides a framework within which individuals can carry out specified duties and a means of implementing administrative procedures'.

For example, every student attending college becomes part of an organization. Timetables, informing them of the time and place for each lecture or workshop activity, place constraints on students and lecturers, requiring them to be in the right place at the right time.

Timetables allow the resources of manpower, rooms and equipment to be used in the most efficient way. The organization then stands a better chance of achieving its objective – the best education of its students.

In principle, this is similar to a business organizing its resources to meet the requirements of its customers.

Structure design

It is what the organization does that determines the way in which the structure develops. What the organization does is subject to change in terms of product demand or technology. Structures which fail to change when required become inefficient.

Many organizations use the so-called **classical structure** as it seems to serve them well. There are a number of variations on this, all of which are governed by the following principles:

1 *Division of labour* This arises from the need to subdivide the activities involved in running an enterprise. The subdivision is decided by the policy-makers in the organization, but is usually based on the categories of personnel, production, administration and finance.

2 *Specialization* This is open to criticism, because it tends to produce a rigid structure. However, it is widely used to subdivide the organization into specialist areas such as accounting and production.

Over-specialization can lead to:
The restriction of inventiveness and initiative
repetitive and boring routine work
departmental loyalty at the expense of organizational objectives

3 *Departmentalization* This is caused by the division of labour. Specialists are grouped into departments with defined responsibilities within the policy of the enterprise. Departments may have rigid or open terms of reference.

4 *Span of control* This is defined by the number of junior managers directly reporting to a senior. A number of factors determine the span of control applied to individual structures:

simplicity or complexity of the tasks undertaken
distribution of the labour force
technology used

Within the constraints imposed, structure design should avoid the two extremes of structures that are too wide or too narrow.

Wide structures These tend to create a span of control where managers have too many junior managers reporting to them. Many writers on organization

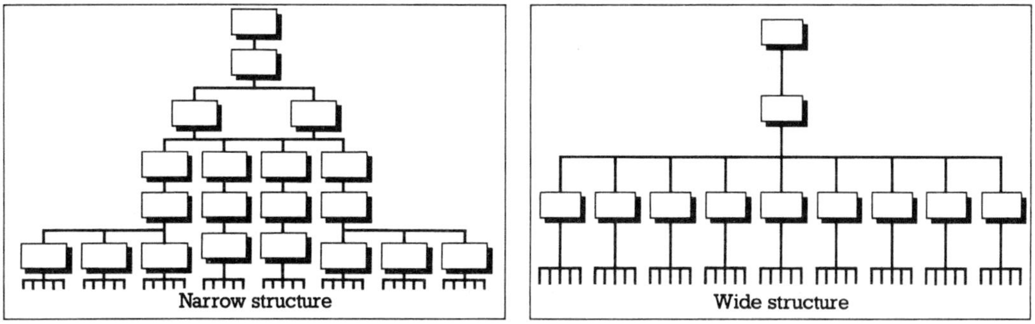

Span of control and structure design.

design share the view that a maximum of five juniors concentrating on different aspects of management specialization should report to any one senior. In practice, this is not always possible.

Narrow structures These create a tall structure with extended lines of communication, making the transfer of information up, down and across the structure more difficult.

Activity 2

Design an organization structure suitable for a charter airline having six twin-engined aircraft, each seating twenty passengers, crewed by a captain and a co-pilot. The airline specializes in short-haul flights. No in-flight service is required, therefore no cabin staff are needed. The division of labour is as follows:

Flight planning and scheduling	Advertising and selling charter flights
Aircraft maintenance	Provision of goods and services
Cleaning and servicing the aircraft	General administration

Keep the span of control within reasonable limits and the lines of communication as short as possible.

5 *Levels of responsibility and authority* Classical structures are subdivided down the structure into roughly three strata of management:

Senior management – responsible for formulation of policy and long-term planning
Middle management – responsible for carrying out the policy formulated by senior management and usually heading up a department
Supervision – responsible for dealing with the day-to-day problems in manpower, machines and materials.

6 *Unity of command* Where possible, a subordinate should receive direct instructions from only one manager. Structures are communication systems. Instructions passed down to a subordinate from more than one source can lead to confusion and loss of control.

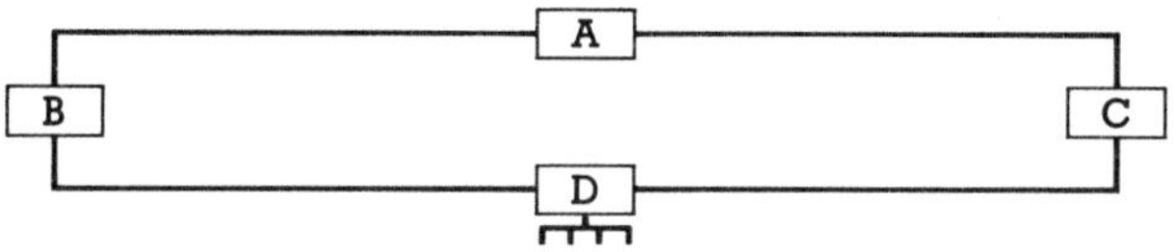

In the diagram above, the structure design has produced a situation where:

A is the senior manager with a span of control over B and C.
D is responsible to B and C, who can both give D orders.

This will give D a problem if B and C fail to co-ordinate their instructions.

7 *Lines of communication* These should be as short as is allowed by the constraints which influence the operation of the enterprise.

Extended lines of communication up, down and across the structure will increase the complexity and formalization of the communication system.

Information is the life-blood of the organization. However, its production, storage and retrieval incur a cost to the organization. And anything that increases the complexity of the communication system also increases the possibility of some mistake occurring within it.

Organizations are a system – a number of component parts (specializations) joined together in some organized pattern (structure) in order to meet given objectives. These parts can only operate in an organized and effective way as long as the communication system functions.

Activity 3

Write a description of the relationship between structure design and the communication system in a business organization.

8 *Co-ordination* Whatever titles are given to individual departments, they represent the specific functions which have to be undertaken if the organization is to achieve its objectives.

These functions have to be co-ordinated within the plan dictated by the policy for the enterprise. Problems would arise if departments were allowed to work in isolation without regard to the parts played by the rest of the structure.

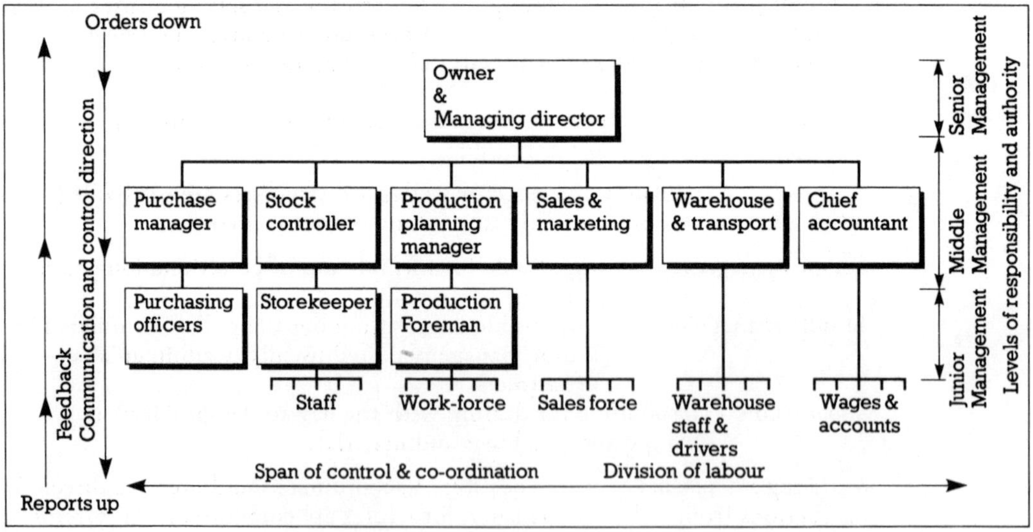

Classical organization structure.

Activity 4

Draw diagrams to show how the following types of organization could be structured:

1 A typing bureau with twenty employees.
2 A large store with several departments, each employing ten to fifteen sales staff.
3 A chain of eight snack-bars in the south of England, each with its own manager and up to thirty full- and part-time staff.

The following list illustrates the interrelationships which would exist between departments in a manufacturing enterprise. Many of the functions described would be equally applicable to other commercial or local government activities. The Civil Service, for example, has to purchase the raw materials for administration, hold stock, recruit and employ labour, and apply costing and budgetary control techniques.

You may find it useful to refer back to this section and use it as source material when you are attempting some of the activities in later blocks in this book.

The interrelationships between departments in a manufacturing firm.

Departmental Function	**Interrelationships**
Marketing function	**Related activities**
Establishes consumer demand for the product or service provided by the organization.	*Distribution* Provides distribution channels for the product. Packaging and shipping requirements.
Samples the potential market through market research, gathering information on a planned basis to allow statistical analysis for market forecasting.	*Research and development* Identification and development of markets for new products.
Defends the product or service by keeping a watching brief on consumer buying habits and the activities of competitors.	*Sales* Identification of markets which the sales force can exploit.
Examines the market for opportunities for expansion of the product range, or for increasing the sale of existing products.	*Production* Provision of an adequate work-load to utilize fully the resources of the production unit. Product policy and product mix.
Promotes the product in the market through advertising, mailshots and promotional activity, eg, competitions, free gifts and sports promotion. Provides promotional display material for retail outlets.	*Finance* Provision of market intelligence for determination of pricing policy.
	Administration Arrangement of export and import procedures and documentation when the company markets abroad.
Sales function	**Related activities**
May be a separate function or part of the marketing function.	*Production* Sales department liaises between the customer and production on matters related to delivery dates, quality standards and viable production quantities.
Deals directly with the company's customer or consumer outlets. Contacts are obtained and maintained by the sales force.	
Obtains orders and negotiates contracts for the provision of goods or services – including discounts, delivery and price – within the company's sales policy.	*Marketing* Market intelligence related to consumer demand and the activities of competition are an aid to production planning.

When the product or service is of a technical nature, the sales force will provide technical advice to the customer. Sales people will be specialists and may need to be highly qualified.	*Finance* Information concerning orders received from customers enables the customers' accounts to be updated.
Provides market intelligence through its contacts with customers. This feedback of of information is an important part of the salesperson's function.	*Quality control* Contractual negotiations related to the customers' quality specifications.
The sales office provides an administrative back-up for the sales force and is a point of contact for customers.	
Provides brochures, price-lists and promotional material for customers.	

Purchasing function	**Related activities**
The purchase of raw materials, components and consumable stores, required for production purposes or for the maintenance of plant, equipment or building fabric.	*Production* Provision of materials to the required specifications. Enables the production unit to produce within the anticipated scrap rates and reduce production costs.
Obtaining quotations from suppliers authorized to supply under the company's purchasing policy. Placing orders on the basis of negotiated contracts with suppliers. Seeking to obtain the most favourable discounts and credit terms.	*Stock control* Ensures the maintenance of adequate stocks to meet production demand by reordering when requested to do so and ensuring that delivery promises are met.
Carrying out purchasing research related to new materials and products, movement in market prices and to advantages of bulk buying specific materials.	*Warehouse* Informs the warehouse of incoming material and the delivery date. Storage space can then be made available. This information is vital if the material requires special storage conditions.
Progressing orders placed by the purchasing department in order to maintain delivery promises made by the supplier. Keeping and updating supplier reliability ratings.	*Finance* Passes invoices to authorize payment for goods received when the supplier sends in the account.
The sale and disposal of scrap materials and redundant plant or equipment.	
Maintaining a reference library of price-lists, catalogues and specifications.	

Research, Development, Design function	**Related activities**
Research into new materials and processes related to the company's markets and products.	*Production* Improving production methods and processes. Designing products with standardized components that are easy to manufacture.

Development of new production methods and technology to improve output or reduce production costs.	*Quality* Quality standards and material specification are set by the designer.
Developing new outlets for existing products and services.	*Marketing*
Liaison with customers to advise on matters related to the end use of the product, or the introduction of a new technology.	Developing of marketing ideas and/or providing new products to be marketed. Provision of technical service in the promotion of a new product.
Examining ways in which the company could diversify into new products or markets closely related to existing markets.	*Sales* Improving and providing new products for the sales department to enable them to meet and beat competition.
Design and redesign of the product to meet market requirements and the threat of competition. Product design covers these areas: 1 Appearance 2 Cost 3 Durability 4 Reliability All of these factors are related to the end use of the product.	*Engineering* Installation and trials of new production methods, or modification of existing production methods.

Production function	**Related activities**
Co-ordinates the activities of manpower, machines and materials to achieve the desired output at minimum cost.	*Stock control* Provides raw materials in the right quantity and at the right time to meet production schedules.
Translates customer orders into detailed instructions for work to be carried out. These instructions will include quantity to be produced, quality standards to be met and materials to be used.	*Quality control* Ensures that the materials used are of the required specification. Checks the quality of the production output and warns when the product is going outside specified limits.
Schedules the incoming orders into the existing work-load and establishes the order of priority of each order.	*Production planning* Work flow and working methods based on the application of work study techniques. Design and provision of equipment needed for production.
Maintains the flow of production and prevents bottle-necks by progressing the work in progress.	*Engineering* Responsible for machine setting and maintenance.
Reschedules orders if necessary to meet a change in sales policy.	
Plans tool changes and tool setting as required by the production plan.	*Warehouse* Provision of storage for raw materials. Delivery of raw material to the production unit. Provision of storage space for the finished product.
Works within the standards and limits laid down by quality control.	*Purchasing* Buying materials and components suitable for production methods.
	Personnel Recruitment and training of suitable labour force.

Quality Control function	**Related activities**
Works within the quality control policy of the company in relation to its market and the end use of the product.	*Production* Provides a quality check and early warning when something is about to go outside the set standards.
Tests and checks incoming materials and components against specifications laid down in purchasing contracts.	*Purchasing* Ensures that incoming materials are of the standards set by the purchasing specification.
Provides the gauges and testing equipment necessary to check production standards.	*Stock control* Informs stock control when the material delivered has passed inspection and may be included in the stock control records.
Provides inspection staff to examine the product at specified intervals.	*Engineering* When production is in danger of going outside the specified limits, makes request to the engineering department to alter the machine setting.
Warns the production unit when the product is in danger of going outside the limits laid down.	*Sales* Ensures that the customer's specification is met, in order to encourage the customer to reorder.
Rejects products which do not conform to the required standards.	*Design* Puts the specifications laid down by the design department into effect.
Decides which rejected products might be reworked to pass inspection standards.	

Stores, Warehouse, Transport function	**Related activities**
Storage and safe-keeping of goods and raw materials delivered to the company by its suppliers.	*Purchasing* Receiving and checking the goods ordered. Informing the purchasing department that the order has been received and checked.
Checking the quantity of incoming goods against the delivery note from the supplier and notifying the purchasing department of any discrepancies.	*Production* Providing a buffer between incoming materials and the production unit. Providing internal transport. Providing storage space for the finished product.
Issuing raw materials as requested by the production unit for the completion of a specific order.	
Issuing consumable goods and materials necessary for production, maintenance and administration of the company.	*Stock control* Providing stores for materials and components. Providing storekeeping staff to issue, safeguard and record stock movement.
Providing internal transport as required by the production unit for the manufacture of the product.	*Finance* Issue of payments for the external transport contracted by the transport unit. Payment of rental for company cars hired for the sales team.
Providing the external transport required for delivering the product to the customer.	

Providing and maintaining the company fleet of cars for sales staff and other employees.

Sales
Undertaking delivery of goods to customers within the contracted delivery date.

Administration
Processing relevant transport documents required by law. Routing invoices and delivery notes to appropriate departments.

Finance function

Financial accounting – providing balance sheets, profit and loss accounts for management decision making.

Management accounting – costing and budgeting for control of expenditure on production procedures and processes.

Financial planning – expenditure on capital equipment and buildings.

Preparation of accounts to submit to customers for goods and services which the company has provided.

Wage/salary administration – calculating the amount to be paid, making statutory deductions, making up wage packets.

Preparation of data and statistics for management planning and decision making.

Formulating and administrating a system of budgetary control.

Maintaining control over the cash flow position by the application of credit and debt control.

Related activities

All other departments
Payment of wages and calculation of incentive payments. Preparation of departmental budgets.

Purchasing
Payment for goods and services ordered by the purchasing department.

Sales
Preparation of statements and invoices for goods and services supplied to customers. Receiving payment from suppliers and processing credit notes.

Administration
Payment of bills related to the running of the business; eg, rates, insurance, taxes. Banking procedures related to the financial aspects of the business.

Board of directors
Provision of data to assist the board in:
1 Corporate planning
2 Capital investment
3 Budgetary control

Personnel function

Provides a well-trained and motivated work-force able to make best use of the company's resources.

Produces written job specifications as a basis for recruitment and training of the labour force.

Recruits labour at the request of the department heads.

Devises and administrates a suitable training programme for the labour force.

Promotes safety and implements the legal requirements imposed by the Health and Safety at Work Act 1974.

Negotiates and implements a satisfactory wage/salary policy for the company.

Negotiates and enters into agreements with the relevant trades unions, concerning conditions of service and discipline.

Promotes joint consultation between the management and the work-force.

Related activities

All other departments
Provision of a manpower plan for the organization on which to base:
1 Training programmes
2 Educational courses
3 Safety training
4 Incentive schemes
5 Recruitment
6 Staff development
7 Redundancy
8 Industrial negotiations
9 Welfare and pension schemes

Putting the principles into practice

Case study

A skilled woodworker decides to go into business on his own, having identified a market for handmade furniture. He will have to organize everything as a one-man business on the following lines:

Buy wood, metal furnishing, adhesives, screws
Arrange storage for raw materials.
Plan the manner in which the furniture will be produced
Establish what market is available for the product
Make furniture to orders received
Arrange delivery to customer
Get payment for goods delivered
Arrange payment for goods purchased.

The organization structure would be very simple and could be represented as follows:

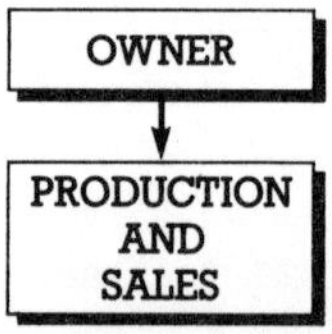

However, the activities that the sole owner of the business will become involved in are more complex than the simple structure indicates:

Purchasing – wood, screws, metal furnishings, etc
Stores – of the purchases made
Planning – production of orders
Sales – selling the product
Marketing – establishing customer demand
Transport – getting the product to customers
Accounts – getting payment for goods and paying for goods received.

Provided the market demand remains small, the sole owner may be able to deal with all these activities. If demand increases, he will not be able to cope and one or more of the activities will suffer as a result. Eventually, the owner will employ other people to **specialize** in certain activities. He will be dividing the running of the business into departments, each run by a specialist in one activity. It follows that as the business grows, so the organization structure changes. The **division of labour** can be represented in this way:

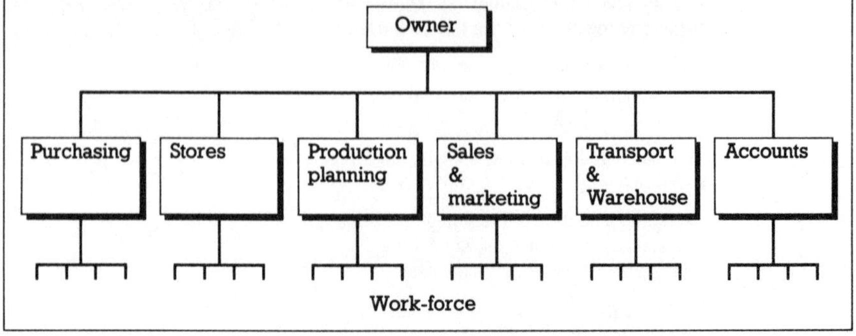

The role of the owner has now changed from manufacturing the product to supervising the work of the specialists. His main function is now to **co-ordinate** the activities of the six specialists in order to meet the demands of the customers. Structure design has given the owner a **span of control** of six, ie, he has six specialists in the management team who report directly to him. There are now two levels of **authority** and **responsibility** – the owner, who is senior manager and policy-maker, and the management team of specialists, who are each responsible for one function in the business.

Continued growth of the business would give one or more of the six specialists a work-load beyond the point where they could cope. Some of the work would in turn have to be delegated to subordinates and as a result the structure would develop along these lines:

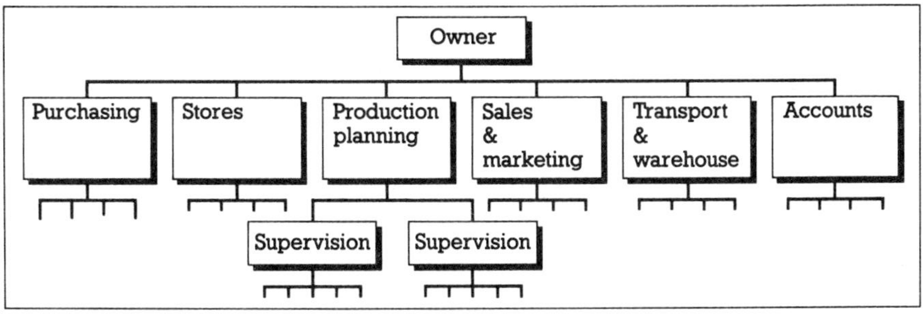

Three strata of management can now be identified in this organization structure:

Senior management (the owner)
Middle management (department specialists)
Junior management (supervisory grades).

The owner of the business is becoming further removed from the production function, but it is as essential now for him to know the current situation at all levels of the business as it was when he was the sole person in the business.

This makes clear the need for an efficient communication system for passing information up and down the structure.

There are many ways in which efficient communication can be achieved. They range from paperwork systems based on clerical procedures to integrated electronic technology combining computers and the communications industry.

What can go wrong with the system?

A communication system will only work well if the structure design facilitates the flow of information. Accurate information delivered to the wrong department will at best cause unjustified delay. In extreme cases, it could cause the business to fail.

Structure design and systems design are closely related. Good structure design can minimize the amount of information which has to be processed. This in turn reduces the cost of administration, which is an overhead cost to the business.

In common with other organizations, the furniture manufacturing company would have to communicate with the outside world (its environment) as well as conducting internal communications related to the running of the business. The external communications would be carried out by a number of different employees. To avoid mistakes, each employee must know what their role in the company requires of them. Good structure design aids the definition of individual roles.

Other types of organization structure

Structures tend to be designed to suit the objectives of the enterprise. There are no set standards which dictate the way in which organizations should be subdivided and titled.

Many activities are given different titles from organization to organization. For example, the activity which deals with the storing and provision of materials may be called **stock control** in one organization and **materials control** in another.

Titles are not important. What is vital is that the function of the department and its part in the following cycle of activity are clearly understood.

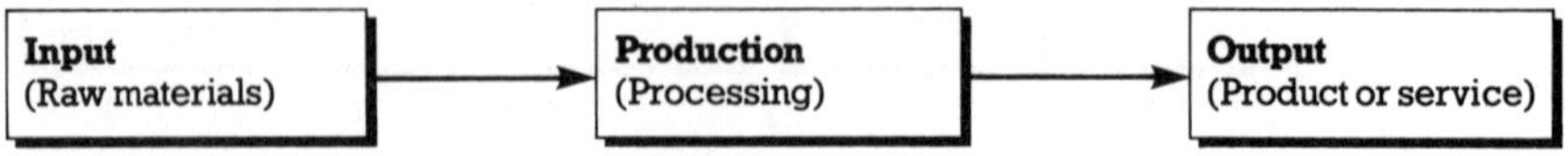

Examples of the model applied to various organizations.

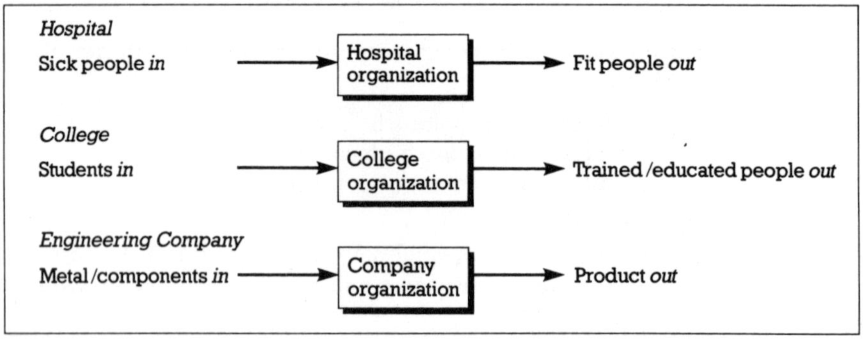

Activity 5

Design simple structures for the above examples. Show the subdivision of departments in each of the organizations and examine the way in which departmental titles are determined by what the organization does.

Line and staff structure

This type of structure arises with the increasing complexity of organization structures and the demand for specialization. It has its origins in the way in which the Army organizes its resources with line officers directing the activity of the troops and staff officers planning the battle and arranging the supplies. The difference between line and staff managers can be defined as follows:

Line manager – gives direct orders to subordinates and is accountable for the outcome of the actions taken as a result of those orders being carried out. Staff manager – provides advice or a service to other managers in the organization on the basis of some specialist knowledge or professional competence.

An individual manager may well have a line function in his own department and a staff function in relation to other managers, as shown in the diagrams below.

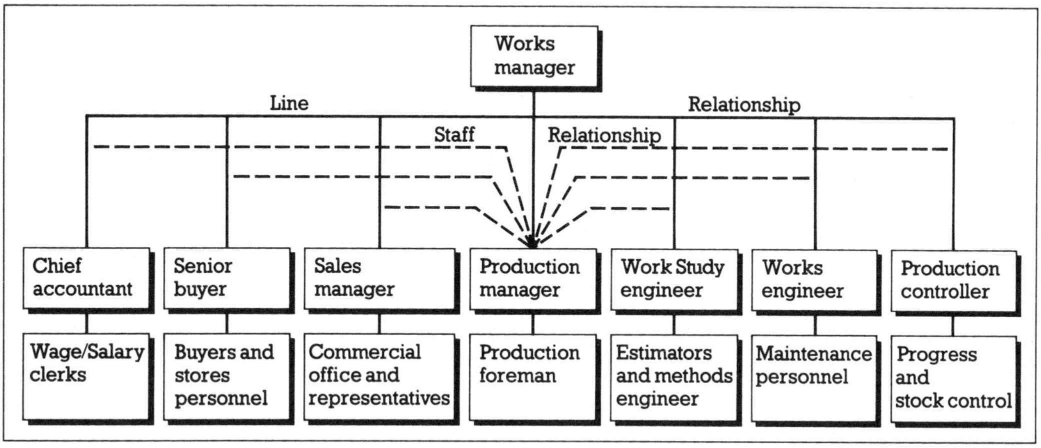

Line and staff structure in manufacturing company.

Staff managers should pass advice or instructions through the line manager to avoid the confusion of orders coming from two sources. Co-operation between line and staff managers is essential. It is usually achieved by a combination of formal meetings and informal compromise. However, human relation problems cannot be avoided in any system involving the co-operation of a number of people.

Activity 6

Examine the way in which your college is organized and draw up an organization chart which will identify:
a departmentalization
b levels of authority and responsibility
c line and staff management functions.

Patterns of behaviour related to line and staff organizations

With increased growth and complexity in the structure, defining the authority and responsibility of line and staff managers becomes more difficult. Some organizations feel that it is advisable to have 'grey areas' where authority is not clearly defined. This solution has the drawback of creating potential conflict within the management team.

Line managers sometimes think that staff managers take decisions based purely on specialist knowledge without proper consideration of the problems those decisions can cause. A work study specialist may propose a change of working methods to increase output. The line manager may see this as a potential source of industrial relations conflict. Conversely, staff managers get frustrated when their advice meets with opposition from line managers.

People do not always conform to the ideals behind the structure design. Individuals may indulge in internal politics and power struggles. This is the inevitable outcome of setting up a formal structure.

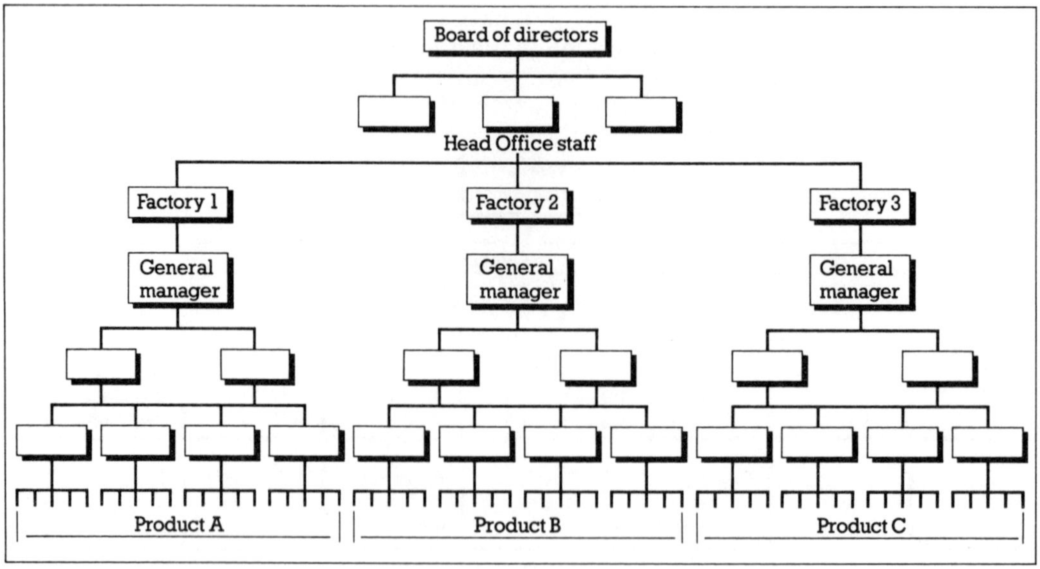

Organization structure – division of labour by product grouping.

Behaviour patterns related to product grouping

As organizations grow, they may reach a point where each product or service is capable of supporting a self-contained organization structure. When this stage is reached, it is an advantage to treat each product or service as a separate **entity** or **group**. The diagram above illustrates this.

The product grouping structure tends to develop strong group loyalty, which can minimize conflict between specializations. Competition develops between the groups, which can be beneficial or damaging, depending on how it is channelled. Job satisfaction can be attained by employees working in smaller groups within the organization, which provides opportunities for wider experience. See the diagram, 'Blankshire County Council'.

Activity 7

List the information you would expect to be able to gather from the examination of a company's organization structure.

Behaviour patterns related to matrix structures

Matrix structures were developed in the aerospace industry when it became desirable to arrange the utilization of resources in ways different from conventional structures.

Whilst traditional structures are based on divisions into specialities, the **matrix structure** is built around individual products or projects with team leaders co-ordinating the provision of resources from the various functions of the management team. Functional management remains, but has to change its directional role to provide services across the structure.

Employees working in the functional departments remain accountable to their functional manager, but they also report to the project team leaders. This runs counter to the principle of unity of command as each employee is accountable to more than one person. All members of the management team have to co-operate closely to make this system work.

Matrix is particularly suited to the long-term routine activities such as medical research or the production of consumer goods on a large scale within large organizations. Employees within matrix structures are usually project or producer orientated. Subordinates of the functional managers feel committed to the projects to which they are allocated. Executives co-ordinate their efforts to supply each project team with the support it requires. Any conflict within the management team can be arbitrated by a senior manager.

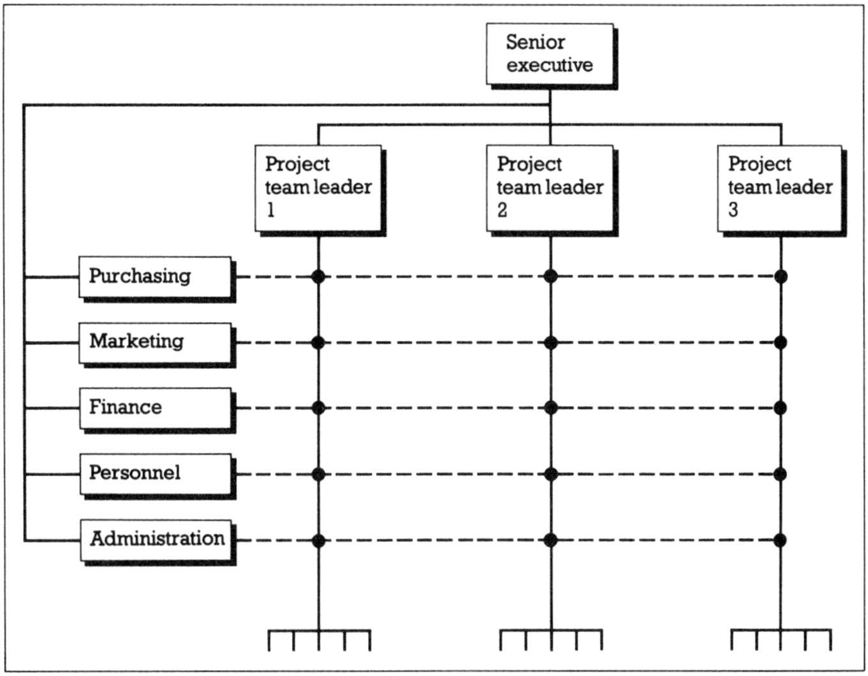

Matrix structure.

Those responsible for planning and control in an organization must have the authority which allows them to carry out their duties. **Authority** has been defined as the legitimate power which is delegated to an individual within the organization to give orders and expect to be obeyed.

The degree of authority given to an individual will stem from the task designated by their **job description**.

Referring once again to the classical structure as a model and expanding on the definitions, three distinct levels of authority can be identified.

Senior management – have the authority to determine policy and take the necessary decisions to implement policy without reference to higher authority.
Middle management – are given the authority to take decisions within the policy laid down by senior management and defined by the **division of labour** within the structure.
Supervision – are given authority to deal with day-to-day problems related to the resources of manpower, materials and machines; at this level decisions to take action outside defined tasks have to have the approval of the appropriate middle manager.

When an individual accepts a post within an organization, he or she also accepts the responsibility of ensuring that the tasks related to that post are

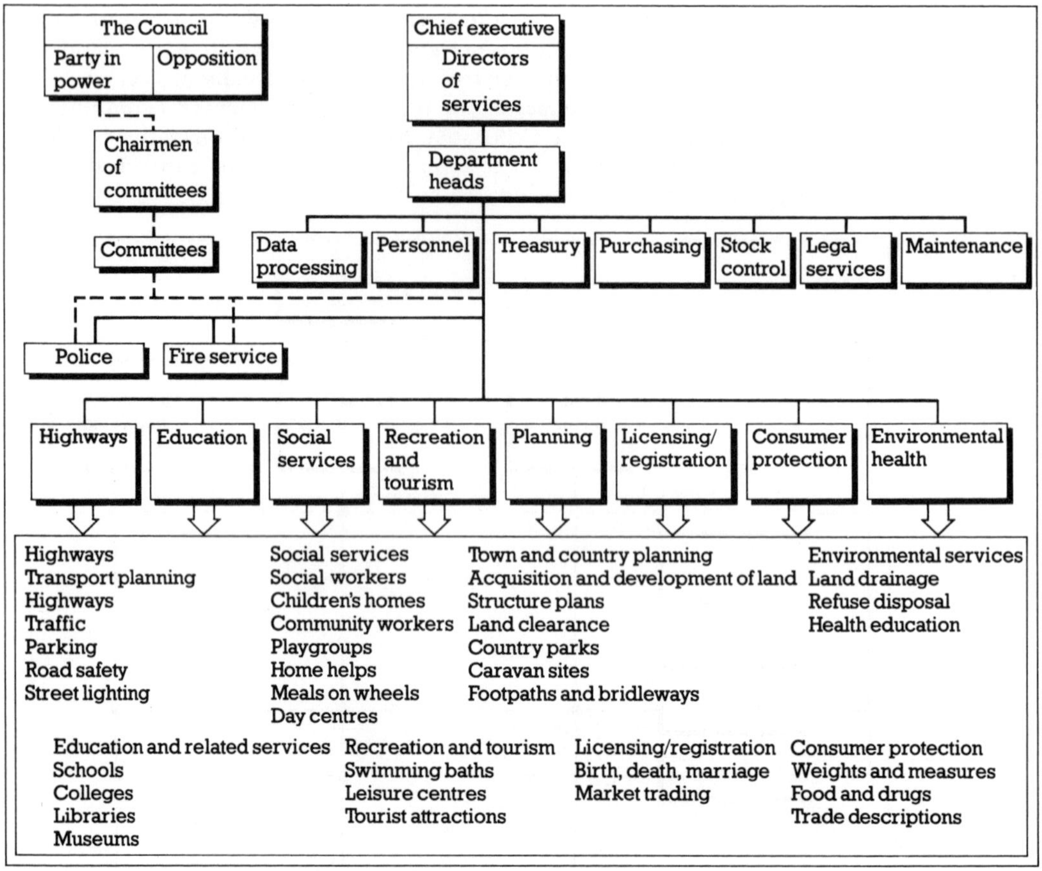

Blankshire County Council – A large organization structure.

carried out to the best of his or her ability. *All* employees take this responsibility on board – there are no exceptions. Taking the classical structure once again:

Senior management – are responsible to the owners of the business (eg, the shareholders) for the outcome of their decision making.
Middle management – have a responsibility to senior management for the implementation of policy within their department.
Supervision – are responsible to middle management for the day-to-day running of the department.

Responsibility is defined in the **job specification**, or subsequently given in the form of an instruction from a senior manager. In the latter case, the responsibility would be *delegated*, the senior manager giving a junior a task to perform and making the junior *accountable* for its completion to the senior. By delegating the task in this manner, a senior will not relinquish the ultimate responsibility he has for seeing that the task is done.

Activity 8

A middle manager is said to have responsibilities up, down and across the organization structure.

a Define these three dimensions of responsibility.
b State the problems which would arise if middle managers could delegate the responsibilities defined by their job description.

The function of authority and responsibility

Refer to the diagram 'The basic principles of structure design', which illustrates the organization structure and demonstrates the principle of **division of labour**. From this it can be seen that:

'ORGANIZATIONS ARE PEOPLE'

A complex structure of:

TASKS
Requiring SKILLS and KNOWLEDGE and carried out by EMPLOYEES

in order to meet
OBJECTIVES

If the organization is to meet its objectives, it is vital that each individual employee should know exactly what is required of them and the degree of authority they have to discharge the duties imposed by the task they are given.

The basic principles of structure design.

Division of Labour	– breaks the structure down into specializations at the administrative level and defines the job that each function must perform
	– breaks complicated tasks down into simplified jobs, some of which can be repetitive
This	
Determines the job	– its scope
	– the duties involved
and the	– responsibilities involved
	– limits of authority
Job description	– position in the organization
	– department or section
allowing the	
Analysis of the job	– breaking down the job into its component parts and the circumstances in which it is performed
	– deciding *how* the job is to be done
To determine	– skills and knowledge required and appropriate levels of authority and responsibility

(Factors taken into consideration will vary according to the level of the task in the organization structure.)

Organization structures – a case study

This section introduces a case study describing the manufacture of plastic tubing, a product widely used in the engineering industry.

The purpose of the case study is twofold:
1 to demonstrate the various principles and techniques encountered in the course work;
2 to provide a source of reference when you undertake the various activities in this book.

Information is provided about the product and the method of manufacture, the layout of the factory, the management team and the organization structure. You will be asked to carry out a few simple tasks to start with to give you the feel for using case study material. At a later stage, you will be given tasks which are related to the course work and asked to apply them to this particular organization. So, make yourself familiar with the company and its structure from the information given below.

Case studies are inevitably contrived, but they do provide the opportunity for you to use course material in a practical way. In this instance, a small- to medium-sized manufacturing company with a standard product has been chosen in order to avoid getting into the complications of administrating a complex product. The basic principles that you will be introduced to are equally applicable to standard and complex business operations.

The company

The name of the company is Extruded Plastic Tube Limited. It is a private limited company with the members of the board of directors holding 85 per cent of the shares, the remaining 15 per cent being held by the senior management employees of the company.

In common with similar business organizations, its main objective is to make a reasonable profit whilst maintaining its share of the market in the face of competition. It can only meet these objectives if it is able to co-ordinate the activities of its employees at all levels of the organization structure. It follows that the active co-operation of its employees in the performance of their various tasks is of the utmost importance.

People will perform best when they know what is expected of them. This is why it is important to have a well-defined structure identifying the task that each individual has to perform.

An organization structure is provided within the text. You should examine this critically from time to time as the course proceeds and try to identify any weaknesses and suggest improvements that could be made.

You should now look at the sales promotion information sheets given below. These are issued by the company as part of its sales and marketing campaign. They provide background information on EPTL which you will need to use for activities in later blocks.

Sales promotion information sheet.

EXTRUDED PLASTIC TUBE LTD

Who Are We?

A privately owned limited company who specialize in the extrusion of high-grade plastic tubing. During the fifteen years we have been in the extrusion business, our Research, Design and Development team have refined our production methods to the point where we can guarantee the quality of our products to meet customers' specifications over a wide range of applications. Our directors, who are engaged in the management of the company, head a team of specialist managers; this ensures that our products are competitively priced.

Who Are Our Customers?

They are many and varied. We supply the needs of the small business with the same detail and attention that we give to our customers in the multinational and nationalized industries. Our products have been used to convey water, effluent and chemicals and to provide conduit for a variety of services. They are to be found in factories, down mines, in ships, on oil rigs and on building sites – in fact, any place that high-quality plastic tubing is required in the UK, the EEC and the Middle East.

Our Sales Force

We have a team of sales-people in the field covering the United Kingdom. Each individual in the sales force is a qualified plastics technician, specifically trained by the company to be able to advise our customers on the application of our products. They are each allocated a region of the UK where they live. Thus, they will know the requirements of firms in that area and build the relationship between our company and each individual customer.

Our Board of Directors

Bill Southgate – Managing Director is a qualified engineer and plastics technician. His career in the plastics industry began twenty years ago as a graduate apprentice engineer. On completion of his apprenticeship, he had five years in Research and Development before moving over to the Marketing Division of a large plastics material manufacturer. This was followed by a period as General Manager of a plastics moulding company before being approached by EPTL to take up the post as MD. In common with our other directors, Bill is a major shareholder in the company.

John Appleton – Production Director A Member of the Institute of Production Engineers, John has been with the company for eight years, joining us in the first instance to reorganize the factory layout and mechanical handling in the production process. He was invited to join the board on completion of his studies for Membership of the Institute of Plastics Technology.

Bryn Roberts – Chief Accountant and Company Secretary
A Member of the Chartered Institute of Company Secretaries, Bryn has had considerable experience in accounts and costing in a number of well-known companies. He has been with EPTL for twelve years and has been a director for the whole of that time. Bryn is the instigator of our costing and budgeting procedures, which enable us to function efficiently.

Our product range

Dia (cm)	Bore (cm)			Weight in kilos (per metre)			Output in Metre/Day
20	18	17·5	17	8·95	11·0	13·0	65
15	13	12·5	11	6·55	9·54	12·26	75
10	8	7·5	7	4·25	5·2	6·0	100

Tube is manufactured to customer requirements between 3 – 6 metres

The above range is manufactured on our ten modern six-inch bore extruders, capable of high output throughout the range. During production, which is carried out on a three-shift system, seven days a week, the product is constantly monitored by our quality control inspection procedures against agreed customer specification.

Output per shift – 6-inch bore extruder

20 cm Dia. : Output per shift per bore dia.		
18 cm bore	17·5 cm bore	17 cm bore
581·75 kilo	715·0 kilo	845·0 kilo

15 cm Dia. : Output per shift per bore dia.		
13 cm bore	12·5 cm bore	11 cm bore
491·25 kilo	715·5 kilo	919·5 kilo

10 cm Dia. : Output per shift per bore diameter		
8 cm bore	7·5 cm bore	7 cm bore
800·0 kilo	750·0 kilo	700·0 kilo

Calculation:

Output in metres/day × Weight per metre length = Total capacity per day

Type		Radius		Volume in cm³ $\pi \times 100$ (outside radius – inside radius		Material density 1·5	Weight in grams per metre (Volume × density)	Weight per metre in kilos $\left(\frac{\text{Weight in grams}}{1000}\right)$
OD	ID	(OR) Outside	(IR) Inside					
20	18	10	9	314·2 (100 – 81)	314·2 × 19 = 5969.8	1·5	8954·7	8·96
15	13	7·5	6·5	314·2 (56·25 – 42·25)	314·2 × 14 = 4398.8	1·5	6598·2	6·60
10	8	5	4	314·2 (25 – 16)	314·2 × 9 = 2827.8	1·5	4241·7	4·30
				314·2 (–)	314·2 × =	1·5		

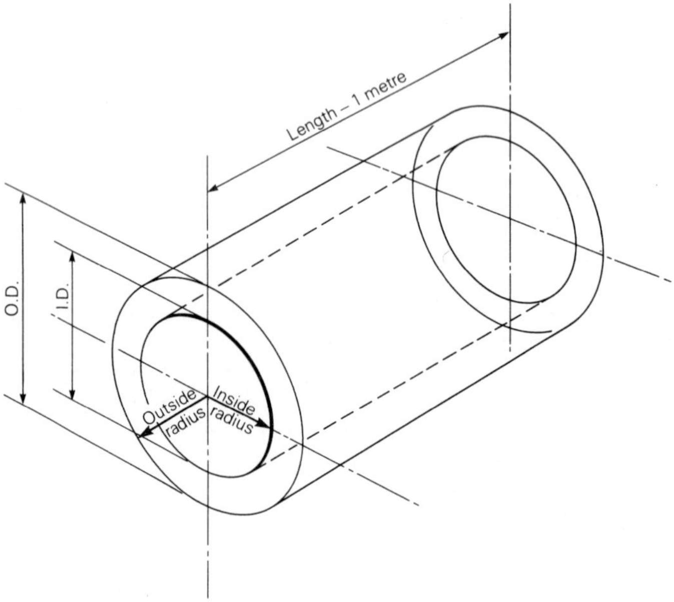

Product Familiarization – calculation weight per metre length
Volume = Area × Length
Area of an annular ring = π (outside radius^2 – inside radius^2)
Volume of a tube = Area of annular ring × Length of tube
To calculate volume of one metre length of 20/18 tube in cm^3
π (outside radius^2 100 – inside radius^2 81) × 100 cm
π (100–81) 100
= 3·142 × 19 × 100
= 5969·8 cm^3
Weight of a body = Volume × Density of material
Density of the plastic material used: 1·5 g per cm^3
Weight = Volume (5969·8) × Density (1·5)
= 5969·8 × 1·5
= 8954·7 grammes/metre
To convert to kilos divide by 1000

The production unit

Extruded Plastic Tube Ltd has a modern factory on an industrial estate. The layout follows the principle of straight-line flow production to minimize the movement of materials during production. In this respect, it follows the simple model of production previously referred to:

Raw materials IN – Production – Finished goods OUT.

Diagrams of the factory layout are given below. They are not to scale, but it can be assumed that the production area containing the extruders covers an area of 100 metres by 50 metres. The first diagram represents the ground floor, including the ground-floor office accommodation, and the second diagram represents the total area of the factory, also showing the first-floor office accommodation.

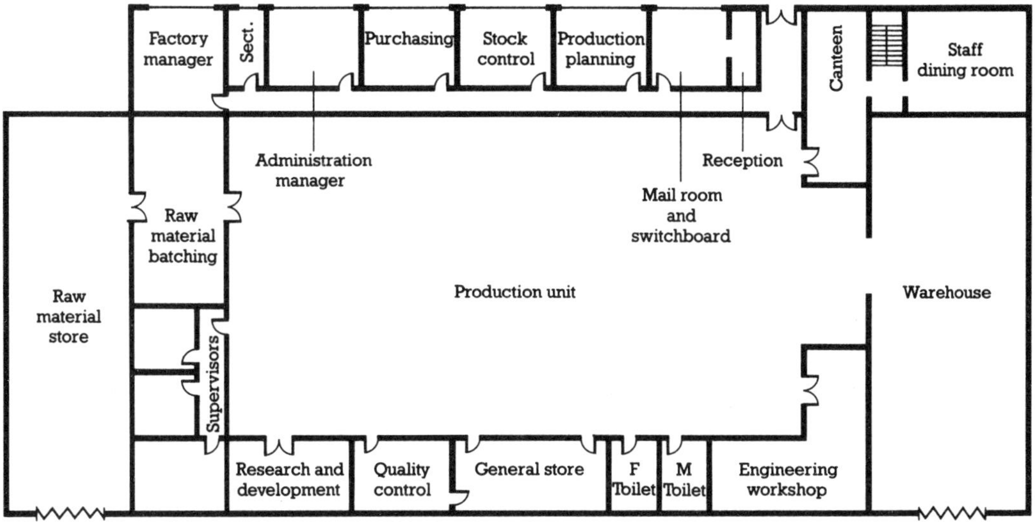

Factory layout – extruded tube production.

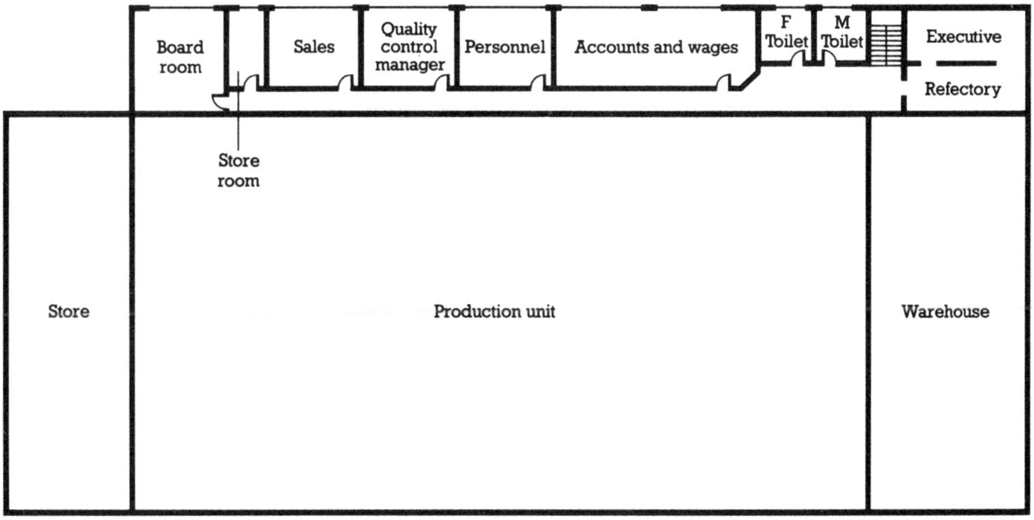

Factory layout – first-floor office.

The production method

To manufacture its products the company uses a machine called an extruder. These machines are standard equipment in the plastics industry and the manner in which they operate is briefy described below. To give you an impression of what these extruders look like, they can be compared with the machines used by butchers to mince meat products.

Extruders used to produce large-bore tubing, which is made by the company, are complex in their construction and controlled by a sophisticated system of electronics. Purchasing these machines involves considerable capital expenditure. The extrusion machines must be kept in full production over the working week to recoup this capital expenditure over the shortest possible period of time.

Extruded Plastic Tube Ltd works on a system of three shifts per day and a seven-day working week. In order to do this, they have to employ sufficient labour to run four shifts. This allows three shifts on to cover the twenty-four hours and one shift off on rest days. Shifts rotate in the order of morning shift, afternoon shift, night shift, rest days.

The factory ceases production for one week at Christmas and three weeks in August, when routine maintenance is carried out.

The extrusion process

As you will be looking at the way in which EPTL operates in detail, you may like to know a little about the manufacturing process which they use.

Materials in the form of plastic granules are stored in the material stores until called off by the production unit, when they are delivered to the designated machine and fed into a feed hopper. The granules are gravity-fed down from the hopper onto a rotating screw contained within the extruder barrel.

Granules are driven forward by the rotation of the screw providing a thrust to the material and forcing it up the barrel of the extruder. As it moves forward, the material passes through a number of heating zones located round the outside of the barrel. The granules become molten and are compressed as the core diameter of the screw is increased to aid the flow of material along the screw. Considerable pressure is generated by this compression and the thrust of the granules at the cooler back end of the extruder barrel. This forces the molten material through the die at the end of the barrel into the desired shape – in this case a continuous tube.

On leaving the die face, the material is cooled and resumes its solid state, thus retaining the shape dictated by the die form.

Administration procedures

The company has not yet introduced a modern data processing system and still relies primarily on clerical administrative processes. Its organisation structure is shown in the diagram. Control over the use of its resources is established through paperwork systems. This will give you the opportunity to look at the various adminstrative systems which can be used to control a business, before being introduced to the modern technology being implemented in many businesses today.

Using EPTL's system of administrating its resources as a basis, you will be given a number of tasks directly related to the function of a clerical assistant in a similar organization structure.

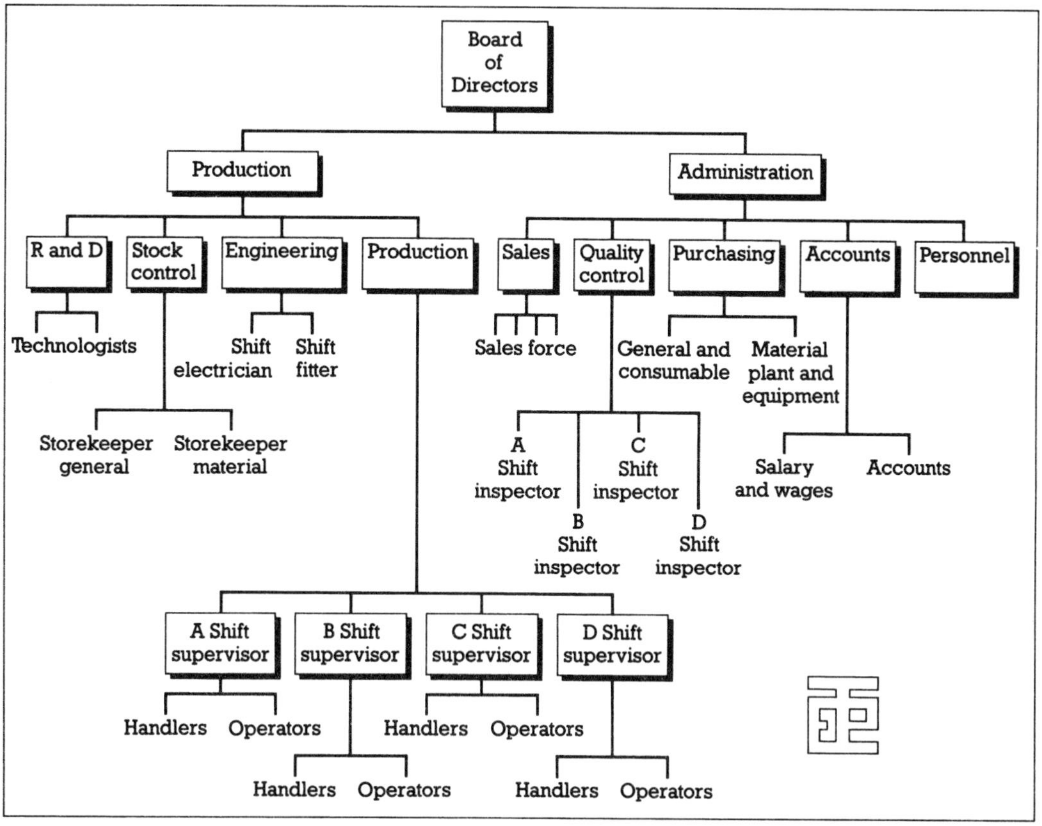

Extruded Plastic Tube Ltd – organization structure

The previous simple model of an organization, Raw Material IN – PRODUCTION – Finished Goods OUT, can be related to Extruded Plastic Tube Ltd:

Raw material IN

Plastics material delivered from the supplier in 20 kilo bags, 50 bags per pallet.

Materials stored awaiting call-off from the production unit.

On receipt of call-off from the production unit, the required materials are transported to the batching department.

Production

Materials batched into batch bins for individual extruders, according to the order each extruder is working on.

Batch bins transported to the designated extruder and loaded on to the machine.

Material gravity-fed into the extruder and extruded into a continuous tube of the required diameter and bore.

Extruded tube cut to lengths required by the customer's order.

Cut lengths placed onto a truck in batches of 50.

Roving inspection checks the tube against the required specification.

Batches of 50 tube lengths transported to the warehouse.

Finished goods OUT

Batches of 50 tubes received in the warehouse from the production unit.

Batches racked in space allocated for the customer's order until the required delivery amount is accumulated.

Transport for delivery to customer arranged to comply with the delivery requirements.

Orders loaded and despatched.

Activity 9

a Assume that EPTL have decided to introduce microcomputers and other data processing equipment into the organization. Outline the changes that are likely to take place in the organization structure.
b Identify the line and staff functions in the EPTL structure.
c Write a short description of the way in which the EPTL structure design has overcome the span of control problem faced by most large organizations.
d Using the factory floor layout, trace the progress of an order through the various departments concerned.
e Assuming that the principle of division of labour has not been applied to the EPTL structure, describe the problems that would arise when progressing an order through the factory.
f Trace the line of communication through the structure which would allow the managing director to be informed of a breakdown of the factory floor.
g State which of the resources of the organization you would expect to be the direct responsibility of an employee in a supervisory grade of management.
h Examine the EPTL structure and suggest changes which could sensibly be made to the individual responsibilities of the two senior executives for the grouped activities of production and administration.

Correspondence

Although the use of electronic means of carrying messages is rapidly increasing, the chief methods of written communication are still the **business letter** for outside the firm and the **memo** for the firm's internal correspondence. Reports may be used to convey information both inside and outside the organization. We shall look at these in Block 2.

Business letters

Organizations are invariably anxious to create a good impression in any contact with the outside world. You will be expected to be able to produce visually attractive and technically accurate business letters. The overall effect is achieved by the letter-head, the content of the message and the tone used to convey that message.

Letter-heads The company's headed notepaper plays an important part in creating the company image. A firm of solicitors, for instance, might select a plain white notepaper with black italic lettering; a school might display its badge and motto in the school colours; a firm selling by mail order might choose a bright and bold heading with several colours and typefaces. The quality of the paper will contribute to the total picture by conveying perhaps, 'only the best is good enough' or, maybe, 'we don't waste money on inessentials here'. Many firms incorporate into the letter-head a logo. This may be an arrangement of its initials or a symbol designed to convey the company's leading characteristic – a bulldog for tenacity might be suitable for a glue manufacturer, and a cheetah for an express delivery firm. Many firms use their logo in their advertising campaigns and their packaging.

The legal requirements for company notepaper have to be met, of course. We have shown these under the EPTL letter-heading. People will need to know your phone number (with STD code) and your telex or fax number if you have one.

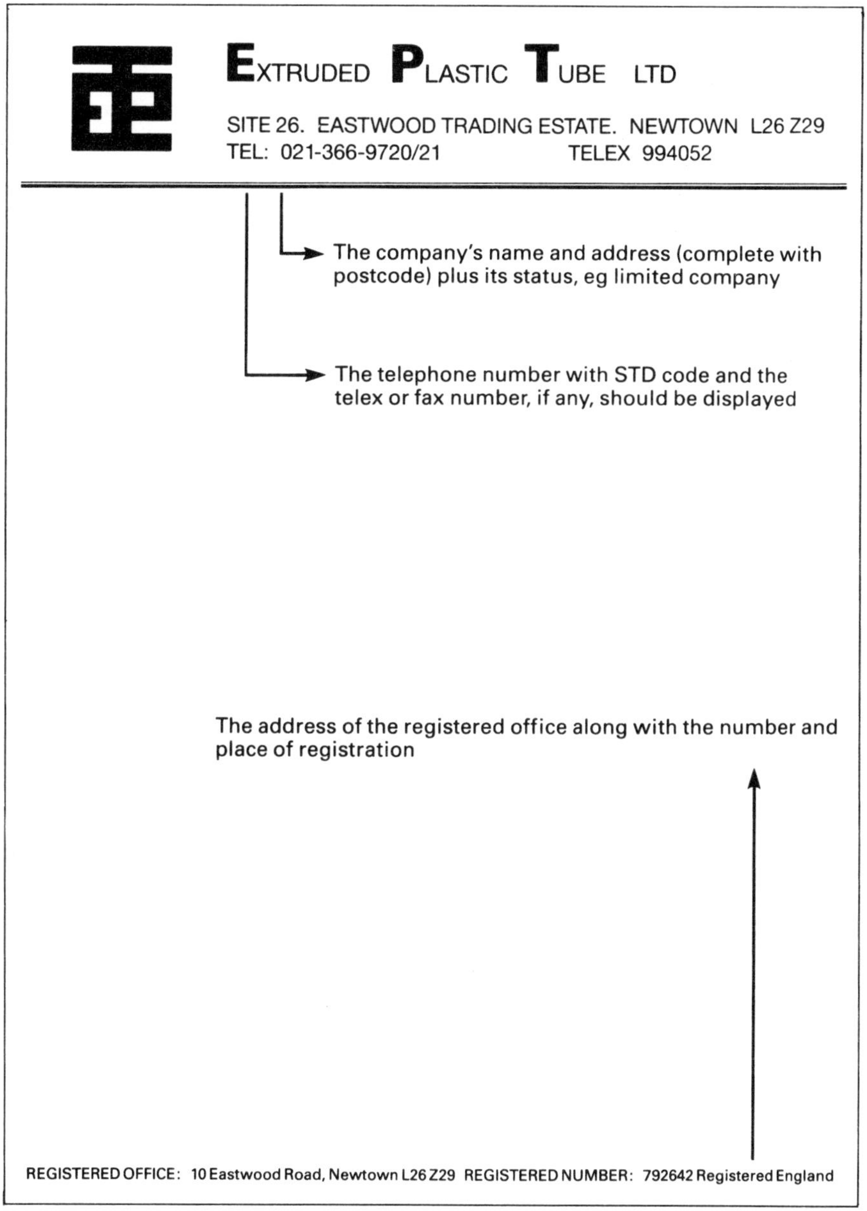
EXTRUDED PLASTIC TUBE LTD
SITE 26. EASTWOOD TRADING ESTATE. NEWTOWN L26 Z29
TEL: 021-366-9720/21 TELEX 994052
The company's name and address (complete with postcode) plus its status, eg limited company
The telephone number with STD code and the telex or fax number, if any, should be displayed
The address of the registered office along with the number and place of registration
REGISTERED OFFICE: 10 Eastwood Road, Newtown L26 Z29 REGISTERED NUMBER: 792642 Registered England

Laying out a letter

Every organization has its own preferences for layout and you are expected to fall in with whatever the **house-style** happens to be. You will need to be flexible in this, of course; circumstances may make it necessary to adapt the rules sometimes.

However, certain conventions are generally observed, though subject to modification – generally more for economic reasons than for aesthetic ones.

The usual layout, known as **fully blocked**, goes along with **open punctuation** to reduce keyboarding time to an absolute minimum.

Fully blocked letters have the typing lined up straight down the left-hand margin, ie. no indentations in addresses or for paragraphs. Open punctuation uses no punctuation outside the main body of the letter. (You must have punctuation in the text of the letter itself, of course.) The 'st' in 1st, 'nd' in 2nd, etc is omitted in the date at the head of the letter and also in dates quoted in the text itself, eg 'Thank you for your letter of 10 March 19..'. The time saved by reducing the number of key depressions for commas and spaces in every letter produced represents a considerable sum of money over a year.

BALTIMORE PIPING LTD
CANNING HOUSE
CLOCK SQUARE
CRAWFORD CR6 1RD

Phone (STD 0239) 6842 Telex 260739

Your Ref

My Ref TJJ/264

21 March 19..

Sales Manager
Extruded Plastic Tube Ltd
Eastwood Trading Estate
Newton L26 Z29

Dear Sir

<u>Standard Range Extrusions</u>

Please let me have a copy of the specifications you offer in your standard range along with a current price list.

Yours faithfully

T. J. Jackson

Production Manager

Company Registration Number 819830 England

Registered Office 45 Cavendish Square London W1B 2EB

Letter seeking information – fully blocked layout with open punctuation.

Although there are other methods of laying out letters, the one described is by far the most common now. A typing manual will give you plenty of examples of alternatives.

Activity 10

You are the assistant secretary of the staff association at Extruded Plastic Tubes Ltd: you are planning a mystery tour for the office staff for the last Friday of next month. There will be supper at a pub in the country at about 9.00pm.

Invent a pub and write to ask if they can cater for a party of about fifty people on that date. You would like a supper choice of chicken in the basket or hot pot. Ask them to quote a price.

Use open punctuation and a fully blocked layout. Sign it yourself.

Getting started

Confidentiality If necessary mark both the envelope and the top of the letter confidential. Such letters usually have one person as the addressee.

Reference numbers If you are replying to a letter which gave a reference number, you should quote it as 'Your ref' at the top left when you reply. In the letter from Baltimore Piping, the production manager is initiating a new correspondence, so there is no EPTL reference to quote. They do, however, give their own reference number (TJJ/264) and will expect EPTL to quote it in their reply.

There could be some difficulty in getting your letters to the right desk if you fail to quote reference numbers, especially if the organization is large and impersonal. Avoid anything that may delay a quick response to your communication.

The date The date should be written out with the month in full, not expressed as numerals. Always put the year in: correspondence can drag on for years and incomplete dates can lead to confusion. Occasionally, a date can be crucial in legal matters.

The inside address This is the name given to the name and address of the recipient of your letter. The inside address usually appears at the top of your letter, but sometimes it is located elsewhere, either by company preference or to fit into the window of a window envelope.

You should write out 'Street', 'Road', 'Avenue', etc in full, but abbreviated names are acceptable for counties, eg, Lancs, Northants. The name of the town and the postcode should be in capitals, with the postcode on its own line at the end.

Addresses[1] If you are writing to a company or other large organization, you should address your letter to the head of the appropriate department (eg the sales manager), especially if you have no reference to quote. This saves the people who open the post having to read your letter to find out whom to give it to and will speed up the response.

Some organizations will not open letters addressed to individual members of staff (eg Miss Copthorn) in their absence. This can lead to delay and is best avoided if you have no reason for wanting to address that person in particular. However, if you do want one particular person to read your letter you can mark it '*personal*' and it will be dealt with by the person named.

2 Sometimes the name of the firm is composed of the personal names of the partners (eg. Smith, Meakin and Shaw). This often happens with solicitors, accountants or brokers. If they are not a limited company, you should address them as 'Messrs' (short for the French, Messieurs).

3 If you are writing to individuals, there are several options open to you.

To a man you can put 'Mr J.C. King' or 'J.C. King Esq.'. Esq. stands for Esquire and is mostly used for people with some standing in the community or when you are trying to compliment someone. You can only use it if you know the man's initials and you must never use both Mr and Esq. Use Esq. if the man has letters after his name.

Mr and Esq. indicate masculine gender, but say nothing of the marital status of the man. Mrs and Miss indicate both gender and marital status, a feature which some women prefer to avoid by using just Ms. If you are replying to a letter from a woman, she will probably have indicated at the end of her letter the style she prefers and you should follow that in your reply. There is no equivalent to Esq. for women.

4 If you are in a job which calls for correspondence with people who have titles, you would be well advised to get a specialist book on the subject. It will also tell you how to cope with letters after the name.

Salutations or openings 'Dear Sir' or 'Dear Madam' is now thought to be rather cold and formal in tone. There will be times when coldness and formality are required, but generally a more affable note is desirable and the personal surname is used if known, eg, 'Dear Mr King' or 'Dear Mrs Thompson'. (Note that the initials are dropped in the salutation).

Letters to the editors of quality newspapers sometimes still start 'Sir', but check in the newspaper to keep abreast of practice.
It is sometimes helpful to give a heading to indicate the subject matter, or to give the account or order number the letter refers to.

Finishing off

Complimentary closures It is conventional if you start your letter with 'Dear Sir' or 'Dear Madam', to end with '*Yours faithfully*'.

If you started 'Dear Mr' or 'Dear Ms', you should end with '*Yours sincerely*'. If the spelling of 'sincerely' gives you trouble, just write down 'sincere' and add 'ly'. You must get this right in business correspondence in England.

'Sincerely yours' is a variation considered somewhat warmer in tone; 'Yours very sincerely' even more so. 'Yours truly' is a possibility, but 'Yours very truly' is an American phrase, rarely used in correspondence.

If you started with just 'Sir', to a newspaper editor or in some other extremely cold or formal letter, omit the complimentary close and go straight on to the signature.

The existence of all these variations and the levels of warmth associated with them show how important the appropriate tone is in business communication.

Enclosures If something is to be enclosed with the letter – such as a cheque or a price-list – it is usual to type 'enc.' either in the margin where the enclosure is referred to or at the bottom of the letter. The people in the post room can then make sure that the enclosure is not thrown away by mistake when the post is opened. Conversely, if an enclosure is left out, the post room can draw the recipient's attention to that.

Signatures The writer will sign by hand and the name will be typed underneath the signature. Under that it is usual to put the writer's position, eg, 'Works Manager'. Sometimes someone else will sign instead of the writer; then 'p.p.' or 'for' should appear by the typewritten name, eg:

> I do hope the information given will be of benefit and enable you to decide your future actions. Please let me know if I can be of any further help to you.
>
> Terry Shaw
>
> p.p. R.C.J. Jones
> Research and Development

Postscripts These are to be avoided. If necessary, rewrite the letter.

Carbon copies If you are sending a copy to another interested party you should indicate that at the head or the foot with the letters 'c.c.' eg, c.c. Miss Franks.

The body of the letter

Customers, clients and suppliers form an opinion of an organization from its business letters. You should draft and redraft as many times as is necessary to get a perfect letter. Presentation, grammar, spelling, punctuation, content and tone are all registered by the recipients and can affect future relationships.

Choosing your approach

Unlike the spoken word, your letter cannot be modified in the light of the recipient's immediate reaction to it. No smile or gesture can soften its tone; no frown or straight look indicate that you really mean to press your point. It is very easy to upset people in letters, even people whom you know well, so you should make every effort to match your approach to the known or supposed characteristics of your correspondent.

Tone of voice

Just as you vary your tone of voice according to circumstances when speaking, so you must vary it when writing.

If someone is cross or indignant when they speak, they tend to use short sentences with very little padding in them. Similarly, in written correspondence a sharp tone is achieved by conveying your message in a few words, eg, 'Please reply without further delay.' Be careful not to overdo it. The idea is to be firm, not rude.

If you are trying to placate someone or persuade them to do something they are reluctant to do, you will get a softer tone by using more words, wrapped up in 'courtesy clauses'. For instance, 'I would be very grateful if you could find time to let me have another copy of your list of requirements, so that we may process your order without any further delay.'

The parallel between the spoken and the written word must not be pressed too far. It is seldom appropriate to use in business correspondence the kind of vocabulary and sentence structure that is perfectly acceptable in speech, as the following shows.

Appropriate language

Jargon Jargon is the word for the vocabulary that belongs to a particular trade or profession. When used between members of that profession it is an economical and accurate way of conveying information. To use it to someone who is not familiar with it, or with the intention of impressing or even confusing your correspondent, is poor communication.

There is a kind of business-letter jargon which survives from days gone by, but you should find a simple and elegant equivalent and use that instead.

Please advise....	Please let me know....
Enclosed please find....	We enclose....
We acknowledge receipt of....	Thank you for....
Despatched by Parcel Post.	Sent by Parcel Post.
Your esteemed order....	Your order....
We have despatched same....	We have sent it....
We remain....	This means nothing. Delete it.

Slang This should be avoided. It lowers the tone of your letter; furthermore, it goes out of date very rapidly, so you are likely to be out-of-step with a correspondent if they are not of your generation and background.

Ostentation Attempts to raise the level of vocabulary in correspondence can be problematical. Long words and dignified phrases may be appropriate in certain circumstances, but you must learn to judge these circumstances. A sentence like, 'The commencement of the staff toddler's party will be at 3.30pm' is inappropriate; say instead, 'The toddler's party will begin at 3.30pm.' Similarly, a statement about a garden fête such as, 'The location may subsequently be amended to take account of changes in climatic conditions' is better expressed as 'If wet, in the hall.'

Speaking for the firm

Junior members of staff generally speak with the company's voice rather than their own, eg, 'We see from your letter that...'. A senior person or one expressing a strong personal opinion would use the first person singular, ie, 'I see that...'. The impersonal 'It is apparent that...' strikes a very formal note.

```
Dear Mrs. Prescott,

Thank you for your letter of 19 May, enclosing your order for a
hanging cabinet type K26.

We were not able to decide from your letter whether you would
like the cabinet with wooden doors or with metal ones.  On the
whole we would recommend the wooden ones for both appearance
and durability although they are a little more expensive.

If you could let us know within the next seven days, we could
still send the cabinet in time to meet your deadline.

We look forward to hearing from you.


Yours sincerely


Edith Harper (Mrs)
(Sales)
```

The body of the letter.

Salutation – warm and friendly use of personal name

Opening paragraph – refers to Mrs Prescott's letter by date and subject matter

Paragraph 2 – says what the problem is and suggests a possible solution

Final paragraph – says what Mrs Prescott should do to make progress

Complimentary close – required by the use of 'Dear Mrs Prescott' as the salutation

The writer will sign above her typewritten name

'Sales' is a piece of information for Mrs Prescott to use when she replies to this letter

Section structure

Letters should be paragraphed and the paragraphs kept as short as possible. The sight of long blocks of text is likely to make people put off reading your letter.

First paragraph The first paragraph is used to set the scene, usually either by referring to a letter received from the correspondent or by stating the reason for initiating the correspondence.

Getting onto the page often causes problems. Phrases like 'I am writing to you' are redundant and should be avoided. 'Referring to your letter...' and 'With reference to your letter...' either lead to incomplete sentences or oblige you to cram most of the message into the opening sentence: avoid these too. A simple and grammatically correct opening is 'Thank you for your letter of...'; you can hang another clause on the end of it if you like.

Second paragraph This is the start of the centre section, which may need two or three paragraphs if the material is long or complex. This paragraph constitutes the substance of the letter and goes into detail about its subject matter.

Final paragraph The final paragraph typically states what the next action is to be, so that the reader can see what to do to make progress.

With practice, writing a business letter will cause you no problems. While you are gaining experience, make use of the checklist provided every time you have a letter to write. You will find it helpful when you work through Activities 10 to 12.

Activity 11

You work as clerical assistant at a garden centre. You are to hold a special Flowering Shrubs Week from 2 to 9 May to boost your sales and you have been asked to draft an unsolicited sales letter to be distributed in your area. Customers can enter a prize draw for a collection of three shrubs by completing and sending in a tear-off slip.

The garden centre offers the following:

a 10% discount all that week
b Large selection of herbaceous and bedding plants
c Water garden section
d Sheds and greenhouses
e Tea-room
f Children's play area.

Draft a lively and inviting letter, likely to appeal to gardeners, including a tear-off slip at the bottom. Invent a suitable name and address for the centre.

Letter checklist.

Will it be easy for the firm you are writing to to get your letter to the right desk quickly?	**• Quote a reference number • Designate particular section,**
Have you picked a salutation that sets the right tone for your letter?	**• Dear Madam – formal • Dear Mrs Green – friendly**
Does the structure of your letter follow a logical pattern?	**• Para – Introduction • Para 2 – Main message • Para 3 – What next?**
Have you signalled any enclosures or carbon copies?	**• Enc • c.c. Mrs Charlton**
Have you chosen the complimentary close that matches your salutation?	**• Dear Sir – Yours faithfully • Dear Mr Jones – Yours sincerely**
Have you read it through to be sure it is all right?	**• Tone of voice • Punctuation • Grammar • All the facts • Spelling**

Activity 12

You work for the Sri Lanka Bond Tea Company, which markets a range of quality teas and teabags. You have received the following letter of complaint.

Spider Cottage,
The Green,
Linkworth,
Glos.

16 May 19..

Public Relations
Sri Lanka Bond Teas
The Tea House
Nicholas Street
Howe HA26 4TR

Dear Sir,

I recently purchased a packet of 80 of your Morning Brew Teabags for use in the Teasmaid machine bought for me by my colleagues on the occasion of my retirement.

It had been my intention to stay in bed late every morning for the rest of my life, but alas every day so far your teabags have burst and I have had a mouthful of tea leaves and have had to get out of bed instantly.

This bad start to the day is souring my outlook on life and I wonder what you would like to do about it.

Yours faithfully

Alan Smith

Upon investigation you find that there had been a mechanical defect on the Morning Brew teabag machine a month ago and that one morning's production had been scrapped. Apparently, one case of teabags got through inspection unnoticed.

Though the customer is complaining, he has chosen to use a light-hearted tone of voice.

Company policy is to send complimentary packets in such cases.

a Design a letter-head for the Sri Lanka Bond Tea Company, and invent a suitable logo.
b Write a letter of adjustment (so-called because it adjusts the situation) to Mr Smith, using your letter-head.

Activity 13

Write a letter of adjustment to Mrs Jones in response to her letter of 24 March 19— — below.
To promote good customer relations, write also to Miss Dilys Roberts, the assistant who fits the description, outlining the attitude you expect your staff to have.

14 Rock Gardens
Little Hampden
Cambridge

24 March 19..

The Manager
Barnolds Bakeries
Southland Road
Cambridge

Dear Sir,

I enclose the remains of a sliced loaf purchased at your Campion Street shop yesterday. A careful examination will reveal that it contains a piece of rubber glove.

I have already complained to the green-eyed assistant who sold it to me and wish to make a strong protest at the way she laughed when she saw it. This matter could easily come to court if I cared to make an official complaint. I should like to hear what you propose to do.

Yours faithfully

Amy Jones.

Amy Jones (Mrs)

The memorandum

The **memorandum**, usually called a *memo,* is used to convey messages within an organization.

The **communications** network in an organization of any size needs a means of keeping all departments or sections informed about what is happening so that they can co-ordinate their efforts. Most organizations have printed memo forms, sometimes in pads, sometimes interleaved for carbon copies, sometimes with a colour-coded series of copies. The coloured copies indicate to the recipients whether they are responsible for taking action themselves or whether they are simply to take note of someone else's action.

The memo in the organization structure.

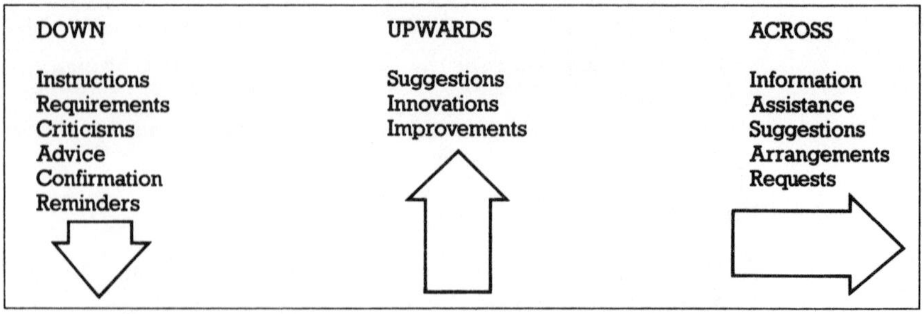

DOWN
Instructions
Requirements
Criticisms
Advice
Confirmation
Reminders
UPWARDS
Suggestions
Innovations
Improvements
ACROSS
Information
Assistance
Suggestions
Arrangements
Requests

The memo provides a written record of what someone was asked, instructed to do, etc. It should therefore always be dated and initialled and written in a businesslike manner.

Memos usually travel down the organizational tree from more senior to junior personnel, or across it between people of equal rank. A junior clerk could send a copy of a memo to his supervisor 'for information' but if he is writing to his immediate supervisor it is usually more appropriate to send a letter. An exception is the unsolicited memo, suggesting an improvement or floating an idea up to someone in authority.

Layout

Memos generally have a layout along these lines, though organizations have their own preferences:

Memo heading.

MEMORANDUM	
TO:	SUBJECT:
FROM:	DATE:

Usually memos are on A5 paper (ie half the size of A4) though A4 memos may be needed for complex or detailed mesages. It is considered acceptable to put the date in numerals, and your initials are sufficient at the end. There is no salutation and no complimentary close. If you are sending copies to others, or if you are enclosing anything, you should indicate that as in a letter.

Style

The memo's style will vary according to the needs and positions of correspondents. The style of a directive from the chief executive to all staff may be extremely impersonal; see below.

FROM:	G.T. Jones	SUBJECT:	Security
TO:	All Staff	DATE:	25.7.19..

All members of staff are reminded that they are held personally responsible for the safety of documents in their keeping. In particular, confidential papers should be lodged overnight in the safes provided on each floor for that purpose.

G.T.J.

The style of a message slipped onto the desk opposite yours may be friendly and informal:

TO:	Harry	SUBJECT:	Stats
FROM:	Jane	DATE:	9.3.19..

I've got the Stats for last month now. Can you spare half an hour tomorrow morning to have a look at them?

J.

However, because the format invites brevity, it is easy to adopt a harsh tone unintentionally:

TO:	Barbara	**SUBJECT:**	Sales figures
FROM:	Brian Edwards	**DATE:**	12.11.19..

```
 When will you have finished analysing the sales returns?  I
want them by Friday at the latest.
                                                  B.E
```

A harsh tone is especially unwelcome between colleagues, so you should find space for 'please' and thank you' and check your phraseology to make sure you have not been rude:

TO:	Barbara	**SUBJECT:**	Sales figures
FROM:	Brian Edwards	**DATE:**	12.11.19..

```
 Mr Jones is pressing me for the sales figures.
Could you get the analysis done by Thursday evening, do you
think?

Many thanks.
                              B.E
```

As before, we have supplied a checklist of the things to watch out for when writing a memo. You will find it useful when you work on Activity 13.

Should you send a memo or a letter	• Memos move down and across, letters move up as a rule.
Have you used a suitable tone with regard to your respective positions in the firm?	• To colleagues a friendly but business-like approach. To subordinates a more impersonal approach may sometimes be appropriate.
Does your memo sound civil?	• Check that brevity has not produced rudeness. Find space for 'please' and 'thank you'.
Have you initialled it?	• Your name will be at the top, so initials are generally sufficient.
Have you dated it?	• Necessary in any correspondence. Numerals are considered acceptable.
Is the layout correct?	• No salutation. No complimentary close.

Memo checklist.

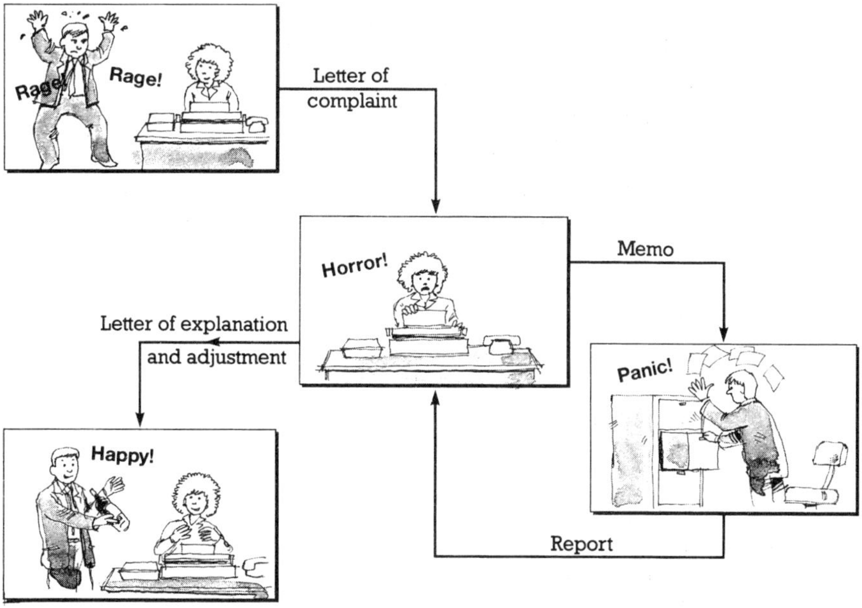

Correspondence chain.

Activity 14

Using a fully blocked layout with open punctuation, write to a local firm asking if they will let you have a specimen of their headed notepaper. If you are in employment, bring in a sheet of your company notepaper as well.

In due course, critically inspect the letter-heads your class has collected and afterwards design a new headed notepaper for Extruded Plastic Tube which you think will be more effective than the existing one (you will find an example earlier in this block).

Send a copy of your new design to the marketing manager with a memo saying you would like to suggest a change in the firm's letter-head and logo.

Summary

In this block we have established that organizations are people and that an organization is structured in a way that will allow the people to contribute effectively to achieving the objectives of that organization. The structure defines levels of responsibility and authority and divides the available labour into specialisms and departments. We considered the desirability of limiting the **span of control** to produce **unity of command** and to provise speedy lines of **communication**. Various structures of increasing size and complexity were studied in relation to the objectives a particular organization may have. The formal and informal groupings among employees were contrasted, and the difficulties which may arise from group pressure and role conflict were considered.

Part of a company's communication takes place through business letters and memos and the guidelines for writing these were introduced.

We were introduced to the manufacturing company EPTL, whose fortunes will be followed throughout this book.

We have introduced the concept of organizations consisting of people working within some defined structure of relationships.

The manner in which structure design determines the degree to which an individual's responsibility and authority allows them to contribute to the objectives of the organization has been discussed.

The function of the structure as a communication system has been emphasized and the role of the informal structure introduced.

Skills

Skill	*Activities in which skill is developed*
a Information gathering	1, 6, 11
b Learning and studying	1, 2, 3, 4, 5, 6, 7, 8, 9, 10, 11, 13
c Working with others	1, 6, 13
d Communicating	1, 3, 4, 5, 6, 7, 8, 9, 10, 12
e Design & visual discrimination	2, 4, 5, 6, 10, 12, 13
f Identifying and tackling problems	1, 2, 7, 8, 9
g Numeracy	
h Information processing	8, 10, 11, 12, 13

Block 2
Systems Modelling

Introduction

In this block we shall see how models of systems can be designed to allow us to test the viability of a projected sequence or routine. Systems for transferring information and setting up paperwork routines will be considered. Not even the best-designed system can cover every possibility; there will be numerous occasions when 'one-off' reporting will be needed. Some possible formats will be considered towards the end of the block.

System modelling

System modelling is a problem-solving technique which aids decision making by indicating what the problem is and identifying its component parts. When a problem is broken down into a number of smaller problems and the relationship of the smaller problems to each other is understood, the approach to a solution can often be more clearly defined.

Definition of a system

1 An organized assembly of component parts.
2 As a general rule, the component parts are affected by being in the system – they undergo some change if they are removed from it.
3 The assembly of component parts does something.

Familiar systems

You are constantly encountering systems in your everyday life. Examples are central heating, transport, weather and telephone; and solar, political and education systems.

Many systems are interrelated. For example, the internal combustion engine consists of the mechanical system, the electrical system and the fuel system. The **model** of these systems – in the form of engineering drawings – allows the mechanic to diagnose the problem when a car refuses to start.

Sometimes the interrelationship between systems affects the survival of mankind. For example, the destruction of the ecological system of the rain forests affects the world weather system.

Systems modelling can be used as a means of analysing, planning or testing a theory. It allows a problem or situation to be studied in a representative form; a road map is a familiar example.

Activity 1

Examine three maps of different areas and write a short description of the information they supply about the territory covered. In particular, outline the way in which an Ordnance Survey map describes variations in the height of the countryside.

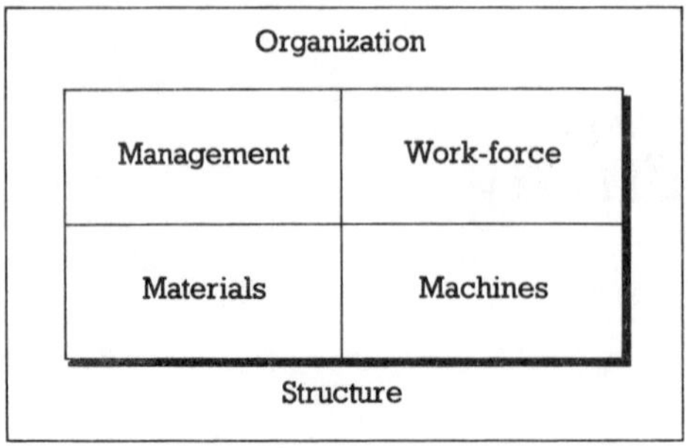

Manufacturing System

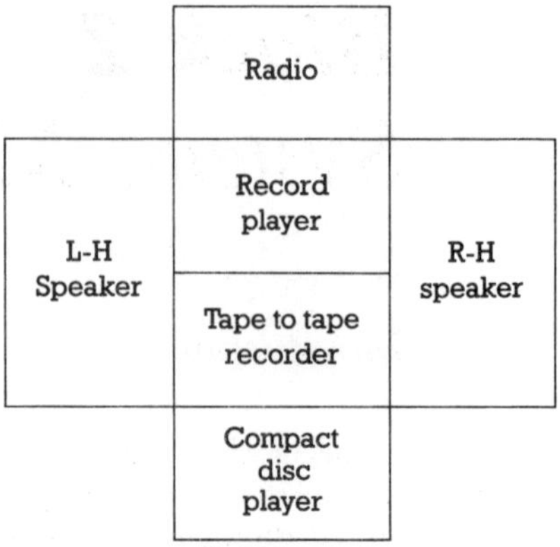

Hi-Fi System

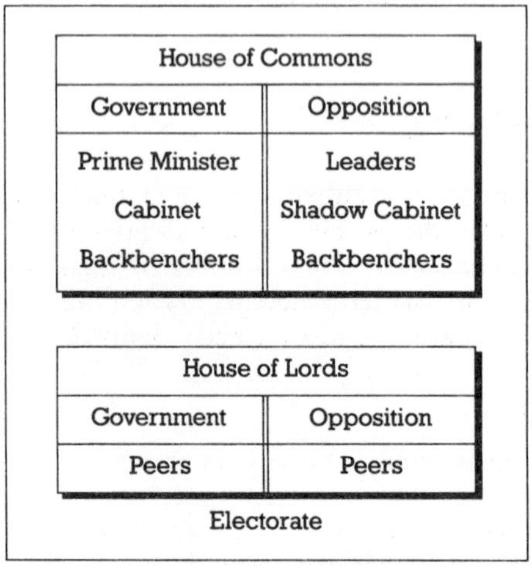

House of Commons
Government
Opposition
Prime Minister
Cabinet
Backbenchers
Leaders
Shadow Cabinet
Backbenchers
House of Lords
Government
Opposition
Peers
Peers
Electorate

System of Government

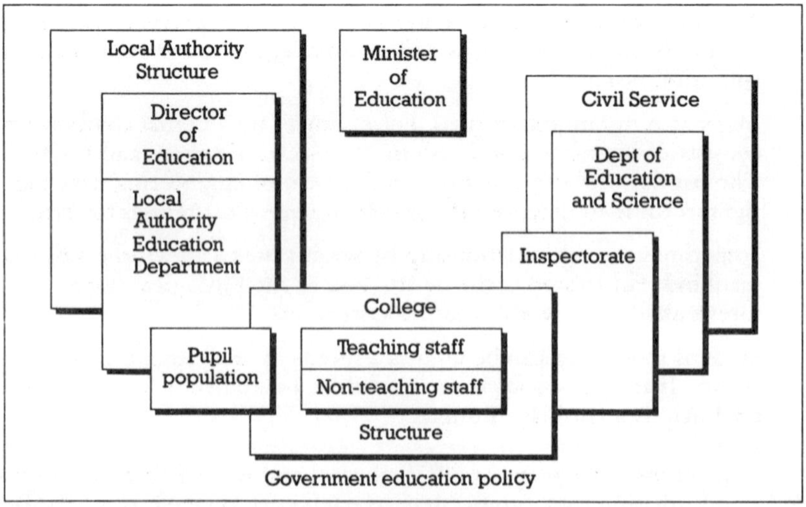

An Education System

Examples of systems.

Throughout this book a number of principles and workings methods are demonstated in a representational form and you are given tasks to develop your skill in recognizing and applying the technique to the study of people in organizations.

The objective of studying organizations as systems is to establish the way in which the component parts of organization structures interact. Central to the types of organization structure we shall examine in this block are the technology and the control systems used and the people employed. These three have to be kept in balance.

Activity 2

Using simple sketches, devise representative forms to describe the following:

a The events which led up to a road accident involving a road tanker, a saloon car and a motor cycle. Assume the accident has occurred at a crossroads' junction controlled by traffic lights.

b The ground movement of an aircraft, from the time it lands on the runway to arrival at the airport terminal.

An introduction to algorithms

A system often involves a sequence of operations. This is particularly true of business and commercial activities. These systems can be diagramatically represented by a **flow chart** using the two symbols shown here. The first represents some form of activity, the second represents a decision point where alternative courses of action may present themselves.

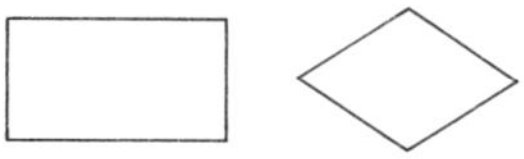

Activity 3

Before reading any further, complete the following flow diagram to demonstrate the procedure for removing all the red cards from a pack.

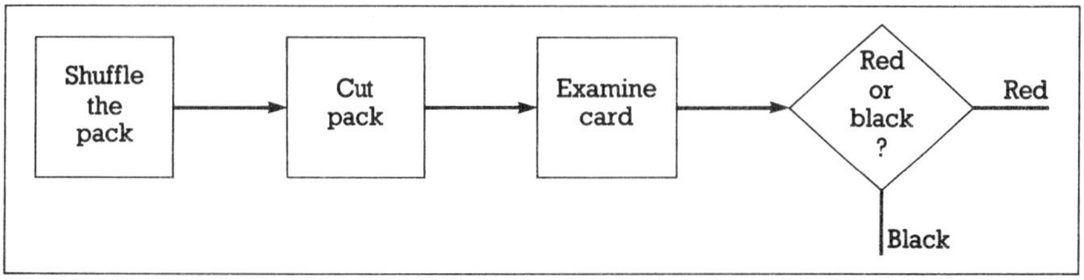

When you have done that, draw a diagram showing the sequence of operations required to remove all the black cards with a face value of 6 or less.

You will find that you have to return to the point where you 'examine card' in order to continue the process until the task is completed. This loop back originates from the decision symbol.

Taking the following simple sequence of activities a **flow chart** can be constructed as shown below:

1 Go to front door.
2 Open front door.
3 Check if raining or dry.
4 If dry, close door and go out.
5 If wet close front door.

The first activity must be to go to the front door and the final activity must be to close it, whether you go out or stay in.

The algorithm for this would take the following form:

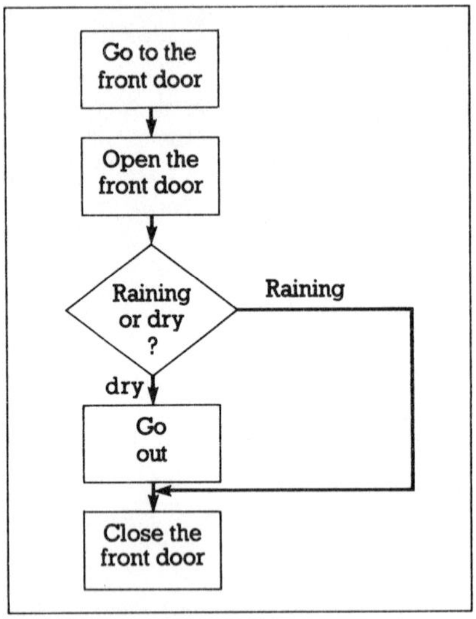

However, the system might have to take into account the possibility of going out when it is raining. This introduces the need to have more than one decision point. This need not present flow charting problems (you may have already found this out when you constructed the flow chart to sort out black cards under the value of 6). Any number of decision points can be introduced if the logic of the diagram is correct.

The flow diagram will now be expanded to look like this.
1 Go to front door.
2 Open front door.
3 Check if raining or dry.
4 If dry, go out and close front door.
5 If raining, check if rain is light or heavy.
6 If rain is light, take umbrella and go out.
7 If rain is heavy, take raincoat and umbrella and go out.

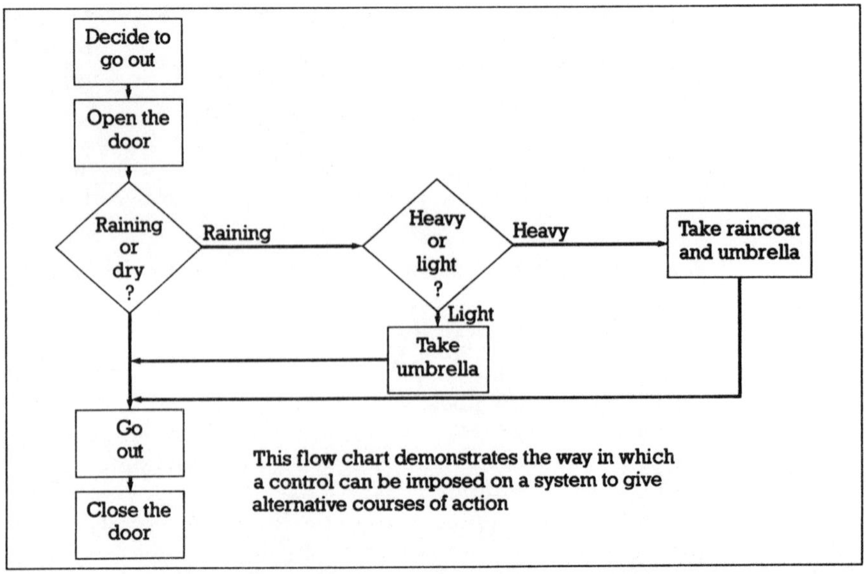

This flow chart demonstrates the way in which a control can be imposed on a system to give alternative courses of action

You can see this in the following simplified model of the control function applied to administration procedures in a business organization.

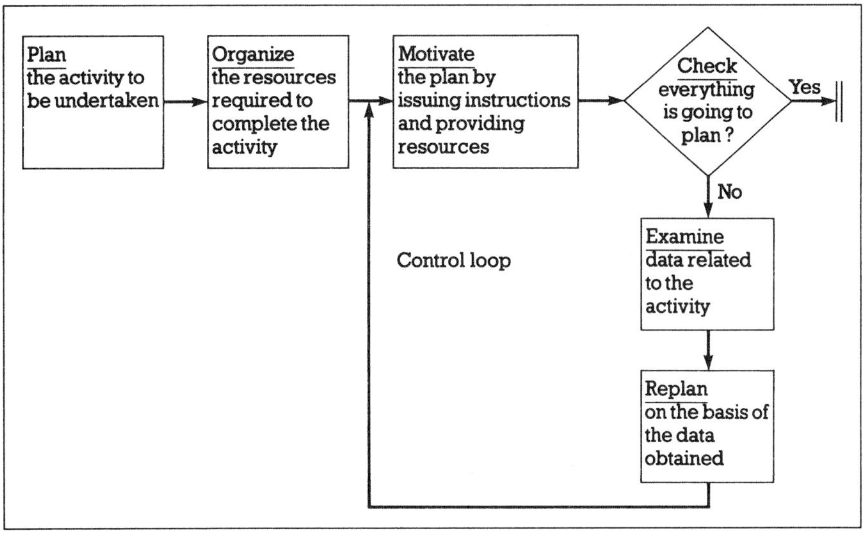

When designing new systems and procedures, it is most important to ensure that control over the events is exercised. Feedback of information is vital to the well-being of the organization. Well-designed administration procedures will aid control, but in the final analysis it is the human factor which determines the degree to which any system is successful.

Activity 4

Using the principle demonstrated in the diagram above, draw an algorithm for starting a car from the following information:

1 Get into the car.
2 Start the car.
3 Check rear mirror.
4 Signal to turn into traffic.
5 Release hand brake.
6 If traffic is clear, pull out.
7 If not safe to start, wait till traffic is clear.
8 Start journey.

Activity 5

A wedding is to take place in four months' time. The bride-to-be's family is spread around the UK and the Continent. That family has to make the arrangements for 150 guests. As a starting-point they have drawn up the plan shown below.

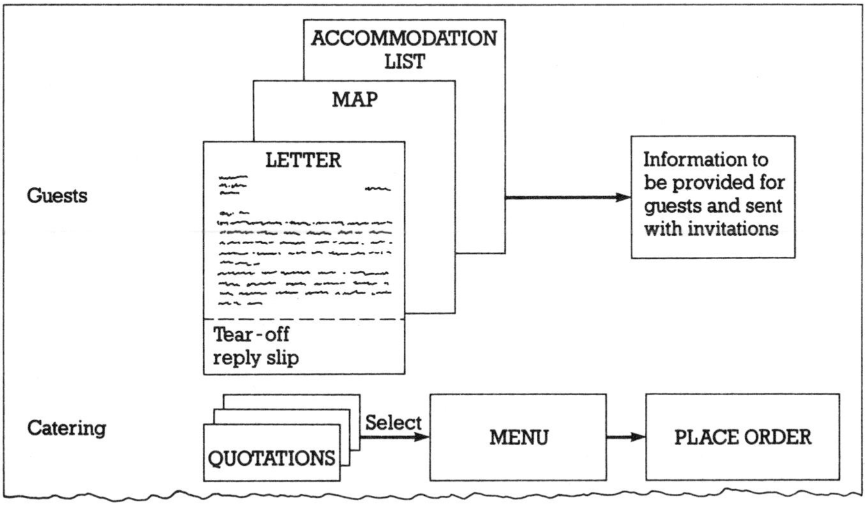

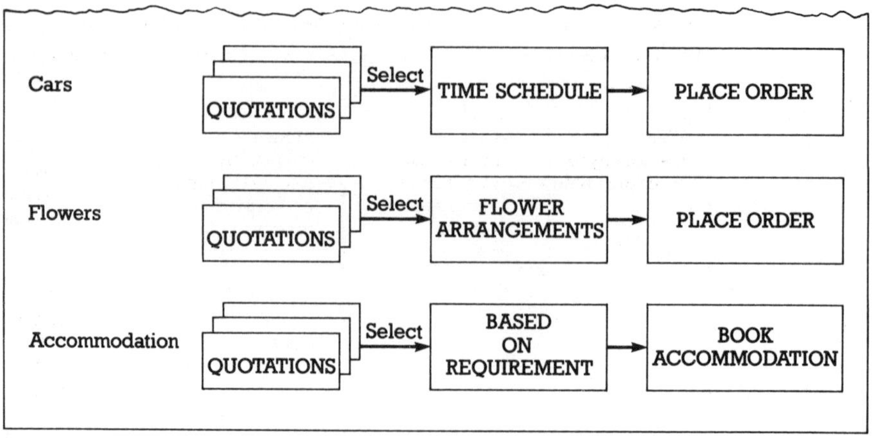

Systematic approach to planning a family wedding.

a Design the standard letter and tear-off reply slip to be sent to the invited guests.
b Suggest a system of dealing with the replies which will prevent anyone being overlooked or being without accommodation.
c Suggest the order in which the activities should take place, explaining what determined your choice.

Systems confirmation

A number of separate components connected in some way need not be a system. They may be merely a collection. You have learned that a group of components comprises a system if removing one component results in a change in that component or in the system.

When we examine the central heating system, we find that the component parts are:
a water
b a source of heat
c radiators
d pipes
e a thermostatic control.
Note that each component is complete in itself. It is only when they are assembled and made to interrelate that they become a system. This relationship can be represented in the following manner:

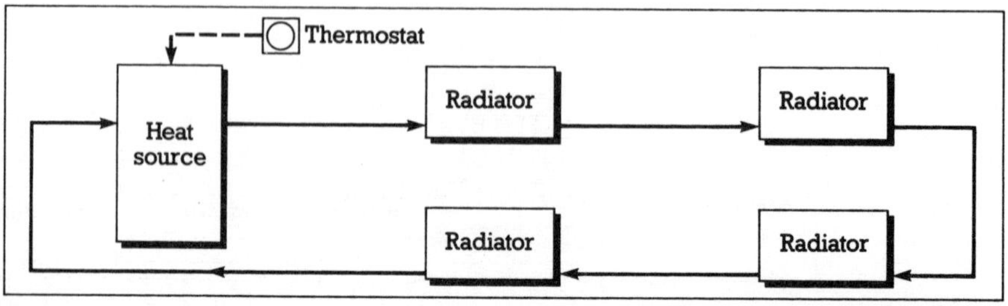

When you apply the test of removing one component, you will see that the system will fail to work, regardless of which one is removed.
This diagram shows that the system has a built-in **control** in the form of a thermostat which constantly monitors the air temperature. How it does this need not concern us; it is its function and its relationship to the **feedback** from the air temperature that are important.
These principles can be applied to administrative systems in a business organization, whether it uses basic clerical procedures or sophisticated electronic data processing.

Systems design

In a large organization systems design is usually the responsibility of the management services function. Smaller organizations will use established systems sold by stationery manufacturers, often adapting standard documents for their own use.

The function of the management services department and the techniques of **organization and methods** are dealt with in Block 7. We shall consider the general principles and procedures here.

Design considerations

Systems design needs the same care in planning and attention to detail as that which would be applied to the design of a product.
Any system transmitting information within the organization, or outside to its suppliers and customers, must be cost effective.
Ideally, the cost of obtaining information should not exceed its value to the organization, but this is not the only criterion. Any deficiency in the **communication** and **feedback** system can cause the organization to lose control.

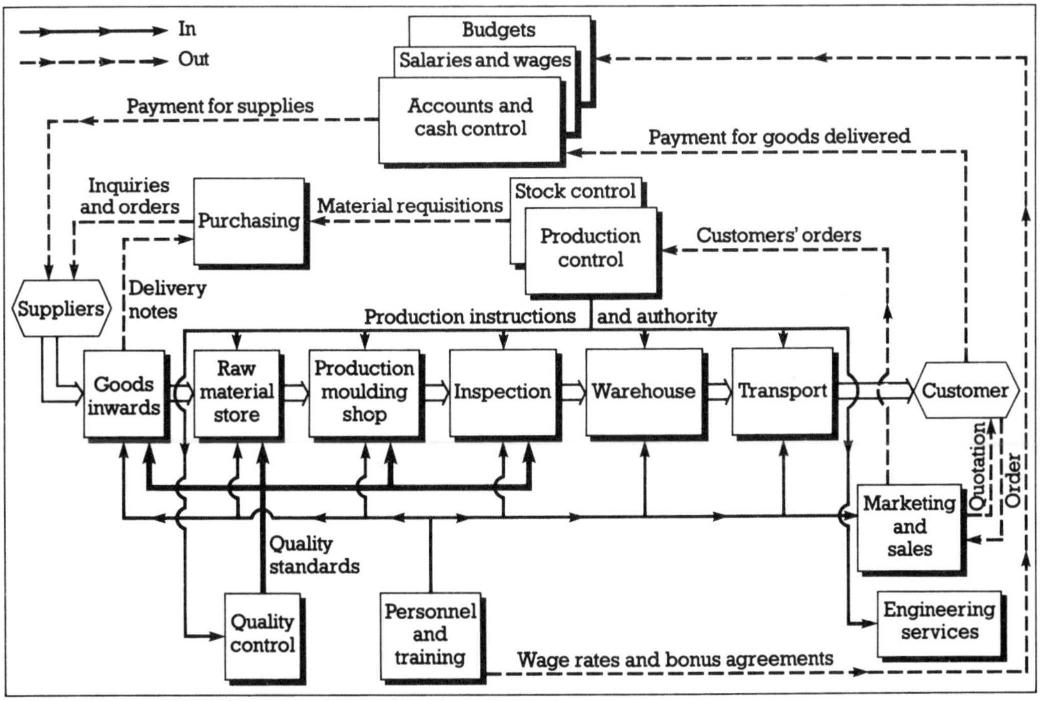

Production organization administration system.

Good systems design is a trade-off between simplicity, cost and the degree of control required. To achieve a reasonable balance between these factors, two questions have to be asked of any administration routine:

Who wants to know this information?

Why is the information needed by any particular person?

To get the correct answers to these questions, systems designers have to know about the organization structure. **Lines of communication** up, down and across the structure have to be identified, and the function and size of each department have to be understood. A knowledge of the organization's product or service is also essential.

Paperwork routines often require the active co-operation of other departments in the organization structure.

Forms

Who needs them?

If you have the very common mistrust of forms, then think again. A well-designed form makes communication very simple by reducing the possibilities of error; therefore much of the information circulated around an organization is carried by forms of one kind or another. Unfortunately, the tendency is for too many forms to be created and for them to be completed diligently long after their usefulness is finished.

The initiation of new forms should be controlled by one person or section. They should keep a record of the forms in use (and their distribution) and issue identifying numbers for them. From time to time, the initiating departments should be asked to justify their continued use.

Pre-planning

The form should cover all eventualities in the area it relates to, not just the current situation. Think about every possibility before you send a form for printing. If there are many possibilities, you should limit the form's application to a manageable part of the area, giving it an appropriate restricted title. Another form may be needed to cover the excluded cases; if so, make sure its title differentiates it clearly from the original form – if you don't people will fill in the wrong one.

Layout

The form should be simple to read and to fill in, and it should be in a logical order. Allow enough space for the answers (eg, long addresses) but don't allocate large spaces where the answer is likely to be very short.

If you are giving instructions for filling in the form (eg, 'Please use a black pen'), do that at the top of the form and specify dense print. If many lines of information are needed, break them into blocks of five to ten lines with a space between. Use ruled lines of various densities to separate sections.

Other aspects of preparation

You may have to consider what sort of paper your form should be printed on; it may, for instance, have to be filled in or consulted on an outside location. Copies may be required and these can be colour coded to help in distributing them to the correct sections. It could help to include a numbering sequence for copies.

Try to avoid being rushed into producing a form, especially if you will have to order a large quantity straight away. A trial run to allow any modifications to be made is desirable.

Computer input forms

You probably know that in computer input forms the layout is entirely governed by the requirements of the related computer program.

Typically, there will be details written on the form which are never inputted – eg, the customer's name. Instead, numerical codes will be entered in exactly the order demanded by the program. As each program is likely to be a unique creation, you will have to discover its sequence before you can design the input form.

Reports

You will need to be able to produce a pithy, well-organized and informative report. This is a key communication skill in any organization.

Reports are usually called for by someone higher in rank (but you may sometimes initiate a report yourself to go up the organization). It follows that your reputation and career prospects are often at stake when you are reporting and you will want to present what you have to say as well as possible.

Reports can be either written or oral. A variety of styles of presentation are possible for each, according to the complexity of the material and the expertise of the audience.

The five parts of a report

The structure of a report remains constant. You should include the following categories of information in any report, written or oral.

1 *Terms of reference* – who asked you to report on what, and when.

The instruction to produce a report can come in any form ranging from a request for information shouted down the stairs to a formal memo giving an exact specification of the material to be included. You must get clear terms of reference before you begin, and you must state them in your report: both you and the person you are reporting to will be annoyed if your report is off the point.

2 *Procedure* – what you did to find out.

This may have been: asking someone, measuring something, analysing something, going to have a look, working out the figures etc, or combinations of such activities. Listing these allows your reporting officer to identify any source of information which you may have missed.

3 *Findings* – what you found out (also called evidence).

In this section you present systematically everything you have managed to find out. Information from various sources is brought together to produce a coherent picture of the situation. The most important items come first; subsidiary or support material back them up.

4 *Conclusions* – what you deduce from what you found out.

Bear in mind that 'conclusions' is used in the sense of 'deductions' – not of 'ending'. Your findings will have led you to some particular view of the situation – eg, somebody should be fired, new equipment is needed, the system needs revising.

5 *Recommendations* – what you suggest should be done.

You are not always asked to make recommendations, especially if you are a junior member of staff. If you are asked to do so, do recommend something positive. The people you are reporting to will ignore your recommendations and make their own decisions if they feel like it, but they will be irritated by non-specific suggestions like 'I recommend some changes should be made.' If cost is involved in your recommendation, give some idea of what this might be.

Letter format reports

Much reporting is done within the format of an ordinary business letter, especially where the report is going outside the organization to a client or customer. The letter format is perfectly suitable if the information is short and simple and if there is an obvious way of marshalling the facts.

Sample letter format report.

The first paragraph will contain the **terms of reference** and the **procedure** (but not labelled as such). The **findings** will come in the second paragraph and the **conclusions** and **recommendations** (if any) in the last paragraph.

```
                                          DATA REMEMBER
                                          1 High Street
                                         Wigfall WF2 6RS

19 June 19..

Mr N. Smith
6 Hillside Road
Ty Draw
Clwyd

Dear Mr. Smith

Thank you for your letter of 10 June 19..
asking me to find information on JOHN CLARE.
I approached Northampton Public Library who
were able to give me these facts.

Clare's library of over 400 volumes is housed
at the Public Library and is listed in D Powell's
'Catalogue of the John Clare Collection' (1964)
The transcribed manuscript of 'The Midsummer
Cushion' is apparently in Peterborough.

I think you could well obtain additional detailed
information if you contacted the Peterborough
Museum Society direct.

Yours sincerely

Jo Waller

Jo Waller
(Researcher)
```

Terms of reference

Procedure

Findings

Conclusions

Schematic reports

The schematic report presents information in numbered and labelled sections using the five-part layout already outlined. If necessary, a section can be subdivided, each subsection being given a label to make the structure of the report clearer.

You will find this layout suitable where the material is fairly complex, particularly if it is to be considered by a group of people who each have a specialist interest in some section of it.

A schematic report is a formal document. It calls for formal expressions – if it is going up to the management you should use impersonal constructions (eg, 'it was noted that') rather than personal ones (eg, 'I noticed that'). Absolute correctness in facts, spelling and layout are important.

If you are reporting to a colleague of equal rank, you may decide that impersonal constructions are too formal. You will still need to be absolutely correct, of course.

In either case you should take up a neutral position as a purveyor of information – though doubtless personal bias will creep in if the topic matters to you.

You should devise an *informative title* for your report. Managers are inundated with reports and have no time to read through them to find out what the topic is.

The first section will be labelled *terms of reference*. You should decide whether to write this at the margin or centre it, to put it in capitals, to underline it in red etc. However you display this section heading, the other four must be displayed in the same way: uniformity allows the reader to run his eye down the page and pick out the major sections easily.

Follow this with *procedure* (note how it is spelled!), saying what you did to find out your information (going to stores, phoning sales statistics, talking to people etc).

The *findings* section will almost certainly need splitting into subsections; you must devise appropriate titles for these. Analysing the items into subsections is an exercise in logical thinking, as is deciding the order of the subsections. The numbering of these should be done with great care (see 'Layout of a schematic report'). Any muddle will make it impossible for readers to find their way around or to refer each other's attention to specific items.

Remember that *conclusions* covers what you have deduced about the situation (avoid restating the findings).

In the final section make the *recommendations* you think fit. Try to express each recommendation in the same style.

EITHER

1 Introduce all with one clause:
   It is recommended that:
   1 a new fork-lift truck be bought
   2 a new member of staff should be appointed.

OR

2 Use 'that' to introduce each item:
   It is recommended:
   1 that a new fork-lift . . .
   2 that a new member of staff . . .

OR

3 Treat all as imperatives:
The following recommendations are made:
1 Obtain a new fork-lift . . .
2 Appoint a new member . . .

Make sure you spell 'recommendations' correctly. Here is a tip: remember that the word consists of 're' (a prefix meaning 'again') and commend (which never begins with a double 'c' when used on its own).

Sign and date your report. It will have given you a lot of work, so make sure you get credit for it.

If you have tables of figures or charts, refer to them in the text and add them at the end as Appendix I, Appendix II etc. That will prevent the thrust of the report being weakened.

In the layout in the illustration you will see that the subsections for the findings are indented more as they become more subsidiary – this is another device which allows readers to concentrate on the points that are their special responsibility.

TITLE

I TERMS OF REFERENCE

II PROCEDURE

III FINDINGS (OR EVIDENCE)

A Subsection heading
- 1
- 2
- 3
  - a
  - b
  - c

B Subsection heading
- 1
- 2

C Subsection heading
- 1
- 2
- 3
  - a
    - i
    - ii
  - b
    - i
    - ii

D Subsection heading
- 1
- 2

IV CONCLUSIONS

V RECOMMENDATIONS

It is recommended that:
- A
- B
- C

Signature.................................
Date...

Layout of a schematic report.

The **numbering** of a schematic report often causes an undue amount of trouble. There are several methods.

In a very long report you can use the **taxonomy** system, which is easily extended. You number the first item in the first section 1.1, the second 1.2 and so on. When the topic changes, start numbering again at 2.1, continue with 2.2 etc. You can insert headings if you wish.

For less lengthy material it is usual to alternate the numbering between numbers and letters. If your report breaks down into five levels of importance (and it will be pretty detailed if it does) you can use this system:

1 Roman upper-case numberals (I, II, III, IV) followed by
2 Capital alphabet letters (A, B, C, D) then
3 Arabic numbers (1, 2, 3, 4) then
4 Lower-case letters (a, b, c, d) then finally
5 Roman small-case numerals (i, ii, iii, iv).

If there are only four levels of importance, drop 5, the Roman small-case numerals. If there are only three levels, drop 1 and 5, ie, use no Roman numerals.

You are strongly recommended to leave the numbering until you can see how it will develop – and then to do it in pencil first.

REPORT ON PARKING ARRANGEMENTS AT
Chetwood Town Hall, December 19__

A TERMS OF REFERENCE
On 30 September 19__, following complaints from the Police Superintendent (Traffic), the Town Clerk instructed the Premises Section to report on existing conditions in the car park and make recommendations for improvements.

B PROCEDURE
1 The existing parking procedures were ascertained.
2 A week-long count of vehicles using the car park was undertaken.
3 Car park users were asked to state their reason for parking there.
4 Members of staff and councillors were invited to submit their views.

C FINDINGS
1 *PARKING PROCEDURES*
There are 50 Parking places, 20 of which are reserved. Senior members of staff and councillors are issued with stickers entitling them to an unspecified parking space at the north end of the car park (marked 'Reserved' in white paint). There is no car park attendant. There is no actual barrier, though there is a sign saying 'Official Business Only'.

2 *COUNT OF VEHICLES* (See Appendix I)
More cars were left in the car park in the afternoons than in the mornings and more at the end of the week than at the beginning.

3 *REASONS FOR PARKING* (See Appendix II)
About half the cars parked during the 5 days were left by people who could be considered to be there on legitimate business. The rest were simply using a convenient space in the centre of town. Parking at the adjacent supermarket is charged at £1.50p per hour. There is no parking space at the Library.

4 *VIEWS OF STAFF*
a Senior staff
Senior staff entitled to parking stickers complain that though they can usually park at 9 in the morning, they can seldom extricate their cars during the course of the day if they need to go out on business. If they do vacate their place, they claim that they can never return to it because a councillor will have taken it.

Sample schematic report.

b Junior staff
Staff not entitled to stickers admit to using the places intended for official visitors 'sometimes' or 'now and then'. They justify this on the ground that the nearest public car park is 500 yards away and costs £2 per day. They complain about shoppers and tourists filling the car park.

c Councillors
Councillors are incensed that they have to cruise around waiting for a space and then often find their exit obstructed by a tight array of badly parked non-authorized vehicles.

D CONCLUSIONS
It appears that parking provision is inadequate even for legitimate users and that the lack of means to limit access to the general public was the direct cause of the mêlée of which the Superintendent (Traffic) complained.

E RECOMMENDATIONS
In order to prevent a recurrence of this situation it is recommended that:
1 no public parking places be offered at the Town Hall;
2 an electronic barrier be erected at the south end, operated by discs to be issued to 40 authorised persons;
3 the 10 remaining places be held for important visitors whose arrival would be notified to the Premises Section ahead of time;
4 efforts should be made to obtain contract parking elsewhere for those members of staff not issued with parking discs.

FRANK GRIFFITHS
Head of Premises
9 October 19 --

APPENDIX I

Number of vehicles using Town Hall car park

	MON	TUES	WED	THURS	FRI	TOTAL
am	49	86	42	100	120	397
pm	70	94	46	108	143	461
Total	119	180	88	208	263	858

APPENDIX II

Reasons for using Town Hall car park
1 – 7 October 19--

Staff	100
Town Councillors	80
Visiting Housing Department	140
Visiting Rates Office	102
Attending Art Exhibition	36
Shopping At Supermarket	150
Going to the Library	108
Sightseeing	142

When presenting a schematic report it is usual to send a covering letter or **letter of transmittal**, a title page and a brief summary of the main findings. See the next illustration.

CHETWOOD TOWN HALL

Car Parking Arrangements

Report to Town Clerk from the Premises Section
9 October 19__

CHETWOOD TOWN COUNCIL
Town Hall, Chetwood, CH1 1SR

9 October 19__

The Town Clerk
Chetwood Town Council
CHETWOOD CH1 1SR

Dear Sir,

You instructed me on 30 September 19__ to report on the situation in the car park and I now have pleasure in attaching my report.

Yours faithfully

F. Griffith

Head of Premises

SUMMARY

CAR PARKING ARRANGEMENTS

The 50 available spaces are inadequate for the demand and the position is exacerbated by unauthorized parking by the general public.

Steps to limit access, reallocate places and acquire further contract parking have been recommended.

Title page, covering letter and summary of report.

Activity 6

You work in the front office of your college and your job specification includes two days a week giving clerical assistance in the student services department.

The head of student services believes she has noticed a feeling of unrest amongst the students recently and would like to find out what is bothering them. She has asked you to prepare a schematic report for her based on information which you are to get from the students.

Using your own college as a resource, draw up a list of questions and put them to a sample of your fellow students. You might like to include questions on the library, the study facilities, the student common-room, the food, the lectures etc.

Base your report on these findings and make any recommendations you think fit.

EXTRUDED PLASTIC TUBE LTD
SITE 26. EASTWOOD TRADING ESTATE. NEWTOWN L26 Z29
TEL: 021-366-9720/21 TELEX 994052

1 November 19__

The Office Manager
EPT Ltd

Dear Sir

FIRE DRILL

You asked me on 30 October 19__ to report on the success or otherwise of the fire drill to be held that afternoon. I, therefore, arranged for the landings and collection points to be supervised from 4.00 to 4.30pm and made the following observations:

FIRST PARAGRAPH
Terms of reference and **Procedure**

1 The fire-bell on the first floor, south corner failed to operate.

2 Many of the younger staff ran about in an undisciplined fashion, jostling each other on the stairs.

3 One meeting of executive staff (room 15) refused to suspend their meeting.

4 About a quarter of the staff failed to arrive at the collection points and are assumed to have gone home.

MIDDLE SECTION
Findings in indented numbered paragraphs

I therefore conclude that the staff's attitude to fire regulations is unsatisfactory and recommend a poster campaign giving the correct procedures, backed up by a directive from the management. The technical fault in the fire-bell has already been corrected, but we should institute regular weekly checks of the alarm system.

FINAL PARAGRAPH
Conclusions and **recommendations**

Yours faithfully

Harry Owen
Safety Officer

Sample mixed-form report.

Mixed-form report

As the name suggests, this is an amalgam of the two preceding formats – the **letter format** and the **schematic format**. You will find it suitable for use when the material is too lengthy or complex to fit well into a letter but not long enough to warrant a full schematic treatment.

The mixed-form report starts off like a letter. The salutation is likely to be 'Dear Sir' because of the formality of the situation. The first paragraph of the letter will cover (without labelling) the **terms of reference** and the **procedure**.

The change comes with the **findings** section. This should be displayed as indented numbered points. Six to eight points will be the most you can comfortably accommodate; any more will require a different format.

The report will finish like a letter, with a final paragraph giving **conclusions** and **recommendations** followed by the complimentary close, the signature and the designation.

Activity 7

The production unit of EPTL is complaining that the plastic granules coming from the materials store are in damaged sacks, with the result that about 20% are spilt on the shop-floor as the men are loading the hoppers.

The production manager, Mr Blossom, sends you along to materials where you learn that the problem arises from a damp floor and has only recently developed. You then fetch the maintenance engineer to have a look. He says there is probably a seepage from the central heating pipes which are sunk in the concrete slab at that point. He thinks the only cure is to break out that section of floor and re-lay the pipes.

Write a mixed-form report for the production manager incorporating this information.

Marketing reports

Marketing reports are intended for clients. You should therefore pay particular attention to presentation and grammar and to matching the style of writing to the needs of the particular client.

Opening Paragraph A marketing report calls for a slightly different layout, the main conclusions being brought forward to follow the introduction and being expressed in summary form.

Methodology and findings The centre section will give an outline of the **method of research** and detailed **findings**, with any tables and diagrams. Such tables need captions, and the units used and sources must be clearly stated.

Final Paragraph In the last paragraph you should summarize the survey findings and give your general **conclusions** in more detail than in the introduction. Your **recommendations** will close the paragraph.

Finally, you should separately list all the tables and diagrams you have used, give a list of references and attach any appendices.

Title page

Contents page

List of appendices

Text of report

– Introduction (purpose of report)
– Main conclusions (series of short statements)
– Methodology (outline of research)
– Survey findings (text and tables and diagrams)
– Summary of survey findings
– General conclusions and recommendations

List of tables

List of diagrams

References

Appendices

Format for a marketing report.

The informal report

The **schematic report** can be too formal and complex in certain circumstances. An **informal report** is suitable when the report is going to a colleague of equal rank in another department or to your immediate superior, or when the material does not lend itself to numbered points.

The material is organized into three sections:

1 *Introduction* – giving a picture of the situation or the background of the report.

2 *Evidence* – this is the old **findings** section, usually short paragraphs of continuous prose under subheadings.

3 ***Conclusions*** – what has emerged from your investigation and what you think should be done now.

Plastics Trade Fair - Escrix Exhibition Centre

INTRODUCTION

Following the Board's decision to exhibit at this year's Fair, a pre-visit was made to investigate the space and facilities available.

EVIDENCE

Display Stands	Stands vary in price according to location but all seemed of adequate size and were well provided with electrical connections and the like.
Facilities	Stands in the price range £3000-5000 offer a reception suite for entertaining clients.

The central commissariat provides secretarial and tele-communication services to exhibitors.

An executive refectory provides cordon bleu meals and an excellent wine list - a bit expensive perhaps

The technical team of fitters, riggers etc. needs booking in advance.

CONCLUSIONS

The environment was pleasing and the facilities meet our requirements. This smallish exhibition centre would provide us with the kind of exposure we seek. I would certainly recommend going there.

Omar Kalifa (Marketing)

13th NOVEMBER ____

Sample informal report.

Memorandum reporting

The memorandum report, as you might imagine, is a report written in memo form, generally on A4 memo paper.

This layout is suitable for occasions when you wish to suggest an improvement to an existing routine or the introduction of a new idea to your superior or to someone on the same level as yourself. Your relative positions in the organization will dictate the tone. You should use the formal diction that goes with report writing.

The format is very flexible within a general framework. Use the opening paragraph to set the scene. In the second paragraph you should state your main points as succinctly as possible. In a final paragraph you could suggest a sequence for implementation, a time-scale or whatever is appropriate. If you want to introduce many figures or extracts from publications in support of your idea, you should attach these as appendices.

FROM: Jane Moss, Accounts **SUBJECT:** Purchasing - Form 36D
TO: Mr Watson, Purchasing **DATE:** 13 December 19__

Form 36D is issued in triplicate on the 8th of each month by Purchasing to Production, with copies to Statistics and Stores.

The system was started five years ago at the time when we were first moving into the Trulex market and was designed to facilitate decisions on the viability of the move. Accounts received the information late via Statistics.

Since we have become firmly established in this market, neither Production nor Statistics has any further interest in 36D. Accounts, however, still need these figures for the monthly return (AC 26) and a member of staff goes every month in person to collect the copy which is still being filed in Statistics.

I would like to suggest that this form is redesigned as:

1 top copy to Stores
2 copy to Accounts
3 flimsy filed in Purchasing.

It would also be desirable from Accounts' point of view to change the date of issue to the 1st of the month and there appears to be no objection to this.

J. M.

Memorandum report.

Eye-witness reports

You may be called upon on occasions to give an eye-witness report. These are most often needed when there has been an accident. The narrative of events should usually be given in chronological order and in the form of a standard business letter.

The five-part structure of a report does not apply in these circumstances. You should simply state what the accident is and when it happened in the opening paragraph and then elaborate on your part in or view of it in the second. You may sometimes be able to suggest a way of preventing a recurrence, but usually no recommendations are required or possible.

The chief difficulty in writing eye-witness reports is in making clear who was in what position and/or in what direction the participants were moving. Very often a diagram will help you to cope with this problem.

You should be careful not to make any sweeping statements in the heat of the moment about who was to blame for an accident. You may be called upon later to substantiate your view, possibly in a court of law. A short cooling-off period before allocating blame is advisable.

SEMPER TRADING
Industrial Estate
PILBEAM
PL6 4MT

Today's date

The Managing Director
Semper Trading

Dear Sir

You asked me to report on the accident I witnessed this morning on Factory Way involving a company van and a green Ford car.

I was cycling to work at 8.15am behind a van being driven by Mr. Tom Sharp, travelling west to east along Factory Way. Mr. Sharp was passing the mouth of Acker Lane indicating to turn right into the Industrial Estate, when a green Ford suddenly pulled out of Acker Lane across his path to turn right, ie west.

The van struck the side of the car behind the passenger seat and badly damaged the panel. The car driver was knocked out for a minute but soon came round. His face was cut.

Mr. Sharp asked me to cycle on to work and phone for an ambulance, which I did.

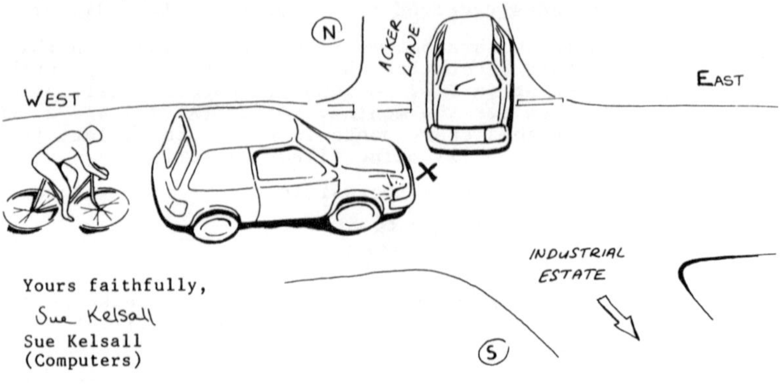

Yours faithfully,

Sue Kelsall

Sue Kelsall
(Computers)

Eye-witness report.

Activity 8

You are in charge of the customer records section in the sales department. One of your duties is to report any accidents that occur in your section.

On Monday morning Mrs Mary Carlisle, the cleaner, told you that as she was leaving at 7.00pm the previous Friday evening she tripped over her mop and fell down four steps. The only person still on the premises was her friend, Kate Farmer, who took her to the hospital outpatients' department where she was diagnozed as having a sprained ankle. She ruined her tights on the bucket as she fell.

The hospital strapped Mrs Carlisle's ankle and she was taken home to 7 Dundee Place, Heworth in a taxi.

Make a copy of the accident report form illustrated below and complete it for Mrs Carlisle's accident.

Routine reports

You will find that the vast majority of reporting in any organization is done on a regular basis – every week, every month or perhaps even every day. This kind of report is most often made by filling in a form called a **return**; examples are illustrated below.

Because of the legal implications of accidents at work, staff involved in any accident, however slight, are usually required to report it at once. A standard form of the type illustrated will be available for this too.

POST RETURN

Week no..Week ending ....
Name ....
Section ....

Pieces of post in hand end of wk.......	Rec'd in Week no.	Cleared Week no.	Outstanding at...............
41	126	111	56

Signed......

STAMP RETURN

Week ending Friday ....

Value	B/fwd	Used	In hand	Required
5p	6	5	1	10
10p	7	7	0	12
15p	8	6	2	15
20p				
24p				
28p				

DINNERS SERVED

3 months ending ....

TIME	CANTEEN	REFECTORY
12 – 1	46	9
1 – 2	62	28

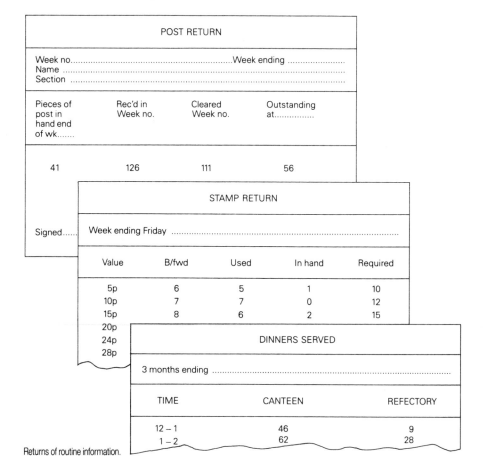

Returns of routine information.

ACCIDENT REPORT FORM

Name of person involved or injured

Home address

Department/Section

Name of foreman/section leader

Date and time of accident

Injuries received

Did the injured person report to first aid post? YES/NO (circle one)

Was the accident reported to foreman/section leader? YES/NO (circle one)

If YES give name

Name(s) and Department(s) of the witness(es)

Damage to company property

Damage to personal property

Signature ....

Department ....

Date ....

NB: Eye-witnesses should immediately submit a detailed account of the incident to the Personnel Officer on company notepaper.

Factsheets

You may be asked to present a factsheet or briefing when your superior starts to take an interest in a situation – often when matters need the intervention of someone with more authority.

The factsheet needs a title. It is usual to say at the beginning who has asked for it, but there is no need to give your sources of information as usually you will have been asked to write it because you have detailed knowledge.

The main body of the document will be taken up with a clear picture of the situation. If it is complex, headed and numbered paragraphs or numbered points indented in sections may be needed.

The purpose of the factsheet is simply to inform, so neither conclusions nor recommendations are needed.

FACTSHEET ON SITUATION RE: MISS S BARNES AND A WALLIS
At the request of Mrs A J Simmons (Personnel Officer) to report on the position regarding the dispute between Sally Barnes and Arnold Wallis on 1st October 19__

I inherited this file on 1st September 19__ when Miss Carruthers's work-load was split.

The situation at that time was that Miss Barnes (Sales) was proposing to sue Mr Wallis (Records) for insulting behaviour alleged to have taken place in the filing stack on 2nd August when Miss Barnes visited the Records Office looking for a missing customer record file.

On 2nd September I arranged interviews in the Personnel Office with each party individually. Both appeared quite reasonable and Mr Wallis agreed to apologize to Miss Barnes.

When I interviewed them together on 6th September, however, they both became very irate. Mr. Wallis refused to apologize and Miss Barnes subsequently, on her own admission, let down all Mr Wallis's car tyres. Mr. Wallis responded by removing the H.T. lead from Miss Barnes's vehicle the next day.

Since then there have been a number of moves and countermoves against each other's cars and the work of both the Sales Office and the Records Office is suffering. Furthermore, as the Sales Staff are nearly all female and Records are all male, the whole firm is starting to take sides on a gender basis.

I understand that a women's committee is to be formed to support Miss Barnes's demand for an apology from Mr Wallis and/or his dismissal.

Edith Harper
Personnel
1 October 19__

Activity 9

Your employer, Mr Edward Rabat of Red Guide Tours, asked you yesterday to prepare a report on the facilities in Bankside, a Midland market town, to help him decide whether to include it in his list of overnight/weekend stopping places.

Bankside is one of three towns you have surveyed recently and at that time you obtained the information below. From this prepare a factsheet for Mr Rabat, inventing any necessary detail.

BANKSIDE – results of survey

1 1 cinema
2 3 discos
3 1 bingo hall
4 8 AA or RAC hotels
5 5 AA approved garages
6 Market every day except Wednesday
7 1 4-star hotel
8 2 garages specializing in motor cycles
9 Early closing day Wednesday
10 27 guest houses and B & B acommodation
11 1 caravan park
12 1 museum (folk collection)

File minutes

A minute in the context we are considering is a report of the current position in a situation, or of the latest developments, or of a recommended course of action.

Minutes live in files and are intended to brief the people working on that particular file or case. They may be written on the file jacket itself or they may be on file paper and attached to metal-ended tags inside the file. It is usual for new file-paper minutes to go on top of the heap so that the latest information reaches the eye first. If you file your minute out of order, the reader may not discover it and may take inappropriate action.

An informative, succinct, even witty, minute is much appreciated. Your minute will remain on file for ever, so you should be particularly careful. A study of the style of other minute writers to the file will help you.

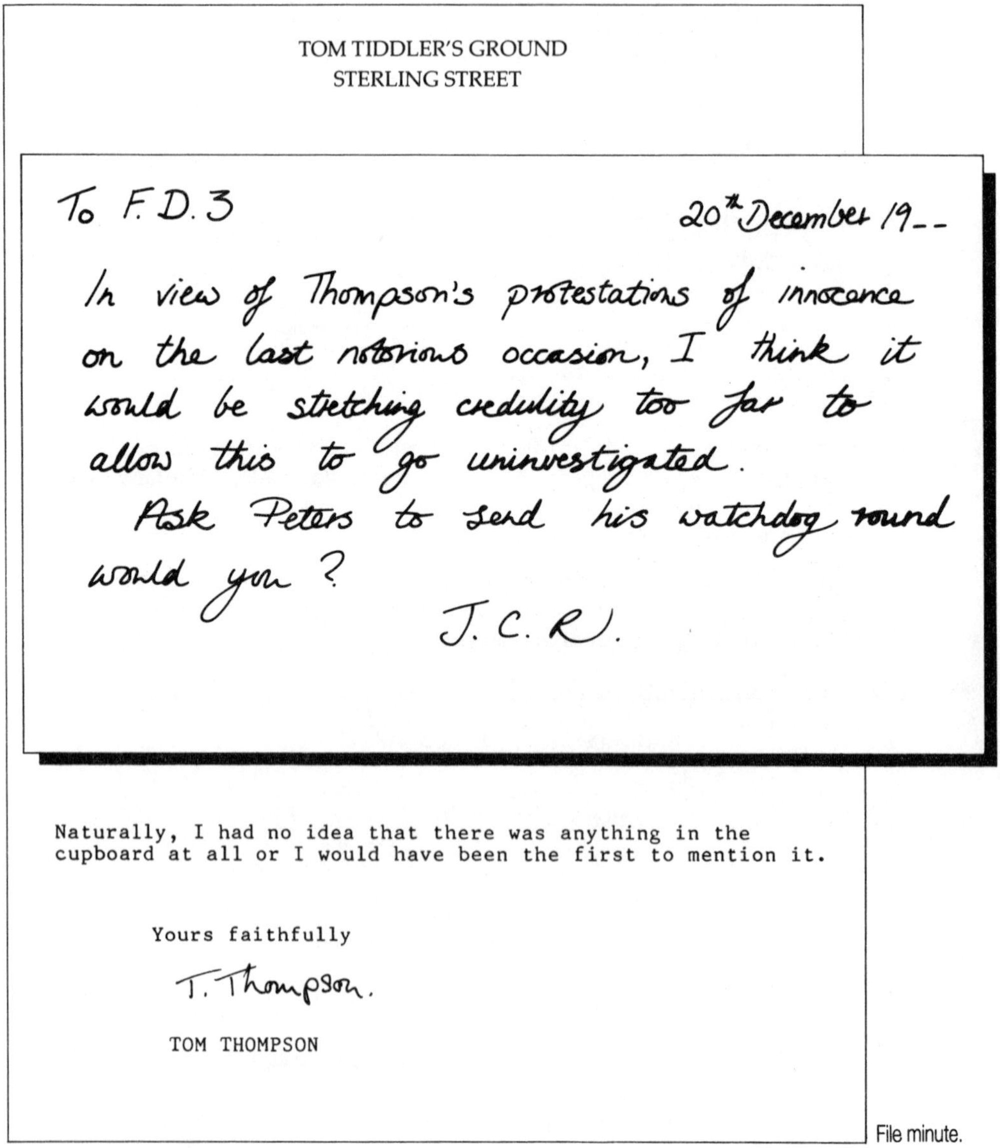

TOM TIDDLER'S GROUND
STERLING STREET

To F.D.3 20th December 19--

In view of Thompson's protestations of innocence on the last notorious occasion, I think it would be stretching credulity too far to allow this to go uninvestigated.

Ask Peters to send his watchdog round would you?

J.C.R.

Naturally, I had no idea that there was anything in the cupboard at all or I would have been the first to mention it.

Yours faithfully

T. Thompson.

TOM THOMPSON

File minute.

Summaries, abstracts and précis

There is so much written information reaching most executives these days that they frequently ask junior members of their staff to do some of the reading and present the information to them as a short summary.

Sometimes the executive will know which topics he is interested in and will ask you to **summarize** only the relevant parts. An **abstract** is the name given to a very brief summary of points of particular interest in a long text. Sometimes they will want to know what total theme is being developed and will want a short version of the whole text, ie, a **précis** – usually about one-third of the original length.

Summarizing is an advanced skill. You need to be able to comprehend the text, to process it through your brain and reproduce it, reduced to its major ideas, in a concise form.

When deciding whether to use continuous prose or numbered points under headings, consider the purpose of the summary – it may be for quiet appraisal in the privacy of the office or a brief to take to a meeting.

You first need to read the article or text, perhaps more than once if it is complex or technical. From that you will get an idea of the subject matter and will be able to identify the key ideas. They will come wrapped up in illustrations, anecdotes, jargon, repetitions etc. These probably add a good deal of interest to the text, but they are not essential to the meaning.

Jot down some rough notes covering the major points. Rearrange them into a logical order if necessary.

From your notes, produce a rough draft, writing on alternate lines to make changes easy. You should aim to express the ideas in your own words. However, some of the writer's words may be so technical or so appropriate that you will have to use them in your version. You should make a word count now – a reduction to about one-third of the original length is considered about right, unless you have had different instructions.

If your summary is very short, check to see if you have omitted any major ideas. If it is too long you will have to prune it. Try rephrasing parts of it, perhaps combining pairs of sentences or clauses into one. There will be odd words you can dispose of, but be careful. It is easy to lose the sense at this stage or to produce an ungrammatical and disconnected version.

If you are using numbered points, you do not need whole sentences to carry the ideas. But take care that your notes are not so brief that the reader cannot follow them.

Now read right through your summary, remembering to check the spelling and punctuation.

Finally, make a fair copy, taking trouble with the presentation. Give it a relevant and informative title and state the source of the original text.

Activity 10

Work through the various stages of the summarizing of the newspaper article 'Take an efficient look at time wasting' to see how the procedure outlined is carried out in practice.

Take an efficient look at timewasting

● If executives kept tabs on their every move they could do a lot more with their day, says WINSTON FLETCHER

HOW MUCH time do we all waste at work? How inefficient are we? How disorganised? Couldn't we all, with a little thought, effort and training, squeeze an extra 10% out of each day by minimising interruptions and using our time more effectively?

The recent spate of takeovers suggests that many leading companies believe executives in other leading companies are not using their time as effectively as they could. Yet surprisingly little research has been done on how managers occupy their working hours; still less on how they could occupy them better.

All executives, whether in private or public industry, in national or local government, admit that a vast amount of each day is spent in futile meetings; in handling unnecessary phone calls; in unproductive travelling; in dealing with trivia; and in coping with interruptions.

How much of this derives from organisational inadequacies, and how much is the executive's own fault varies from workplace to workplace. Once again, no analytic data are available. Yet it seems certain that many of the problems could be overcome.

One of the few extensive surveys of how management spends its time was made by IBM in 1979. It showed that over 50% of the average executive's day was spent on just five activities: writing, meetings, telephoning, travelling, filing. (Top management spent over 60% of its time on these activities – 22% on meetings alone.)

All five activities, and especially the first four, can be prodigious timewasters. Yet there is now a plethora of information, accumulated from small studies and case histories, that could help executives to improve their performance.

Take just a few examples. Time management can be greatly improved by anyone who keeps a personal time chart for a couple of weeks – a detailed hour-by-hour diary in which all activities are recorded, and a note made of their usefulness. It is a chore to begin with, but quickly becomes routine. And I have yet to meet a single person who was not astonished by the results and who did not find them exceedingly useful.

Writing, to take another example, is something most of us do inefficiently. Indeed, writing by hand , as opposed to dictating, is itself a considerable timewaster.

An American study has shown that dictating to a secretary or a machine will normally increase an executive's output by as much as 400%. Yet, even when dictation facilities are available, many executives are too conservative, or too uncertain, to use them.

Perhaps they are hoping to leap over the secretarial stage and are looking forward to the day when every manager has his personal computer or word-processor, but meanwhile they are wasting endless hours scribbling unimportant notes in longhand.

When you do dictate, a few tips will help ensure the outcome is less garbled than is all too often the case. Before you start:

● jot down headings of an outline of what you want to say and tell your secretary (or dictate into the machine) what the document is going to be about;

● pause before each statement

● emphasise consonants such as "b", "p" and "d" which can easily be misheard.

● spell out proper names and unusual words.

All simple stuff, but rarely done.

Similarly, most of us constantly misuse Alexander Graham Bell's wonderful invention – and misuse our own time as we do so. Modern equipment has greatly improved the mechanical aspects of phoning, but the human aspects have remained as inadequate as ever.

How often do you accept calls when you know you should not because you are completing an urgent job? How often do you find yourself unable to bring telephone conversations to an end as quickly as you should? How often do you ring off without having mentioned something you intended to?

Just as you could improve your performance on the telephone, so you could almost certainly use your travelling time more productively. You probably spend at least 250 hours each year (about 30 full working days) shuttling between home and work. It is inconceivable that you couldn't use that time more creatively than you do.

In the car, you can dictate into machines, rehearse speeches and presentations, take cassette courses or set yourself mental management problems. In the train your briefcase should become a travelling writing desk, as in days of yore. Lengthy air journeys can be the most productive of all if you can discipline yourself to eschew too much sleeping and the bar.

The areas in which we could all improve our efficiency are innumerable. But wouldn't too remorseless a drive for greater efficiency make working life even harder and drearier than it is? Possibly, but far more often it will have the opposite effect.

If you organise yourself better, you will find more free time to concentrate on the things you enjoy doing – problem-solving, thinking, planning.

You may enjoy spending endless hours in fruitless meetings or incessantly searching for mislaid documents, but if you do, you are an exception bordering on an eccentric. And British management could do with becoming rather less charmingly eccentric.

● *Winston Fletcher is the author of The Seven Keys to Superefficiency, published by Sidgwick & Jackson £9.95*

How to summarize an article.

SUMMARY OF ARTICLE ON TIME MANAGEMENT

ROUGH NOTES

Para 1	Is it possible for management to make more efficient use of their time?
Para 2	Little research available
Para 3 + 4	Generally admitted that much time is wasted. Organizational or personal faults
Para 5	IBM survey showed 50 per cent of time devoted to 1) writing 2) meetings 3) telephoning 4) travelling 5) filing. First 4 very wasteful.
Para 7	Improvements possible – activities and usefulness. Personal time-use diary.
Para 8 + 9	Writing by hand very inefficient. Dictation increased output by 400 per cent.
Para 10 + 11	Before dictating a) jot down outline of letter under headings – inform secretary of general purpose; b) pause before each statement; c) emphasize consonants, particularly 'b' 'p' and 'd'; d) spell out proper names or unusual words.
Para 12 + 13	Limit phone calls, end them quickly, make sure you deliver main message.
Para 14	Travelling time; a) dictate to a machine; b) practise speeches; c) take cassette course; d) solve management problems in heads) e) don't sleep or drink on planes.
Para 16	Lead to overwork or strain? Beneficial effect on person and management.

TIME MANAGEMENT

ROUGH DRAFT

Scope of article

Could executives make better use of their time?

Research

There is little research available on

Very little research has been done on how managers use their time but a general feeling that a great deal of time is wasted either because the organization ~~of the firm~~ is at fault or because the person is at fault. *inefficient*

individual

An IBM survey showed that managers spent half their time on five occupations:

1) writing

2) meetings

3) telephoning

4) travelling

5) filing

were prodigious time wasters

and that the first four of these wasted a lot of time.

Time use

scheduling *can be very revealing*

It can be h~~elp to s~~chedule every activity undertaken - and its usefulness ~~- in a~~ personal time-use diary. Writing by hand is a very bad *TIME CONSUMING* ~~way of usin~~g time. DICTATING can increase output by 400%. ~~To be successful one should, before dictating:~~

per cent if a few simple tips are followed.

a) jot down outline of letter under headings

b) tell secretary the main drift of the letter

c) pause before each statement

d) emphasize consonants 'p' 'b' and 'd' especially

e) spell out names and difficult words

Telephoning

e *decisively*

Limit incoming calls when busy, ~~a~~nd them ~~quickly~~, but make ~~sure you have covered all the main points you want to cover~~.

all the necessary points have been covered.

Travelling

Executives could ~~use their~~ travelling time ~~gainfully~~ by:

make more productive use of

1) dictating to a machine en route

2) practising speeches

3) taking cassette courses

4) *reviewing* ~~solving~~ management problems

5) limiting sleeping and drinking on *aircraft* ~~planes~~.

Outcome

It is possible *operate such remorseless schedules but*

It ~~is a~~ possibility that executives could suffer even more from stress and overwork if they ~~fit all these other things in.~~ ~~I~~t *it* is more likely though that ~~this regime~~ would have beneficial effects on both the firm and the individual.

there would be

FINAL DRAFT

FINDING TIME

Summary of an article 'Take an efficient look at timewasting' by Winston Fletcher in ***The Sunday Times***, 27 July 1986.

SCOPE OF ARTICLE

Could executives make better use of their time?

RESEARCH

There is little research available on how managers use their time but a general feeling that much time is wasted, either because the organization is inefficient or because the individual is at fault.

An IMB survey showed that managers spend at least half of their time on these five activities, the first four of which are prodigious timewasters:

a) writing

b) meetings

c) telephoning

d) travelling

e) filing.

POSSIBLE IMPROVEMENTS

Time-use diary

Scheduling every activity undertaken - and its usefulness - in a personal time-use diary can be very revealing.

Dictating

Writing by hand is too time consuming. Dictating can increase output by 400 per cent if a few simple tips are followed before starting:

1) jot down outline of letter under headings

2) tell secretary the main drift of the letter

3) pause before each statement

4) emphasize consonants, 'p', 'b' and 'd' especially

5) spell names and difficult words.

Telephoning

Limit incoming calls when busy, end them decisively, but make sure all necessary points have been covered.

Travelling

Executives could make more productive use of their travelling time by:

1) dictating to a machine en route

2) practising speeches

3) taking cassette courses

4) reviewing management problems

5) limiting sleeping and drinking in aircraft.

OUTCOME

It is possible that executive could suffer from even more strain and overwork if they operate such remorseless schedules, but it is more likely that there would be beneficial effects on both the firm and the individual.

Activity 11

MEMORANDUM	
TO: You	SUBJECT: Customer Care
FROM: B. Milner	DATE: Yesterday

Summarize this on one side of A4 for me, would you?
I want it for the P.R. Conference next week so make it easy to see on the page.

Many thanks,

B.L.M

Summarizing correspondence.

Why it pays to make the customer king

● Companies are slowly realising the value of courteous and helpful staff in improving customer care, reports CONRAD BRUNSTROM

Imagine the scene. The electricity man has come to read the meter. But he won't come in because your dog is growling. You know the dog is "a nice old thing – it wouldn't hurt a fly." If the meter man simply tells you to lock him up, you will resent it. So what should he say to you?

And what should the meter man say to the dear old lady who offers him a cup of tea? (He has more than a hundred meters still to read). Or to the householder who asks him to give a rough estimate of the bill? Or when it is clear that someone is fiddling the meter? In all these cases how the meter man behaves affects how customers feel about the Electricity Board.

Take another kind of problem. You are the manager of a wines and spirits shop, owned by a national chain. A customer returns to your shop saying "I gave you a £20 note. You've only given me change for £5." The customer is a regular. What do you say? What do you tell your staff – some of whom are part-timers? And would it make any difference if the customer were a skinhead?

More and more companies are recognising that they must improve customer care – which means they must make it a business objective. To achieve it they must set standards for the service required. They must also train staff to deal with customers.

The days of the meek undemanding customer are over. There can be no justification for having to queue up to pay for an indifferent service. In local government, in the health service, even in social security offices, customers are becoming more vocal. And where they can't take their custom elsewhere, they are giving support to pressure groups to force improvements.

These pressures have a compound effect. Why do you wait hours in the out-patients' clinic even though you made an appointment for a particular time – especially when you find your estate agent is ready for you at the agreed time?

In both cases you are paying for the service. More people are making such comparisons.

There are three basic rules for a good customer care policy.

● Top management must give its commitment to the policy at the outset and continue to give it. Customer care is a policy, not a campaign.

● Management and staff should agree on practical measures to make customers feel wanted. These could be as simple as always giving your name on the telephone so that the customer knows who is dealing with his business and feels that an individual in the company has taken personal responsibility for him.

● Management must get it across to staff that the customer is the person who is paying their salaries.

But the drive for better customer care has to be properly planned. If not the results can be bizarre.

Take, for instance, the "smile" campaign of one of the big banks. It festooned staff restrooms and toilets with big, red smiling lips. Staff treated the campaign with contempt. They knew they needed to improve customer service but this would not be achieved by grinning like clowns all day.

Surely a better objective would have been for the staff to think of ways of getting customers to smile their thanks to the staff.

Companies should also beware the whiz-bang approach to improving customer care.

These campaigns use "star personalities" on videos, bright folders, posters and stickers supported by lavish conferences.

They often make a high-toned demand for courtesy – with the implicit suggestion that staff are naturally discourteous. Such campaigns can signal management's concern, but unfortunately they do not make a lasting impact.

An allied danger is the big image-creating campaign which is not backed by practical measures to make sure the reality approximates to the image.

If you are told that British Rail is "getting there" but find that your local service is no better than before, then mood-setting television adverts that tell you what a wonderful job everybody is doing could be counter-productive.

Getting staff to adopt customer care standards and practices is a long and difficult task that needs management effort at all levels. Without it the staff are likely to say: "Why pick on us? We don't get the back-up, only the complaints."

Half the battle is to identify the problems that staff face and provide help to overcome them. If their background does not provide the skills they need, exhortation is a waste of time.

Often so-called discourtesy is merely a failure to be articulate. A simple formula of words for a difficult situation can work wonders and can earn the employees' – and customers' – gratitude. Once staff realise that management is not criticising them but is trying to make their life easier, they will respond.

There are other points to bear in mind, too. Too often staff do not even know of the achievements of their organisation. Knowing might make them proud to work there. For example, people still look back with pride to the old Great Western Railway – 40 years after its incorporation into BR

The fundamental message is simple: "the customer expects to be king. He is no longer amenable to massaging by bland marketing messages. He simply wants better service.

Organisations that fail to pick up the warning signals will lose out – but please, please, don't rush into a "courtesy campaign". The overtones of forelock-pulling doom it to failure.

On the other hand, thoughtful, expertly designed and monitored customer care programmes with do-it-yourself input are paying off. Their success will increasingly be a matter of public debate over the next few years.

● *Conrad Brunstrom is manager, learning systems, with Inbucon Human Resources.*

Summaries of correspondence

You will need a special form of summary when you have to summarize a series of letters, perhaps where solicitors are to be called in or when your supervisor needs a brief statement on a situation and how it has developed.

Your summary will need an informative title giving the subject and the date-span of the correspondence. It may be worth giving full details of the names and addresses of the correspondents at the start; it will save you having to repeat them throughout.

Some of the letters may be so routine that they can be omitted. You must give the dates of significant developments in the correspondence; for instance, time-clauses in a contract or service may be involved.

Some firms routinely summarize correspondence as each letter is received or sent, using a tailor-made section like the one illustrated for this purpose.

FILE JACKET TOWNROW BUILDING AND CONSTRUCTION CO			BC 28
CORRESPONDENCE			
DATE	WRITER	SUBJECT	
14 · 2 · 19..	TOWNROW	Sale of property to Mr Peter Binks	28 BROWNING CLOSE
16 · 3 · 19..	BINKS	Cracks under kitchen window	
18 · 3 · 19..	TOWNROW	Inspection arranged.	
24 · 3 · 19..	TOWNROW	Superficial cracks only. Will be re-pointed.	
1 . 6 . 19..	BINKS	Window glass cracking. Serious subsidence suspected. Urgent action required.	

Summarizing correspondence.

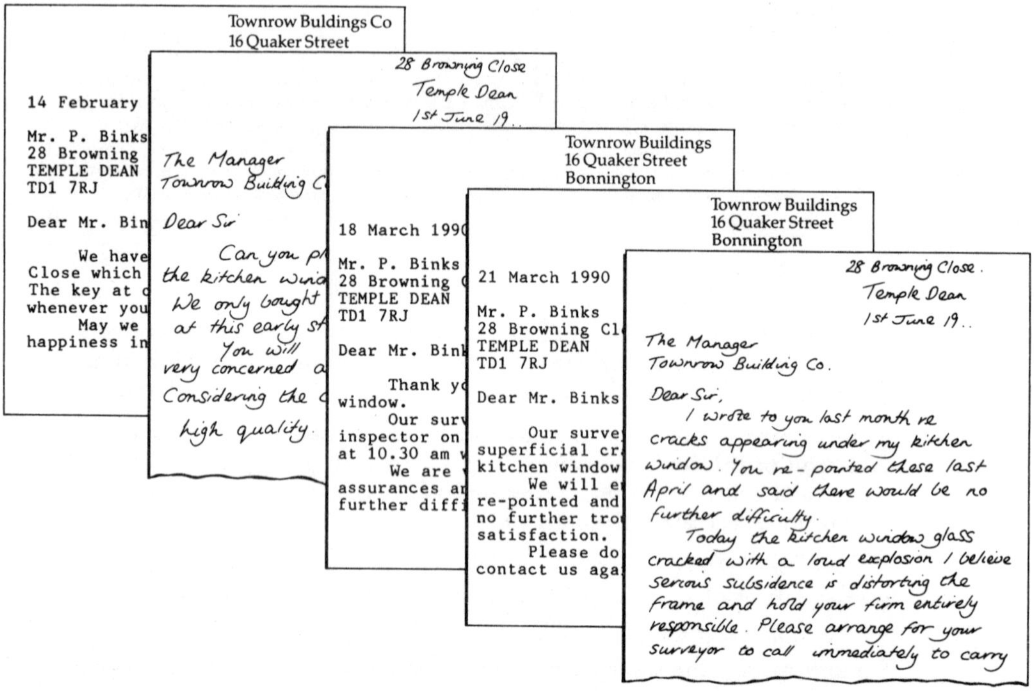

Summary

We have seen how systems modelling allows management to consider possible solutions to problems prior to introducing modifications. The elements of **flow charting** were introduced and emphasis placed on the necessity to build in **control** and **feedback**. The general principles of care and attention to detail in **systems design** were extended to include the design of the **forms** which carry so much information around organizations. Finally, we looked at various formats for **report** writing and at **factsheets**, **file minutes** and various kinds of **summary**.

Skills

Skill	*Activities in which skill is developed*
a Information gathering	2, 6, 8, 9, 10, 11
b Learning and studying	1, 2, 3, 4, 5, 6, 10, 11
c Working with others	6
d Communicating	1, 3, 5, 6, 7, 8, 9, 10, 11
e Design and visual discrimination	1, 2, 3, 4, 5, 9
f Identifying and tackling problems	1, 2, 3, 5
g Numeracy	1, 2, 3, 5
h Information processing	1, 2, 3, 4, 6, 7, 8, 9, 10, 11

Block 3
Managing People at Work

Introduction

Managing people is the heart of running any organization. In this block we shall look at ways of motivating the work-force and ways of reducing conflict. The psychological characteristics of people in groups will be examined, as will various leadership styles.

Management techniques

Management can take two views of the rules and regulations affecting individuals in organization structures.

1. They are there to facilitate the efficient running of the organization.
2. They are there as a threat and constant reminder of what will happen to the individual who does not conform.

Those who take the latter view can be a menace to the organization. Managers with no authority other than that given them by the rule book tend to lack original thought and to stifle any that their subordinates may have. People prefer to be led rather than driven.

A number of techniques for successful management are outlined below.

Communication

So much lip service is paid to communication in some organizations that it can become a bad joke. However, the ability to communicate ideas and commands is an essential skill for the manager. The role of communication in motivation is often overlooked. As a result, the team spirit suffers.

The most important rule in face-to-face communication might well be 'Communicate for tomorrow as well as for today.' Normal courtesy and respect for subordinates leads to respect for the manager as a leader and willingness to co-operate.

Leadership

A few are born leaders; most have to learn to be leaders. Modern management tends to emphasize democratic leadership, but there are times when the autocratic style will best serve the interests of the organization and the individual.

Wise leaders keep the use of autocratic methods to a minimum, knowing that this approach closes the door to communications with the group they control.

The acid test of leadership is the ability to achieve the objectives set by the organization.

Given the ability to sense how the group thinks and reacts to any given situation, the manager can lead successfully – even if the group does not much like him.

Motivation

A major part of the manager's task is the motivation of subordinates. It is much easier to control a bunch of 'self-starters' than a group who have to be told exactly what to do and to be supervised while they do it. The smart manager realizes that it is not possible to stand behind everyone all the time they are working.

Motivation is based upon the realization that each individual has certain needs, such as those for recognition, status and self-development.

Career and job satisfaction are long-term motivation factors. In the short term the manager can motivate by a simple word of encouragement or the recognition of a job well done.

Some consider that this is pandering to the subordinates' egos and that they should perform well because that is what they are paid for. If you think that, consider the fact that the performance of managers can only be as good as the performance of the team they lead.

Delegation

Motivation involves participation by individuals. They need to feel part of any activity they are engaged in. In order to satisfy this need, the manager must be prepared to delegate responsibility.

Delegation prevents the manager from becoming overloaded with work. Overworked people can endanger the organization: they tend to concentrate on the easy tasks and lose all sense of priority. Note also that the continuity of the work of the organization should not cease because an individual manager is absent. There are risks involved in delegation, but many of these can be eliminated by efficient **communication** and training. Managers should not plead inefficiency of subordinates as an excuse for failing to delegate.

Assessment and appraisal

The manager who can **delegate** with an easy mind is a manager who knows his people. Few are blessed with the gifts of making accurate snap judgements about people, and appraisal of performance must be based upon continuous assessment. The performance of each individual may improve or deteriorate as time passes.

Appraisal interviews should be a two-way **communication** exercise, giving the employee an opportunity to voice hopes and aspirations. Any criticism should be constructive – some plan to improve weaknesses should be presented by the manager.

Assessment and appraisal must be carefully planned and implemented so that they meet the desired objectives.

Morale and discipline

It is helpful to consider these two jointly. It is easy for a group to have high morale if it is allowed to do just as it pleases, without regard to the objectives of the organization.

Measurement and assessment of morale has been the subject of investigation in many large organizations. Complicated data processing systems have been designed, searching questions asked, tables and learned papers produced. Some managers have a less complicated approach, simply asking the questions, 'Do they perform well and willingly? If not, what appears to prevent them?'

Sure-fire success cannot be guaranteed, whichever approach is chosen–but when employees feel that they are getting reasonable pay and working conditions they are usually motivated to co-operate.

Discipline is necessary for the promotion of good morale. Those who confuse discipline with oppression will be disappointed by the results; those who have a fair and equitable discipline policy will maintain morale.

Few people like to work for an organization with slack discipline. The novelty of 'getting away with it' soon wears off and self-respect begins to suffer. On the other hand, few people wish to work in the shadow of the rule book. Managers must bear in mind that rules are for the guidance of the wise and instruction of the foolish.

When disciplinary action is needed, management should have the courage to proceed within the disciplinary code, tempering any action with justice.

Training

Many jobs require the employee to complete some form of training within the working situation. Others involve some form of training or further education outside the organization.

Training is related to **morale**. Those who are well trained and competent will be likely to achieve job satisfaction.

Planned training will ensure that money budgeted for this activity is well spent. This means that the training needs of the individual employee must be identified. For this the organization has to rely upon the observations of the immediate manager or use the **assessment and appraisal** system.

Barriers to communication

Communications are vital for the control of organizations. Most problems that arise in implementing policies, transmitting orders and obtaining feedback can be traced back to a failure in communication.

When communications fail we talk of barriers which have prevented the message getting through or distorted it during transmission. When considering structure design, these barriers can be subdivided into the **physical** and the **psychological**.

Physical barriers

These are related to the geographical layout of the departments, factories, and units that make up an organization. They may be separated by walls and passages or by several miles.

When data have to be moved physically from one place to another, occasional problems of delay and mislaid documents can not be avoided. The cost when data are moved has to be reflected in the cost of the product or service. Problems can be reduced by using modern office technology, but technology does not come free of charge.

Many offices have developed into large purpose-built units, and attempts have been made to reduce barriers by introducing open-plan and landscaped offices.

Psychological barriers

Many of the components of complex communication systems are not visible to us. These are the psychological barriers present because of attitudes and beliefs we have, which we accept without question.

Some are embodied in day-to-day sayings which are accepted at their face value, for example, 'All Chinese are cunning.' A moment's consideration of this type of statement reveals how invalid it is: as there are several million Chinese, there must be one or two who are trustworthy.

What we believe determines the way in which we view the world. The way in which we view the world can affect the way in which we communicate and set up a barrier.

If we could visualize the barrier that we create, it might look something like this:

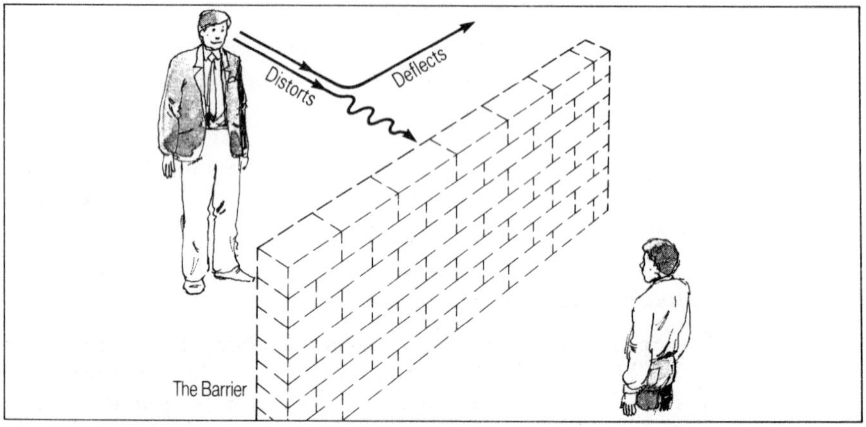

and as a result, the message can be deflected or fail to be transmitted.

Our own barriers are made up of a number of 'bricks' representing our individual make-up. They present us with a number of problems.

The following are examples of 'bricks' people carry into the communication field:

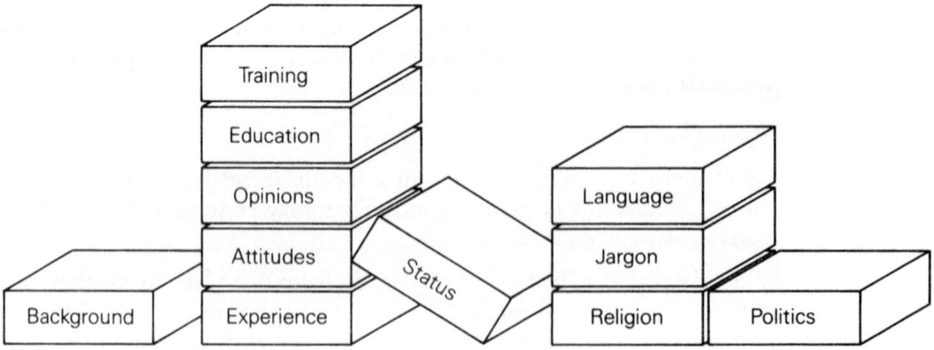

All of these influence the way in which we look at the world. For an example of this, listen to two politicians of opposing parties discussing an aspect of government such as defence.

Good communication can be achieved when:

1 A real message is being sent.
2 The sender is articulate.
3 The receiver is willing to listen.

Activity 1

List some bricks–in addition to those illustrated–which you can identify in your day-to-day communications.
Apply the extended list to the following situations:
a A teenage girl asking her parents if she can go on a holiday abroad with two friends of the same age.
b A customer asking the bank manager for a large overdraft on a current account.
c An elderly person attempting to understand a form for claiming extra benefits from the social services department.

In business communication, *simplicity* is the keyword.

Leadership and management style

People in organizations have to be directed and motivated; this organizing and directing is the function of management. The manner in which the leadership function is discharged has come to be designated the **management style**.

Leadership

A cynical definition of leadership goes as follows: 'Getting others to do what you are not able to do yourself.'

Before reading any further, consider the following jobs, which involve getting other people to perform certain tasks.
a a cabinet minister
b the senior executive of a county council
c the managing director of a multinational company
d the manager of a football team
You may come to the conclusion that the cynic's definition is not far from the truth. Those who supervise the activities of specialists may not necessarily have their specific skills, yet this lack of skill does not prevent them from successfully managing.

To take one example, the managing editor of a newspaper does not have to be printer, compositor, editor, photographer etc in order to understand the function of those within the organization and direct their activites. The managing editor's success in getting the best out of the people in the organization depends on the example set by the leadership/management style.

What characteristics identify a leader?

To answer this question we ought to ask first, 'What is a leader?' There are both good and bad leaders, good leaders being those who are acceptable to society in general and bad leaders being those who are not. An example of the latter is the leader who can organize a group of people to commit a major robbery. For either type, the ability to persuade others to act in a certain manner is essential.

Activity 2

A master criminal is considering the possibility of robbing a bank during a public holiday period. The outline of the plan is to break into an empty shop next door to the bank, tunnel into the vault during the holiday weekend, force the safe and take cash and valuables from deposit boxes.

The operation will require a confidence trickster to rent the empty shop, a building expert to tunnel through into the vault and a safe breaker to get access to the money and open the deposit boxes.

A number of well-known experts are being considered for the break-in. Each tends to be a loner and is not noted for willingness to accept the discipline of working in a team.

Discuss this leadership situation with others and draw up a mental picture of the characteristics the master criminal requires to ensure a successful, co-ordinated operation.

Opinions vary about what characteristics a leader should have. The US Army has a list of 32 for potential officers; presumably a reasonable selection from the list is considered to be evidence of suitability.

Many industrial psychologists would agree that the following four characteristics cover what is desirable in any leader. The leader should:

1 *Possess intelligence* To the degree that the leader should be slightly more intelligent than the group he or she leads. This should enable him or her to exercise the communication skills required to convey objectives to the group.

2 *Demonstrate social maturity* In the sense of having broad interests and being emotionally secure, which includes the ability to take defeat and start again without being frustrated, having self-respect and projecting self-assurance.

3 *Have inner motivation and drive* Seeing the completion of one level of achievement as the platform for the next; welcoming responsibility as the means to progress and achieve personal goals.

4 *Possess human relation skills* Realizing that nothing can be achieved without the willing co-operation of other people and that a healthy respect for the well-being and dignity of others is vital.

Experience suggests that a sense of humour is also an asset.

Activity 3

How many of the above characteristics would you apply to your mental picture of the master criminal? Make a numbered list of criminals in the news recently and note beside their names the relevant numbers.

Choose a socially acceptable leader from any section of society. Discuss as a group the extent to which they display the above four characteristics.

If there is clear evidence that they do not display all four characteristics, can you determine what makes them a successful leader?

At this stage you may have concluded that:

a it is not easy to identify what makes a successful leader,
b a leader may not conform to the popular concepts and yet still be successful,
c different situations call for different leadership skills,
d all leaders work within the constraints of the organization and the situation.

Situations can produce leaders who take the initiative and persuade others to follow. History provides many examples of people who have come from relative obscurity to lead nations or great campaigns. The manner in which they have achieved their goals ranges from cruelty to charisma, but each one have had to practise some style of management.

What determines management style?

You have learned that the manner in which one individual manages the activities of others is identified as the **management style**.

These styles are categorized by industrial psychologists, who study their effectiveness in a variety of management situations. Management style has been the subject of considerable research and is not explored in depth in this book. However, in order to understand the problems involved in getting people in organizations to work efficiently, you will need to be able to identify the general styles practised.

The Autocratic style Autocratic managers believe that the role of management is to tell the working group what to do. When they give instructions, people are expected to obey without question, for they have complete authority to command because of their position in the organization. In accepting this authority, autocrats also accept full responsibility for the action taken.

This description makes the autocrat appear to be a somewhat unpleasant person to work for, but that is not always the case. The autocrat can also be a benevolent manager, able to establish good human relations with the working group. If so, the group will work effectively. Some problems can arise because the autocrat will decide what is good for the group without consulting the members. This can lead to autocratic managers being disappointed with the results of their benevolence: for example, the industrialist may build his work-force a sports club when what they really want is a fair and equitable wage structure.

Some people react favourably to an autocratic style of management. It gives them a sense of security and relieves them of any responsibility apart from carrying out instructions. Those with any initiative tend to leave the group or to become frustrated.

Autocratic managers are not good at communicating with the working group. In extreme cases they make attempts to isolate themselves by putting up barriers to prevent the group from approaching them.

One advantage of this style of management is that it allows a quick decision to be made and implemented. On the other hand, the decision taken may not be the best one as it has not involved discussion with anyother person. Where an autocratic decision is made on the basis of some specialist training or knowledge, then the autocratic approach will be in the best interests of the organization.

Activity 4

A company employing over 1000 people in a branch of the engineering industry has in its maintenance department a group of unskilled labourers who specialize in the movement of plant and equipment within the works. This group is known as the heavy gang and is distinguished from other labouring staff in that its members are not required to perform any routine tasks such as sweeping up or cleaning.

The group is supervised by a charge hand, an ex-dock worker with skills in the use of ropes, cranes and slings and the movement of heavy loads. His management style is completely autocratic to the point where he could almost be said to rule by fear. Two factors allow him to take this approach. Owing to the nature of the work, the heavy gang works a considerable amount of overtime; much of it is at weekends when the plant is shut down and it attracts enhanced rates of pay. The charge hand is a former professional wrestler and appears well able to deal with any attempt to intimidate him.

In terms of productivity and efficiency, this group has a recognized reputation. Once a task has been explained to the charge hand, it can be left to the group. It is a matter of pride to them that they have never failed to meet any target set for them.

Although the charge hand's style of management is well known in the factory, when the gand was expanded to include two more members, 80 per cent of the labouring staff in the factory applied for the vacancy.

Consider what makes a dictatorial approach to management so successful in the case of the heavy gang.

The Persuasive style There is some similarity between the persuasive manager and the autocrat: they both expect orders and instructions to be carried out. The difference is that the persuasive manager will seek to give reasons for the decisions taken.

Autocratic decisions are often better received and acted upon if those involved are told how their role fits into the overall scheme. This tends to boost the **morale** and **motivation** of the working group.

Activity 5

A company has employed a new sales manager to control its UK sales force of thirty. The terms on which she has accepted the job require the sales turnover of the company to increase substantially within six months for her to keep her position.

A preliminary investigation into the activities of the sales force has revealed the following:

1 Each sales representative arranges their own working day, including the number of calls made on customers.
2 It would be possible to increase the number of calls made by each representative by at least 20 per cent.
3 Expenses claimed by the representatives are not backed up with any documented evidence.
4 Representatives are never called back to the sales office to confer on sales policy.

Prepare the outline of a plan for the sales manager to deal with this problem. Discuss, with your group, the degree of autocratic and persuasive management the situation imposed on you when you made the decisions in your plan.

The consultative style The consultative manager is prepared to consult with the group and to modify plans and decisions as a result of comments and advice given by members.

Note that the manager makes the plan before consulting with the group; no original thought is expected from individual employees until an overall plan has been decided upon.

Consultative managers are good at communicating ideas; they make their subordinates feel part of the decision-making process. Their success in management is related to the type of labour and working methods they control. Very little consultative management can take place on the production line of a car factory where the individual's activity is dictated by the work-station and line speed.

Activity 6

John Webb is the manager of the research and development laboratory of a major pharmaceutical company.

John controls the activities of a team of scientists engaged in testing the side-effects of the company's products and conducting research into new drugs for the pharmaceutical market. He is expected to work within the broad policy laid down by the board of directors, which states that the research and development laboratory should not engage in pure research.

The company operates on a strict budgetary control system, allocating costs to each department and expecting a reasonable return on its investment in research. Managers are assessed annually on the degree to which the performance of their department compares with budgeted performance.

Taking the role of John Webb, write an outline of the advantages and disadvantages of practising consultative management in the research and development laboratory.

The participative style This takes the principle of consultative management a stage further. Participative managers put the problem to the group and involve them in the decision-making stage. Ideas and suggestions are encouraged.

A number of factors have contributed to the growth of this form of management in recent years. Industrial and commercial processes have become more technical, demanding the employment of skilled technicians and specialists who want a say in the way in which their work is carried out. Trades unions have had considerable power and have demanded greater involvement in the management decisions which affect the working conditions and terms of employment of their members. Participation has been shown to be a successful motivator.

Case study–participative management

RN Resins, a small company manufacturing technical resins and adhesives for industrial applications, found that its management team had expanded to the point where its overheads were a threat to its competitiveness. A major reorganization reduced the management to a level where close supervision of all activities became impossible. Senior management had always worked in close co-operation with the work-force, maintaining an easy relationship in which communication presented few problems.

Transportation of the finished product to customers was carried out by the company's own van, or by using road transport hired from a local haulage firm. Selection of transport was simply made on the basis that the haulage firm was called in if the company van was out on deliveries.

Two men employed as storekeepers were responsible for preparing the loads and loading the transport for delivery. They approached the management and suggested that it might be worth examining relative costs for delivering by company transport and by hired transport.

Management asked them to devise a scheme for planning the use of transport and within a relatively short time this scheme was produced and adopted. On being put into operation, it produced £2000 savings in the first month.

The two storekeepers are now on a bonus payment system. They are completely responsible for the selection of methods of transporting deliveries to customers, with authority to negotiate terms with hauliers they select. Management has extended the participative system to the resin blending section, where savings have been made by reducing the wastage in resin processing.

Activity 7

Make a list of the possible reasons why the employees in the case study were motivated to produce a scheme to reduce the transport costs in the first place. Suggest why their interest should be sustained.

The free rein or laissez-faire style Free-rein managers see themselves primarily as the providers of resources for their group to use as members see fit. This type of manager does not give the group they control any great degree of leadership-inspired **motivation** in the form of a general policy or by setting objectives.

The group is left to establish its own goals and solve the problems. Abdication of power by the free-rein manager will frequently result in friction within the group and the abandonment of its objectives.

There are times, however, when a free-rein style will be the correct approach. Think back to the heavy gang – the wise manager in that company left the gang to get on with the task once it had been explained to the charge hand. Any attempt to oversee the work or give detailed instructions would have resulted in delays.

If it is used as a predominant style, free-rein management will demotivate the group and be seen as a sign of weakness in the manager.

Activity 8

A group of twenty women are employed as inspectors for a product manufactured by a continuous flow technique. Inspection is carried out by holding each unit of production over a light source to examine it for defects. The work cycle is short and repetitive with little job interest. A specified number of units has to be inspected by the group in each hour that the machine operates. Failing to meet this number results in a back-log on the production line and stops production.

Management insists on strict control over the working group, discouraging the women from talking whilst working and keeping a tight control over the time taken for recognized tea-breaks.

A new supervisor has been appointed to the group. During the three weeks she has been in control there has not been a single delay caused by a backlog in inspection. The manager of the deparment is aware that the new supervisor is breaking the rules laid down about talking and that the women are allowed to get drinks from a vending machine without seeking her permission. He is about to see the supervisor to remind her of the disciplinary code laid down for the department.

Given the chance to talk to him before he leaves his office, what would you say?

Management could almost be considered as a branch of the acting profession. The manager perceives the scene presented by a given situation and plays the appropriate role.

Whilst the majority of work tasks in industry and commerce respond to participative management, there are extremes where authoritative management is required for the good of all concerned. Situations arise where only the manager has the necessary knowledge, expertise and authority to make the correct decision. Other situations arise in which free-rein management is the best approach – turning a blind eye on occasions may allow a manager to gain in the long run.

It is the role that the manager plays in a given situation which determines the response from the work group. This role is subject to a number of constraints within specific organization structures, such as company policy, the type of process or production being managed, the layout of the working environment, the attitude of the working group and standards of discipline.

Although there are undoubtedly a number of charismatic leaders who are natural managers, most people require training. At least, training instils an understanding of the complexity of controlling the activities of others. Management skill tends to develop as a result of experience; management training allows the skill to be developed without too many mistakes being made.

The voice of experience

A world-weary and very experienced supervisor once gave a newly appointed and rather green manager the following good advice: 'If you ever get to the point where you do not know the answer, assume a quiet air of confidence and walk slowly away!'

Motivation – human relations aspect

It has been said, 'If you dig deep enough into any problem you will eventually come down to people.'

Human relations is the study of people at work in organizations, the aim being to predict the behaviour of the individual in the working environment and establish ways of improving the results of human efforts.

Human relations have existed since mankind started to live in groups. The scientific application of human relations skills in the work situation is a relatively new technique.

Before the industrial revolution, workers were organized into small groups with simple work relationships. Conditions were often bad.

The industrial revolution did little to improve the lot of the work-force; in many instances it made them worse. In the new mills and factories the work-force was viewed simply as an extension of the machinery and referred to as 'hands'.

Fortunately, some employers took a more humanitarian approach. Notable among these was Robert Owen, who refused to employ children, taught his work-force the need for cleanliness and temperance, and improved their working conditions. Owen was one of an exceptional few. Most employers in the 1800s were slow to accept the ideas of those few.

In the 1900s F. W. Taylor drew attention to the role of people in the work situation in improving efficiency in production. Taylor maintained that just as there was a machine for the job, there were also appropriate working methods to enable people to do the job. He is recognized as one of the founders of scientific management and work-study techniques.

During the 1920s and 1930s, Elton Mayo carried out a number of experiments at the Hawthorne Electrical Works in the USA. As a result, he came to the conclusion that the organization is a social system in which the worker is an important element.

Taylor sought to improve production by rationalizing the way in which the working methods were planned. Mayo attempted to increase production by humanizing it and recognizing the social interaction which takes place in the working group.

Investigative work by social scientists has continued into the present. Industrial scientists are now attempting to cope with the problems being posed by the matching of the work-force with modern technology.

Do people want to work?

It is often claimed that people do not want to work. Such claims tend to be made by people who are themselves in well-paid and satisfying jobs about in the less gratifying areas of employment.

Work makes the individual feel part of society, with a purpose in life. Recent studies carried out in the UK revealed that a sense of deprivation is experienced by the long-term unemployed. In the USA, a study carried out by P. M. Morse and Weiss on the function and meaning of work concluded that work is more than a means of providing the income to sustain a reasonable standard of living: many people interviewed said that they would still want to work if they had sufficient income to satisfy all their needs without working. This goes some way to explaining the phenomenon of the millionaires who work an 18-hour day.

It seems that people do want to work, not just for money but for other motives – such as job satisfaction, self-respect, ambition and recognition.

Activity 9

List a number of occupations which do not attract high rates of pay, but do not seem to have a problem in attracting people to them.

Identify three jobs in which there is a distinct possibility of being killed in the course of working.

Consider what motivates people to undertake these two types of task.

There are said to be two main reason why people work:
Intrinsic satisfaction – where the job is an end in itself. Involvement in the work satisifies the needs of the individual.
Extrinsic satisfaction – where the job provides a means of achieving the satisfaction of some need outside the working environment.

Intrinsic satisfaction may be the motivating factor for a research scientist with an ambition to find the cure to some illness.

Extrinsic satisfaction may be the motivating factor for a worker on a production line who submits to the boredom of repetitive working cycles and unpleasant working conditions because the high earnings allow him to pursue some hobby or support a desired life style. Work provides money; money provides the things which satisfy the needs.

This is, of course, a very simplistic explanation. We all have a complex mixture of needs.

Motivation – techniques

Motivation is one of the most difficult areas confronting those who have to manage the activities of others. Human beings present multiple motivation problems. We are all individuals, and, when a number of us are placed in a regulated situation such as an organization structure, we are likely to behave in different ways.

To motivate someone is to cause a certain behavioural pattern. Our behaviour patterns are determined by our **needs.** We are motivated to fulfil our needs as we perceive them, not neccessarily as others see them.

Some needs – such as food and drink – are very basic and essential to survival. Others are very complex – such as the need to be recognized and valued in a group or organization.

Human behaviour is determined by the individuals's **need structure**.
Motivating people in organizations can be accomplished by:

a getting them to see that the desired behaviour will fulfil their needs;
b indicating that if a certain course of action is not followed, opportunities to fulfil needs will be restricted.

Distilled down to its basics, this approach is a crude reward and punishment system which has many weaknesses if it is not applied with some subtlety. In the first case, the satisfaction of needs must be genuine; in the second, the punishment has to be the last resort.

A number of motivation theories have been advanced which are related to the need structure; for example, the need hierachy of Abraham Maslow (1943).

Maslow described motivators as a series of ascending needs which, while remaining unsatisfied, act as motivators. Once satisfied, the need ceases to be a motivator and another need arises to take its place. This can produce a **cycle of motivational activity** as follows:

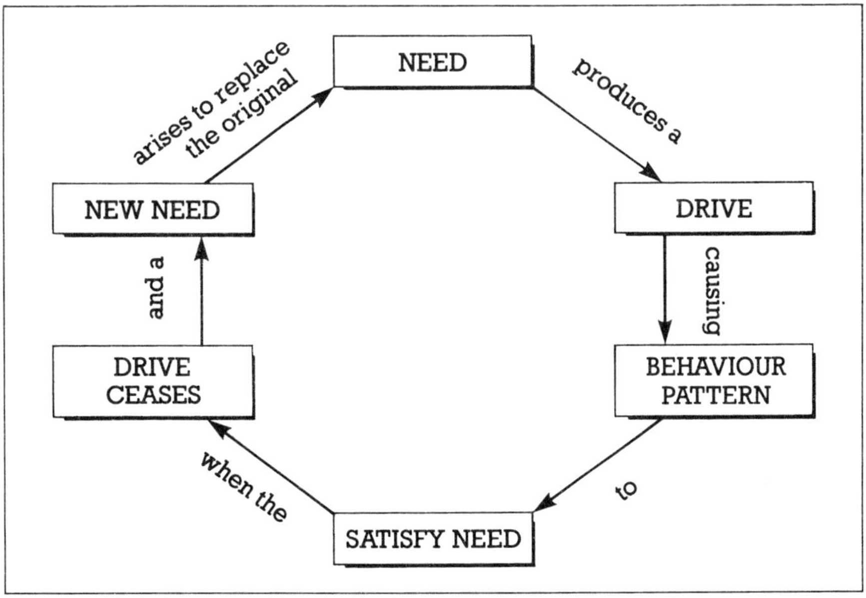

In fact, the new need may arise during the satisfaction of an existing need. In the situation of being both hungry and thirsty, you may decide to drink. In the act of taking a drink, your thoughts will turn to food and the need to satisfy your hunger.

A practical application of the theory will show the way in which needs dictate the way in which people behave in given situations. Do not try to read too much into the following activity; simply use the cycle of motivational activity described above to formulate your answer.

Activity 10

Part of the production process in an engineering works involves cleaning grease from components before they are assembled. The cleaning is carried out in a department isolated from the rest of the factory to protect the employees from corrosive fumes.

Management recognizes that operating the cleaning equipment is an unskilled, dirty and unpleasant job. They have introduced a rate of pay which is well above that paid to skilled operatives in order to reduce labour turnover and the cost of retraining.
In spite of the high pay, employees in cleaning tend either to seek a transfer to another department or to leave the company. The average time for any employee to remain in the cleaning section is twelve months.

Write a short report to the management explaining:
1 Why people are prepared to accept the job in the first place.
2 Why the high rate of pay fails to stop people seeking ways of leaving the job after relatively short periods of time.

Most people seek the esteem of others. This is why we adopt a certain style of dress or join certain groups. These are the badges which proclaim to the world what we are.

The badges which motivate people at work can be many and varied. Two of the better-known ones are job titles – such as manager or personal assistant – and privileges – such as eating in a separate canteen, starting work at a different time from others and being paid monthly rather than weekly.

Badges denote the status of people in organizations and people tend to guard their status jealously. Any attempt to deskill a job will meet with considerable resistance, even if no loss of earnings is involved.

Status can relate to working environment as much as to title and privilege. The situation described below is factual and took place in the 1950s, when the type of employee described was in very short supply. It could be argued that in the present climate of unemployment this would not have happened, but it is quite likely that the reaction would be just the same.

Case study

A company decided to transfer the stock control office from its main office to combine it with the production control office which is situated on the factory floor.

When the decision was made known, the stock controller's private secretary and two typists gave in their notice. On being interviewed by the personnel manager, they all gave the reason for leaving the company as being a reduction of their status in the company arising out of the move from the main office to the factory.

Maslow is not the only one to have suggested some form of need hierarchy; others have made similar suggestions with a variety of levels in the hierarchy.

The proposal that the levels in hierarchies can be closely defined and related to all employees has never been substantiated and must be viewed with some reservation.

Activity 11

1 Taking as a model the organization in which you are employed or the college at which you are studying, identify how the motivation factors suggested by the Maslow need hierachy model apply.

2 Consider your intended career and identify the way in which the need to pursue that career has changed your life style.

3 List the jobs/studying you have done since starting work/college which, given the choice, you would not have done.

4 Write an essay in which you explain why you chose to carry these tasks out.

Now you have completed Activity 11, do you think that there might be something in the idea that people have needs which determine the way in which they behave?

Motivation and maintenance factors

Fredrick Herzberg made a significant contribution to the study of motivating people at work by distinguishing between **motivation** and **maintenance** factors.

The research

Two hundred engineers and accountants in Pittsburgh, USA, were interviewed and asked to state what made them feel good about their job and what made them feel particularly bad.

The findings

When some conditions in the working situation are absent, their absence will cause considerable dissatisfaction. However, when those same conditions are present, they do not motivate in any significant way.

These conditions Herzberg named **maintenance factors** because their presence is necessary to maintain a reasonable degree of satisfaction in the employee. They are also known as **dissatisfiers** or **hygiene factors** because they are related to the 'health' of the organization.

The significance of the findings was that many factors which management had perceived as strong motivators were found to be more potent as demotivators.

Other conditions in the working environment operate primarily to build motivation and job satisfaction. When these are absent, they rarely cause dissatisfaction. These are known as **motivation factors** or **satisfiers**. They are the factors which make up successful motivation schemes.

The following are said to be motivation factors:
- Recognition
- Advancement
- Type of work done
- Responsibility

Do you think that they could be applied to any occupation?

These are said to be maintenance factors:
- Company policy
- Relationship with supervision
- Relationships with peer group
- Salary
- Job security
- Working conditions

Are there any that you would consider to be motivation factors?

You may not entirely agree with the above classifications since you will rank them according to your individual needs. Nevertheless, it is important to recognize that Herzberg's theory indicates that employees are motivated best by what they do for themselves – by taking on responsibility, gaining recognition, promoting their own ideas and so on.

Subsequent research has tended to confirm this theory, but there are some limitations to its application in different environments:

1 Herzberg's study was carried out in the USA and is relevant to the attitudes of the American worker.
2 Research carried out on white-collar workers has indicated that some factors considered as maintenance ones (such as pay and security) are frequently seen as motivation factors by these workers.
3 Job security is seen to be a motivation factor by both white-collar and blue-collar workers in times of high unemployment.

Activity 12

1 Consider the problems associated with the motivation of production line workers in a car factory. What solution does management usually apply?
2 Identify the motivation and maintenance factors Herzberg might relate to personnel employed as senior administrators in local government or the Civil Service.

The achievement motive

Another motivation theory is that of David McClelland, set out in *The Achievement Motive* (New York: Appleton-Century-Crofts, 1953). There is a similarity between McClelland's approach and Maslow's theory in that both are based on **needs.** McClelland suggests that, amongst others, we each have a need for **power**, **affiliation** and **achievement**. The degree to which these motivate us differs from person to person.

Need for power

When this is dominant, the person will get satisfaction from the ability to control the activities of others. Influence and control are highly valued. People are seen as a means to an end and are valued for their use to the leader rather than as individuals.

Need for affiliation

People who have this as the dominant need will value personal relationships and want to be liked by those they work with. Satisfaction is derived from social contact and activities. Recognition as being someone who is 'easy to get on with' is very rewarding.

Need for achievement

People with this need seek out areas of work where personal responsibility can be exercised and successful completion of targets is assured. Achievements are collected like trophies. Failure is avoided at all costs and this may lead to seeking projects which are sufficiently complex to attract attention but are well within the individual's capabilities. Achievers tend to be loners as they want to take the kudos of success. They are, however, usually prepared to take the blame for failure.

As individuals, few of us slot neatly into any one of the above three categories. Human beings are a complex mixture of fears, desires and needs.

The lesson to be drawn is that it might be advisable to try to match individual needs to the type of job to be done.

McClelland claims that the need to achieve can be taught. This has been challenged by psychological research, which indicates that motivation is determined during childhood. This is not the place to enter into academic discussion of this complex subject, but there is evidence that people's motives do change as a result of adult experience and training.

Activity 13

The management team of Extruded Plastic Tube Ltd includes the following specializations:

Managing director
Sales manager
Personnel manager
Chief accountant
Production controller.

Applying McClelland's theory, draw combined bar charts to show the percentage that each need should dominate to fit each of the managers to their task.

The human side of enterprise

We shall now turn to Douglas McGregor. In *The Human Side of Enterprise* (McGraw Hill, 1960), he examined the concept of management's task from two points of view which he labelled the **conventional view** and the **new theory**. The propositions in these concepts are described as Theory X and Theory Y.

Theory X

The **conventional view** of management's task in directing resources to meet the organization's goals:

1 Management is responsible for organizing the elements of the enterprise – manpower, money, materials equipment – to meet some predetermined goal.
2 In order to meet this goal there must be a process of directing, motivating, controlling the actions of employees and modifying their behaviour to conform to the needs of the organization.
3 Management must intervene to ensure that people do not become passive, or even resistant, to organizational needs. Therefore they must be persuaded, rewarded, punished, controlled. Management's task is to direct their activities.

These conventional views are based on a pessimistic view of people at work arising out of a number of beliefs which were widespread during the Nineteenth century and not entirely without support in the Twentieth. McGregor sums them up as follows:

1 The average person is by nature lazy and works as little as possible because he or she lacks ambition and dislikes responsibility, prefering to be led.
2 This leads him or her to be self-centred, indifferent to organization needs and, by nature, resistant to change.

Social scientists do not challenge management's perception of human behaviour in organizations. What they do challenge is the view that people are like that in any inherent sense, suggesting that it is the nature of the organization that makes them react in this way.

Maslow, Herzberg and McClelland all suggested that people have needs and that these needs can provide a motivating force. The working population has become better educated to meet the demands of industry. As a result they have become increasingly interested in having a say in matters which affect their working lives. Recognizing this, McGregor suggested that a new approach to the management of people was desirable.

Theory Y

The **new theory of management** takes a more optimistic view, recognizing that people at work do have needs that motivate them:

1 Management is responsible for organizing the resources of the enterprise to achieve predetermined goals, but at the same time should accept that people are not by nature passive or resistant to organizational needs. They have become so as a result of experience in organizations.
2 Management must make it possible for people to recognize and develop the potential present within themselves to assume responsibility and direct behaviour towards organizational goals.
3 Where possible, the essential task of management is to arrange organizational conditions and methods of operation in such a manner that people can achieve their own goals by directing their own efforts towards organizational objectives.

The problems in establishing a method to motivate the employees of an organization arise out of the fact that what motivates some does not motivate others. Many theories have been proposed, but management still finds the problem at all levels of the organization.

Attempts have been made to solve it by applying the **economic man** theory. This approach is based on the idea that if they are paid enough, people will be motivated to work hard. Unfortunately, this has not proved to be true. The car manufacturing industry is positive proof that the theory has its weaknesses. Everyone likes to have sufficient money, but there comes a time when jobs can be so unpleasant or tedious that people are inclined to seek a change, even when this means a drop in earnings.

Activity 14

You have been given the opportunity to do any job you choose. Describe your choice and then give an order of priority to the following list of job factors, indicating their influence in making your choice.

a Good prospects of promotion
b Status of the job in society
c Status of the job in the organization structure
d Authority to make and carry out decisions
e Working for a competent management
f The status of the organization
g Good salary or wages
h The opportunity to take responsibility
i Working as part of a closely knit team
j Security of employment
k Good working environment
l Exciting, but unstable employment.

Select two factors which you feel would be a constant motivator to you to perform at a high level.

Select two factors which you consider would not greatly motivate you, but would make you discontented if they were removed after you had completed twelve months in the job.

Your choice will have been a purely personal one. What will have been revealed is that some factors would have provided long-term motivation for you, while others would either have been short term or not very significant unless you were deprived of them.

In many occupations, the manner in which the work has to be done will prevent a number of motivation factors being applied. This is why the task of motivating a work-force tends to be complex and subject to failure.

Consider once again your priority of job factors in Activity 14. Some factors will have been chosen on the basis of how you would like the world to view you. We all like to feel that we make a favourable impression and it is right that we should have a certain amount of self-esteem. When that self-esteem comes under attack, we either feel inferior or react in an angry manner.

People are more inclined to be motivated towards meeting the organization's goals if they know that they are trusted to get on with their job and that their efforts are appreciated.

Those who manage the work of others can motivate them regardless of the type of work undertaken, provided they do not fall into the trap of assuming that the odd word of appreciation and thanks is not necessary because people get paid to do a job.

Where do we go from here?

Even a brief look at the motivation problem shows that there is no clear solution. This will not have surprised you. Organizations are composed of individuals, all of whom differ in their needs and aspirations. They are also performing a variety of tasks.

The manner in which those tasks have to be organized will determine the constraints placed on both management and managed in providing the satisfaction of needs which will motivate each individual. Many companies have turned to the technique of **job design** in an attempt to increase the motivation of their staff.

Job design – motivating the work group

Job design encompasses three approaches to reorganizing working methods in order to improve the motivation of the employee.

Job rotation

This is the most basic form of redesigning a job. Employees are trained in a number of different tasks and moved from job to job at predetermined intervals or at the discretion of management.

Job interest is increased through training in new skills and sustained by being moved from one work routine to another. Management is able to make better use of the work-force because the increased training produces more flexibility.

The frequency with which moves are made requires careful planning if the working environment tends to produce strong social relationships. In this situation, people may resent being moved from their group.

Job enlargement

The movement of the employee from job to job is replaced by a horizontal enlargement of the individual job, expanding the operation by the addition of new tasks. These additional tasks are usually at the level normally carried out by the employee.

Application of job enlargement is often successful in mass production industries where the work has been broken down into short cycle, repetitive activities. By adding a number of short work cycles, the worker is given a number of different tasks to perform and boredom is reduced. Greater job satisfaction comes from completing a subassembly than by simply adding a single component to the product.

When applied to production units, the approach has given good results in terms of productivity and improved quality control.

Job enrichment

A vertical enlargement of the job, differing from job enlargement in that it involves the worker in planning and controlling the resources and working methods related to the task. Job enrichment goes a long way towards satisfying the individual's need for status and recognition.

Where the type of work being undertaken dictates strong management control, this approach is more difficult to apply than the previous two. Nevertheless a number of companies have found it worthwhile radically to change production methods to accommodate the introduction of job enrichment.

The redesigned job

For a redesigned job to be successful it should:

a have a variety of tasks in the work cycle;
b either be a completed task or make some significant contribution to the finished product;
c Provide opportunity to make decisions, plan or control work cycles;
d provide feedback to check on results;
e Stretch the capabilities of the individual employees without taking them outside the bounds of their capability.

Does job design provide the answer?

ICI, Volvo, Phillips and the Civil Service are organizations which consider that they have benefited from job design.

On a smaller scale, go back to the case study of RN Resins (participative management) for an example of job redesign improving both efficiency and motivation, to the benefit of management and work-force.

Does it always work?

Well, no; it does not! As always, we come back to that basic resource of management, the human being. There is evidence that some people are not adverse to doing a repetitive job and do not want their field of activity expanded.

Research into reaction to job design has suggested that **job enrichment** might be most effective when applied to supervisory and white-collar grades. The effectiveness of the technique has never been proved conclusively: there are too many variables, such as the skill with which the design has been carried out, the attitude of the trades unions, the type of work being undertaken, the commitment to training etc.

Managers have voiced some doubts about the value of job design, citing the problems and the cost of retooling and restructuring working methods. Job enrichment is often seen as negating management's power to control. It carries the risk of demands for higher pay being made to compensate for accepting greater responsibility.

Trade unionists are always suspicious of changes in working conditions as these may adversely affect their members. They are particularly wary if there is a possibility of improved output reducing the number of employees required.

Activity 15

A number of Japanese companies have become established in the UK and appear to have little difficulty in using the Japanese style of management to motivate British employees.

Nissan is a typical example. The firm has built a car factory in the North East where the long-established heavy industries have a history of militant trade unionism.

Find out about the Japanese technique of involving the individual employee in the management of their particular work area and identify the extent to which the techique of job design is being applied.

Conflict in organizations

There is always some conflict in organizations employing the services of others. It arises out of the differences which exist between the main objectives of the employer and the employed.

Objectives of the employee	Objectives of management
1 Maximize earnings	1 Minimize costs
2 Security of employment	2 Maximize profit
3 Safe and pleasant working conditions	3 The right to manage
4 A say in matters which affect working conditions	4 Meet responsibility to the investor
5 The right to union representation	5 The survival of the business

These objectives are clearly not compatible. As each side will try to maintain its position, conflict is inevitable.

Organizations are a collection of groups, each with its own loyalties and objectives. When these groups come into contact in carrying out their allotted tasks, conflict is bound to arise at some point. It takes the form of interdepartmental rivalry, empire building, industrial relations and internal politics. In extreme cases conflict may manifest itself as vandalism of projects and property.

Activity 16

Industrial and commercial organizations are not the only collections of people that are subject to conflict. It happens in social clubs, political parties and families.

Make lists of some of the differences in objectives which could develop a conflict situation in:

a the local committee of a political party, where one would expect a consensus based on the common purpose.

b A family with a teenage son and daughter.

Is conflict always bad for the organization?

It need not be. Conflict between individuals or groups can motivate people with the will to win. In certain circumstances it can be a creative force. An individual or group in conflict with the system will strive to prove that they are right. Many advances have been made in the scientific field by people who were in conflict with the establishment view of what they were doing.

On the other hand, conflict can cause considerable waste of human resources – time and energy can be spent in political in-fighting.

Executives and specialists often fight for what they believe to be right and this can develop into a power struggle which can seriously damage the organization.

Different interpretations of religious and political beliefs all too often lead to the original organization splitting into different factions. You will be able to think of examples for yourself.

Problems arising out of conflict between groups

Groups tend to have norms and values which they promote and defend. This makes one group look upon others with a different point of view as competitors.

Having a common purpose will strengthen the morale and solidarity of the group when it is faced with a challenge. This makes it difficult for the group to see any point of view other than its own.

Attempts to consult or conciliate in order to settle differences may deteriorate into open conflict. Consultation is used as a platform to air grievances, publicize strongly held beliefs and attack the opposition.

Activity 17

Hogsnorton-in-Marsh is a small county town situated on the main route to a popular holiday resort. Built in the times when a farm cart was the fastest thing on the road, its winding streets are not suitable for modern traffic and a bypass has been proposed.

Two routes have been suggested. One passes close to the town and would border parkland and a number of sites of historical interest. The other would take a wide sweep round the town and cut through farm land. Since the publication of the two proposed routes the local population has divided into town and country factions, each opposed to the route that will affect them most.

A public inquiry is to be held at which protestors are to present their views to an independent chairman.

Outline the main points that each side will make in support of the route they prefer.

Obtain information about the various pressure groups each side could contact to support their point of view.

Write a short article for the local paper to support your claim that the public inquiry will be a waste of time since it will not settle the conflict between the two contesting parties.

Sources of conflict

We all want a big slice of the pie Resources in any organization are finite and the demands made upon them by various groups may not be satisfied. Each group will protect its own interests and in doing so will deny the claims of others.

A typical resource involved is **money**, involving the ratio of wages to profit margins and the maintenance of a competitive position in the market. Salary and wage differentials within the organization are often a source of group conflict and industrial dispute.

We do not all want the same things Those who manage the organization see their success in terms of productivity and efficiency, their ultimate goal being the survival of the organization and the progression of their careers.

Those who are managed, on the other hand, see their goals as security of employment and the provision of an adequate standard of living.

The former leads to cutting costs and the reduction of the labour force to the absolute minimum consistent with meeting organizational objectives. The latter leads to lines of demarcation and restrictive practices to protect jobs, regardless of the organization's objectives.

We do not like to be told what to do The degree of authority and control at different levels in the organization may be a cause of resentment. Improved standards of education in the work-force and the strength of trades unions have led to people wanting a greater say in decisions which affect them.

Style of management, leadership and span of control can all have a bearing on the way in which people perceive authority being imposed.

We do not like what we do Where the job they do lacks responsibility, is highly boring, is badly managed or provides no group identity, people become alienated and anti-organization.

Case study

On being instructed to move from being a receptionist to being an accounts clerk in a large solicitor's office, an employee lost her temper and swore at the managing clerk.

There are a number of possible sources of conflict in this situation:

1 Interpersonal friction between the two people concerned. They may not be able to get on in their daily work routine.
2 Resentment of authority. The managing clerk may be autocratic in his approach; the employee may be a malcontent.
3 Conflict of goals. The managing clerk may be moving the employee to a less rewarding job in order to meet a staffing crisis.
4 Conflict of values. The managing clerk may have broken a well-established practice that no employee is moved from one job to another without prior negotiation.

Conflict resolution

In any organization there is usually a range of values which are shared by management and the work-force. These provide common ground for agreement, and give management a degree of legitimate power which they can exercise by general consent.

When this consensus breaks down and a conflict situation arises, power becomes the major factor in resolving differences. This raises the question of where the power resides in the organization. If it is in the hands of the management, then it will be applied to meet organizational needs. If it is in the hands of the work-force, the management may have to modify its plans to meet the work-force's demands to have a say in the decision-making process.

Management may respond to the participation of the work-force in decision making in one of two ways:

1 See joint participation as being advantageous in that it will improve the co-operation of the work-force by demonstrating some of the problems facing management in meeting objectives. In some cases, the structure of the industry or its markets would allow the organization to benefit from employees and management jointly determining terms and conditions of employment.
2 See joint participation as a direct attack on management's right to manage resources for which they are ultimately responsible. Where the product is highly technical, or the market very complex, management will view the work-force as not competent to make decisions in the best interests of the organization.

The degree to which management can maintain its legitimate authority by general consent is vital. Where sources of conflict are minimized, the number of rules and regulations required to control the work-force can be reduced, to the benefit of management and work-force.

A variety of approaches are available to management for the resolution of conflict in the organization. Those which have found the widest acceptance are described by R. Blake and J. Mouton in *The Managerial Grid* (Houston: Gulf, 1964), and are summarized below:

1 Forcing the issue Using authority, fear, coercion to bring about a quick solution to the conflict. For example, using the threat of redundancy to solve a conflict over the demand for a wage increase.

The effect may not be long term. Resentment at having a solution imposed will continue and the conflict may break out at a later date with renewed vigour.

2 Smoothing the way By the use of tact or diplomacy seeking a compromise between the conflicting parties.

The success of this approach will be limited if one party sees the desire to compromise as being a sign of weakness in the other, or as showing favouritism to a third party.

The suspicion that this form of compromise might be viewed as a sign of weakness keeps the armaments trade in business.

3 Abiding by the majority rule Dispute is resolved by having a vote, with all parties agreeing to abide by the result of the ballot. It is used in committees, where the chairman will put an issue to the vote. On a wider scale, the trades unions use this method to decide matters of policy or to end a dispute.

This solution is usually proposed by those who expect the vote to go their way; but whatever the outcome, there is always a losing side and it may react in much the same way as it would if the issue were forced. Losing an election does not stop the opposing parties from trying to promote their own political policy and attacking the government.

4 Compromising In this, each party is prepared to modify its objectives in order to establish grounds for a settlement of the conflict. This is often a face-saving situation in that it gives both parties an opportunity to say that they achieved something from the negotiations. It is typical of negotiation between management and unions and in international diplomacy: one party asks for more than it expects to get; the other party offers less than it is prepared to give; and the nation is treated to eleventh-hour discussions which go on far into the night.

Having said that, we must recognize that a great many of the negotiations between management and representatives of employees are amicably settled by compromise.

5 Reaching a consensus In order to get a consensus, the conflicting parties must be willing to work together to achieve a solution. This is the best method of solving a conflict since all concerned have a common goal.

Consensus may be forced on conflicting parties as the only way to survive in a given situation. Faced with the possibility that the organization may go out of business, management and work-force may reach a consensus on matters of pay and conditions previously seen as insoluble.

6 Going for confrontation In this, each party will openly state its views and objectives and its intention to promote them. The stance may be firm or aggressive, signalling to the opponent a determination not to give way. This is sometimes used as an opening gambit to see if the other party will back down. It may also be a deliberate strategy: one party may see a distinct advantage in a conflict situation developing. A shop steward who wants the support of his members on some future issue may promote conflict on a minor issue to make management appear unwilling to negotiate.

Management might see an advantage in promoting conflict in a group which is unwilling to accept change as a means of successfully applying the principle of divide and rule.

7 Absorbing the problem This is achieved when one party in the conflict is able to absorb the other party within the system involved. This places a constraint on the absorbed party to conform to the rules and norms of the system.

Many union representatives display the qualities of leadership that management seeks for supervision. It is not suprising therefore that many representatives have been promoted to supervisory jobs. A problem for management is that the former representative may continue actively to oppose them in union negotiations after being promoted.

Activity 18

You are one of a small group of survivors from a sinking ship who have managed to launch a lifeboat.

In the ensuing panic, people have thrown into the boat a variety of things which they consider to be important; also one passenger has brought his dog. Taking stock, you find the following items: two crates of canned food, two ten-gallon drums of fresh water, twenty kilos of ship's biscuit, one sheet of polythene 4 metres by 6 metres, a sextant, a pack of playing cards, a first-aid kit, four bottles of brandy, a coil of rope, a leather case containing maps, four thick woollen blankets, a box of signal flares.

Assume that in order to reach the safety of the shore, you must each day dispose of one item or of the dog.

Working individually without reference to anyone else, decide upon the order in which you would carry out the daily disposal.

You should then join a group, each member of which has drawn up their own list, and come to a group decision on a composite list for the daily disposal. Failure to produce a composite list will result in everyone in the boat dying before a rescue vessel arrives.

When you have finished the second part of the activity, write a short analysis of the group exercise, identifying the cause of any conflict and stating the method by which it was resolved.

Informal leadership

Informal leaders are selected by common consent of the group. They may assume the leadership role for a short period of time only. They arise to to serve the interests of the group and may be selected on the basis of factors such as:

a personality
b technical ability
c communication skills
d understanding of the groups's aims
e planning skills
f being the 'old hand' who knows the ropes.

In return for serving the group, the informal leader will be given the respect of the group and may be accorded certain privileges.

Leadership may pass from person to person in the group to meet given situations, but in practice there is usually one predominant informal leader whose influence is greater than the others.

The role of predominant informal leaders is important. If they are pro-organization, they will work for the good of the organization. If they are anti-organization, they can influence the group's attitude towards meeting organizational goals.

Does the informal leader make a good formal leader?

Formal leaders are appointed to designated posts in the organization and given specific tasks and responsibilities. They are made accountable for the performance of the resources they control.

Informal leaders may display leadership skills, but they are not accountable for their actions in the way that a formally appointed leader is. The career of the informal leader will not suffer as the result of making a bad decision. Informal leaders usually deal with one situation at a time; the formally appointed manager works in a dynamic situation and has to deal with different situations simultaneously.

Activity 19

Return to Activity 18. Assume that the survivors in the lifeboat include the following:
a navigator
a priest
a fisherman
a doctor.
1 Decide which of these would be most likely to emerge as the predominant leader and justify your choice.
2 Describe situations in which each of them might emerge as an informal leader.

Formal power – related to the delegated position the person has within the organizational hierachy.
Informal power – given to a person by the group; not delegated and therefore not part of any specific chain of command.

Most managers would prefer to work without an informal structure. They are uneasy about the way in which informal groups modify instructions, resist management plans and cause instructions to be carried out in a manner different to that which management intended.

One of Elton Mayo's Hawthorne experiments demonstrates the point. Observations showed that a department which carried out wiring operations had the formal organization structure illustrated here.

This type of group is known as a **primary group**. In the group, formal leadership was weakened because the supervisor's duties frequently took him away from the department for long periods.

Division of the group into smaller, more stable groups was prevented by the inspectors being responsible to the quality control manager, who had no administrative function in relation to the wiring room, and also by both wiremen and inspectors being moved from job to job in the department.

Observations of the group's activities revealed the following situation:
1 The way in which work was being carried out differed considerably from what the management intended.

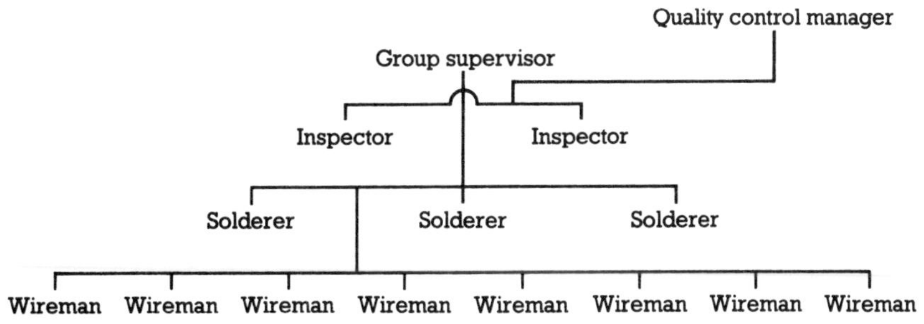

2 The group limited the productive output by time wasting, stopping before the official time and setting a limitation on the amount of work produced by each wireman and solderer. Output figures were falsified by recording fictitious machine breakdowns.
3 The most efficient workers in the group were prepared to reduce their output to conform to the norms set by the group. Those who failed to

do so were punished by the rest of the group, the punishment ranging from verbal abuse to physical attack.

4 Members of the group considered that the unofficial roles and relationships were the most important ones for the group. Conforming to group norms made each person acceptable to the rest of the group.
5 Group norms and practices were by and large opposed to the general aims and objectives of the organization.

Elton Mayo's work drew attention to the importance of the primary group in the work situation, in particular to the way in which it affects both the individual and the relationship between management objectives and actual performance.

Managers may view the informal group structure as a barrier to efficient and effective utilization of the resources of the organization but they accept the fact that the formation of informal groups cannot be prevented. In fact, the manager himself is almost certainly a member of an informal group.

Activity 20

Are you a member of an informal group? In work or college, do you seek the company of one group of people more than another? If so, it is likely that something other than personalities attracted you to it. You may even dislike one or more members of the group.

List the reasons why you prefer to join a certain group, either at work, college or during leisure time.

Examine the way in which you change your behaviour or opinions when you are with the group. Why do you think this change takes place?

Roles played by informal leaders

Keeping the group informed Some people seem to have access to information about the organization which is not generally known. This information can be highly valued. The status of the leader will depend upon the accuracy of the information.

Putting the group's point of view Possession of the skills and courage needed to represent the interests of the group to management will ensure group support for this type of informal leader. Do not confuse the role with that of the shop steward, who represents the interests of union members on a recognized formal basis.

Maintaining discipline When existing or new members of the group do not want to conform to the group norms, a member of the group will try to persuade them to fall into line, or will ensure that the group applies the agreed sanctions.

Defending the group When the group comes under attack from either the formal organization or other informal groups, it will seek advice from the member who is capable of devising a scheme to defeat the attack.

Informal communications

Communications within the informal structure are carried out on a face-to-face basis and do not have to rely on formal lines of communication such as memoranda, reports, notice-boards etc.

The system is usually referred to as **the grapevine**. The information passed has a variety of labels, such as the **buzz**, the **gen** and the **info**, and is usually sought after by those in the organization.

The term 'grapevine' has its origins in the American Civil War, when military intelligence telephone wires were strung from trees and bushes, resembling a grapevine. It was a notoriously unreliable system and the messages transmitted could be easily misinterpreted.

Grapevines in organizations have their origins in people and are therefore subject to any unreliability present in those involved. They arise out of the natural desire of people to talk to each other about matters which affect them.

There are times when the management may regret the existence of the grapevine with its lack of accountability for what it might do to morale. Conversely, management might be more concerned if there were no grapevine for that would indicate that the employees were uninterested in what was going on.

Features of the grapevine Because it passes information from person to person, the grapevine has the capacity to carry a lot of information (accurate or inaccurate) at high speed. Again because of the person-to-person links, it can crack security screens put up by the management.

It is always busy when the situation increases the demand for information – for example, when there is a take-over bid or when redundancies are pending.

The grapevine.

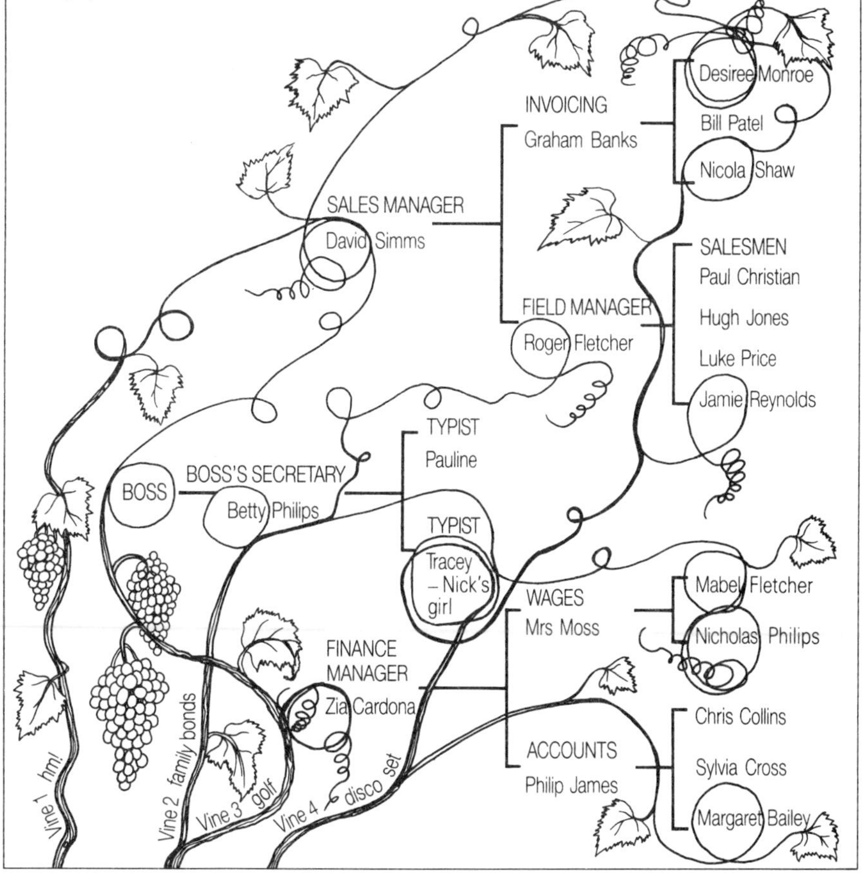

In most organizations, the grapevine is influential in that most people are ready to listen to the information being passed. When the situation is right, they will be ready to believe what the grapevine tells them.

The grapevine and rumour Rumour is an undesirable feature of the grapevine and is very often the only aspect of it that many people recognize.

Rumour differs from grapevine information. The grapevines carries a high proportion of factual information, whereas rumour is started before any fact has been established. If rumour turns out to be fact, that is usually simply a coincidence. The problem with rumour is that the recipient of informal information has no means of distinguishing between it and grapevine information.

Grapevine patterns Gordon Allport and Leo Postman, in *The Psychology of Rumour*, reported the finding that rumour arises out of **interest** and **ambiguity**. If there is no interest in a given situation, then a person will not start a rumour about it or feed the grapevine. If there is no ambiguity in a given situation, then the facts are known and therefore not a subject for speculation.

The assumption that information is passed from one person to another in the form of a long chain may be true in some situations, but the pattern may differ: one person may tell a small number of others and only one or two of those told may pass the information on. The result is a **cluster chain.** Obviously, those who pass the information will be those who are interested in the situation. They in turn will be anxious to attract the attention of others and will often embellish the story to gain that attention.

Activity 21

In 1956 the board of directors of a company were discussing the possibility of closing their Birmingham factory and centralizing production at the main works in London.

Before the final decision was made on this issue, the Birmingham workforce found out what the board had in mind and the union called an official strike.

How might the information have been transmitted to the Birmingham factory?

FORMAL GROUPS	INFORMAL GROUPS
* Are created by management	* Are self-selecting
* Implement company policy	* Set their own standards
* Expedite the work flow	* Collect and disseminate information quickly
* Provide a means of control	* Are not under management's control

Formal and informal groups.

Can the informal group benefit the organization? The organization can benefit from informal groups. It has been suggested that the formal and informal organization can be compared with the two blades of a pair of scissors – one cannot function without the other.

The management of any organization is subject to change, which can be rapid and frequent. This makes it virtually impossible to plan for every event. The existence of the informal structure tends to smooth out the anomalies in policies and instructions.

Management's work-load can be lightened if the informal structure is working with them as activities will need less supervision.

The informal structure can make a significant contribution to the job satisfaction of the employees and stabilize work groups. Social acceptance in the working group may compensate for a lack of other factors which would motivate employees.

The informal communication system can be used by management as a source of information concerning the attitudes of the work-force, or to convey certain types of information to test reaction.

Activity 22

The office manager in the head office of a building society controls the activities of thirty clerical grade employees. They are divided into teams of five.

One team gives the manager considerable trouble through their constant spreading of rumour about the way in which the company treats its employees. Much of what the groups says is unfounded and seems to stem from one person, John Beale. To date, John has been smart enough to prevent the office manager from being able to challenge him directly.

On the first day back after the annual holiday, John telephoned the personnel department to say that he was ill and would return to work when he was better. The manager had to farm some of the work out to another group to cover John's absence and chose one which had always been co-operative. When discussing the rescheduling of the work, the group's supervisor mentioned that someone had told him that John had stated an intention to have a few extra days 'on the sick list' in order to attend a vintage car rally.

John did not answer the telephone when personnel tried to contact him at the request of the manager. The manager then asked the personnel department to start disciplinary procedures with a view to dismissing John on his return.

After an absence of five working days, John returned to work with a sick note from his doctor saying that he had been suffering from influenza. The manager wanted to pursue the dismissal procedure on the grounds that if he had been ill at home, he would have answered the telephone.

1 Assuming the personnel manager agrees to go ahead with the dismissal, what do you think the reaction of John's group will be?
2 What justification does the manager have for suspecting John of not being off work as a result of illness?
3 What will the influence of the informal group structure be in this situation?
4 To what extent will the rest of John's group see this as an attack on the group as a whole?
5 If the manager succeeds in getting John dismissed, would this solve the problem of the group spreading rumours?

Group pressures

There has been a great deal of research on how groups of people work together and what pressures they exert to get individuals to conform to group standard. In the 1930s a psychologist called R. C. Sherif did an experiment to discover how a group of people established what was 'right' or 'proper' in the first place. (You can read it up in detail in any standard psychology textbook; it is likely to be in a chapter on social influences.) He used a phenomenon called the autokinetic effect in which a tiny point of light fixed in one spot in a totally dark room appears to rove about. Sherif first asked his guinea-pigs to watch this light, on their own, and estimate how far it was travelling. Some people said a few inches and other said several feet. Then Sherif put them into groups and asked them to try again. After a few attempts, when they heard each other's responses they began to agree on a certain distance and in the end the whole group decided on one particular 'right' answer. Further research (by Rohrer) revealed that their conviction about this answer persisted for months and that they would try to pass this standard on to any new group they were put into.

Activity 23

Write down in one paragraph how you think the kind of group behaviour described above could operate to the benefit of a firm.

Another researcher, Soloman Asch, did some follow-up work to see if he could get people to conform to the standards of a group even when it was clear from the evidence of their own senses that the group was making a wrong decision. He sat his guinea-pig down with a group of about seven others – all of whom were Asch's confederates – and asked them to reach a group decision on which of three lines on one chart was the same length as the line on another chart.

Pick a line.

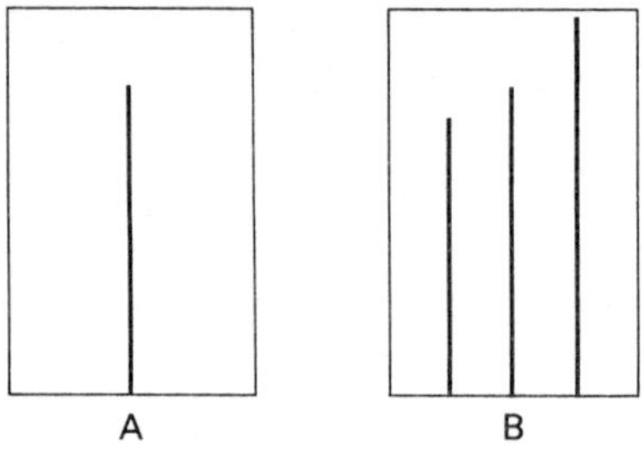

It is abvious that the middle one of the three lines in Chart B corresponds to the one in Chart A, but the confederates refused to admit this in a certain number of trials and 74 per cent of the guinea-pigs – though very embarrassed and obviously not really agreeing – went along with the majority decision. Most of us are reluctant to take an independent line in opposition to the rest of our group – a factor which can be important in business, especially in matters of honesty.

Activity 24

Divide your group into seven to nine discussors and an equal number of observers.

The discussors, working individually, rank in order the items on the list of points of value to an employer.

Meanwhile, the observers are each allocated to a discussor, and discreetly place themselves in a position where they can see him or her well. The observers are given a copy of the list so that they know what is going on. They also get a copy of the checklist of behaviours on which to note down all the utterances of their discussor.

The discussors now sit in an open circle and are filmed as they try to agree on a correct order for the items. They must arrive at a consensus of opinion by explanation and discussion. They are not allowed to have a chairman or to vote or to trade items off with each other. Differences of opinion should be regarded as opportunities for further explanation and no one should give in for the sake of peace. The discussors note down the new order as they agree it.

Afterwards the discussors add up the differences between their original order and the one finally arrived at by the group. They should note how far they were prepared to comply with the opinion of the others (eg, if your no. 1 item is the group's no. 10, you have conceded 9 points).

The observers are now filmed as they announce the type of utterance favoured by their discussor, and give an assessment of their overall peformance. The discussors should now complete a group members' report on their experience in the group.

When this part of the activity has been completed, the group should re-form. The discussors and observers should exchange roles. This time, the list of points an employer might disapprove of should form the focus of attention.

CHECKLIST OF BEHAVIOURS

Name of discussor	①	②	③
Explaining			
Being the expert			
Pouring oil			
Blocking			
Arguing			
Insulting			
Sulking			
Accepting			
Seeking information			
Agreeing			
Encouraging			

POINTS OF VALUE TO AN EMPLOYER

Place in order of importance the following points that an employer might value in an employee:

Initiative
Pride in work
Good personal relations
Wide viewpoint
Seeks work when slack
Quality conscious
Good timekeeper
Asks questions
Reports faults
Follows instructions
Remedies problems
Versatility

POINTS AN EMPLOYER MIGHT DISAPPROVE OF

Place in order of importance, worst first, the qualities which an employer might disaprove of.

Doesn't follow instructions
Bad timekeeper
Dislikes supervision
Careless about quality
Can't concentrate
Chats, gazes around
Personal problems
Bad relations with other people
Doesn't pull weight
Doesn't like change
Doesn't report faults
No loyalty to company

GROUP MEMBER'S REPORT	Yes	No
1 Could you get the group to listen to what you had to say?		
2 Did you influence the group much?		
3 Were you in agreement with the group's final decision?		
4 Did you think everyone took part in the decision-making process?		
5 Was your group co-operative?		
6 Which of these statements best describes your behaviour? Tick one:		
a I tended to stay in the background and listen, letting others decide.		
b I was keen to convince the others that what I thought was right.		
7 Select one of the options below to complete this sentence: The best way for a group to reach a decision would be by		
a Voting		
b Letting the strongest person decide most things		
c Reaching a unanimous decision by voting		
d Letting the person with expert knowledge decide		
e Tossing a coin and leaving it to chance.		

Role conflict

You have probably come across the term 'role conflict'. The fact that one person has a role in several groups leads to conflicts of loyalty if the requirements of those roles are contradictory. The trade unionist who has been promoted to a management function is in an embarrassing position if industrial action is taken. The father of a young child is in difficulties when a meeting called late in the afternoon runs into the time his child's birthday party is being held.

The problems can be even more acute when the standards of the organization with regard to working practices and output vary from those of the work group. Individuals may have great difficulty in deciding which set of responsibilities and obligations has the strongest claim on them.

Changing hats

This situation is so well known that a certain amount of leeway is usually given to people who 'wear a number of hats' so that they can define which role they are fulfilling at any particular moment. Colleagues do, however, become extremely unsympathetic if they feel that the hats are being changed for reasons of self-interest.

Which hat?

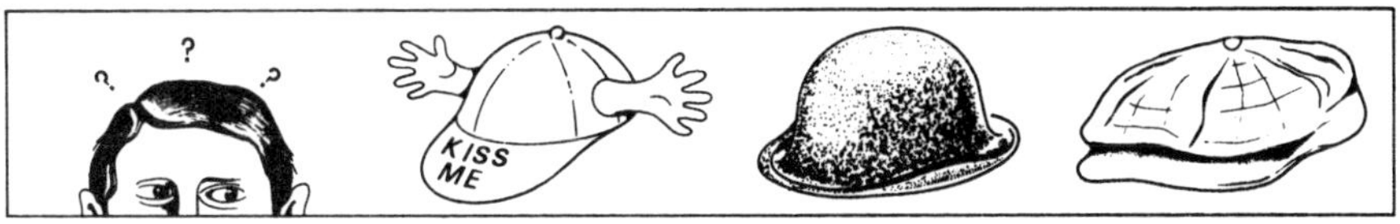

Activity 25

Some of the younger element at Extruded Plastic Tube Ltd are starting an action group to try to introduce some more enlightened attitudes to the firm. You are asked if you would like to join and you go to a tea-time meeting in the staff dining-room.

The issue they decide to start on is equal opportunities at work, beginning with the problem of men's predominance in supervisory/executive posts. The first thing they want to establish is that such predominance exists. You are asked to find out the facts.

Using your personal knowledge, your experience of your workplace or college, and newspapers and the library service, prepare a set of notes to form the basis of discussion at the next meeting.

In small groups, each operating as EPTL's action group, discuss the question of men's predominance in supervisory/executive posts, considering the following points:

1 Is there such a predominance, generally speaking?
2 Are there any areas where women have most of the top jobs?
3 Why are women not appointed to senior posts from outside?
4 Why are they not promoted to them from inside?
5 Is there any significant difference in education/qualifications between likely candidates of opposite sex for a given post?
6 What other factors are at work?
7 What action could be taken to redress the balance?

After discussion, summarise on one side of an A4 sheet what was said for each of the numbered points, under subheadings.

Attitudes

A person's attitude can be defined as the way in which they respond to a given situation or visual stimulation. This reaction need not be based on any sound basis of reason. It may be entirely unconscious on the part of the person concerned.

For example, what rational explanation is there for the average person's reaction to the spider?

Where do the attitudes we each have about various aspects of life come from?

Why do our individual attitudes so often vary from the attitudes of others?

The formation of attitudes is a complex business which goes on throughout our lives.

The illustration of the socialization of the individual shows some of the many factors which go to forming the way in which the individual perceives the world.

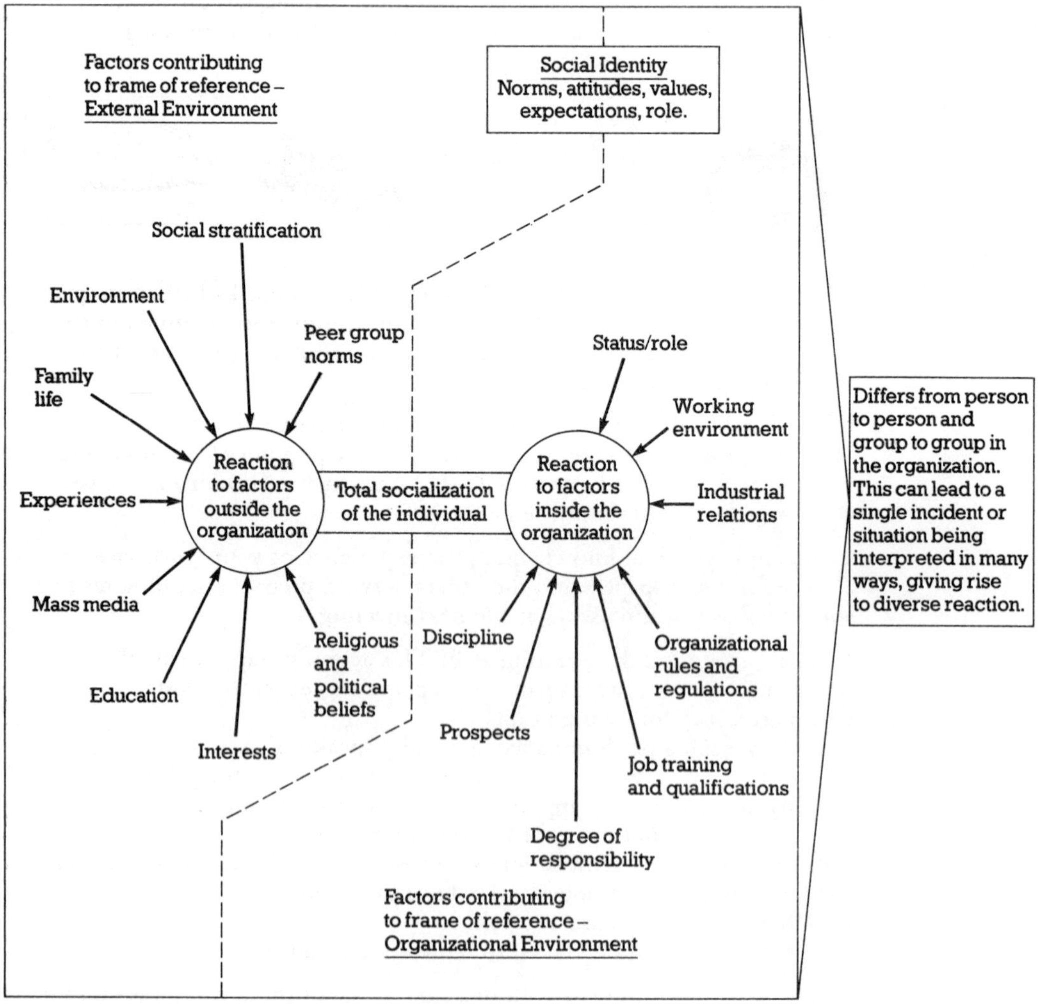

Socialization of the individual

Activity 26

Test your own attitudes by placing a tick under 'Good thing' or 'Bad thing' for the following:

	Good thing	Bad thing
Overseas aid		
Nuclear power generators		
The European Common Market		
Punk rockers		
Trades unions		
Drink-and-drive legislation		
Religion		
Marriage		
Fast foods		
Income tax		
Traffic wardens		

Check your list with whose of others in the class for similarities and differences in attitudes.

Conduct a survey in your college or at work, using the above list. Compile a bar chart to show the results.

Whatever your attitudes were in Activity 26, they were based on the way in which you perceive the subjects listed.

You probably had less difficulty in making a decision between good and bad for those things which you have experienced or which have had some bearing on your life – for instance, if you have had a parking ticket recently, you are likely to have decided that traffic wardens are not a good thing.

Perception of a situation can be preset by information gained before the situation arises. Imagine that you are about to meet the group you will be working with when someone tells you that they are not very friendly to newcomers. Although you do not know any of the people, you are likely to be put on the defensive.

Training for a specific job or profession will have a bearing on the way in which you perceive situations. An experiment conducted in a New York police academy revealed that the trainees who had completed initial training saw violence more often in a set of visual stimuli than a control group which had received no police training.

Our view of the world about us is governed by our ability to perceive. The boundaries of our perception are in effect a frame and we all have a different one. These **frames of reference** determine the meaning we attach to events and to the behaviour of others. They may also prevent us from understanding the attitudes of others. Management and unions in negotiation tend to take the view that the problem could be solved if the other party would see reason. What they want is for the other party to accept their frame of reference.

Can attitudes be changed? Some attitudes remain with us for life; others are changed by training, experience, age and the need to conform to the groups we associate with.

Activity 27

A company has a disciplinary code with provides for a final 'court of appeal' in the form of a committee of union representatives and management. The committee is about to meet to consider the case of an employee who has been suspended pending dismissal for repeated acts of 'horse play'.

The employee's manager considers that these pranks put the other employees in the department at risk. Repeated warnings have been ignored. She quotes the Health and Safety at Work Act in support of her recommendation that the employee be dismissed.

Assess the possible differences in the frames of reference of the union and management representatives when considering this appeal.

What do you think has determined the manager's attitude to the employee?

Change and resistance to change

Organizations undergo constant change as a result of growth and the way in which they operate. Some changes are sought; others are forced on the organization through market pressures, developments in technology and changes in legislation. Whatever the reason, some people will see any change as adversely affecting them and will react against it.

Agents of change in skilled industrial crafts

FROM

The original concept of a craft tradesman's role, based on:

- Five to seven years' apprenticeship in a specific skill
- A lifetime of employment in a specific trade
- Lines of demarcation to protect the work of craftsmen in their trade
- Rate of change in technology having no marked effect on the application of skills during the working life of the individual craftsman

TO

- Increased application of mass production methods
- Mechanization of production tools – leading to
- Automation of production methods – leading to
- The introduction of computer controlled machines and processes

Application of the change described above will only be successful if working methods are simplified. The agent for change in simplification of working methods has been the application of **work study** and **data processing** techniques, which have led to the deskilling of a number of trades. Many applications of engineering crafts have become the province of the production planner and the computer programmer.

Agents of change in commercial employment

FROM

A relatively small number of clerical employees specializing in some aspects of the administration of the business such as sales, accounts, stocks.

Concept of employment based on:

- Long-term service with the organization
- Some form of career advancement, often based on length of service
- Close relationship with the management of the organization
- Different terms of employment from those of hourly paid and craft workers
- Development of clerical and administrative skills through experience over long periods of time
- Development of skills and knowledge of procedures making the individual employee become valued by the employer

TO
A substantial increase in the proportion of administrative workers to production workers with associated increases in the amount of paperwork to be processed.
The result has been:

The introduction of mechanization and increased use of business machinery
Simplification and standardization of routines
The introduction of computers and other business machinery based on microchip technology to enable the design of integrated technology systems linked to external communication systems
Many of the office skills being no longer required, having been replaced by technology
Clerical and administrative workers can be employed on flow-line methods similar to those used in production units
The size and complexity of administration diminishing the personal contact between the clerical worker and management

The agents of change have been **Organization and methods** techniques, **integrated technology**, and the advanced design of **business machinery** and **communication systems.**

Resistance to change

You will be aware that change is inevitable in organizations. However, when the changes affect us as individuals, we tend to seek reasons to attack a change in working methods rather than support it.

We feel comfortable with things the way they are, even though they may not be the best things in a particular situation. If you return home and find that the furniture in the living-room has been rearranged, the odds are that you will protest, failing to see any advantages in the new layout.

What causes resistance to change in organizations? Organizations are complex structures of human interaction. The causes of resistance to the aims and objectives of the organization can stem from a variety of factors. Identification of causes is complicated and requires in-depth investigation of individual cases, but there are three factors which will promote resistance in any given situation.

Fear of the unknown
a What the effect of change will be on job security, job satisfaction, job status and earnings.
b Suspicion that relocation or break-up of an established working group will take place.

Ignorance
a A lack of understanding of what is involved in a given situation of change or impending change.
b When people are not sure of what is going to happen they tend to prepare for the worst possible outcome.
c Under these circumstances the **grapevine** will be very active and rumours are likely to be taken as fact.

The way in which change is put into effect When change is instituted without consultation with the employees or their elected representatives, or when methods of communication between management and employees are poor, reaction is bound to be unfavourable.

Resistance to change can have a significant long- and short-term effect on the organization. It can manifest itself in low productivity, poor morale, increased industrial action, lack of co-operation and, in extreme cases, sabotage.

Activity 28

Blanks & Sons are well-established wholesalers whose business is the distribution of newspapers and magazines over a wide area of the Midlands. The area is sub-divided into sections, each containing a number of retail outlets which order from the wholesaler.

Contact for the placing of orders is through a staff of order clerks, each of whom has a specific section to deal with. The bulk of ordering is done over the telephone or by the retailer calling at the firm's premises. On receipt of the order, the order clerk is responsible for instructing the warehouse to batch up and despatch to the customer.

Customer records are kept by each order clerk on a Cardex system from which the details of the customer's orders are extracted and sent to the accounts department.

Order clerks have been encouraged to develop personal contacts with their customers by visiting on a twice-yearly basis. The firm also invites the customers to a number of social gatherings.

Twelve months ago the firm's accounting system was put onto computer, bringing advantages to both customers and the firm. The data processing manager has put a proposal to the owners of the business that the ordering system should now be centralized on a data base, with customers keyboarding orders directly into the system.

Identify the likely causes of resistance by the order clerks to the change.

Outline a plan for the management to implement the change so that conflict and resistance are minimized.

Conclusion

In considering the management of people at work, we have looked at a number of interrelated aspects under separate headings. Here we draw those aspects together and offer a brief revision of what has been covered.

Management of people at work would be simpler if people would behave in a predictable manner. Management is often faced with a difficult situation without being sure how it developed. Managers who conscientiously practise man management techniques may still be very disappointed with the result.

Problems arise because management is forced by the constraints of working in a defined organization structure to apply standardized working methods to individuals.

Motivation techniques can go a long way towards gaining the co-operation of the work-force, but management has to accept that the people they control have unique aspirations, likes, dislikes and attitudes which are important to their well-being. These will generate a form of behaviour which does not always suit the objectives of the organization. The problem posed for the management is to decide how far these individual characteristics can be tolerated.

Some **code of discipline** is essential in any organization if it is to regulate behaviour towards achieving its aims. To ensure the disciplinary code is upheld, some form of sanctions has to be applied to those who do not conform. However, the application of sanctions should be the last resort – it could be considered as representing a failure to motivate the individual.

Management and leadership style can do much to minimize the problems encountered in fitting the individual into the organization. Managers who concern themselves with the individual's needs for recognition and status, and who aim to preserve the dignity of the employee, have a greater chance of motivating the individual. Demotivated personnel are not working for the organization – they are too busy trying to spread their despondency to others.

Demotivation raises the question of **morale**. When morale is low, the efficiency of the organization suffers. Individuals with low morale may sometimes act out of character, often finding this the only way of relieving the tension set up by frustration.

Managers should be aware of the cause of this frustration. In many instances, it will be the organization itself – through its working practices, pay and promotion policies, working conditions etc, and these are difficult for the manager to control. However, if the manager is seen to be trying to improve things or is making it possible for employees to live with the situation, then they may well support the effort being made on their behalf.

There are many recorded instances of the morale of a group being maintained at a high level under very poor conditions. Strength has been drawn from overcoming them. It could be concluded that people act in a way that benefits the organization when they have pride in themselves, their skills and the group to which they belong.

Most individuals who work within the formal framework of an organization's structure belong to an **informal group** of fellow workers with common interests and objectives which are often in conflict with the aims and objectives of the organization.

Individual group members can have the dilemma of conforming to requirements of the formal structure and meeting the demands of the informal group. This puts the individual into a **role conflict** situation, making them subject to considerable pressure. Because of its ability to apply pressure to individuals, the informal group can alter attitudes and dictate patterns of behaviour which appear unreasonable.

Informal groups are formed spontaneously; they are not hired by management and they cannot be dimissed. Like it or not, management is stuck with them. Appreciation of this fact is an important step towards turning the objectives of the informal group towards those of the organization.

You will have learned that there are no set answers to the many problems in fitting individuals into organizations. This must not deter those who have to manage the activities of others from attempting to understand what motivates those who work for them.

Summary

In this block we have taken a broad look at the problems that can arise between management and managed and have considered various managerial techniques for reducing friction and promoting the well-being of the work-force. Managers need to manage, and sensitivity to the feelings of others and knowledge of how groups operate will make a major contribution to the efficient working of the organization.

Skills

Skill	*Activities in which skill is developed*
a Information gathering	1, 3, 7, 11, 12, 13, 15, 16, 17
b Learning and studying	All activities
c Working with others	1, 2, 4, 5, 6, 8, 17, 18, 19, 20, 24, 25, 26
d Communicating	All activities
e Design & visual discrimination	1, 10, 13, 17
f Identifying and tackling problems	All activities
g Numeracy	28
h Information processing	15, 17, 22, 24, 25

Block 4
Information Technology

Introduction

This block starts with a description of the function of the office in an organization as a collector, classifier and processor of information. Changes in the office environment are considered and lead into a general introduction to the role and function of the microprocessor in modern information technology.

The application of computer hardware and software is outlined, and examples of some of the software in general use are given.

The role of the modern System × telephone system is described, the importance of efficient use of the system by office personnel being emphasized.

In conclusion, the block considers the effect on the people in an organization of the introduction of office technology.

Information technology

To meet their objectives, all organizations – whether commercial, political, social or governmental – collect data. This data is usually related to obtaining supplies, providing a product or service, meeting legal requirements and controlling cash flow.

Organizations also generate data through giving instructions to members, keeping accounts, budgeting expenditure and communicating with other organizations.

Services provided by the office
The collection of data will only be effective if it can be used to exercise efficient **control** over the management of the organization. The function of the office is to provide systems whereby data can be stored, collated and retrieved to provide the organization with a 'working memory' and the management with relevant information.

A business needs to keep records to know what procedures need to be carried out and to provide a memory bank of communications and commercial links with other organizations.

The service provided by the office procedures allows the control function to be installed and maintained. Like other forms of control, office procedures have to be well planned and constantly updated.

Regardless of the size of the organization, this service remains virtually the same in principle, but the manner in which it is performed can vary considerably depending upon the methods used to process the data.

It is not possible to give an extensive treatment of the technology available for data processing here; the purpose of this block is to introduce types of office technology which are used fairly widely. As you will be well aware, microprocessors have transformed the role of the office worker and are certain to affect more clerical and administrative procedures as time goes by.

Activities undertaken by the office can be subdivided into four categories:

1 **Keeping records** – routines related to the function and control of the business. These records have to be stored so that they can be easily retrieved for reference. 2 **Collecting data** – information fed into the organization from external sources, such as customers, suppliers, government departments. 3 **Processing data** – collating, extracting, modifying data; preparation of instructions, orders, statistics, budgets. 4 **Communicating data** – data prepared has to be circulated through recognized channels within the organization and to outside contacts.

Changes in office equipment

In the late nineteenth century, when the industrial revolution had replaced cottage industry with the factory unit, each manufacturing unit had its counting-house where clerks dealt with correspondence and cash transactions. This work was carried out with basic equipment, data being entered in handwriting using quill pens, and it was very time consuming.

As manufacturing processes became more sophisticated, the amount of office work extended to cover other activities and more office staff had to be employed. The increased cost of administration generated an interest in speeding up the data processing function in the business. The first major step towards mechanization was the introduction of the typewriter, the forerunner of modern office equipment.

Invention of the telephone allowed business communications to be speeded up. Handwriting was replaced where possible by shorthand systems.

The twentieth century saw the application of electrical power to office technology and the introduction of the dictaphone. By the middle of the century, the office was geared towards the processing of data on a large scale using reprographic equipment, Comptometer calculators and Power Samas punch-card machines. Telephone and telex provided speedy communications within the organization and outside.

Manufacturers continued to make improvements to office equipment, but the major breakthrough came with the arrival of the microchip. This enabled complicated operations to be performed with equipment small enough to be located in the office.

Initially, computers were the responsibility of specialists and had to be locked away in air-conditioned rooms. Today they are the everyday desk-top tool of the office worker. Sophisticated software allows complicated operations to be performed and data to be transferred from one computer to another.

Information technology may still be in its infancy, but the present state of the art provides some impressive equipment, such as the desk-top computer, the word processor and computer networks with electronic filing and mailing facilities. Reproduction of data has been improved by high-speed laser printers, facsimile machines and high resolution photocopiers.

The telephone system has also been computerized. It can now carry data at speed throughout the world through a satellite system which works twenty-four hours a day.

All this is a far cry from the quill pen, yet within the space of ten more years these modern marvels may be seen as very basic technology.

The purpose of office services

Any activity which involves getting people to meet some objective requires planning. If you have been involved in preparing for a family holiday you will know about the problems which can arise if some seemingly small matter is overlooked. Once a plan has been formulated and put into action, some form of control must be exercised if its objectives are to be met. To achieve this control, an organization sets up a system which allows **communication** to take place up, down and across its structure, providing feed-back of information which indicates that all is going according to plan or draws attention to the fact that something is amiss.

You will appreciate that the faster the feedback takes place, the more efficient the control over the situation is likely to be. At this point, it would be worthwhile to refresh your memory regarding the **control loop**. See Block 2.

Modern data processing equipment works at speeds which are difficult to comprehend. Feedback information can be produced at a rate which no human operator could hope to achieve. This technology can now be applied to a wide range of business equipment, a fact which is extending the influence of office services into the field of management services.

Internal and external data.

Some examples of external data
- Letters
- Quotations, estimates, invoices, delivery notes
- Accounts, statements – for goods and services supplied
- Catalogues and price-lists
- Advertising and promotional materials
- National and local Government publications

Some examples of internal data
- Personnel records
- Wage and salary records
- Cost control and budget records
- Stock control records
- Production control records
- Memoranda
- Reports

Activity 1

Choose six examples from the above list of internal and external data which you would use for the application of electronic data processing.

Compare and discuss your choice with other members of the class.

Computers in the office

The introduction of electronic data processing has revolutionized the way in which the office functions. Examples of advantages computers can bring to business management and administration are given below; others will be presented as you progress through your course within other disciplines, such as financial control and economics.

Management An important part of the management function is forecasting such things as market demand for goods and services. Software computer packages provide methods of assessing information and aid decision making.

Administration Administrative functions such as budgetary control, stock control and financial control can be programmed as standard procedures with data processing equipment.

General The microchip has brought about desk-top computing in the form of personal computers and word processors.

The changing environment of the office

There are some organizations where the mass processing of data is still achieved by pools of clerical workers and typists, sitting in rows in large open-plan offices. Other data will be processed by administrative staff, secretarial staff and clerical workers, many of whom work in the isolation of separate offices. In these circumstances, the distribution of data often involves physical transportation, which is both costly and time consuming.

The modern office employs sophisticated electronic equipment which processes and distributes data, not only within the organization but also between the organization and its working environment. As a result, many tasks which used to be performed by office staff have been taken over by technology or have been radically altered.

Activity 2

A manager attending a conference on office automation was heard to say, 'Do we have to go mad and automate everything?'

Discuss with other members of the class what should influence the automation of office procedures. Take as the starting-point the consideration of what type of organization the manager quoted is likely to be employed in.

Changes in office equipment.

BEFORE IT	AFTER IT
Typewriters	Computer/word processor
Spirit duplicator	Networks
	Sophisticated photocopier
Ink duplicator	High-speed laser printer
Filing cabinets	Electronic filing
	Electronic mailing
Telephones	Integrated telephone system
Telex	
PBX switchboard	PABX switchboard
Punch-card machines	Telex and teletex
Pocket calculators	Facsimile
	Microfiche

The diagram above sums up the changes in office equipment. Telephones are in both lists, but the function of the telephone has changed with the introduction of System X. This is a computerized communication system capable of carrying information in digital form.

Computers

Originally, computers were large installations requiring many thousands of valves and complicated wiring. The heat generated by such installations was so intense that air conditioning and cooling were necessary.

Advances in microtechnology have reduced the size of the computer to the point where it can be placed in the office or workshop without needing a protected environment.

Computers can now be designed to perform a specific task or provide a particular service.

Main frame computers

These are large configurations with central processors capable of handling huge quantities of data. The installation includes back-up storage on tape decks, hard disk and memory storage. Peripheral equipment such as printers and input devices are provided according to what is required from the system.

Main frames are essential where data has to be processed on a large scale – this is known as **number crunching**. They are very useful in the research field, in government offices and for storage of large data bases.

Main frames can be accessed by smaller computers which can be **logged on** by a user code.

Minicomputers

These are smaller installations than main frames, with a central processor which is interactive with users. They are able to interrogate the system through user terminals with visual display units (VDUs) and obtain speedy solutions to problems. Minicomputer systems can be programmed with packages which deal with specific applications such as accounts, personnel records, stock control and scientific data bases.

This system provides the user with many of the advantages of the main frame, but is considerably cheaper to purchase and maintain.

Microcomputers

Complicated communication networks can now be miniaturized onto a silicon chip to produce a microprocessor. In effect, the central processor of the main frame computer is reduced to a component which would fit onto the end of a pencil, yet contains all the circuits required by a central processor.

The chip has led to the desk-top computer, the word processor and many other computer applications – such as the supermarket checkout computerized till. Reduction in size and cost, resulting from the silicon chip, has made the computer available to wide sections of industry, commerce and schools and also in the home.

The basic unit of the minicomputer consists of a keyboard, a VDU and a printer. Other input devices available will be described later. A wide range of software packages is available for minicomputers, from commercial and business applications to computer games.

Machine language

Computers have one thing in common with human beings. In order to communicate they have to have a language, and like human beings they do not all speak the same one. This causes some inconvenience, but does not prevent one machine 'talking' to another because of the common factor in all processors, which allows translation from one language to another.

Electronic data are processed by means of switches contained in the central processor of the computer, in the form of minute silicon chips in the various types of equipment.

Machine language is composed of bits – which are individual switches – and bytes – which are groups of bits. Using a binary system, the number of bits in a byte determines the combination of letters/figures which can be used in each piece of information fed into the processing unit.

Example

A four-bit byte provides the following combination for coding information by raising each switch by the power of 2 instead of the more familiar 10 used in the decimal system, and counting the total of the switches in the ON state.

8	4	2	1				
0	1	0	1	=	0101	=	Binary 5
1	1	0	0	=	1100	=	Binary 12

An eight-bit byte would give a total of binary 0 to 255 and provide a considerable coding combination to provide a language.

Fortunately, we do not have to be electronic engineers in order to work with computers and related data processing equipment. However as a user of the equipment, you have to understand that it will not understand any instruction not presented in its language.

Data entries have to be accurately presented. American data processing experts have coined the term 'GIGO', which means, 'Garbage In = Garbage Out'. A computer understands what is fed into it within the parameter of its language. It might not understand if the data fed in does not make sense. It will carry out any instruction given to it within its programmed capability.

Activity 3

Given a machine language consisting of four bits and using the grid shown below, devise a binary system for coding the documents used in the personnel department of EPTL. Take as your starting-point the application form for employment.

Document title	Code			
1 Application for employment				
2				
3				
4				
5				

Putting the computer to work

Multi-user systems These are based on a main frame or minicomputer, with a number of terminals connected by keyboards and having VDUs. A central processor controls the flow of data in the system. Keyboards act as **dumb terminals**, that is to say, they are able to access data stored in a central processor, but are not capable of modifying it in any way. Terminals are not able to address each other as they would in a network system.

Where a number of people need simultaneously to access a common programme, such as a data base, the multi-user system can save considerable time. The central processor achieves multiple accessing by **time slicing** the flow of digital information. In effect, this means that when dealing with information from one terminal, it isolates itself from the remaining terminals in the system. Switching from one terminal to another takes something like one-thousandth of a second, therefore the flow of data is effectively continuous.

Software packages for accounts, sales and data base are available and are widely applied in banking, insurance, currency exchange markets and travel agencies. In these applications, advantage is taken of the speed at which the system works and the way in which data can be made secure from the sight of unauthorized users.

Problems may arise for the user when the traffic flow is heavy, as this will delay the feedback to individual terminals. If the central procesor goes down, then the whole system will be out of action.

Stand-alone computers Modern microprocessors are so compact that computer installations with sufficient power to cope with a wide variety of control functions will fit onto the desk top. A central processor is built into the equipment, allowing it to be programmed with a wide range of software.

Once programmed, the stand-alone computer is capable of working as an independent unit or in conjunction with other data processing units.

The home computer is an example of the stand-alone system. Each one will have a central processor capable of accepting programmed instruction from magnetic tape or disk, a QWERTY keyboard with a number of extra function keys and some form of VDU, either a monitor or the domestic television set. The rich and dedicated computer buff will add other refinements such as a printer and disk drive.

Network system Stand-alone systems are able to transfer data from one processor to the VDU or printer of another system. This capability allows them to communicate with other computers or peripheral equipment and to be configurated into **networks**.

Features of the network system The ability to pass data from one VDU to another allows the network to be used as an internal mailing system. Information transmitted in this fashion can be edited, electronically filed or disposed of.

The system can access data base information such as Prestel, or be connected to a main frame or minicomputer providing a common file of information and acting as a server for the network.

Microcomputers linked in this fashion within one building are called **local area networks** (LANS).

Networking allows a high volume of data to be transmitted and peripheral equipment to be shared. The latter ensures that the use of the peripherals is maximized and reduces the cost of providing equipment.

The particular configuration used will depend upon what is required of the system. The three currently most common are illustrated: **bus**, **star** and **ring**.

1 Bus system

Processors are connected as illustrated, with one processor acting as a server. In a bus system, each work-station will only pick up data addressed to it. This can be a distinct advantage where a high volume of data is being transmitted. Extra work-stations can be added without too much trouble, making the system flexible.

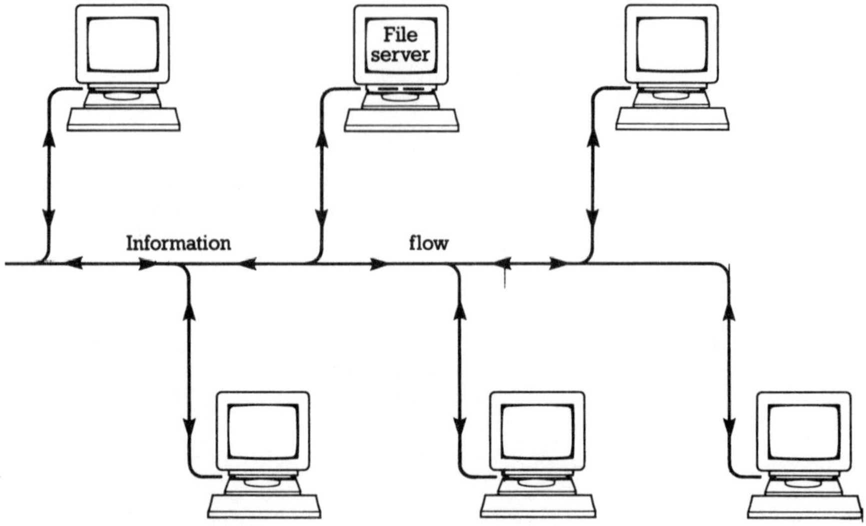

Local area network – 'bus' system.

2 Ring system

Processors are connected to a closed circuit cable. Data passes round the ring in one direction until it reaches the designated work-station.

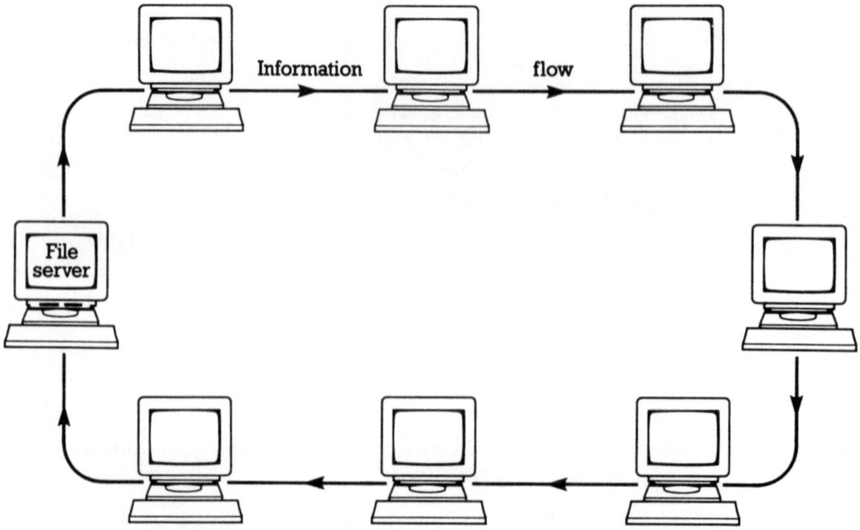

Local area network – 'ring' system.

3 Star system

Processors are individually connected to a central processor acting as a server for the system. The server receives and directs the data flow round the system as required.

Local area network – 'star' system.

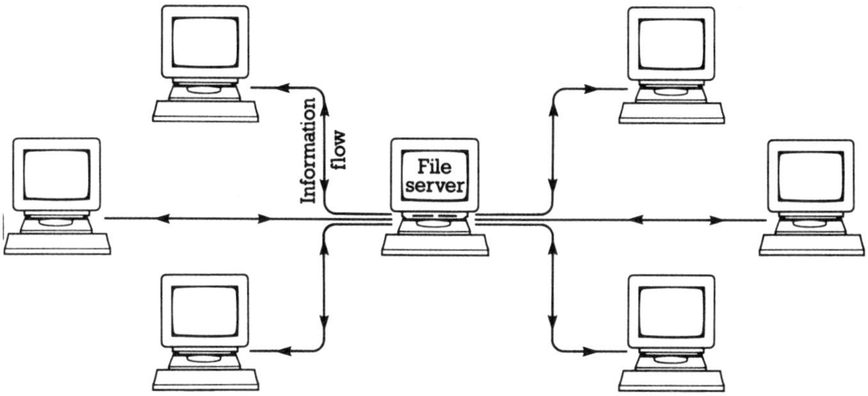

Work-stations connected into the network system are capable of working independently as stand-alone units. The efficiency with which data is transferred in any one system depends upon a number of factors, apart from the particular configuration used. For example, the type of cable used to connect the work-stations can affect the rate at which data can be transmitted, and the number of users in the system can determine the speed at which each work-station can be served.

Installation of a network system has to be based on careful planning, starting with an analysis of what will be required of the system when it is in operation.

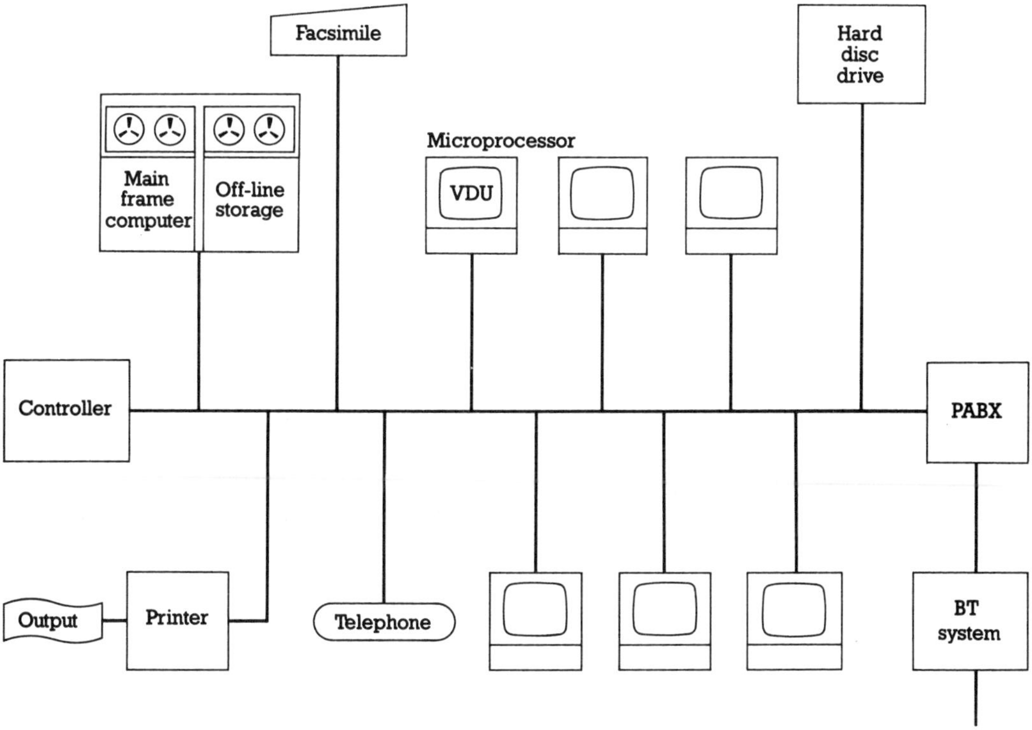

Local area network and related information technology.

Word processing

Until recently the work of transferring draft letters or reports onto paper fell to typists and secretaries. They performed an invaluable function as editors, checking grammar, spelling and punctuation. This ensured that regardless of the way in which the letter had been dictated or drafted, it would be correct when sent to its final destination.

Many secretaries and typists are now changing to word processors, which offer many advantages over the typewriter. However, there is a trend towards providing networked work-stations, allowing administrative staff to draft and edit their own letters and reports on a VDU before directing them to a shared printing facility.

When this happens in your organization, you will be required to learn the word processor package for the machine your company has installed. Having mastered this, you may be required to generate your own written communications and will no longer be able to rely on the skills of secretaries. You will have to take responsibility for the technical accuracy of your own work and will need to develop an eye for layout on the page. Fortunately, word processors provide you with the opportunity for getting a communication right in every respect before printing it.

The impact of these changes on the role of typists and secretaries will be significant. If every manager starts producing his own mail, many jobs may be lost. On the other hand, the introduction of the word processor could expand the role of secretarial staff, enabling them to move into the management structure which has often been closed to them in the past, even though they often undertook tasks which involved the acceptance of considerable responsibility.

Word processors

Dedicated word processor This is an electronic typewriter. The facility is limited to this function, but it does have considerable data manipulation capabilities. Where the application of office technology is confined to the processing of documents, this type of equipment improves efficiency and productivity.

Computer word processor Combines the function of word processing with computing facilities. The silicon chip has enabled the microcomputer to be designed as a compact, desk-top personal computer word processing unit, capable of handling the data processing requirements of a small business, or a department in a large organization. This capability can be further extended by linking the PCW into network systems or a central processor with backing store and data bases.

Word processing Except for some electronic typewriters which have a small memory capacity, the typewriter prints directly onto paper as the keys are struck. Any subsequent alteration or correction either involves extensive use of correction fluid or a complete rewrite. Extensive communications such as reports have to be written in draft and corrected by the author before the final version can be typed.

With a word processor you can enter the data onto a VDU. The information is stored visually before printing or transferred to hard or floppy disk for permanent storage.

Both during and after processing documents, data can be manipulated in the following ways:

Edited Corrections made, text altered or removed, additions made.
Styled Various typefaces can be programmed on one document.
Printed Any number of copies can be printed, and documents can be repeated, as and when required.

Layouts for standard documents, such as letters, reports, invoices and statements, can be stored on disk and retrieved when needed. If certain phrases are used repeatedly, these can also be stored and retrieved.

The cost of word processors now compares favourably with sophisticated electronic typewriters. The manuscript for this book has been prepared on an Amstrad PCW8256 costing less than £500.

Word processing software As with all computer software, you get what you pay for. There is a wide choice but this may be restricted by the processor's capability in terms of data storage or machine language. Examples are WORD STAR, TASWORD, SUPERWRITER, NEW WORD IT and LOCOSCRIPT.

Other facilities such as a dictionary of several thousand words, a spelling checker and an indexer can be added.

Activity 4

Select a suitable type of word processor for the following business activities:

1 The legal department in the county hall of a local authority.
2 The patients' record department in a hospital.
3 The office of a firm of management consultants.
4 An estate agent's office.
5 A medium-sized engineering company employing eighty people.
6 A secretary working for an author writing detective thrillers.

In each case, write a short statement justifying your choice.

Find out what word processing packages are being used at your place of work or college. Try to get some 'hands-on' experience by doing some simple text editing.

Accounts packages	Computers are very good at mathematical operations, which makes them the ideal tool for accounts procedures. Programmes are designed to provide visual information in the form of tabulations or graphs. Statements, wages/salary slips can be printed, payment of suppliers' accounts can be authorized.
Data bases	Extensive files of information can be stored within the computer and in off-line storage. The information can be sorted or collated in any way the organization demands. For example, a company employing several thousand people could select all employees aged between 25 and 30 who have attended a specific company training course during the past five years.
Spreadsheets	Replace the calculator. Answer the 'What if?' questions that management has to ask about many aspects of the business. Spreadsheets are a valuable asset to estimators, engineers production controllers and budget controllers.

Other software available.

Activity 5

Taking the examples given in Activity 4, suggest where accounts, data bases and spreadsheet packages could be usefully employed.

Example of the word processor's capability

Very little typing skill is required. There may be some advantage in having keyboard skills which enable touch typing and therefore faster data processing, but for many applications this is not essential. A relatively unskilled typist can manipulate the typed data on the screen without having acquired layout skills by completing tedious drills. All that is required is for the data to be entered in any form onto the screen. By selecting the required changes from a menu displayed on the screen, the layout and style can be modified by pressing the appropriate function keys.

A menu typed on the screen initially as:

```
EATMORE HOTEL
(Prop: A.B. Goodbody)
LUNCHEON MENU
Entree.  Soup of the Day or Grapefruit.
Main Course.  Lamb Cutlets or Fillet of
Plaice.
Vegetables.  French Fried Potatoes,
Garden Peas, Carrots.
Sweet.  Choice from Sweet Trolley
or Ice cream.
Coffee.
£3.50 (Including VAT)
```

Can be edited on the screen to be printed as:

```
           EATMORE HOTEL
        (Prop. A.B. Goodbody)

           LUNCHEON MENU

              Entree

          Soup of the Day
                or
            Grapefruit

            Main Course

           Lamb Cutlets
                or
         Fillet of Plaice

            Vegetables

            Garden Peas
      French Fried Potatoes
              Carrots

               Sweet

     Choice from Sweet Trolley
                or
             Ice-cream

              Coffee

  Price: £3.50 (including VAT)
```

Activity 6

You work in the benefits office of a government department which is putting its standard letters onto disk so they can be called up on a PCW and sent out as necessary.

You have been asked to write text covering these five frequent causes of delay in working out benefits due.

a Failure to give name and address of last employer.
b Failure to send birth/marriage (etc) certificates.
c Failure to give number/ages/names of dependent children.
d Failure to quote pension/allowance number.
e Failure to keep appointment (therefore another one needed).

Omitting any official letter-head, start with 'Dear . . .' and draft the text.

Computer hardware

Computers manipulate data and provide solutions. In order to transfer, file and print data, other equipment has to be added. This extra equipment and the computer itself are known as **hardware**, as opposed to the operating programmes, which are called **software**.

The amount and type of add-on equipment for a specific data processing installation depends on what is required of it and on whether it will have to react with other data processing systems.

Disks drives Used to record from and address the disk storage of the system. Disk drives contain a read/write head which scans the disk at high speed, allowing the user to access data quickly.

Disk Similar in principle to disks on which recordings are made. A number of grooves represent tracks which can be divided into sectors for storage of data.

Floppy disk The most widely used disk for the personal computer (PC) and personal computer word processor (PCW), it consists of a magnetized metal or plastic disk in a protective cover. The floppy is relatively cheap and efficient, with a storage capacity of about 360 kbytes.

Winchester disks Hard disks stored in sealed units for protection. Unlike the floppy disk, they cannot be removed from the sealed unit. The disk has several hundred grooves per inch, whereas the floppy disk has a maximum of 96 tracks per inch. This gives the Winchester a high individual storage capacity of around 5 mbytes, which can be further expanded by stacking a number of disks in a single unit.

Micro-floppy disk Similar to a floppy disk, with some of the advantages of the Winchester disk. Micro-floppies are stored in rigid cases for protection and have a storage capacity of 300 kbytes at present, but high-storage disks will be made available as the technology advances.

Printers **Daisywheel printer** – characters are held on a flat rotating disk with a number of spokes, each having one character. When the individual spoke is struck, the image is transferred through a print ribbon onto the paper.

Dot matrix printer – characters are formed by a number of dots impinged onto the paper. The system provides a draft quality print with a single strike or a letter quality with a double strike, the second being slightly off-set to produce a higher density.

Ink jet printer – ink is deposited directly onto the paper by high-pressure jet. It has the advantages of being silent in operation and able to produce colour graphics.

Intelligent copiers – electronic printers which convert incoming computer data to produce images. These machines are capable of sophisticated layouts and a variety of typefaces. Laser beams are used to create the image on photo-sensitive drums or belts before it is transferred to the paper. The equipment contains a microprocessor enabling the copier to be instructed to carry out a number of functions similar to those available on the word processor. Standard layouts, different typefaces and editing can be programmed into the machine. When not in conjunction with the integrated system, the machine can be used as a photocopier.

Optical character reader (OCR) Electronic equipment capable of reading typed script by scanning and converting the images into digital form which can be processed by other data processing equipment in the system. A microprocessor memory enables the OCR to recognize over 200 different fonts and stops the machine whenever it fails to recognize the incoming data.

A familiar use of the OCR is at the supermarket checkout where they are programmed to read the bar code printed on the labels of many products. Reading the bar code at the point of sale enables the sales and stock records to be continually updated by a central processor.

Modem (modulator/demodulator) An electronic device which converts digital data into analogue data for transmission down telephone lines and converts it back to digital data at the receiving end. Used to connect computers through a telephone system.

Computer software

Software is the name given to describe any method of putting instructions into a computer memory by some device such as a floppy or hard disk.

Computer users do not have to write programmes. They can be bought as a 'package' from commercial software houses who write programmes for specific machines or for the so-called **compatible** machines. Compatibles are computers which are capable of running software made by a manufacturer other than the maker of the computer.

The following are examples of packaged programmes provided by software houses. Some of these will be dealt with later. The list is not comprehensive, but it does give an idea of the wide variety of applications.

Accounts	Wages/Pay roll	Inventory control
Data base	Electronic mail	Electronic filing
Graphics	Statistics	Word processing
Budgeting	Costing	Estimating

Electronic filing Electronic filing performs the functions that would normally involve the manual sorting of documents, such as placing in filing cabinets, maintaining Cardex systems, taking extracts and updating information.

Storage of data in a filing system creates a data base which can be referenced and edited, but if this has to be done manually it takes a considerable amount of time. Data often have to be stored in more than one filing system. This means that documents have to be reproduced by carbon copies or photocopying and then distributed to the various storage points.

Activity 7

In Block 5 you will find a diagram, 'sales office routine', which shows the paperwork system used by Extruded Plastic Tube Ltd to inform the departments concerned about an incoming order.

Assuming that the company has now installed a network system, outline the way in which these data could now be distributed.

The advantages of electronic filing can be demonstrated by considering the data base generated by a Cardex system.

This type of filing system only orders data according to one criterion, such as customer name, material type or method of payment. There are problems when attempting to extract or cross-relate data stored on lower sections of the card.

With an electronic data base file, the computer can search for any stored item and sort, extract, add/subtract and subtotal as required.

Data bases provide the ability to:	Setting up a data base requires knowing:
Look through stored records	What information will be stored
Make changes as required	What needs to be done with the stored data
Find specific entries	What format the data base will use
Use print-out facilities	

This will define the appropriate software and avoid the purchase of a package which will not perform the tasks required.

As with all computer packages, you get what you pay for. The degree of sophistication depends upon the cost of the programmed package. Bear in mind that the more 'tricks' a packaged program can perform, the more difficult it is likely to be to operate. A golden rule to apply when considering any package is, 'If the simple system does what you want, then that is the one for you.'

Types of data base **Flat file data base** – a simple system similar to a card index. Stores data on a single file.

Multiple file data base – allows access to a number of files at the same time and a search for information stored in its files.

Relational data base – the most flexible system of the three. Allows access to a number of files at the same time and cross-references files in order to extract data and present it in the desired form.

A data base may store information which comes under the Data Protection Act. The Act places an obligation on those storing personal data to register with the Data Protection Registrar. Information must be treated as confidential and accessed only by authorized users. Restrictions are placed on the transfer of data: it is an offence to pass a mailing list to a third party without the permission of everyone on the list.

Where a high degree of data security is essential, the user will have a password to gain access, or data may be subject to **encryption** – a coding system which scrambles data to prevent unauthorized access

Electronic mail

In Activity 7, you may have decided that the data could be transferred from one VDU in the system to those in the other departments concerned. This would involve 'mailing' the data along the cable connecting the work-stations. Each VDU in the system would have to be ready to receive the data being transmitted.

In a busy system it would not be convenient to have work-stations standing by awaiting data transmission. The problem can be overcome by running an **electronic mail package.**

Electronic mail has a number of advantage over written correspondence:
1 Data goes straight to the intended recipient's work-station.
2 The recipient is given a 'mail for you' reminder.

	YEAR 1				YEAR 2				YEAR 3			
	Q1	Q2	Q3	Q4	Q1	Q2	Q3	Q4	Q1	Q2	Q3	Q4
SALES	80	20	38	104	88	22	42	114	96	24	46	125
PRICE	400	400	400	400	400	400	400	400	400	400	400	400
REVENUE	32000	8000	15200	41600	35200	8800	16800	45600	38400	9600	18400	50000
SALES COST	10000	5000	5000	10000	5000	5000	10000	5000	1000	5000	5000	10000
GROSS P/L	22000	3000	10200	31600	30200	3800	6800	40600	28400	4600	13400	40000
EXPENSES												
Salaries	7500	7500	7500	7500	7500	7500	7500	7500	7500	7500	7500	7500
Rent	3000	3000	3000	3000	3000	3000	3000	3000	3000	3000	3000	3000
Power etc.	1800	1000	1400	2200	1800	1000	1400	2200	1800	1000	1400	2200
Deprec'n.	2500	2500	2500	2500	2500	2500	2500	2500	2500	2500	2500	2500
Advertise				5000				5000				5000
Loan												
TOTAL EXP.	14800	14000	14400	20200	14800	14000	14400	20200	14800	1400	14400	20200
NET P/L	7200	-11000	-4200	11400	15400	-10200	-7600	20400	13600	-9400	-1000	19800
B/F	7500	14700	3700	-500	10900	26300	16100	8500	28900	42500	33100	32100
CUM.TOTAL	14700	3700	-500	10900	26300	16100	8500	28900	42500	33100	32100	51900

Example of spreadsheet print-out.

3 The sender can obtain a recorded check that mail has been viewed.
4 Mail can be edited, stored, routed to another work-station, filed or disposed of as required.
5 The amount of paperwork and space taken up in the storage of records is substantially reduced.
6 It is a cheaper communication system than telephone conversation.

Electronic mail (internal) a typical network of PCs or PCWs would carry an electronic mail package which directs mail to each work-station. A 'mail box' stores the directed information until the user is ready to deal with it.

Electronic mail (external) British Telecom provides an external mail service, Telecom Gold. The subscriber is allocated an 'electronic work space' which allows the use of a wide variety of terminals – such as viewdata, telex and data bases – via the standard telephone network.

Mail merge programme

Allows data base records to be merged with a standard letter or other master document. Ideal for the production of personalized communications and mail shots.

Spreadsheets

These differ from a data base in that they are able to calculate the effect of a change in the value of one or more of the units of data entered.

Individual blocks of data are stored in locations specified by X and Y co-ordinates as shown in the illustration. These locations are labelled according to the type of data stored in them.

The layout of the spreadsheet requires careful planning; it can be difficult to modify it once the format has been programmed.

Because of the 'What if?' facility, changes in the various classifications of data can be entered and the overall effect can be automatically recalculated. This enables management to model situations and check the effect of proposed changes before committing the organization to a particular course of action.

Activity 8

Look at the spreadsheet showing a family budget for the first four months of the year.

Spreadsheet Family Budget

	Jan	Feb	March	April	May
Mortgage	180	180	180	180	
Insurance	15	15	175*	15	
Petrol	10	10	10	10	
Car tax	–	–	–	55†	
Food	115	115	115	115	
Hire purchase (car)	20	20	20	20	
General expenses	50	50	50	50	
Total expenditure	390	390	550	445	
Monthly income	600	600	600	600	
Balance c/f	+210	+420	+470	+625	

* The £175 is an annual payment for house insurance.
† The £55 is a payment for car tax made twice a year. The next payment is due in October.

Try applying the following 'What if?' questions to the budget for the rest of the year.

What if:
1 The cost of petrol increases by 5 per cent from the end of April?
2 Food prices increase by 10 per cent from the same point?
3 There is an 8% salary increase at the end of April?
4 The family want a holiday in August costing £1000?

Calculate the balance of the family budget at the end of the year.

Accounts packages You will have seen from Activity 8 that accounts procedures are an ideal application for spreadsheets. Packages can be bought for individual activities such as wages or costing, and integrated packages which provide a number of accounting functions are available.

Activity 9

Draw up a list of industrial, commercial and national/local government organizations which could benefit from using a data base.

Select one from each category. Outline the type of data you think they would store, stating the reasons for your choice.

Design a spreadsheet layout suitable for calculating the net weekly wage in the organization you selected after all stoppages have been made.

The office of the future

We have now looked at the various types of information technology equipment being introduced. Here we summarize how they fit into the office. Typewriters will be replaced by dedicated WPs or PCWs built into **local area networks** and linked through the British Telecom's communication system to **wider area networks** and **satellite systems**.

Technology will lead to reduction in the use of Telex and physical mailing systems.

Telecommunications

The **Private automatic branch exchange** (PABX) will provide an interface for voice, data and facsimile transmission. Telephone conversations will still take place, but on a much reduced scale. Increased use of data facsimile transmission will tend to reduce executive travel.

Internal information will be transferred and filed by electronic equipment.

Electronic mail box

Information received will be passed through a document reader and converted into digital form before being routed to individual work-stations. Mail boxes would be checked at intervals during the day to be passed on, filed or modified.

External electronic mailing will be able to take place when both sender and receiver have compatible data processing equipment.

Printers

Dot matrix printing will be of sufficient quality for most internal printing, high-quality printing and specialized printing being used for the reduced amount of external data.

Activity 10

It has been suggested that the amount of printing will be reduced by the use of VDUs to transmit data.

Make a list of the problems that might arise out of constantly using VDU screens during the working day.

Electronic filing

A number of different methods of storing bulk data will be used, depending on the amount to be stored and the methods used to process it.

Storage methods:
a Floppy magnetic disk
b Hard magnetic disk
c Winchester disk
d Optical digital recording (ODR)
ODRs are capable of storing an impressive 50 000 pages of A4 typing on one 12 in. disk.

Organizations such as banks, credit houses, building societies, government departments and the Stock Exchange are typical of those which will find this type of storage capacity useful.

Staffing

Integrated technology will mean fewer staff are employed. The days of large office blocks may well be numbered.

Routine and menial office tasks will be carried out electronically, no longer providing employment for those with lower standards of education. Those in employment will work at work-stations and will tend to be of a comparable status to one another.

The mass of information available to the individual employee will allow decisions to be taken at a lower level of the management structure.

Work-stations

As technology progresses and the need for integration grows, the system will no longer comprise a number of different peripherals. Work-stations will be designed as single integrated units providing the following facilities:

Computing	Access to local and wide area networks
Word processing	Electronic dictionary
Electronic filing	Spelling checker
Data base	Automatic dialling
spreadsheet	Electronic mailing

The role of the telecommunication system

With the introduction of System × and satellite communication systems, British Telecom will play a vital role in the transmission of data throughout the business world. A great deal of development work has already been undertaken to expand existing services and introduce new technology.

Activity 11

MACROMECHANICS
DALE ROAD
MICKLE TRAFFORD

29th May 19..

Accounts Department
E.P.T. Ltd
NEWTOWN

Dear Sir,

I have just received a second demand for the tube I had off you last month on the 27th.

You want to get up to date. I paid you this £430.99 on the 25th.

Yours faithfully,

John Hardy

Macromechanics.

Your computer runs the invoices each month on the 26th. A second demand clearly crossed in the post with Mr Hardy's payment.

a This problem could occur again and again. Send a memo to the computer section asking them to write a programme to meet the situation – give your suggestions.

b Write to Mr Hardy. He sounded cross in his letter; take this into account in your reply, both in the salutation and the tone.

Technology and people in organizations

The technological revolution is still in its early stages. Few people will not be affected by its impact. In particular, those who are designated as office workers will find that their working environment will change dramatically.

In industrial processes, automation tends to be first applied to production methods on the shop floor. This is because it can be applied to simple repetitive tasks usually performed by unskilled labour. It is now increasingly being used to break down those tasks which have been performed by skilled labour. A similar change is being imposed on the office. Procedures for processing data are becoming less skilled as the sophistication of the equipment available increases.

Those who manage any organization have to be aware of the cost of what they are trying to achieve. This is particularly important where the cost is an overhead, not directly related to production. Office work is in this category. Management will want to invest in equipment which reduces labour costs and improves the processing and transmission of data.

How labour requirements change

When recruiting personnel in the future, organizations will be aiming to obtain a flexible, highly skilled and trained work-force. People will need to be willing to retrain at frequent intervals as new equipment is introduced. Management will be seeking employees who are well educated and able to take a flexible approach to changing jobs and working methods.

In order to retain and develop highly qualified personnel, management will need a policy of on-going training and a system of rewards to encourage co-operation.

For employees, there will be many rewarding jobs which will give greater responsibility and more participation in the running of the business. Technology will make it possible for the administrative worker to make informed decisions and provide a back-up service to management. Greater involvement in the decision-making process will do much to give the individual employee job satisfaction.

A new role for the secretary Typing and shorthand skills will not play a major part in the working life of the secretary for much longer. As the controllers and manipulaters of information, they are likely to have a greater role in the management of the business. To equip them for this, their training will need to concentrate more on business management skills.

Clerical and administrative staff People previously employed in clerical procedures such as filing, classifying and retrieving data will no longer be required on the same scale as before the introduction of office technology. Machines are capable of performing these functions faster and with greater accuracy. As a result, the number of lower grade clerical workers will be considerably reduced. In contrast, the work of the higher grades will become more significant and they will contribute more to the management of the organization.

Activity 12

During the next week, make a note of all the people you see using some form of electronic data processing equipment in the course of doing their work. Compare this with the observations of other members of the class and make a composite list.

Select five tasks from your list and discuss what working methods would have been used to carry out these tasks before the introduction of modern technology.

How technology can change working methods

If you are taking this course at a college, you will be sitting in a classroom with a lecturer giving you information verbally or by some visual aid device. In front of you will be at least one book (this one); others will be used as well. From time to time you will need to go to a library and read books in the reference section, taking notes for your own information. As the course proceeds, the amount of information in your own notebook will grow.

Some technology will be used in your training – video recorders, television, films – but this is only scratching the surface of what is feasible, given the present technology.

Consider the role of the library. This is really a data base; much of the information could be put onto disks and accessed as required. If the information you require is not available in your data bank, a national data bank could be accessed over the telecommunication system or by satellite. Centralization would either reduce the size of college libraries or remove the need for individual colleges to have them.

Lecturers need not stand in front of individual classes. They could stand in front of a television camera and talk to all the students taking their particular subject – Open University lecturers have done that for more than ten years. Colleges could become information centres where students attend for short top-up courses and tutorials.

Do you have to keep a lot of notes? It would be possible to have a floppy disk with basic prepared notes which you could load into a word processor and edit as and when you wanted.

All this would involve a considerable input of capital. In addition, there would have to be a massive retraining programme for college staff .

However, this cost might be off-set by savings in staff and buildings. There would be no need to provide blocks of classrooms if you could get the bulk of the teaching input from a VDU at home and only attend college for tutorials.

Activity 13

Assuming that the government of the day decided to implement the kind of technology discussed above, what new skills would teaching staff have to be trained in to cope with changes in working conditions?

Make a survey of your college and draw up a list of the occupations that would be affected by the changes in education methods described above.

Discuss as a group any disadvantages you consider would arise for the student if technology were introduced on the scale outlined above.

Implementing Change

Introducing new technology always creates problems for both management and managed. Security of employment has been a major consideration in the UK work-force, particularly in the areas of local and national government. Local government officers and civil servants have assumed that they have a job for life, and will gain promotion through length of service and never have to face unemployment.

Many commercial enterprises – such as banks, building societies and insurance companies – also have a tradition of long-term employment. Rates of pay and conditions of service often take this security of employment into account. However, it is within these areas of employment that information technology is having its greatest effect. As fewer jobs for office and administrative workers become available, there will also be less scope for promotion by progression from junior posts within these types of organization.

The immediate effects of change

Technology in the office has contributed to the growth of the white-collar unions such as NALGO, whose aims are to secure employment and improve working conditions. In protecting the interests of their members, the unions inevitably view technology with some suspicion and use delaying tactics if they feel that loss of employment or skill will result.

Managing change in industry and commerce is a skilled business. If technology is changed and jobs are affected, the advantages which are gained can be off-set by loss of morale and motivation. Fear of the unknown makes the work-force seek the protection of the union and become more willing to take industrial action.

Management's task is to communicate with the work-force before change takes place and consult with unions in situations where they represent employees.

Many of the problems related to change in technology can be off-set by a planned approach. The major concern of the work-force will be redundancy. This can be reduced by re-training, natural wastage (not recruiting labour until the work-force is at the required level), adequate compensation for those losing employment and early retirement.

Activity 14

A firm of insurance brokers has been established as a family business for over fifty years. The former senior partner, who recently retired at the age of seventy, took a paternalistic interest in the fifty employees who work in the office and many of the present staff have been with the firm for more than fifteen years.

Consultation between management and the employees has been conducted through a staff association set up by the former senior partner in 1967. Each department has an elected representative on the committee, which meets once a month.

The new senior partner has made it known to the staff association that the firm is about to be 'dragged into the twentieth century'. Consultant system analysts have been employed to introduced office technology as a matter of urgency.

1 Acting in the role of a departmental representative, list the items you intend to mention about the effects of office technology when you report back to the employees in your department.
2 List the problems that could arise if the new senior partner took the view that the firm did not have to introduce modern technology.
3 Select a white-collar union which would best serve the interests of the employees in this situation.

The long-term effects of change

As the number of personnel employed in the office decreases and the office worker becomes more skilled and qualified, relationships between managers and managed will tend towards that of partnership in the administration of the enterprise.

Those who are employed as skilled administrators may not have guaranteed long-term prospects of employment. Promotion will be on the basis of merit or willingness to change jobs rather than on length of service. Salaries and conditions of service will be calculated on the basis of the high productivity made possible by technology.

The wheel will have turned full circle, with office workers identifying with the management of the organization in much the same way as they did before the expansion of administrative procedures. Under these circumstances, the office worker may feel less need to seek the protection of the white-collar unions and prefer to negotiate terms and conditions on the basis of individual skill and ability.

Activity 15

Write to Heating and Ventilation Ltd, of 132 Lime Street, Princes Tilcon, complaining that the air conditioning they installed two months ago (at a cost of £8000) in the computer department of the insurance company in which you work is not functioning properly. It switches itself off at 10.17 every morning and as your premises have a sealed atmosphere you are collapsing with heat in the afternoons. When it is running, it is very noisy. Ask for immediate action.

Activity 16

Listed below are a number of examples of computer hardware. Research the information available in libraries and manufacturers' publications on these and other hardware available. Write a short description of each one and produce an illustrated reference file.

Disk drive	Daisywheel printer
Hard disk	Dot matrix printer
Floppy disk	Ink jet printer
Winchester disk	Intelligent copiers
Micro-floppy disc	Optical character reader (OCR)
	Modem (modulator/demodulator)

Summary

The purpose of this Block has been to provide a general introduction to the wide variety of electronic equipment available in the field of business communications. Some examples of relevant software have been described. This area of business communication is dynamic and subject to constant change. You are advised to concentrate on what I.T. can do for the organization rather than try to understand the complexities of the technology.

As a user of integrated technology, the office worker can be equated with the driver of a car – the user does not have to know what goes on under the bonnet in order to make efficient use of the equipment. We should be interested in what the equipment can do for us rather than alarmed by the intricacies of electronic circuitry.

The question we should ask ourselves is, 'What do we want IT to do?' Organizations can easily go overboard in applying IT to everything in sight without considering the merits of other working methods, or by applying the technology in isolated areas without regard to the effect of that on the overall administration procedures.

In conclusion, you must be aware that regardless of the wonders of modern science, nothing works efficiently unless the organization has well-trained and motivated personnel.

Major changes in working conditions and terms of employment for those working in offices have yet to take place. The introduction of information technology must not happen without full consideration of the effect on clerical and administrative staff.

Skills

Skill	*Activities in which skill is developed*
a Information gathering	1, 4, 9, 12, 13, 15
b Learning and studying	4, 5, 7, 8, 10, 13, 15
c Working with others	1, 2, 12, 13
d Communicating	1, 3, 5, 6, 8, 9, 11, 12, 13, 15, 15
e Design and visual decrimination	3, 6, 9
f Identifying and tackling problems	7, 8, 10, 12, 13, 14
g Numeracy	1, 2, 3, 4, 5, 6, 6, 7, 8
h Information processing	9, 11, 12, 13, 15

Block 5
Marketing and Sales

Introduction

This block defines the difference between marketing and sales and outlines their individual functions in identifying and servicing the organization's market. Various methods of sampling and influencing public opinion are considered. Finally, ways of presenting information visually are described.

The following diagrams outline the structure of two typical departments.

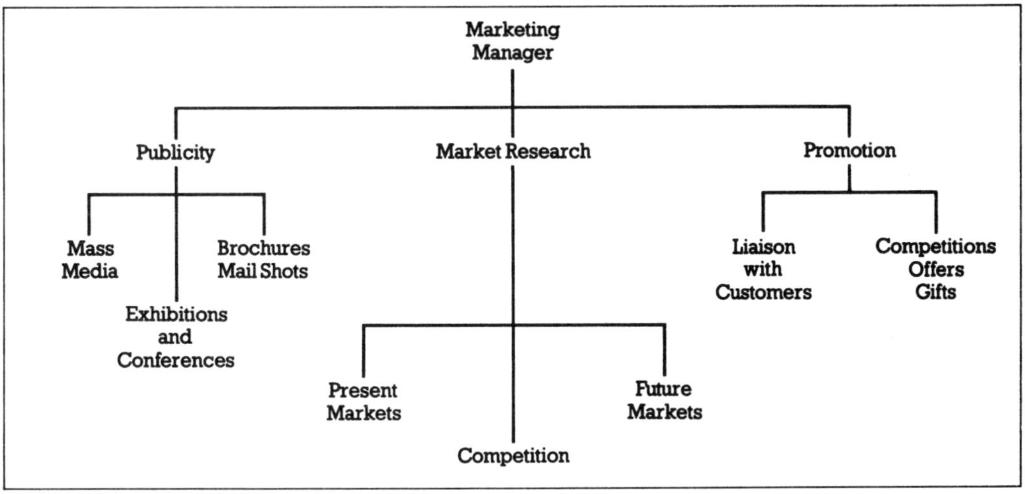

The marketing department.

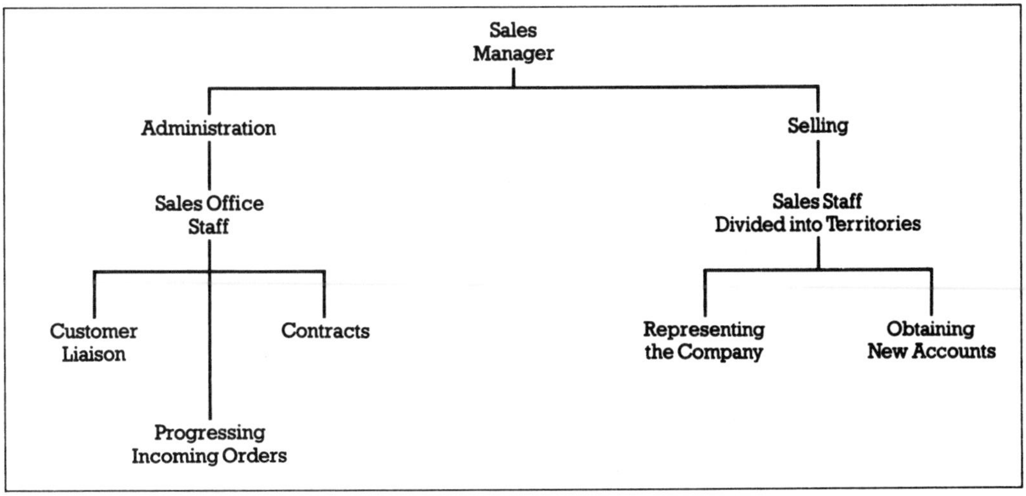

The sales department.

Marketing and sales

You will need to understand the fundamental difference between **marketing** and **sales**. Although the two are closely associated, they have clearly defined functions in the organization structure.

Here is a definition of marketing from the Institute of Marketing and Sales Management: **'Marketing is the creative management function which promotes trade and employment by assessing consumer needs and initiating development and research to meet them.'**

This indicates three main areas of activity:
1. Identify the potential market for the company's goods and services by conducting market research.
2. Introduce the product or service to the purchasing public and create a demand for the goods and services offered. This is an important function when a new product is being launched.
3. In conjunction with the sales function, ensure that the potential demand is satisfied.

What each individual organization considers to be the essential activities of the marketing function will depend upon the type of industry and the products concerned. In general, it can be taken that the main activities will cover:

PRODUCT	PRICE	PACKAGING	ADVERTISING	PROMOTION	BRANDING

The product

A major part of the marketing function is to present the product to the potential purchaser and maintain a favourable product image. Failure to do this can result in a competitor taking the company's business and weakening its market position.

Few, if any, organizations can ignore the dangers of competition. Even those who have a monopoly over the supply of services are not entirely immune from market forces. Before privatization, both British Gas and the Central Electricity Generating Board regularly advertised on television. The considerable expense involved was considered essential in order to expand the use of the service.

Activity 1

You are a clerical assistant in the marketing department of a large furniture manufacturers. You notice an article in a trade magazine describing the improvement made in a competitor's product. Write a memorandum which draws the attention of those concerned in your organization to the article.

Price

Price is a major consideration in selling a product to enable the organization to obtain a reasonable return on capital. The price may have to be very competitive because there are a number of companies willing to supply to the market. If the product or service is in short supply, price could be what the market will stand.

A number of things determine the price. In order to manufacture something, the organization is involved in various costs. Some are accumulated by the purchase of machinery, payment of rent/mortgage on buildings and insurance. These are costs which must be borne whether the business is manufacturing to maximum capacity or is making nothing at all. They are known as **fixed costs.**

Administration of the business, although essential for management and control of resources, does not directly contribute to the manufacture of the product. Provision of services to control the purchase of raw material, payment of wages, selling the product, selection and training of personnel etc, are all considered to be **overhead costs.**

Costs directly contributing to the production of goods, such as labour, raw materials and machine time, will vary with the amount produced. It will obviously take more material to produce a hundred items than it will to produce ten. Direct costs to production are known as **variable costs.**

The relationship between cost and price can be expressed by adding the above three costs, plus the expected **profit margin** on the sale of the product:

Fixed cost + Overhead cost + Variable cost + Profit margin = Selling price

The marketing department will carry out market research to monitor the price charged by competitors and provide feedback to aid the pricing policy of the organization.

Packaging

Most products are packaged in some way because of the practice of presenting products on self-service displays. The package often plays an important role in the promotion of the product image. Few people would be inclined to pay £20 for an ounce of perfume in what looked like a plastic milk bottle wrapped in plain paper. In many organizations, the marketing department pays great attention to this aspect of the product.

In other circumstances, the package may be a means of protection during transport and storage. In this case presentation is not such an important factor to the marketing department. Whatever the purpose of the packaging, it will add to the cost of production and therefore to the price of the product.

Advertising

One function of the marketing department is to stimulate a demand for the product. Some products will sell because a demand exists and the consumer seeks the source of supply. Bread is an example. Others have to be presented so that the consumer feels a need to purchase them. This is the role of advertising. It keeps the product in the public eye in order to maintain or increase sales. Those who manufacture products which are household names do not stop advertising; to do so would give the competitor a chance to attract the consumer. Advertising well-known products is called defensive advertising. Petrol, detergents and canned foods all offer examples.

Advertising on television or in national daily papers is expensive. The marketing department must carefully judge the likely return from additional sales or from the maintenance of sales before a decision is made about wide-scale advertising.

Activity 2

You have been given the opportunity to redesign the cover of your college's prospectus. Make a list of the main points you would emphasize in the layout in order to make it attractive to prospective students and to promote the public image.

Promotion

As stated above, having a well-known product does not in itself guarantee sales. Where the competition is strong, for example in the manufacture and selling of detergents, advertising alone may not be sufficient to maintain the share of the market. A competitor may start to sway the consumer to purchase its brand. Even if this situation has not arisen, the company might feel that it has improved its product and wish to inform consumers and encourage them to try it.

There are a number of ways in which promotion can achieve what is wanted. One way is to offer consumers a chance to win some form of substantial prize, such as a new car or a holiday abroad. This is often coupled with some form of token system enabling consumers to obtain a reduction on the purchase of goods or to claim some form of gift.

Retailers are supplied with promotional display material and may obtain some price advantage or reward from the promoter. Promotion campaigns are coupled with the advertising programme, which may include a well-known personality who endorses the product.

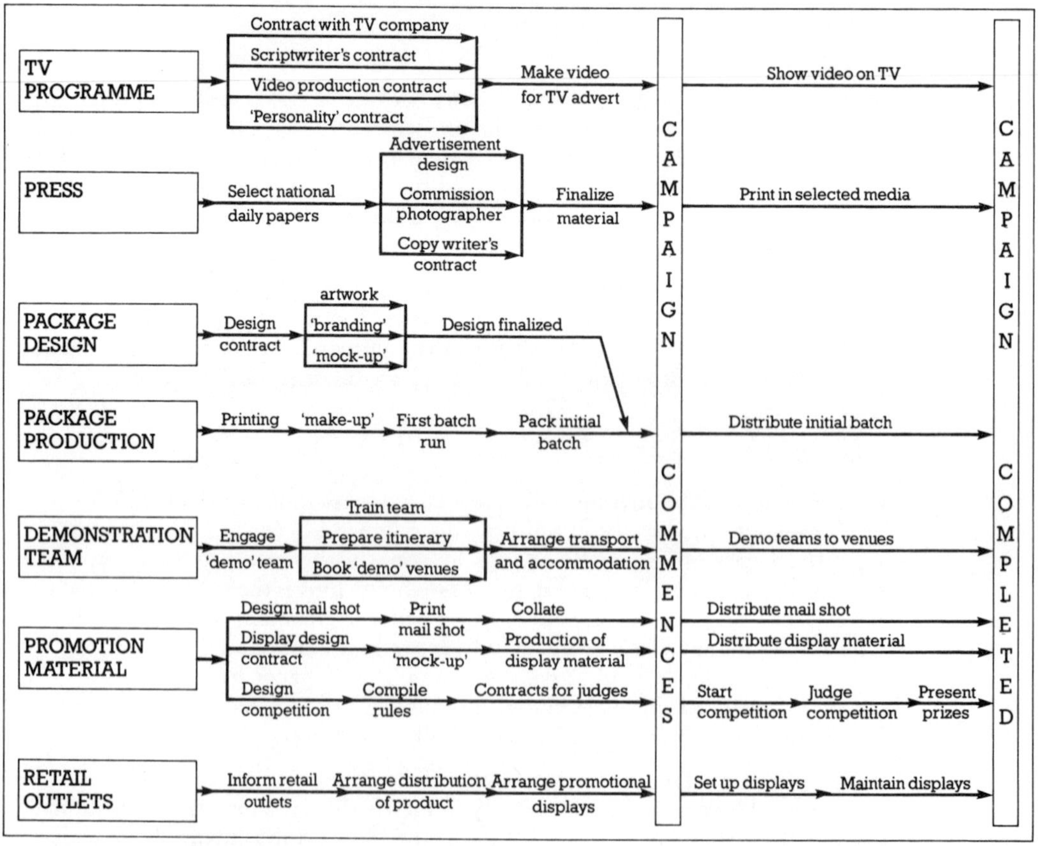

Promoting a product.

Branding

A product's brand is part of its public image. It is most important in the supermarket, where colour and design make certain products immediately recognizable. Companies try to promote brand image through advertising and slogans. These are powerful sales stimulants and will promote impulse buying. Successful advertising, promotion and branding will develop a brand loyalty in the consumer, who will then reject a competitor's product. Brand image can have a considerable influence; more than one motorist with a near empty tank has driven past a petrol station, simply because it does not sell a particular brand.

Activity 3

1 Choose a commercial break you have seen on Independent Television which you consider to be related to the marketing function. Identify the objectives from the content.
2 Select three national daily newspapers you would use to promote the launching of a new credit card which will be in direct competition with American Express. Briefly state why you would select those three in preference to others available.
3 Collect and examine promotional material delivered to your home over a few weeks. Assess the degree to which you think it influences people to buy.

Activity 4

EPTL has a marketing department in its organization structure. Outline how you would expect the department to promote a new range of tubing designed for use in the building industry.

Activity 5

You work for Talbot and Talbot Ltd, a firm manufacturing soaps and toiletries. On 17 September 19__ the board of directors asked you to report on the progress of the new advertising campaign. You spoke to the advertising manager and the sales manager and sent a questionnaire to a sample of the supermarkets you supply. You acquired the following information:

1 Campaign started 1 July
2 TV commercial, two minutes prime time Wednesday and Friday
3 Poster campaign in supermarkets designed to coincide with TV advertising
4 Free offer – bath soap for any three wrappers
5 Turnover month ended 30 June £24 600 (same month in previous year £23 400)
6 Turnover month ended 31 July £24 734 (previous year £22 800)
7 Turnover month ended 31 August £25 630 (previous year £23 536)
8 Prices have risen by 4 per cent over twelve-month period
9 Posters not available until third week in July
10 Customers think TV commercial very poor
11 Considerable interest in free offer.

Make your report, giving conclusions and recommendations.

Activity 6

EPTL are launching an improved tube especially designed for use in the agricultural industry.

There is to be advertising in the farming journals; a demonstration team will tour the country during May, June and July; and a competition likely to appeal to buyers working in agriculture is to be run, with a prestige car as first prize.

You are asked to put in some early work by:
a identifying all the possible publications you could advertise in;
b identifying six or eight locations with excellent road communications that would bring the demonstrations within reach of most areas;
c devising three possible competition formats to be presented at the next marketing meeting.

Questionnaires

Sampling opinion

The marketing department needs to gather information or opinions from the public or from an organization's clients. To do this, usually a percentage of the group being researched is asked to fill in questionnaires. Their answers are taken to be typical of the whole group and form the basis of decisions which will affect the whole group. This sampling procedure requires expert knowledge of statistical techniques, and a specialist firm is likely to be used if the issue is an important one.

Reaching your sample

Questionnaires can be sent out by post or put through letter-boxes, distributed with another publication such as a trade magazine or simply handed to people.

Designing the questionnaire

It is notoriously difficult to get people to fill in questionnaires. You will need to have a leading paragraph explaining the object of the exercise and saying in what way the survey will benefit them. The kind of question you ask will depend on two factors:
1 How you are going to add up the answers when you get them,
2 Whether it is facts or opinions you want.

Simplify your life.

If you are running a large survey and there will be few people to collate the answers, you can simplify the procedure by designing tick-the-box questions; see below:

DO YOU LIKE ONIONS?		Yes
		No
		Don't know

If you will be analysing the results on a computer, you will need a format which provides definite answers. YES or NO has to be the answer to an absolutely specific question, and in order to cover the ground you may have to design many small questions. The question about onions, for example, is much more complex than you may think:

Do you like raw onions?

	Yes
✓	No
	Don't know

Do you like boiled onions?

✓	Yes
	No
	Don't know

Do you like fried onions?

✓	Yes
	No
	Don't know

Covering the ground.

Sometimes the strength of opinion is under review. To cover this you will need to design a continuum of answers, as in the following example:

DO YOU APPROVE OF CHILDREN BEING CANED IN SCHOOL?		Strongly opposed
		Have doubts about it
		Probably OK
		Strongly in favour

The tick-the-box question gives no scope for the circumstantial answer in which the respondent wants to take various factors into account. For answers of this nature, you will have to use the dotted-line approach. The answers will be detailed and informative – but very difficult to add together.

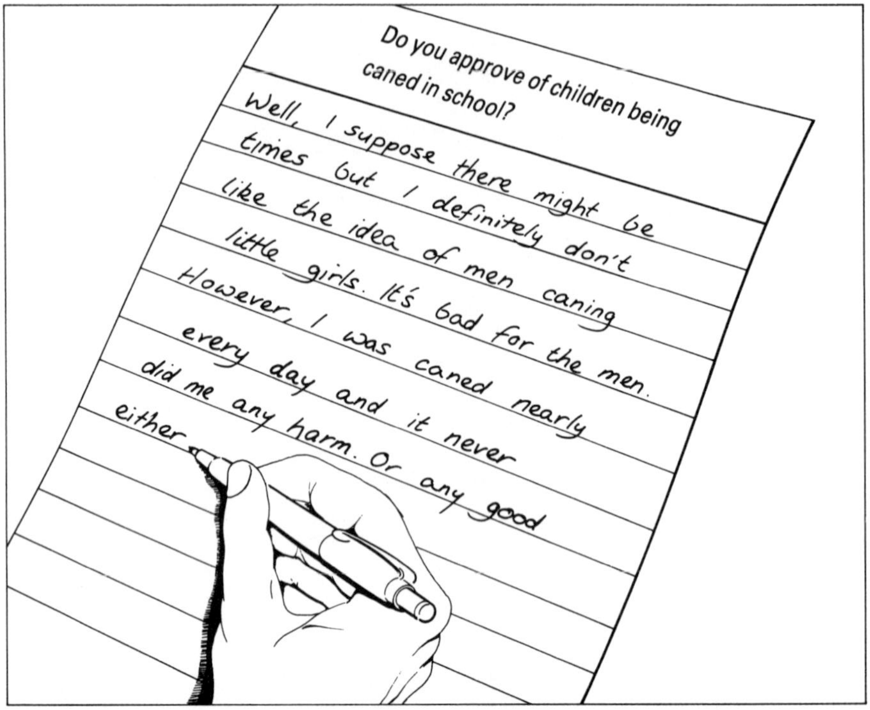

The circumstantial answer.

Phrasing the questions

The person filling in the form will usually be answering in your absence, so the questions must be easy to understand and must not be ambiguous.

Emotional bias Phrasing the questions can be tricky. It is easy to lead people into giving the answer you want by using words with emotional overtones.

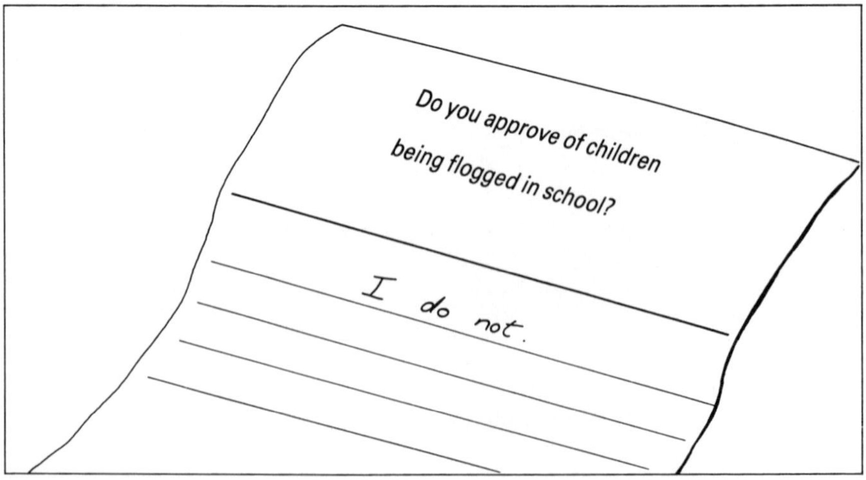

Emotional overtones.

Leading the witness Sentences can be constructed in such a way that they 'expect' a certain answer, a trick frequently used in cross-examination and known as 'leading the witness'.

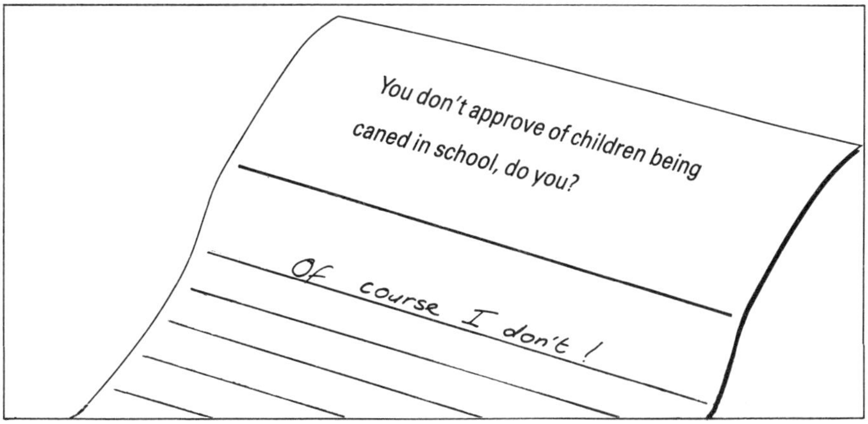

Leading questions.

The 'proper' answer Certain attitudes, often connected with kindness or honesty etc, are considered to be the 'proper' ones. If your questionnaire is covering such a field, your respondents are fairly unlikely to be truthful if their opinion is not the 'proper' one. You will need to bear this is mind.

Proper attitudes

Invasion of privacy Some questions, especially ones to do with age, money, religion and politics, can cause resentment and a refusal to answer. Even asking respondents to give their name can distort all the answers in some circumstances. You should consider carefully whether you really need to know what you are asking.

Distorting the answers.

Getting the forms back You should give instructions about getting the forms back – preferably setting a deadline. Prepaid postage is fairly successful but very costly. A door-to-door collection may be cheaper but is useful on a local basis only. If the survey is being done within an organization, you could have a central collecting point.

Articles for publication

Early in your career you are unlikely to be asked to write press releases, but you may be invited to submit articles for the local paper or for the firm's in-house journal.

Local newspapers

Local newspapers occasionally run features on sections of the business community in their area or on the development of a particular business district. Your organization might wish to benefit from the publicity such features give. For an article of this type you will generally be given a word limit which you should keep to – it relates to the amount of space allocated. Too short a contribution is even more trouble to an editor than one which is too long; the latter can if necessary be pruned.

Catch their attention early

Read the previous week's edition of the paper to get the feel of it. Write an eye-catching headline for your article which will get people reading. The first paragraph should be kept short – about thirty words – and should present the message of the whole article.

The later paragraphs

Develop the rest of the theme in an order which is appropriate in the circumstances. If you want to report what people said, the most economical way is to use **reported speech** (which is explained later), but a few short, appropriate quotations can give life to the presentation. Anything in quotation marks must be actual words uttered. Some personal details about the major people involved are acceptable in local newspapers – you must get names, ages and relationships right.

Final paragraphs

Articles that tail away into silence leave a poor impression with the reader. Take a lot of trouble with the final paragraph. Having done that, make sure you have kept to the stipulated length; you do not want the editor to cut your last paragraph.

The firm's in-house journal

Writing for an in-house journal is particularly testing as it is likely to make a difference to your prospects in the organization. You may be trying to entertain the staff with an account of the events on the last staff outing, in which case a light-hearted, though not slangy, approach is acceptable. You may be conveying information about some organizational change, in which case a more sober and dignified tone will be appropriate.

Layout on the page

You should have your article typed on a typewriter or word processor on A4 paper in double spacing (ie with a line space between two lines of words) using one side of the page only. Use a black ribbon and no more than sixty characters to a line. The left-hand margin should be 4 or 5 cm wide.

If the article runs to more than one page, add a 'catch line' at the top of the continuation sheet, repeating the last four or five words of the previous page. At the end put '–ends–'.

Give the name and telephone number of a contact – perhaps yourself – in case the editor needs extra information. If you want your article published at a particular time put 'Embargoed until . . . [date].'

- Write to length required
- Choose an appropriate tone
- Invent a catchy headline
- Keep the first paragraph short
- Develop the most important idea first
- Make sure quotations are accurate
- Names, addresses and local details can add interest
- Finish on a strong note
- Give the editor a contact for further information
- Set an embargo date if necessary

Checklist for writing articles.

Direct speech

You will sometimes want to report or record the actual words uttered or written by yourself or another.

For direct quotation you should enclose the words spoken (ie the words that would go in a speech balloon in a comic) in inverted commas, either double or single. In a business context, it is usual to put a phrase before the spoken word to show who is speaking; for example: 'Amy Morgan said, 'Our company is actively concerned in the reduction of environmental pollution.'

Activity 7

Using the information given below about student stand-by tickets, write an article to appear in the magazine *The Student*.

Cheap ticket scheme
Operates in London theatres
Arts Council backing
Intended to stimulate interest of young in theatres
Student cards entitle holders to cheap tickets
All but two West End theatres participating
Seats available at cut rates just before curtain-up
£10 seats reduced to £2.50
Spokesman says, 'Students form our most intelligent audience'

> In future entertainment guides will carry symbol 'S' denoting shows which are operating scheme
> Actor Harvey Devereux says 'Acting profession 100 per cent in favour of scheme'.

Proof-reading

Proof-reading is the term applied to checking that the printer or typist has copied your manuscript correctly. It requires considerable concentration and attention to detail. If it is your own manuscript you are checking, it is best to get someone else to read from that whilst you look at the typescript.

You must make any changes needed totally clear. All corrections should be made in ink in the margins. Any marks on the actual text should simply show the place where correction is needed. If there are several corrections in one line, divide them between left- and right-hand margins. When making an alteration to a single character or a word or words, the original should be struck through and the character, word or words inserted in the margin followed by a concluding stroke (/).

There are standard symbols which you should use as far as possible. Write an actual note in the margin if you feel it is necessary to make changes clear.

You should not attempt to 'improve' the style or change the meaning – the writer will become very irate if you do that. Simply make sure that the typist has reproduced what was written, putting any insertions in the right places. Pay particular attention to possible technical errors in the use of English:

1 *Spelling* Check the spelling of both the writer and the typist. Don't forget that your own spelling may be faulty, so use a dictionary if you have any doubts at all.

2 *Typist's errors* These may take the form of transposition, where the fingers have hit the keys in the wrong order, or may be errors caused by striking characters adjacent to the correct one. Look out for incorrect multiples of characters as well.

3 *Punctuation* Few people dictate all the punctuation, so check carefully that the typist has put in the hyphens, apostrophes etc, and has not put them in where they are not necessary.

4 *Grammar* It is easy for a writer to make grammatical errors in a draft, especially if it has had amendments or deletions made to it. Check that the verbs and subjects still agree with each other (eg, plural verb with plural noun) and that the phraseology has not become clumsy.

All this will be a considerable test of your own accuracy in the language. If you can't recognize an error, you will not be able to correct it.

Radio advertising

For radio advertising, your local commercial station will provide a professional broadcaster to present a script devised by you – or you may like to prepare a sound-tape using your firm's resources and voices.

If you want to produce your own tape, you should write a radio script showing exactly what is to be said and with what timing, indicating the background in terms of sound effects or music, before you begin recording. You will need to take care over copyright and union law.

Radio script.

CHOLMONDELEY TOWERS BRASS BAND CONTEST

60 seconds	Voice of Harry Bright over background of band cheering and clapping - from last year's recording of final
At 10 seconds	'The brass band excitement ...
At 25 seconds	For three days every year, Cholmondeley Towers resounds to the music of Souza, while all around colourful stalls and floral displays help create a unique atmosphere
At 40 seconds (for Marcher & Radio City)	The 5th Annual Cholmondeley Towers Brass Band Contest - Derrin Noctorum - Tuesday 9-Sunday 14 August
At 40 seconds (Piccadilly, Beacon)	The Cholmondeley Towers Brass Band Contest, Derrin Noctorum, off the M56, Tuesday 9-Sunday 14 August

TV advertising

If your firm wants a sophisticated TV commercial at prime time, it will certainly hire experts because of the enormous expense involved. However, an enterprising marketing department could itself produce a 20- or 30-second TV ad to go out during the day, using the video cameras and recording equipment now available at relatively low cost.

If you are doing that, write a storyboard with a separate run for the visuals. The visuals need be nothing more than two or three still pictures with a voice-over – a format which can be really effective.

For addresses for all kinds of media advertising, consult a directory such as the *British Rate and Data Guide* (BRAD), published monthly.

① Still of Dreadful 1950s Kitchen

Voice of John Carpenter over blocked-drain noises
'Remember Gran's old kitchen sink? What a nightmare!'

② Still Photo of Shop Front

'Come to Carpenter's sale, 17 Castle Street, Hawsbury, TODAY'
over wood-working noises

③ Still of Oak-fronted Units, etc.

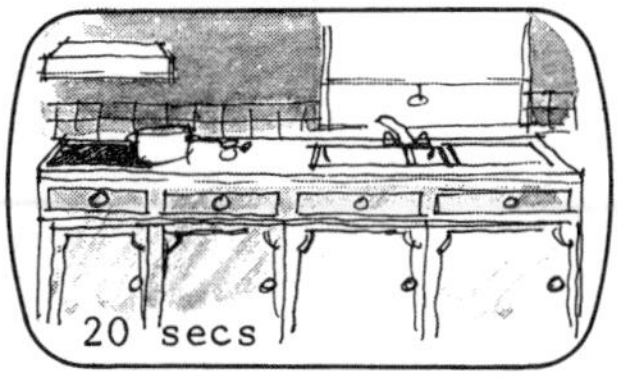

'We have dreams for sale',
over The Supers' track of 'You've never had it so good'.

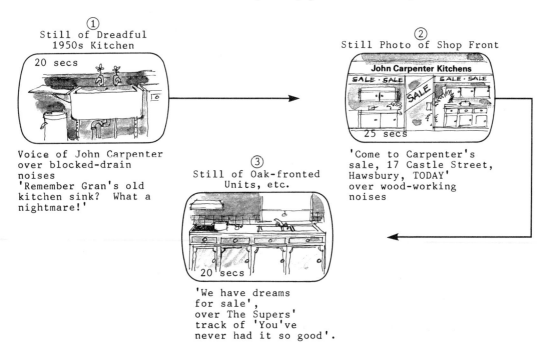

TV ad storyboard.

Sales

Here we outline the sales procedure in manufacturing. In an organization selling a service the procedure is broadly the same; it is only the type of end-product that is different.

The sales function can be divided into two broad areas of activity, covering **administration** and **selling**.

Administration

The sales office is the point at which incoming orders are received. The way in which this happens depends upon the manner in which the company processes orders. Company representatives will be provided with standard **order forms** which are sent to the sales office on completion. If the order is urgent, the representative will telephone the company and the order will be processed by sales office staff.

Instructions from the customer have to be put in a standard form so that they can be carried out by the production unit; this is the reason for the use of the order form.

The next stage is to inform all departments concerned. Routines for this differ: some organizations may process and distribute to the departments concerned, others may forward a copy to the production planning or production control sections (see the diagram 'Sales office routine' for an example of the second method).

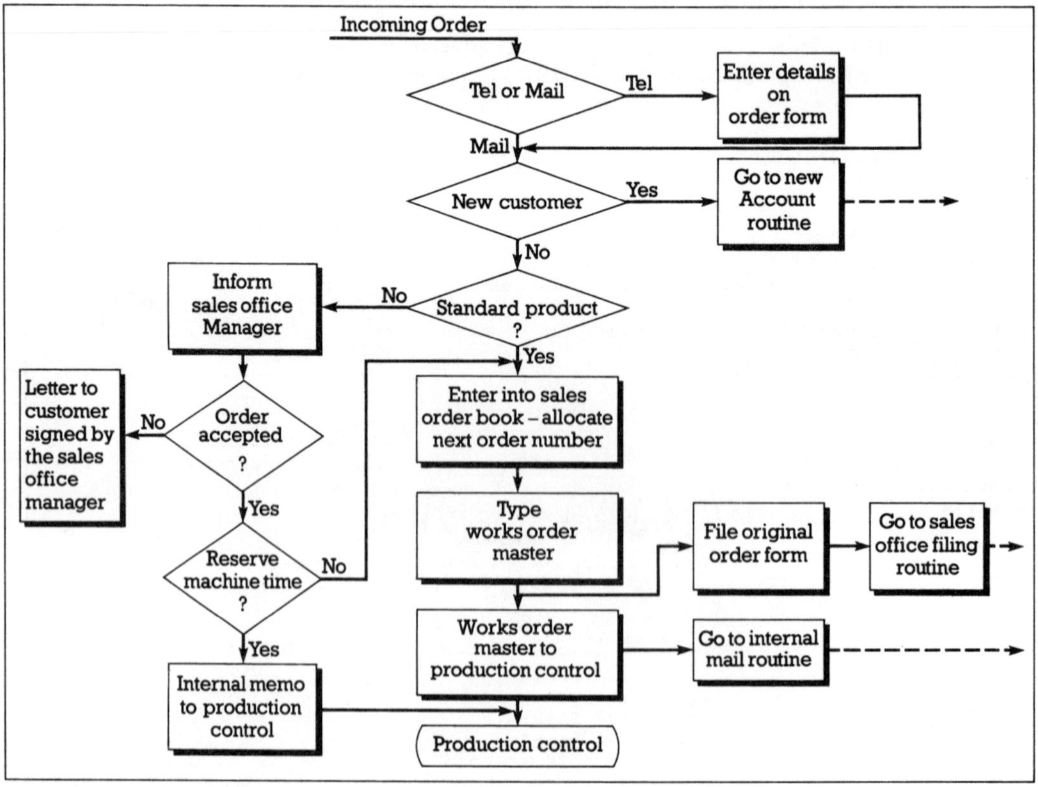

Sales office routine.

Organization of the sales office

Control of the sales office is in the hands of an administrator who is familiar with the sales function and sales routines. The administrator is responsible for the sales force and provides them with a back-up service by:
a communicating company sales policy;
b providing sales literature and price-lists;
c carrying out correspondence with customers;
d arranging sales training and refresher courses.
Responsibility for the performance and efficiency of the sales office rests with the sales manager, whose duties include the implementation of the sales policy, promotion of the various sales outlets, liaison with the marketing department, monitoring the credit control system for the company's customers, following up customer complaints and maintaining records of sales.

Organization of the sales force

The expertise of the sales force will depend upon what is being sold. Expensive capital equipment or highly technical products may require sales staff with degrees in a specific discipline; selling soap to a supermarket may not require staff with anything more than selling ability.

The number of sales staff employed will be related to the number of sales outlets to be serviced and the frequency of calls made. Each sales territory is planned to give the maximum service to the customer and to provide equal opportunity for each representative to develop potential sales.

Representatives make weekly or monthly reports to the sales manager giving:
a the number of customers seen and the person interviewed,
b details of any orders received,
c any comments or requests made by the customer.
This feedback of information is part of the company's market research activity and illustrates the link between marketing and sales.

Checking sales performance

1 **Sales against budget** – each representative has a budgeted figure for their territory in terms of value of sales. This provides a bench mark against which current performance can be measured.
2 **Percentage cost** – the profitability of a representative is based on the total expenditure in keeping them on the road in relation to the turnover percentage in sales.

$$\frac{\textbf{Total expenditure per month}}{\textbf{Total turnover}} \times \mathbf{100} = \textbf{Percentage cost}$$

Documents involved in the selling activity

Inquiry This comes from the prospective purchaser of goods who is seeking information. In certain circumstances it may constitute an order for the goods, but it should not be treated as such if it seeks information concerning price, delivery, terms and conditions of sale. Many organizations have printed **inquiry forms** with the words 'NOT AN ORDER' printed across the document.

Inquiries should bear the name and address of the company initiating the inquiry, a clear description of the goods in question, the quantity required and the department or person the quotation should be addressed to.

Inquiries represent an opportunity to sell. The function of the sales department is to turn an inquiry into a firm order.

Quotation Raised by the supplier of the goods in reply to an inquiry. This document informs the prospective customer of the price, the terms and conditions of sale (including any discounts available), costs of carriage and the time taken to deliver from receipt of the order.

Order On receipt of the quotation, the purchaser can make a comparison with other quotations received. For placing an order with the preferred supplier, customers may use their own **order forms**; some suppliers provide the customer with a form. In general, when one business buys from another, the former procedure is usual. Where the supplier provides the customer with a price-list or a description of the goods coupled with a coding system for ordering, there is no need for a quotation. The mail order catalogue is a good example of how the supplier can provide this sort of information for the customer.

An order should contain the following information:
1 The name and address of the supplier and the purchaser.
2 The address to which the goods are to be delivered.
3 A description of each item required, with the supplier's code or catalogue number.
4 The price quoted by the supplier.
5 The delivery date required by the purchaser.

Activity 8

1 As a clerical worker employed in a sales office, you have been told to let a new customer know that a representative will call to see their chief buyer in seven days' time. Prepare a draft for the letter.
2 Briefly outline the difference between the sales function and the marketing function.
3 Design a sales office record card for storing essential information about individual customers.
4 Your company sells a range of ten distinctive products. Draft a suitable catalogue list to distribute to potential customers.
5 Draft a suitable order form for the sale of the products in the catalogue list you have drawn up.

Activity 9

You are a clerical worker in the sales office of a large insurance company, specializing in life insurance and household insurance. Draw an outline map of the UK and divide it into eight territories, each suitable for one representative.

You should pay attention to the likely location of your company's customers when you make your division.

Visual presentation

The type of communication we have looked at up to now has largely relied on the written word. However, in any organization vast amounts of information are collected, analysed and circulated in the form of figures.

This kind of information is vital to the feedback process by which adjustments needed are made to existing routines. It can be difficult and time consuming to extract the core of the message from a mass of figures. For this reason people

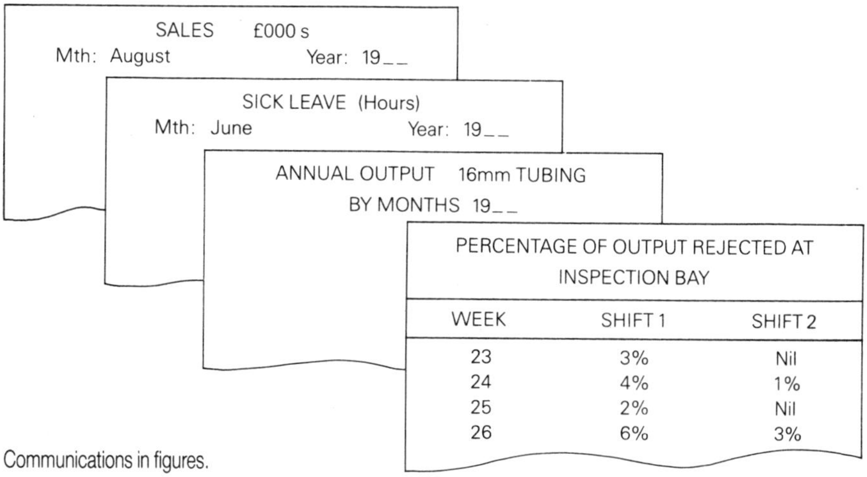

Communications in figures.

are often asked to present the information visually in the form of charts, graphs, diagrams etc.

The opposite problem can occur: a manager or executive may be unable to extract the meaning from information given in a visual form. You may have to interpret for them in words which describe the trend or situation shown.

Both drawing and interpreting charts are a heavy communications responsibility. A failure to see all the implications could lead to a distortion of the picture and to wrong decisions being taken.

False impressions

You will have to be on your guard against the deliberate falsifying or manipulation of the figures by whoever has produced them. We know that words can be used to persuade us that something is other than it is, but we tend to think that figures must be true – perhaps because there was always a 'right' answer at the back of our mathematics textbook at school.

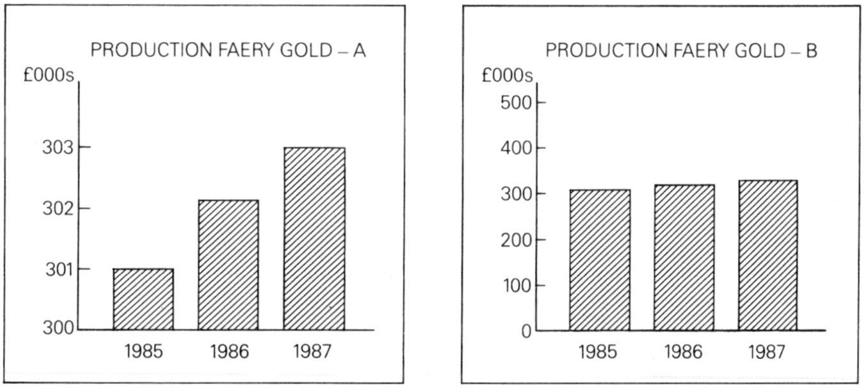

False impressions.

Chart A presents a rosy picture of production to the inexperienced or unwary eye. The scale does not start at zero and is unduly elongated. When it is redrawn as in Chart B, the eye sees at once that productivity is static over the three years. The range of figures to be shown may be so great that you cannot show the whole; if so, leave a gap between the horizontal and vertical axis and insert two little cross-strokes to draw attention to the break. In showing the data in Charts A and B, the bars could be interrupted before they strike the bottom line and given jagged edges, as in Chart C:

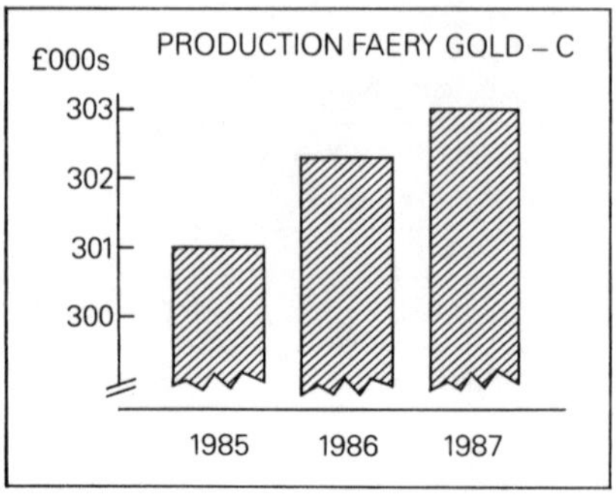

We tend to think that the largest quantity of anything is the best, and the immediate impression conveyed by the ideograph showing dental patients below is that Parlivia is doing better than the others. What is not apparent is that Parlivia has very few dentists.

Average number of patients per dentist

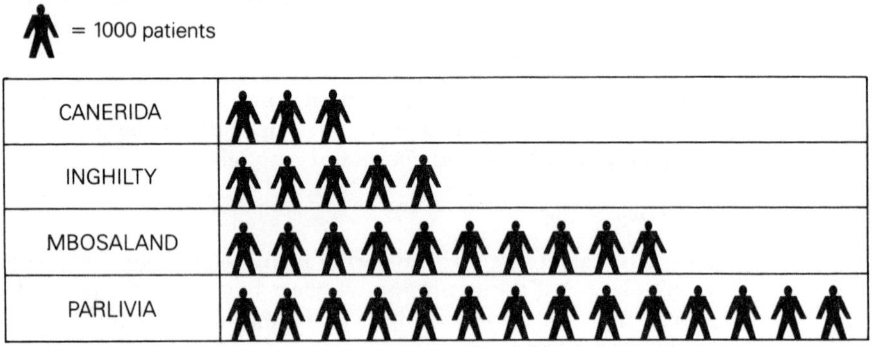

Is most best?

Charts for display

Charts are often pinned on office walls or used to illustrate a talk at a sales conference or some such event. It is essential that ones used in this way can be seen clearly from a distance and have an attractive and professional appearance.

> **SEVEN GOLDEN RULES**
>
> 1 Use a piece of paper of sufficient size for the location or occasion.
>
> 2 Headings should be large and clear and informative. Use bold lettering.
>
> 3 Arrange your chart(s) on the paper in a pleasing way.
>
> 4 Name the unit you are working in at the head of the chart (£ million; metres, etc).
>
> 5 Give the actual figures somewhere on the chart for those people who need an accurate breakdown of the information.
>
> 6 Quote the source of your information at the foot of the chart.
>
> 7 Check your spelling in a dictionary before you add lettering in ink.

Draw it big enough.

Charts for display.

It is important to choose the best form of chart or graph for the information you are presenting. The illustration 'Applications of charts' gives you some guidance about this.

Statistical data can often be represented by bar charts or other diagrams. This enables the relationships and trends and comparisons to be grasped more easily.

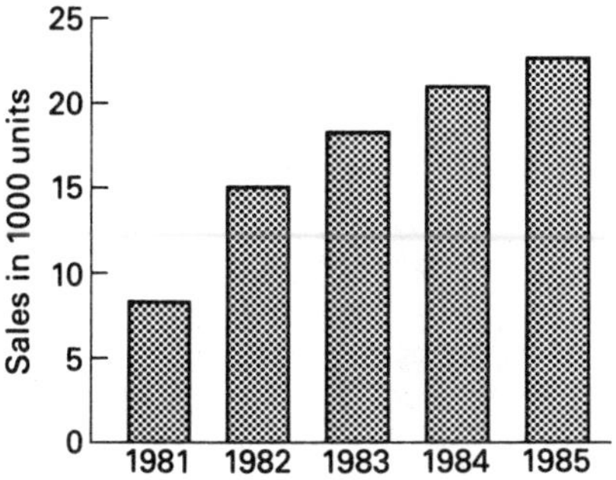

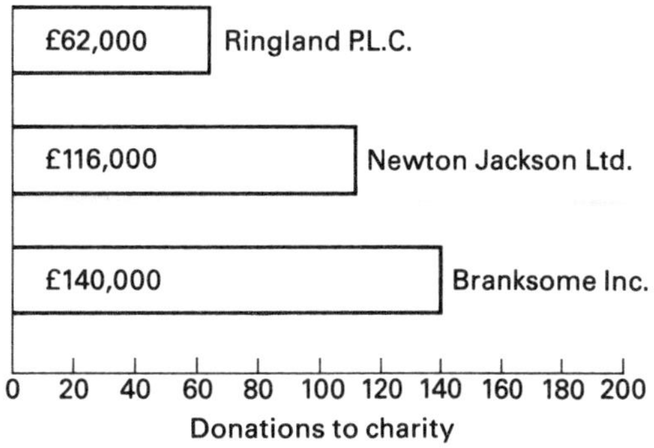

Bar chart
Magnitudes can be compared visually.

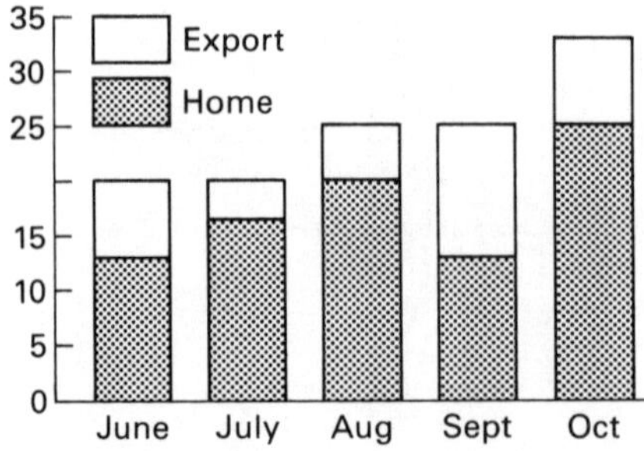

Component bar chart.
Demonstrates visually the way in which a particular set of data is sub-divided.

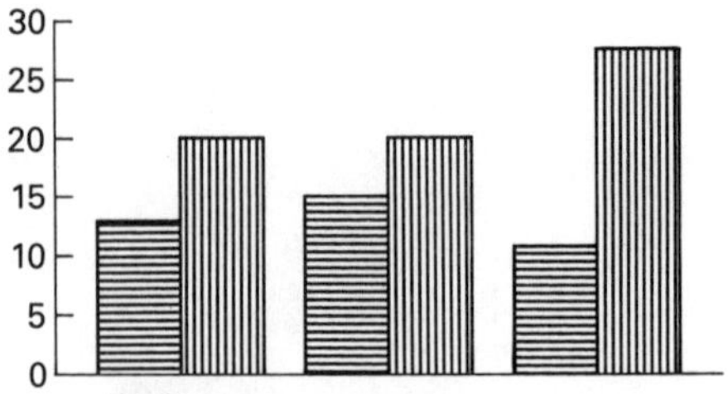

Multiple bar chart.
Sometimes known as a Compound Bar Chart – shows the comparison between two or more bar charts together.

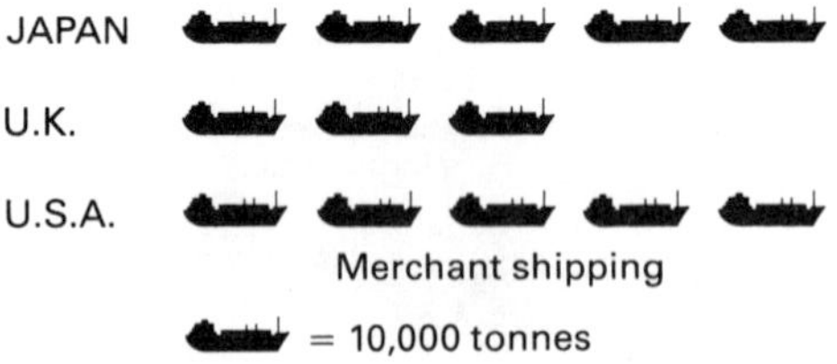

Pictograms.
Used to make a comparison in the same way as bar charts using symbols to represent the type of data under consideration. Good visual impact, aids communication by providing visual interest.

Pie chart.
Used to show the relationship of component parts to the whole. Not so easily interpreted as bar charts.

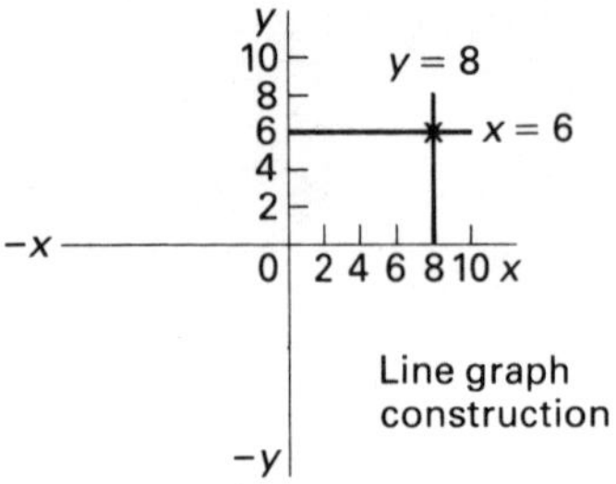

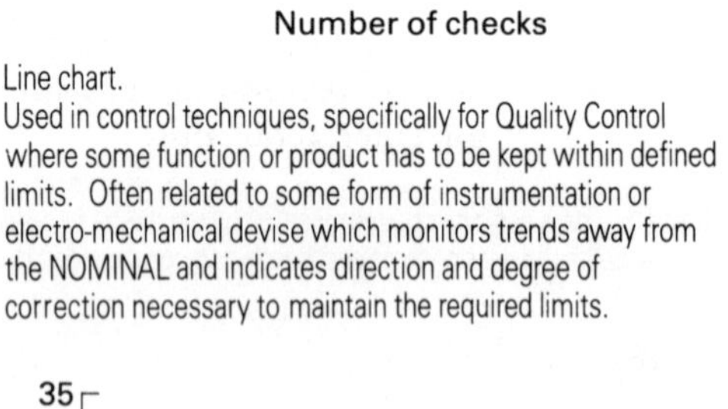

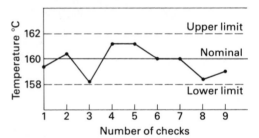

Line chart.
Used in control techniques, specifically for Quality Control where some function or product has to be kept within defined limits. Often related to some form of instrumentation or electro-mechanical devise which monitors trends away from the NOMINAL and indicates direction and degree of correction necessary to maintain the required limits.

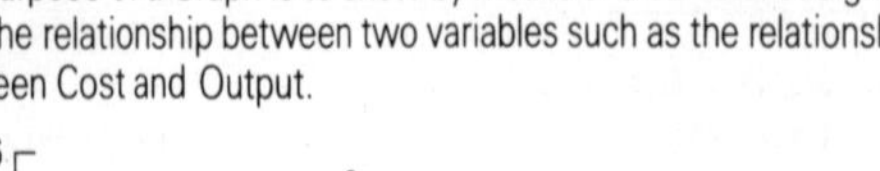

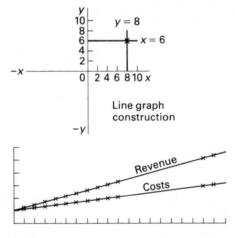

Line graphs 1.
The purpose of a Graph is to show by means of a curve or straight line, the relationship between two variables such as the relationship between Cost and Output.

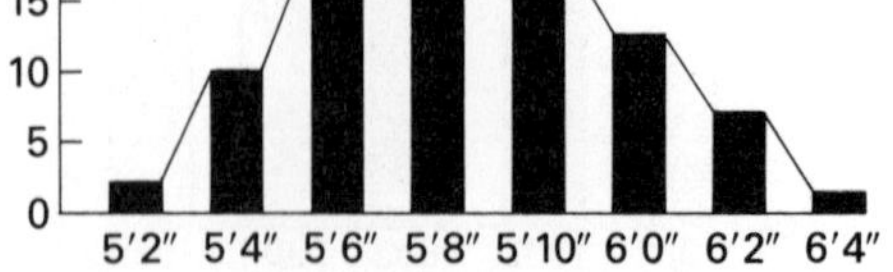

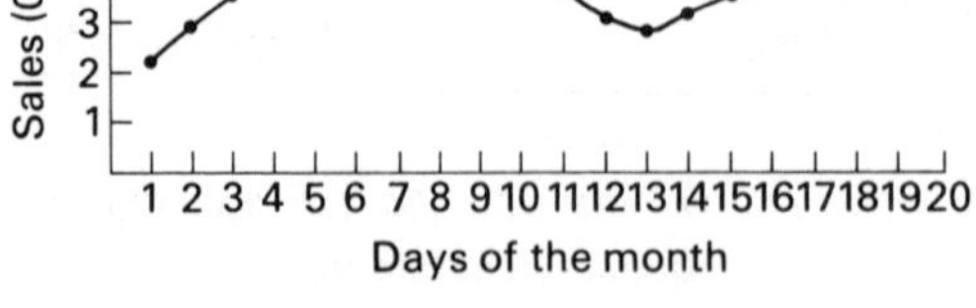

Distribution chart.
Shows the distribution of a sample about some mean point. E.g. Recorded height of a given sample of people between 5′2″ and 6′4″

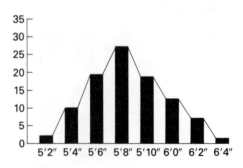

Line graph 2.
Use when variables change over time. E.g. relationship between the quantity of sales and the day of the month.

Activity 10

You are working in the sales department of EPTL. Mr Oxford hands you the following memo.

MEMORANDUM

FROM: Barry Oxford **SUBJECT:** Sales statistics

TO: You **DATE:** Last Friday

Could you produce these figures as bar charts for display in my office please.

I should like:

1) A component bar showing the percentage breakdown of total sales to each of the three diameters. Put actual figures alongside.

2) Three arrays of three bars to show the breakdown of each diameter into £ sales of its various bores. These three on one sheet.

ASAP please

BO

EXTRUDED PLASTIC TUBES LIMITED SALES: PREVIOUS YEAR (ended 5 April)

Figures expressed in £million

DIAMETER	BORE	SALES £m	NOTES
20cm	18cm 17.5cm 17cm	3.24 1.54 0.76	Contract: Wimpey
Total		£5.54	
15cm	13cm 12.5cm 11cm	1.48 1.21 0.48	See K D Korff
Total		£3.17	
10cm	8cm 7.5cm 7cm	1.23 0.48 0.25	New line 1 Oct
Total		£1.96	
ALL SALES	GRAND TOTAL	£10.67m	

Figures From Sales Statistics (EPT Ltd)

Activity 11

Suppose that when you took the bar charts you completed in Activity 10 over to Barry Oxford you called him Barry. He had greeted you by your first name so you thought that would be all right, but his secretary told you afterwards that you had been overfamiliar with him.

Discuss the basis on which you decide how to address your colleagues. Would you call them all Mr and Mrs until invited to do otherwise? Does rank come into it? Does gender? What about age? Would you be completely comfortable calling the whole staff by their first name? At what stage, if any, in your career will you expect to be called by your surname? Does the type of organization make any difference?

After discussion, write down your own views on one side of A4.

Tables of figures

Headings should be clear, with the unit (thousands, metres etc) stated. If the figures are divided into subsections, devise labels for them.

If the table is long, break the data into groups. If the table is very wide, repeat line numbers or labels in the right-hand margin.

The table should be aesthetically pleasing; ie, centred on the page, not too cramped or too widely spread, with tens, hundreds and thousands columns maintained to prevent confusion.

If you are giving totals, it may be worthwhile as an arithmetical check to make your table cross-cast as well as down-cast, with a checkable grand total at the bottom right-hand corner.

Short notes can be put at the foot of the table to explain details omitted from the table. The source of the figures should also be shown at the foot.

The example given here is from *Social Trends*, published by HMSO. If you try to check the totals, you will find that there are some minor discrepancies caused by rounding up or down to the nearest decimal point.

Deaths in and discharges from hospitals due to home accidents, 1974
England and Wales — *Thousands*

	Age group (years)								All ages
	Under 1	1–2	3–4	5–14	15–44	45–64	65–74	75 and over	
Nature of injury:									
Males:									
Fractures[1]	0.4	0.6	0.5	1.3	1.1	1.3	1.4	2.3	9.0
Intercranial injury (excluding skull fracture)	0.7	1.6	1.2	2.3	1.2	0.6	0.4	0.7	8.6
Burns	0.5	1.5	0.5	0.6	0.5	0.3	0.1	0.2	4.1
Adverse effects of medical agencies	0.1	2.4	1.3	0.3	2.9	0.5	0.2	0.1	7.9
Other injuries	0.3	2.4	1.2	2.4	1.9	1.0	0.6	0.6	10.4
All injuries	2.0	8.6	4.6	7.0	7.7	3.6	2.7	3.8	39.9
Females:									
Fractures[1]	0.2	0.4	0.3	1.0	0.9	2.9	4.7	14.3	24.9
Intercranial injury (excluding skull fracture)	0.5	1.4	1.1	1.1	1.3	1.0	0.9	2.1	9.6
Burns	0.1	1.0	0.2	0.5	0.4	0.3	0.3	0.3	3.1
Adverse effects of medical agencies	0.1	1.9	1.0	0.6	7.1	1.4	0.4	0.2	12.6
Other injuries	0.3	1.6	0.9	1.3	1.7	1.0	1.0	2.2	10.0
All injuries	1.3	6.2	3.6	4.5	11.4	6.7	7.3	19.0	60.1

[1] Fractures of skull, spine, trunk, lower and upper limb only.

Source: Hospital in-patient Enquiry 1974, *Department of Health and Social Security, Office of Population Censuses and Surveys*

Tables of figures.

Activity 12

The following memo has reached you in your office in the sales department of EPTL. Read through the documentation and prepare the table as requested.

To: You	**Subject:** Sales conference
From: Ted Flower	**Date:** Yesterday

Have a look at this handout from the Export people for me, will you? Could you put the information into tabulated form with the various features running down the left and the three countries across the top. Many thanks.

Hints to businessmen visiting the Ivory Coast, Niger and Burkina Faso.

Area and geographical features

<u>Area and Geographical Features</u>

The Ivory Coast covers an area of 127 000 square miles and lies on the Gulf of Guinea. It is bordered in the west by Liberia, and in the north by Mali and Burkina Faso and to the east by Ghana. The country is divided into two geographical areas consisting of equatorial rain forest in the south and a drier less humid savannah belt in the north.

Niger has an area of 459 000 square miles and is bounded on the north by Algeria and Libya, on the south by Nigeria, Benin and Burkina Faso, on the east by Chad and on the west by Mali. It has no coastline but the River Niger flows for 185 miles through the south-western part of the country. For 6 months of the year, from October to March, the river can be navigated by small craft from the capital, Niamey, to the town of Gaya on the borders of Nigeria. The only other important mass of navigable water is a part of Lake Chad. Cultivated land amounts to only 2 per cent of the total area and this mostly concentrated in a strip some 100 miles broad running along the Nigerian frontier. The country is a vast plateau with a mean elevation of 1200 feet but a mountainous area in the centre has peaks of up to 6000 feet and the massifs along the Libyan border average about 2600 feet. The north of the country is Saharan and the south mostly savannah.

Burkina Faso is a landlocked country covering an area of 105 900 square miles. It is bounded on the north and west by Mali, on the north and east by Niger and in the south by the Ivory Coast, Ghana, Togo and Dahomey. It is about 500 miles from the sea and has no navigable rivers. The most important rivers are the Red, White and Black Voltas but these become a trickle during the dry season. The Mossi plateau which covers almost the whole of the country is unfavourable to agriculture. There are several small granite mounds of over 500 feet dotted unevenly throughout the country. Climatic conditions are severe and there is a chronic shortage of water.

Ideographs or pictograms

The most visual way to convey information is to draw a picture of it. If the symbol you choose for representing data is recognizable in every country, you can completely overcome the language problems – and also any illiteracy problem.

You will have one or two difficulties, however.

* Can you devise symbols for those abstract concepts?

  Honesty   Diligence   Patience

* If  represents 1000 houses, how much does  represent?

* If  represents 1000 bottles of red wine consumed, how would you accommodate these figures in your graph? Italy 36 338.429 Egypt 5000

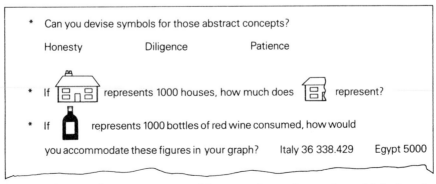

Ideographs are often misinterpreted because the reader tends to think that the biggest is best. For this reason it is better to indicate amount by using a number of equal-sized symbols rather than by using single symbols of different sizes. The example we have given comes from *Social Trends*, published by HMSO.

Ideographs or Pictograms.

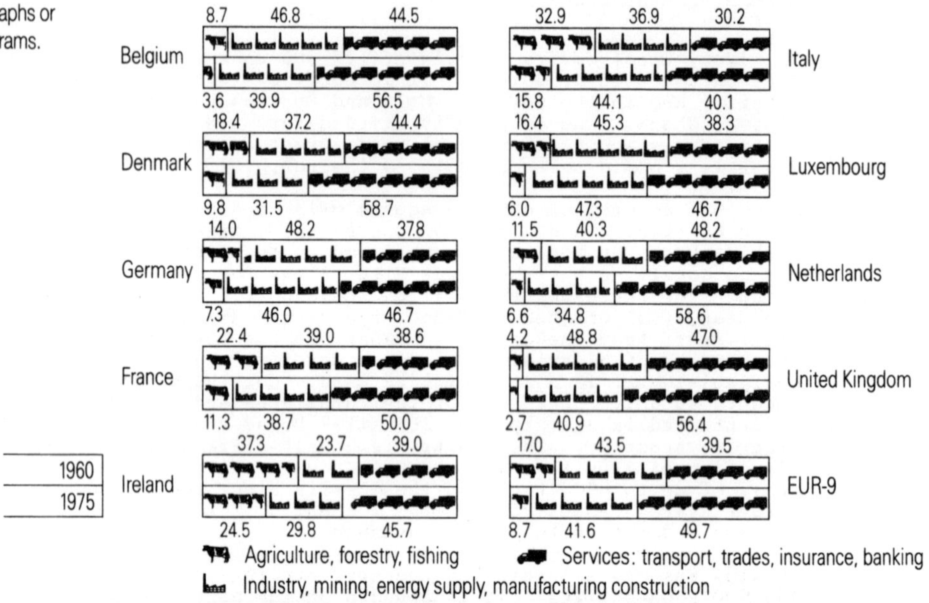

Fig. 13.10 Civilian employment by sectors, as a percentage of total employment, 1960–75
(Source: *The European Community's Social Policy*, Commission of the European Communities, 1978)

Line graphs

The line graph is probably the most familiar visual way of presenting information. It is easy to devise, conveys its message clearly and is simple to interpret. It is particularly useful for handling data with a wide range of numbers in it.

To convey an accurate picture you must choose scales that are neither too elongated nor too compressed. The figures on the horizontal axis should be a continuous series, generally a time series. If you draw a line connecting the plotted points, the assumption is that there is a significant relationship between them. If there is no such relationship, don't draw a line graph.

Line graph.

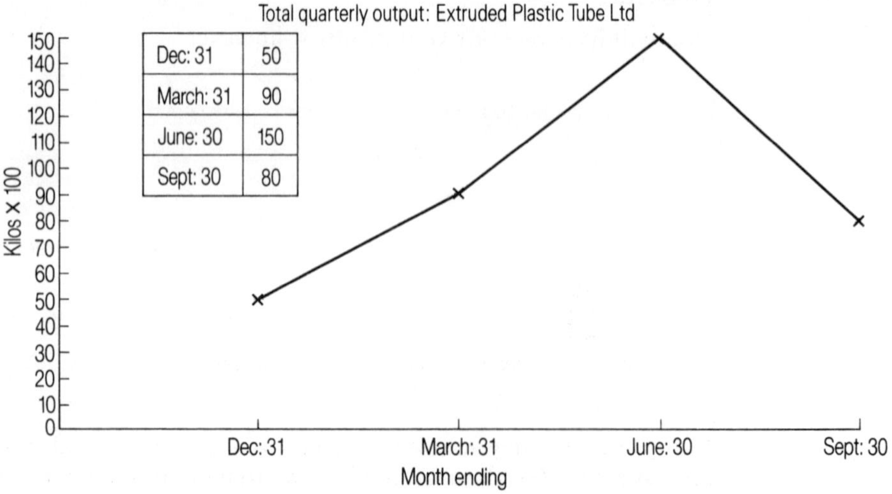

The EPTL output graph shows overall output figures at four points in the year. The overall figures could be split to show distribution over various diameters of extruder, with appropriate changes to the vertical scale.

More detailed line graph.

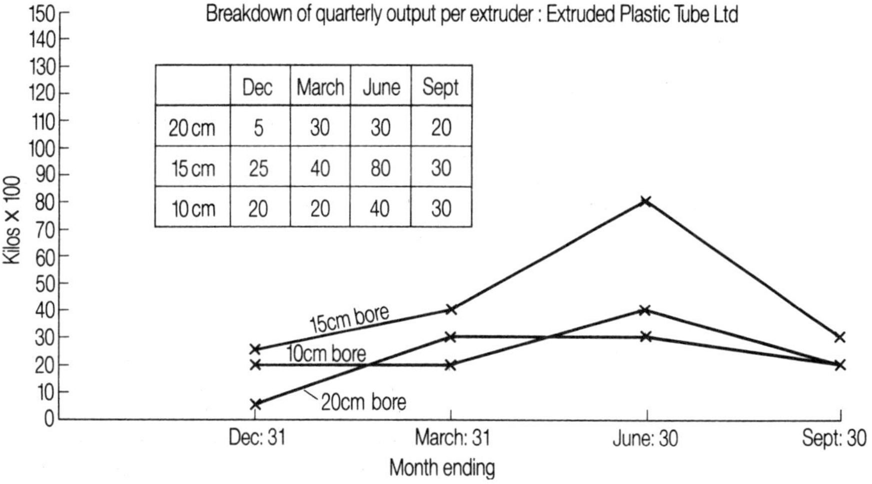

	Dec	March	June	Sept
20 cm	5	30	30	20
15 cm	25	40	80	30
10 cm	20	20	40	30

Note that it would not be possible to determine accurately from these graphs what the output was in any month which falls between the points plotted on the graph. The line connecting the points, therefore, is angled, not curved. A curve is appropriate only where every number on the horizontal axis must have been passed through at some time, eg, in a graph covering raising water to boiling point.

Both the overall output figures and those of individual extruders could have been brought together in one graph, as shown below.

Combined line graph for EPTL.

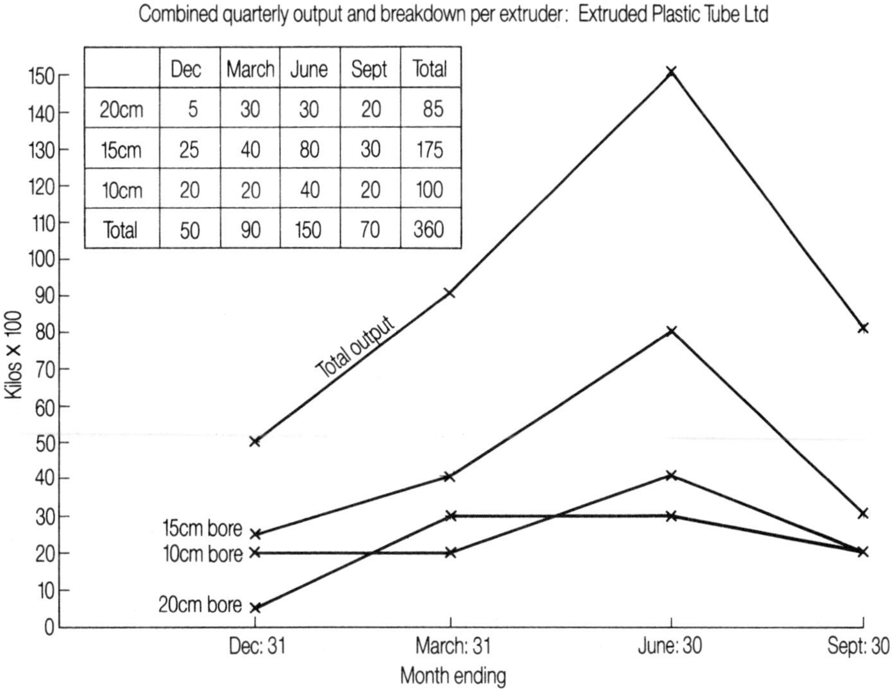

	Dec	March	June	Sept	Total
20cm	5	30	30	20	85
15cm	25	40	80	30	175
10cm	20	20	40	20	100
Total	50	90	150	70	360

Activity 13

Use the output figures shown in the three line graphs as the basis for a multiple bar chart. Draw this up to convey information to the next meeting of the management committee.

Pie charts

One popular method of presenting information is to show the way a whole unit (the pie) is divided into its component parts (slices). The pie can be of any size as each slice will be proportional to the next, but if two circles are being used for making a comparison both must be the same size and the data must be expressed as proportions of 100 per cent. It is usually better to use a bar chart than two pie charts. Pies are suitable only for showing wholes divided into parts.

In a pie chart you should limit the slices to no more than eight as the eye cannot derive any information from very numerous divisions. In fact, the eye is not very good at estimating the comparative value of angles at all, so only a rough picture emerges visually. You should therefore write the actual values on each segment. If you have some very thin segments too small to write on, put them near the horizontal and write the numbers just outside the circle. See the example for Suntan Tours.

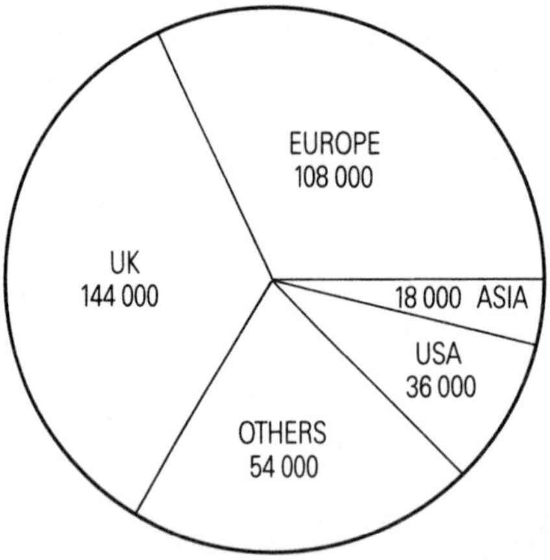

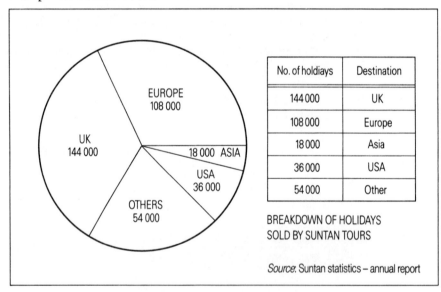

No. of holdiays	Destination
144 000	UK
108 000	Europe
18 000	Asia
36 000	USA
54 000	Other

BREAKDOWN OF HOLIDAYS
SOLD BY SUNTAN TOURS

Source: Suntan statistics – annual report

Pie chart.

Pies will involve you in calculations to determine the angles. You will probably need a calculator and a protractor as well as compasses (or the bottom of a wine-glass). If you reduce your data to percentages of the whole, every 10 per cent is represented by 36°. Make sure all your angles add up to 360° before you start segmenting your pie.

Pies can be coloured, but don't make the colour so dense that you can't see the figures.

Activity 14

Use the figure of total output for EPTL given in the last of the three line graphs and produce a pie chart to show how the £365 000 total was shared between the three extruders.

As there are a number of factors in deciding the best way to show figures visually, we have drawn up a checklist to help you to decide which to use in different circumstances.

APPLICATION OF CHARTS

BAR CHARTS	* suitable for comparing a small number of items * simple to construct * good impact, especially if coloured
COMPOUND BAR CHARTS	* show the components of a whole * can compare components in two or more wholes * maintain the order of the components in each bar
TABLES OF FIGURES	* suitable to convey dense and detailed date * group the data in blocks to assist the reader's eye * build in an arithmetical check
IDEOGRAPHS/PICTOGRAMS	* convey information without words or numbers * use unambiguous symbols * vary the number of equal-sized symbols to show quantity
LINE GRAPHS	* suitable for showing developments over time * easy to construct and read * can compare several items on one graph
PIE CHARTS	* show the components of a whole * restrict number of divisions to eight * require some calculations during construction

Checklist of charts and graphs.

Summary

In this block we have defined the differences between **marketing** and **sales**.

The three main functions of the marketing department were identified and its work in connection with product, price and packaging and with advertising, promotion and branding was described. Questionnaires, articles for publication and media advertising were surveyed.

The sales department, with its reponsibilities for administration and processing of orders and for the running of the sales force or representatives, was described along with the duties of the sales manager. The various sales documents were listed.

The visual presentation of sales statistics and other information as charts, graphs etc and the various methods available were looked at, together with the difficulties that can arise with this kind of communication.

Skills

Skill	*Activities in which skill is developed*
a Information gathering	3, 3, 5, 12
b Learning and studying	2, 3, 4, 5, 6, 9, 11, 13, 14
c Working with others	11
d Communicating	1, 2, 3, 4, 5, 6, 7, 8, 9, 11, 12, 13, 14
e Design and visual discrimination	2, 6, 7, 8, 9, 12, 13, 14
f Identifying and tackling problems	5, 6, 11
g Numeracy	14
h Informative processing	5, 7, 8, 12, 13

Block 6
Production Planning and Methods

Introduction

The block provides an introduction to the principles of controlling the resources of a business. It describes the function of production planning and the methods used to maintain control over the planned output. Routines related to production control and stock control are described and the relationship between the two functions is outlined. The text introduces the Gantt chart and outlines its use as a visual display for scheduling the work-load of an organization.

Production control/stock control structure.

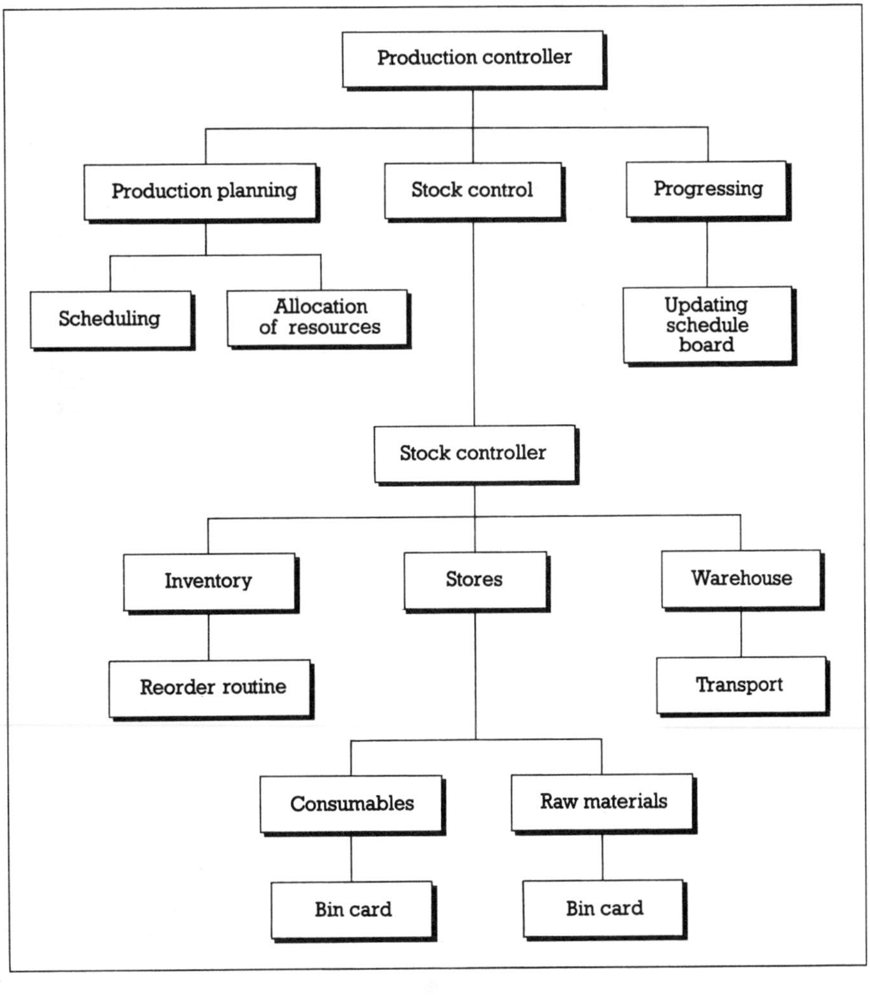

Types of production

Three distinctive types of production methods can be identified. None is necessarily associated with any specific volume of production; much depends upon the production task. In certain circumstances the same task could be undertaken by any of the three methods.

Each method has different characteristics and therefore requires different conditions. Before deciding which one, or which combination of the three, to adopt, the management have to look very carefully at the circumstances.

Some organizations progress from one method to another as the demand for the product grows; others are forced to adopt one because of the nature of the work being undertaken.

Job production

This method is to 'make complete' a single product to the customer's requirements. Production is achieved by a single operator or a group of operators. The project is considered to be a one-off operation and work is completed before the next job is undertaken.

Examples
1 Bridge building
2 Constructing a dam
3 Manufacturing scenery for theatre or film sets

The method is characteristic of many small businesses making specialized products, such as custom-built car manufacturers, bespoke tailors and jobbing builders.

Labour force Highly skilled and versatile, may have to be flexible. The unskilled content tends to be low and confined to servicing the production unit.
Control Not usually complicated as it is largely in the control of an individual operator or a group of skilled specialists.
Capital investment Tends to be high because of the variety of machinery involved in meeting the required flexibility in production.

Batch production

As the output required increases, the work may be carried out in batches. These may be small or large, depending upon the demand and the methods of production. Work is divided into component parts or operations, each operation being completed before the next batch is started. This method of production is the one most widely used in the UK. One purpose of using batch production is to have stock to be held against call-off.

Examples
1 Electronics
2 Petrochemicals
3 Brewing

In **job production**, the operators work on a single job until it is completed. In **batch production**, operators complete the batch before going on to the next one; the batch is transferred from one operation to another and there can be related mechanical handling and work scheduling problems.

Labour force Can become specialized in one aspect of the production process, which leads to a loss of flexibility and 'lines or demarcation' – which make union negotiations difficult in many industries.

Control Keeping machines and operators supplied with batches can be a very complex operation, particularly where production involves batches moving through a number of operations before the product can be completed.
Capital investment Investment in capital equipment and plant may be high, but the cost of producing each unit of work can be kept low.

Factors to be taken into consideration when considering batch size
1 Cost of holding stocks of raw materials
2 Cost of holding stocks of finished goods
3 Maintenance of high machine activity
4 Cost of tooling

Flow production

This can be defined as production during which the unit work content of the product is continually moving towards its final operation and completion. The units of work must be balanced in units of time so that the next stage is not kept waiting.

A predetermined number of products are planned to be manufactured each working day. Sequencing and timing of operations are of prime importance, as is stock control: production must be maintained without tying up capital by overstocking.

Examples
1 Car production
2 Manufacture of consumer goods such as refrigerators and washing machines
3 Manufacture of electronic products such as television sets and computers

Labour force Production-line labour is unskilled, performing simple repetitive tasks which require very little training. Support staff related to the maintenance of the complex equipment are skilled artisans.
Control The control function is complex because of the need to balance the operations to achieve flow-line production uninterrupted by the need to wait for materials, inspection and machines. Computer control is widely used in the industries given as examples above.
Capital investment Flow production is based on mechanization and automation, hence the capital investment is high. Both mechanical and electronic engineering techniques are extensively used. Machinery and equipment must be reliable: the failure of one unit in the flow line brings the whole line to a halt. Continuity of demand is essential to justify the capital investment, and the product has to be standardized with few, if any, variations to the specification.

Production planning

This function has the following objectives:
1 to enable the plant and equipment to work at predetermined levels of performance, given the constraints imposed by the need to carry out maintenance and tool changes;
2 to enable the company to capture and maintain the share of the market determined by its marketing strategy;
3 to achieve a level of profitability which will justify the investment of the resources of the organization.

Planning determines:
a What will be done
b The order in which operations will be carried out

Once the plan has been put into operation, some form of control is essential in order to assess the progress being made in implementing it. Therefore some form of **production control** is set up.

Production planning objectives

1 To transform marketing requirements into instructions to the production unit.
2 To allocate manpower, materials and machines in the most efficient way.
3 To schedule the work-load and arrange for some form of progressing to prevent bottle-necks in the flow of components during production.
4 To arrange the sequence of manufacturing to meet customers' orders.
5 To liaise with sales and production about the priority or rescheduling of orders.

The function of production control

There are many definitions of the production control function and what it comprises. There is no ideal system – each organization selects the one best suited to its requirements.

Whatever system is adopted, production must be planned so that materials, components and products of the right quality are supplied in the right quantity, at the right time and place, at minimum cost. In many small businesses, the experience and memory of the planning staff play a large part in production control. Larger organizations in which a mass of information has to be processed need efficient and flexible systems based on schedule boards, charts or computer services.

The objectives are common to all systems of production control systems:

1 Control of deviations from planned programme.
2 Cost control over the resources allocated to production.
3 Quality control of the product by the inspection of work progress.
4 Control of machine utilization and recording of machine breakdown.

Basic principles of a production control system

1 On receipt of order from sales – break the product down into its component parts.
2 Decide
a what the company will manufacture,
b what will be bought in from suppliers of goods and services.
3 Place purchasing order for bought-in supplies. Obtain a delivery date.
4 Allocate manpower, machines and materials to manufacture the components made by the company.
5 Schedule the new order into the work-load and calculate the delivery date.
6 Produce documentation to issue instructions concerning the work to be done.
7 Circulate documentation to all departments concerned.
8 Progress the order to identify any deviation from planned production.

Three stages of production control

1 Planning Product specifications determine the type and quantity of material for each unit of production, plus the quality standards to be maintained. From the quantity of material required to make one unit, the total material requirements for the order can be calculated:

(quantity per unit × no. ordered) + scrap rate% = total material required

This information is then passed to stock control so that the material can be allocated and stock records updated.

Manufacturing methods will determine the sequence of operations and the time taken to complete the order.

(time to make 1 unit × no. ordered) + scrap rate% = total time required

This information is recorded into the system of scheduling used.

2 Motivating At this stage, the plan for the use of resources is put into action by issuing some form of instruction (**works order** or **job instruction**) to the departments concerned. These instructions constitute an 'authorization to produce', allowing the use of the company's resources. In many instances, the same document can be used as a **progress record** to keep a check on the amount of the order which has been completed.

3 Controlling The systems which can be used to record and control production are numerous, ranging from the back of an envelop to highly sophisticated electronic data processing. However, one kind of display board or bar chart is probably the most widely used. Of these the **Gantt chart** is the choice of many production controllers as it is relatively easy to use, has good display properties and is flexible in the presentation of data.

Gantt charts

This system of charting production activities was developed by Henry Laurence Gantt. It is used in one version or another by many organizations.

Using the Gantt chart In essence, the Gantt chart is a bar chart which lists the units of production resources (machines are one example) down the left-hand side and a time-scale suitable for the production method being used (hours, days, weeks) across the top.

GANTT CHART

Time / Machine	MON	TUES	WED	THURS	FRI
No. 1					
No. 2					
No. 3					

This division provides a grid on which resources allocated can be recorded by entering the estimated time for each activity on individual machines.

GANTT CHART

Machine \ Time	MON	TUES	WED	THURS	FRI
No. 1	ORDER Nº	179			
No. 2					
No. 3					

Sequencing Very few products are completed in one operation. Where a sequence of operations is required, it follows that these will be predetermined by the process of manufacture: you cannot put the slates on a house before the roof is built, or bake bread before the dough has been mixed.

If someone wants to put up a shelf made of wood, the sequence of operations might be as follows:

1 Saw wood to the required length.
2 Plane rough edges.
3 Drill holes in shelf to take bracket screws.
4 Drill holes for wall plugs.
5 Hammer in wall plugs.
6 Screw brackets to the shelf.
7 Screw the shelf to the wall.

In this task it is obvious that the sequence of activities is determined by the sequence of operations required to put up the shelf, which employs in turn the saw, the plane, the drill, the hammer and the screwdriver. To estimate the overall time taken to complete the task, the time taken for each individual activity would be added. A Gantt chart would represent this time in the following manner:

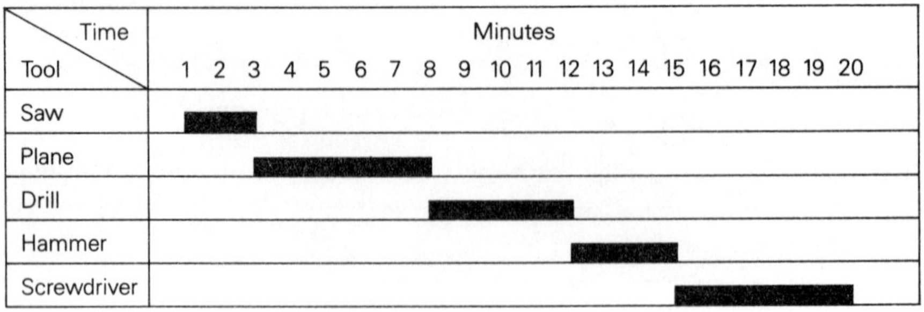

Scheduling the work in this fashion gives a pictorial representation of the work-load and indicates:
a the time that each tool is in use and not available for other work,
b times when individual tools are available for other work,
c the total time that the operator would be occupied on the task.

Other information can be added to the chart to aid production planning and control.

Progressing

An essential part of any control system is the **feedback** of information which allows the progress of any planned project to be monitored. Planning production is an important activity but it does not in itself guarantee that what has been planned will take place. This is particularly true of any activity which involves the co-ordination of a number of resources, all of which may be subject to variation in performance. Manufacturing is a typical example, the resources being **manpower**, **machines** and **materials**.

Fast and accurate feedback of information on the current progress of production enables the planner to detect any deviation from the plan and apply corrective measures. Much of this feedback is channelled through routine clerical and administrative procedures, rather repetitious and unglamorous work whose importance may not be appreciated by those who perform it.

Look at the 'Production control function' diagram to see the importance of feedback. If the question 'Is planned output being achieved?' were not asked, then the system would stop at 'Put plan into effect' and the control loop would not function. As a result, 'No further action' would be the course to follow, regardless of the level of output being achieved.

Progressing is the function of production control, which monitors the progress of the individual components of production from start to completion of the order. It begins with the issue of raw materials from the stores on the authorization of a stores requisition to the production unit.

In a complex manufacturing process, progressing would concern itself with the co-ordination of batches of work and subassemblies to ensure that they arrive at the final assembly point for continuity of production.

Information about the current state of production is fed back to the production control section, who can then update the schedule board or liaise with the departments concerned to minimize the effect of unavoidable delays.

Production planning in the office

Administrative routines are not normally subjected to the kind of production planning applied to manufacturing units. However, the modern office has a considerable capital investment in business machinery and the company will want to be sure that the equipment is used in the most efficient way.

Central and local government and large business organizations such as mail order companies process paperwork in substantial quantities. Routines are often repetitive and carried out stage by stage, and processed in batches. They are therefore comparable with industrial batch production.

Production planning techniques in the office reduce wastage in manpower, improve machine utilization and enable management to forecast the amount of work which can be completed within the working week. It is often essential that the work is completed within a specified time. An example is the preparation of wages and bonus payments, which may have to be completed in time to make a withdrawal of cash from the bank and make up wage packets.

Time taken to complete a given task can be established by the application of **work study** techniques (organization and methods) and scheduling can establish control.

Many modern business machines have a built-in system for checking the output and the errors made by individual operators.

Production control routine.

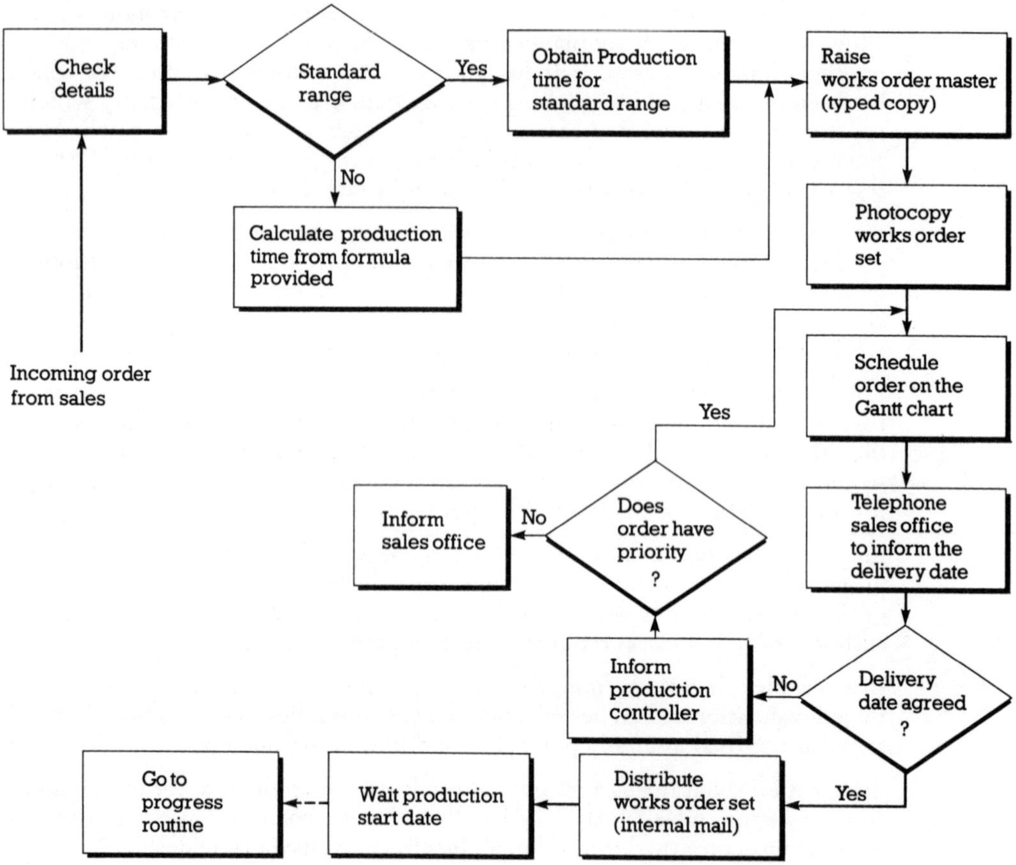

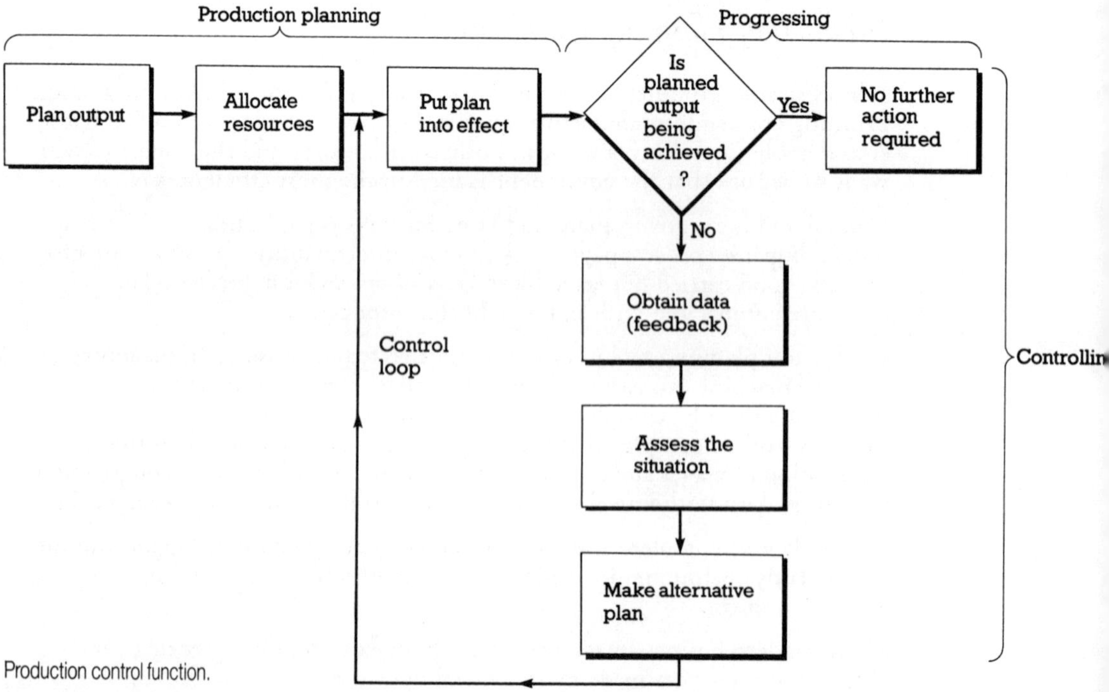

Production control function.

Checking individual output

This can only be checked with any degree of accuracy when the output required does not fluctuate. Ideally, work needs to be fed to the clerical worker in standard batches, the output being subjected to some form of supervision. Recording output establishes the output of each clerical worker.

Checking group output
Some procedures involve a group of people working in a sequence of operations. Work content for each worker has to be balanced to prevent bottlenecks and may have to take into account the variation in ability of individual workers.

Machine activity

In common with production machinery, business machines have breakdowns and require routine maintenance. Planning has to take into account this loss of time, which should be scheduled into the work-load. Records of breakdowns by type may enable the application of preventitive maintenance.

Office management has to be aware that output is related to quality. A clerical worker required to produce a stipulated quantity of work under pressure may find that difficult if the work is demanding in terms of quality or degree of concentration.

Possible effects of failing to maintain quality standards

1 *Inside the organization* Breakdown of communication between departments, resulting in lack of co-ordination between departments.
Lack of communication between management and the work-force, resulting in frustration and lack of motivation.
Loss of control over the business.
2 *Outside the organization* Poor communication with suppliers, which may put stock levels in danger or make the company a bad debtor.
Poor communications with customers, with the organization failing to deliver on time and not producing to the customers' requirements.
Customer accounts inaccurate, lack of credit control, customers being charged the wrong amount.

Effects of business machinery

Business machinery brings the following advantages to producing documentation in bulk:
a Speed: productive output is high.
b Accuracy: this can be maintained regardless of quantity of output.
c Consistency: the predetermined speed of output allows accurate prediction of the time taken to complete a given task.

Activity 1

A new deputy has come into the production department of Extruded Plastic Tube Ltd from another engineering firm. He is producing an article to be published in *Engineering Now* and asks you to proof-read the typescript.

Working in pairs, list the necessary amendments. You may find it helpful to refer back to Block 5 to remind yourself of the procedure.

Computer Numerical Control and Gauging Methods

Anyone who embarks upon using CNC machinery for making precision products must review their guaging methods.

With the old inspection processes, the operator wood measure the finished component as it came off the machine with his vernier guage, and by the time he had discovered that the component was scrap he had probably already produced two or three more which wear also scrap. Now, by using electronic gauges it is possible to detect a drift towards components being out of tolerance. As a result the scrap rate from CNC machineing cells has been reduced to an insignificant level.

Distortion was a particular difficulty with making bodies using heavy duty aluminium alloy with 27 per cent silicon which is easy to machine but susceptable to distortion. The stresses which can be introduced into the components during the initial fabrication and heat treatment result in distortion. It has to be final machined at each end to a tolerance of 0.054 mm on diameter. The cutting prosess itself involves a rise in temperiture and the subsequent expansion of the component can be effected by the holding fixture, causing distortion on removal the depth and number of cuts must be carefully selected to releese enough stress in an minimum total number of cuts overall.

Initially, a nulling operation was used to remove the metal from between the lugs on the motor body but this was found to be the major stress problem causing length to distort. The difficulty has been overcome by developing a method of generating the lugs on a gear shaper. Shaped cutters are made to rotate about the part and are progressivley 'fed in" until iti s reduced to size;

The philosophy adopted for checking is to gauge the most demanding feature produced by each tool in each axis of movement. The known consistency of NC operation can then be relied on to garantee all the remaining features produced.

Printout units for each gauge provide permanent records of each of the measurements and contain calculation rasults indicating average size and taper.

The CNC lathe does not automatically compensate for tool where When a drift towards the edge of the tolerance band for any one dimension is indicated (yellow warning light), the setter must check the Tesa gauge for that dimension, calculate the required tool offset and then enter it himself in the lathe's control unit.

Defects resulting from malfunction of the sell over the first 1,000 components resulted in first 2 components being scrapped with a robot reliability of 100 per cent.

Computer Numerical Control
and Gauging Methods

Anyone who embarks upon using CNC machinery for making ^precision^ products must review their gauging methods.

With the old inspection processes, the operator ~~inspected the finished part~~ would measure the finished ~~product~~ component as it came off the ~~m/c~~ machine with his vernier gauge, and by the time ~~it~~ he had ~~found~~ discovered that the component was scrap he had probably already produced two or three more which were also scrap.

Distortion was a particular difficulty with making bodies using heavy duty aluminium alloy with 17% silicon which is easy to machine but susceptable to distortion. The stresses which can be introduced into the components during the initial fabrication and heat treatment result in distortion. ^It has to be final machined at each end to a tolerance of 0.054 mm on diameter.^ The cutting process itself involves a rise in temperature and the subsequent expansion of the component can be affected by the holding fixture, causing distortion on removal.

Now, by using electronic gauges it is possible to detect a drift towards components being out of tolerance. As a result the scrap rate from CNC machining cells has been reduced to an insignificant level.

STET (Continue ^para^ from 'removal').... ~~To eliminate distortion problems~~ the depth and number of cuts must be carefully selected to release

N.P enough stress in a minimum ^total^ number of cuts overall. [Initially, a milling operation was used ~~for the purpose of detaching~~ to remove the metal from between the lugs on the motor body but this was found to be the major stress problem causing length to distort.

Continue para. (The difficulty has been overcome by developing a method of generating the lugs on a gear shaper. Shaped cutters are made to rotate about the part and are progressivley 'fed in' until it is reduced to size.

~~Development of tooling has further helped to reduce this~~ distortion. We now use Herkel high ~~grade carbide~~ tooling with a top rake angle of about 20°. ~~As well~~ as eliminating distortion this tooling has a life ~~at least~~ twice the length of a nine hour shift, ~~twice that of the tooling previously~~

The philosophy adopted for checking is to gauge the most demanding feature produced by each tool in each axis of movement. The known consistency of NC operation can then be relied on to ~~garauntee~~ ~~garunt~~ garantee all the remaining features produced. [

The CNC lathe does not automatically compensate for tool wear. When a drift towards ~~a tolerance~~ the edge of the tolerance ^band^ for any one dimension is indicated (yellow warning light), the setter must check the Tesa guage for that dimension, calculate the required tool offset and then enter it himself in the lathe's control unit.

Printout units for each gauge provide permanent records of each of the measurements and certain calculations results indicating average size and taper.

~~The~~ Defects resulting from malfunction of the cell over the first 1,000 components resulted in just 2 components being scrapped with a robot reliability of 100%.

Activity 2

1 Illustrate the manner in which the use of classrooms in a college could be scheduled on a Gantt chart.

2 A company receives an order for 1000 units which require two operations to complete the product.

Operation 1 Machine components	10 minutes
Operation 2 Assemble units	5 minutes
Overall scrap rate per machine operation	2%

All the components must be machined before assembly can start.

a Calculate the machine time to be scheduled.

b Calculate the total time to complete the order.

c Assuming that production will start on Monday and delivery will have to be on the Friday after production is completed, calculate the delivery time on the basis of a five-day working week of eight hours per day.

3. Outline the advantages which can be gained from using a computer to schedule the work-load in an organization engaged in mass production.

Activity 3

Schedule the following orders received by EPTL and calculate the delivery date, using a Gantt chart.

1 CJ Constructions plc
500 metres of 10/7

2 BR Engineering
1500 metres of 15/11.

No. 7 extruder has broken down. The engineering department has advised that it will take four days to repair it. Write a memorandum to the sales office outlining the effect this will have on scheduling and delivery. Make a note of the other departments that you will have to inform.

Stock control

Production methods in many industrial and commercial enterprises involve a number of complex operations. The use or assembly of a number of components purchased from various suppliers is often involved. The manufacture of motor vehicles is a typical example, car factories being assembly plants rather than manufacturing plants.

Most companies require raw materials of some kind in order to make goods or provide a service. Components and raw materials must be available to meet the requirements of the customers' orders; therefore some stock has to be held in anticipation of demand. The key question is, 'How much stock to hold?' If buffer stocks are too large, the company is tying up working capital that could be used elsewhere in the business. There is also the risk that stocks held may deteriorate or become obsolete. If this situation is to be avoided, the organization must operate an efficient stock control system.

Managers have become increasingly aware of the importance of **materials management**, which combines the activities of production, stock control and purchasing.

Investment in raw materials and components is often the biggest item on the balance sheet. Relatively small companies with cash-flow problems cannot allow stock levels to exceed those needed to meet commitment to customers.

Conversely, if stock levels are too low, the company runs the risk of having to stop production or refuse orders.

Stock control is a matter of striking a balance between too much stock and too little.

Activity 4

Stock holding can be a problem for many types of business organizations as the stock held can be subject to rapid deterioration or change in fashion. Survey your local shops and draw up a list of items which if held in large amounts would involve a risk.

Stock control function

All materials and components come under the jurisdiction of the stock controller, from when they are delivered to the company's premises until they are issued to the production unit for processing. In some instances, this control extends to the stock of finished goods awaiting delivery to customers, the safe keeping of the stock being delegated to the warehouse manager.

Raw materials and components are kept in designated areas, usually known as stores. Stores are subdivided into spaces allocated for individual items of stock and these spaces are called **bins**. Therefore, each item of stock can be given a **bin number** location.

BIN CARD			
ITEM BRACKETS		STOCK CODE 01 134 / B	
DATE	STOCK MOVEMENT		
	IN	OUT	BALANCE
16 · 4 · 89	500	—	500
17 · 4 · 89		50	450
23 · 4 · 89		25	425
26 · 4 · 89		30	395

Stock control bin card.

Activity 5

You have been given the task of organizing the office stationery stores when the office is transferred to a new building.

Decide on the items of stock you would hold for an office employing twenty clerical and administrative workers. Lay out the bins to contain the stock in a room 14ft long by 8ft wide.

The stores function is closely related to the production control function. In a small organization the two are the direct responsibility of the production controller.

The stores

A store can be considered as a reservoir between the incoming raw materials or components from the supplier and the production unit. As in any reservoir, the demand and supply must maintain a balance between the maximum and minimum planned stock holding.

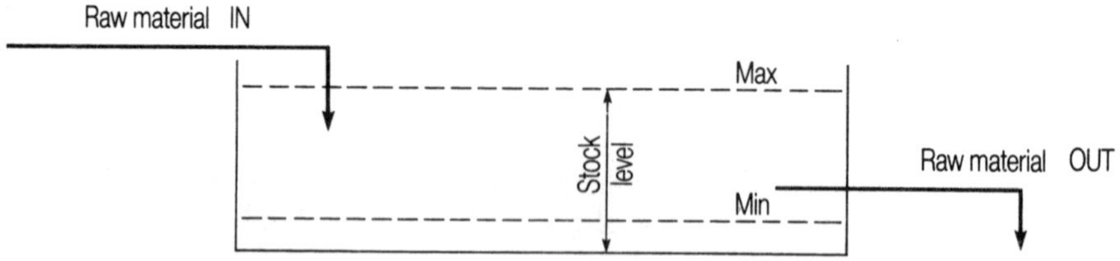

Materials coming under the control of the department can be divided into three categories:

1 *Stores* Raw materials and components directly related to production.
2 *Supplies* Indirect materials such as oils, cleaning materials etc, which are required to maintain equipment and the fabric of the building.
3 *Finished parts* Products that have been fabricated but are not yet assembled into finished products.

Control can be maintained by three documents in a stock control system:

1 *Purchase requisitions* Raised by the stock control department and routed to the purchasing department to request the replenishment of stock.
2 *Issue requisitions* Raised by the department wishing to take stock from the stores (this is usually known as a **call-off**). Issue requisitions must be authorized by a designated member of the department making the call-off and should be regarded as representing cash.
3 *Perpetual inventory* Maintained by the stock control department, this shows the current stock position in relation to the amount of free stock available for orders not yet scheduled into the work-load.

A Perpetual inventory is the key control document in the stock control system, providing information which can be used by the purchasing department, production control and accounts.

For each item of stock, a decision is made about what the **minimum safe working stock** and the **maximum stock** level is. When stock levels fall to the point where the reorder point is reached, fresh stocks should be requisitioned.

The way in which this system works is outlined in the 'Stock control routine' diagram.

Stock control routine.

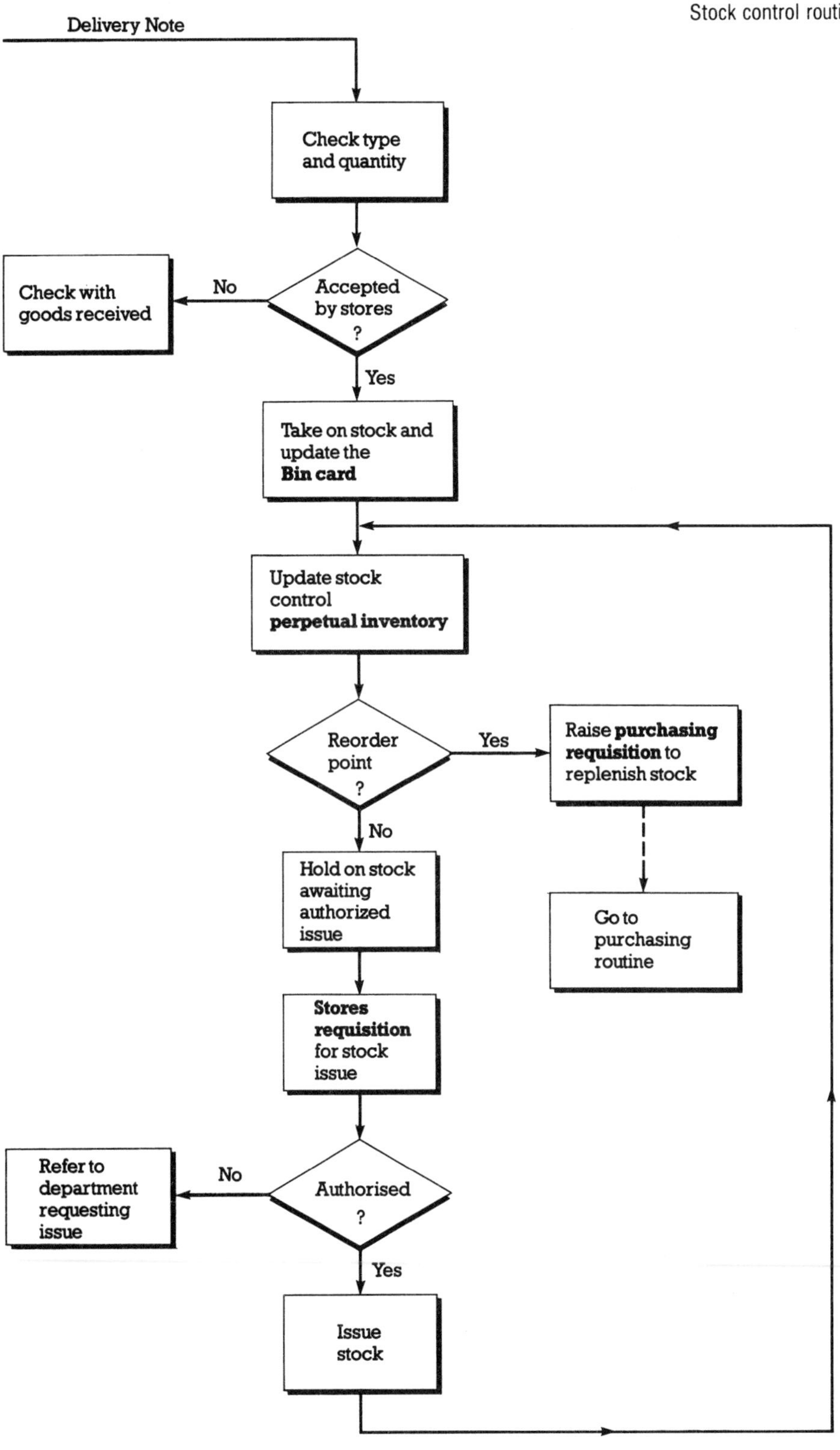

Stores requisition set.

ACCOUNTS COPY

STORES COPY

STORES REQUISITION

DEPARTMENT TOOL SETTING DATE 23·4·19__

ORDER NO.	MATERIAL	QUANTITY
892/78	1" x 5/8" DIA WHITWORTH BOLTS	24

AUTHORIZED ______

MATERIAL 1" x 5/8" WHITWORTH BOLTS				MAXIMUM 1500		MINIMUM 100		REORDER 250
DATE	QUANTITY ORDERED	QUANTITY RECEIVED	PHYSICAL STOCK	ALLOCATED		ISSUED		FREE STOCK
				W/o No.	QUANTITY	W/o No.	QUANTITY	
3·5·19__		C/F	1000					1000
5·5·19__			800			146/2	200	800
6·5·19__			"	152/1	150			650
9·5·19__			800	"	"	151/3	100	550
12·5·19__			700			152/1	150	550
15·5·19__			550	153/5	300			250
15·5·19__								

Perpetual inventory.

PURCHASING REQUISITION

PLEASE ORDER THE FOLLOWING MATERIALS | DEPARTMENT ______

QUANTITY/ WEIGHT	DESCRIPTION	CODE NUMBER

FOR DELIVERY TO: | DELIVERY DATE

SUPPLIER: | SIGNED ______ APPROVED ______

ROUTE TO PURCHASING DEPARTMENT

Purchasing requisition.

Calculating the reorder point for a given stock item

All items of stock should have a designated maximum and minimum level. These levels are shown on the previous 'stores reservoir' diagram. By removing the right-hand side, as illustrated below, the diagram can be coverted into a graphical representation on which the stock levels and rate of issue can be shown.

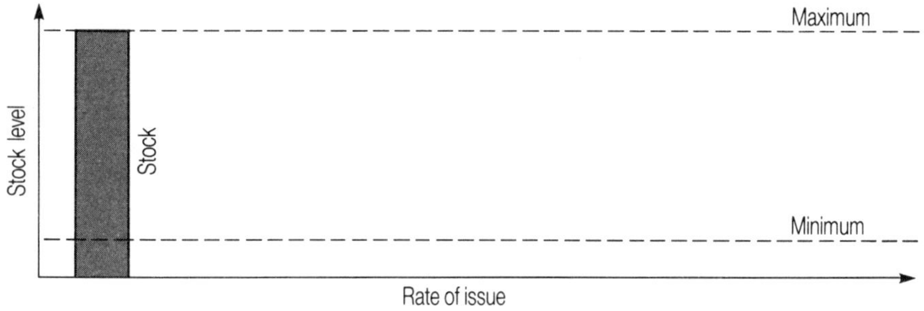

As the call-off is made for the stock held, the stock level remaining in the store will fall and can be recorded as shown below:

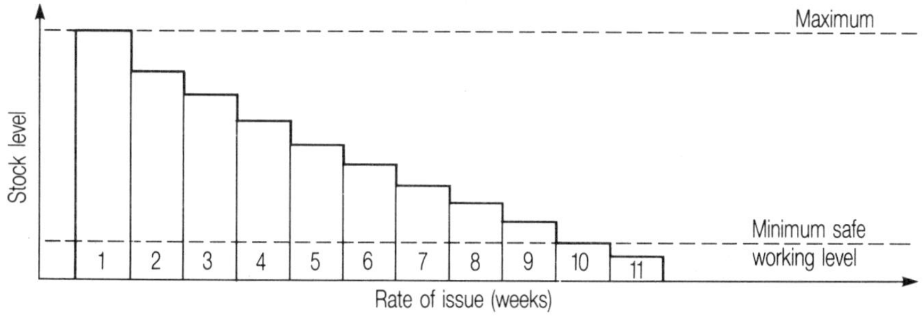

In the diagram, a constant rate of issue has been assumed. Where the rate fluctuates, the average expected rate of issue can be calculated. The graph shows that the stock will run out in week 11. At this point the company would begin to suffer the penalty of lost production if no re-stocking were done.

Ordering stock on the day that stock runs out will not reduce the risk of lost production unless immediate delivery can be guaranteed. This is not likely to be possible.

As an alternative, stock could be reordered when it reaches the **minimum safe working level**. This would be satisfactory only if the stock is delivered one week or less after being ordered. Should it take two weeks, stock will run out one week before delivery takes place.

This indicates that the **time** which elapses between ordering and receiving stock is an important factor in the stock control function. The time delay between ordering and delivery is the **lead time** for a specific stock item. *Lead times* are used to calculate the **reorder point**, when the stock reaches the stock level at which an order should be placed for replenishment. A safeguard may be built into the system by adding a small amount to the minimum stock levels to introduce a **safe working stock level**.

Example. The previous graph shows the stock falling to *safe working level* in week ten. At this time, stocks should return to maximum level, which means that delivery must take place on that day. Assuming that the *lead time* for this item of stock is two weeks, it follows that the order has to be placed two weeks before *safe working stock level* is reached. In order to establish the *reorder point*, the stock level two weeks before reaching the safe working level has to be calculated.

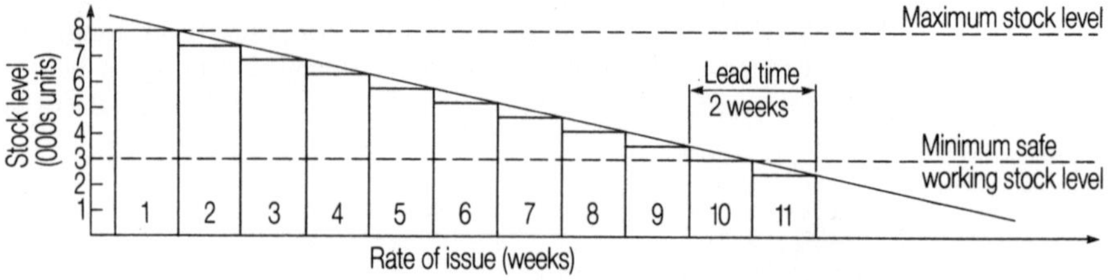

In the graph the calculated rate of issue shows that the safe working level will be reached in week 11. A two week lead time means that the replenishment should be, in the graph which appears above, the safe working level will be reached in week 11. A two-week lead time means that the replenishment should be ordered in week 9, when the stock level will be 300 units. Therefore the re-order point for this item of stock is 300 units.

Activity 6

Complete the example of the perpetual inventory by adding the following stock movements:
15.5.19__ 1000 ordered through the reorder routine.
17.5.19__ 1000 received as a result of the reorder.
18.5.19__ 100 issued from stock.
19.5.19__ 300 allocated to Order No. 153/5 are issued.
20.5.19__ 800 allocated for Order No. 156/2.

Activity 7

The production director of EPTL, Mr John Appleton, has been invited to address a meeting of the plastics section of the CBI in London next month. He asks you to do two things for him:

a Summarize the attached article in note form.

b Write to the CBI conference secretary at 22 Bloomsbury Square accepting the invitation for the 27th at 3 pm in the afternoon. Request any provision you think he will need in the lecture hall. He plans to use a slide/tape sequence. As the engagement will entail an overnight stay, ask them to book accommodation for him.

RESEARCH PROGRAMME AND THE NEW BRITISH STANDARD

The majority of PVC supplied today for use in pipe manufacture is produced by suspension polymerisation, and it is crucial that the polymer producer achieves a high degree of consistency in the quality of the materials he offers. A modern PVC plant represents a massive financial investment. Adoption of full computer monitoring and control throughout the manufacturing process ensures that output is consistent and meets the requirements of polymer users.

Recent years have seen many improvements in the quality of vinyl chloride polymer available to pipe manufacturers, and that has done much to increase the level of confidence in the material on the part of both manufacturer and user.

Many of these developments, and the investment, by ICI in particular, in new highly effective plant, have been reported in earlier issues of *Plastics Today.* There has also been a considerable increase in the understanding of the technology of processing PVC. In particular, the paramount importance of proper gelation of the PVC during pipe manufacture is now fully recognised: it is, indeed, absolutely essential if the effectiveness of the material in pressure pipe applications is to be ensured.

ICI has been very closely concerned with the growth of the market for uPVC, and has supplied material in the form of both polymer and compound to this sector since the early 1960s.

The increasing use of twin-screw extruders and of powder-blend feedstocks resulted in an intensive programme of development by ICI to produce specialised polymers that could be processed readily into pipe.

The grades of 'Corvic' polymer available today for use in pipe extrusion offer a combination of powder properties designed specifically to meet the challenge of tighter specifications for the pipes themselves. In particular, 'Corvic' polymers have easy-gelling properties combined with high bulk density that enable the pipe manufacturer to produce pipe of high quality at optimum rates of output. However the principal characteristic of 'Corvic' polymers available to pipe producers is their very high degree of consistency in quality that enables the producer to keep his processing costs down and the quality of his products high. ICI's very modern plants at Runcorn in England and Wilhelmshaven in West Germany each produce grades of uPVC suitable for pipe extrusion that are sold worldwide.

In 1977, manufacturers of pressure pipe in the United Kingdom invested nearly £500 000 in a programme of research, undertaken by three of the country's leading academic institutions, and co-ordinated by the British Polymer Engineering Directorate with additional support provided by the British Plastics Federation. Although the programme was not seen primarily as polymer-based, polymer suppliers supported the work, and ICI were particularly active in that respect. Consequently it involved a range of professional bodies encompassing the complete plastics industry.

Essentially, the purpose of the research was to investigate methods for measuring the quality of pipe and to determine ways of improving them, so that service performance of the pipe over a long period could also be improved. Detailed study was made of fracture mechanics, crack initiation, rupture, and creep, and the work took the level of technical understanding far deeper than it had been previously. One result was a significant improvement in the technology of the extrusion process.

The next objective was to produce a revised British Standard Specification for pressure pipe that would set higher, but more realistic, standards correlating with the levels of excellence that pipe manufacturers were already achieving. For instance, the revised Standard requires pipe manufacturers to meet new requirements for 'fracture toughness' that will ensure that the product will be of the highest quality and easily able to satisfy the rigours of continuous service, and so provide the water consumer and taxpayer with a cost-effective system of water distribution. Inclusion of fracture-toughness levels will not only tighten the requirements but will also put the UK criteria ahead of those applicable on the Continent. Another of its provisions is the use of a methylene chloride test to measure gelation levels: this is more demanding than the acetone method previously employed.

It is expected that the revised British Standard Specification, BS 3505 will be a major development for the industry, and one that has been welcomed by all parties to it as being a means for ensuring that standards of quality are the highest that can reasonably be achieved.

(From *Plastics Today*, No. 23 'The Hidden Giant', Summer 1985)

Activity 8

Use the following information as the basis of the 'findings' section for a schematic report to the production planner, Sally Price. If necessary, refer back to Block 2 for guidance.

The production line is brought to a standstill in the afternoon because of shortage of raw materials.

The production planner calls in the shift supervisor and tells him off for failing to foresee the problem. The shift supervisor blames internal transport, but they say there were no materials batched for them to transport and they are sick of doing other people's work. The storekeeper is then sent for and he reports a shortfall of actual stock against the bin cards.

All this takes more than half an hour to sort out. Meanwhile a whole shift is being paid to stand idle, and valuable time is being lost.

Everything on the Gantt charts will need rescheduling. The production planner sends you off with the storekeeper to find out exactly what has gone wrong and instructs you to write her a report recommending necessary changes as soon as possible.

You jot down the following points during the course of your investigation:

1 Deliveries of plastics materials from suppliers have been subject to delay.
2 Stores have been a man short for more than six months.
3 Bin cards are filled in manually.
4 Stock records are kept manually on cards held in boxes in numerical order in the raw material stores.
5 Internal transport sometimes help themselves if no storeman is available.

6 Sales statistics 'borrow' the stock records to compile their figures.
7 There is some bad feeling between the staff in stores and in internal transport.
8 It is company policy to reduce the work-force wherever natural wastage makes it possible.
9 Sales statistics report that doing the stock figures is a very tedious job that everyone avoids if possible.
10 In the recent reorganization, transport drivers were promoted to Scale 3 pay, but storekeepers remained on Scale 2.
11 Stores should record issues as they are made but because they are short-handed they often leave it until the end of the shift.

Assessing efficiency

Whatever type of production method is adopted, efficiency is of paramount importance. A number of techniques can be used to increase the efficient use of resources. Each technique requires in-depth study. We confine ourselves to a brief description to demonstrate their application at this point.

Work study

Mention work study to most people and they get a visual impression of someone in jackboots toting a stop watch, with the aim of making them work harder for less money. This view is not altogether unjustified. In the past management has been guilty of abusing the technique by misusing it.

Properly applied, work study can benefit both management and work-force. It is not a substitute for good management; it is one of the 'tools' management can use to produce the results required.

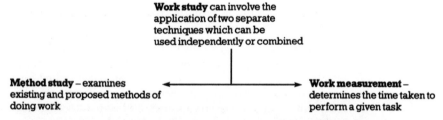

Work study can involve the application of two separate techniques which can be used independently or combined

Method study – examines existing and proposed methods of doing work

Work measurement – determines the time taken to perform a given task

There is nothing new in method study: the pyramids were not built by accident! Careful planning and standardization of the input of manpower and machinery can improve any activity. We are in the logistics age. Increasingly, things are done on a larger scale and efficient methods become more important.

Briefly stated, the objectives of method study are:
1 To use human effort in the most economical way.
2 To improve the working environment and develop safe working methods.
3 To improve the design and layout of the workplace.
The technique has been successfully applied to manufacturing industries, administration procedures, hospitals, retail outlets, space travel and the armed forces – to name but a few.

Building a modern jet airliner is a complex planning operation. The achievement would be somewhat diminished if some method of handling large payloads were not established before the first one landed at an international airport.

Method study procedure

To examine a particular situation so that it can be analysed, the following procedure is followed:

SELECT	the work to be studied on the basis of: *a* the possible economic returns on the cost of carrying out the study, *b* the possible effect on morale and industrial relations, *c* the need to improve safety;
RECORD	the present working methods, using the relevant techniques;
EXAMINE	the recorded existing working methods critically;
DEVELOP	the alternative working methods presented by the critical examination;
SELECT	the most practical and efficient method from the alternatives developed;
INSTALL	the new working methods with planned training for those concerned;
MAINTAIN	by supervision until the new method is established.

Recording the present method It is essential that recording is carried out to enable the analysis to be undertaken efficiently. A number of methods are described below, starting with the five American Society of Mechanical Engineers (ASME) symbols. These are used to construct activity charts.

○	OPERATION	– any activity taking the job a stage nearer completion
□	INSPECTION	– verifies that what has been done is satisfactory or that it is safe to proceed to the next stage
⇨	TRANSPORT	– indicates that something or someone has been moved without any change in the state of the end-product
D	DELAY	– temporary delay in production, such as waiting for materials
▽	STORAGE	– something held in permanent storage and needing authorized release

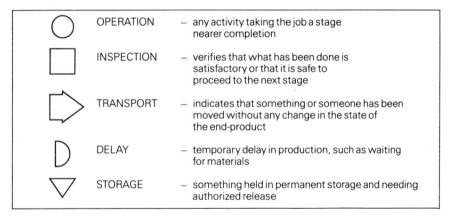

Much of the recording employed in method study is in the form of charts. The most commonly used types are:

PROCESS CHART	– a graphical representation of a sequence of events or steps in a working method, using symbols to indicate the nature of the event
OPERATION PROCESS CHART	– a graphical representation of all operations and inspections involved in a process or procedure in which entry points of materials are indicated
FLOW PROCESS CHART	– a chart setting out the sequence of flow of work or product, or any part of it, through the factory or department by recording all the events under review, using the ASME symbols

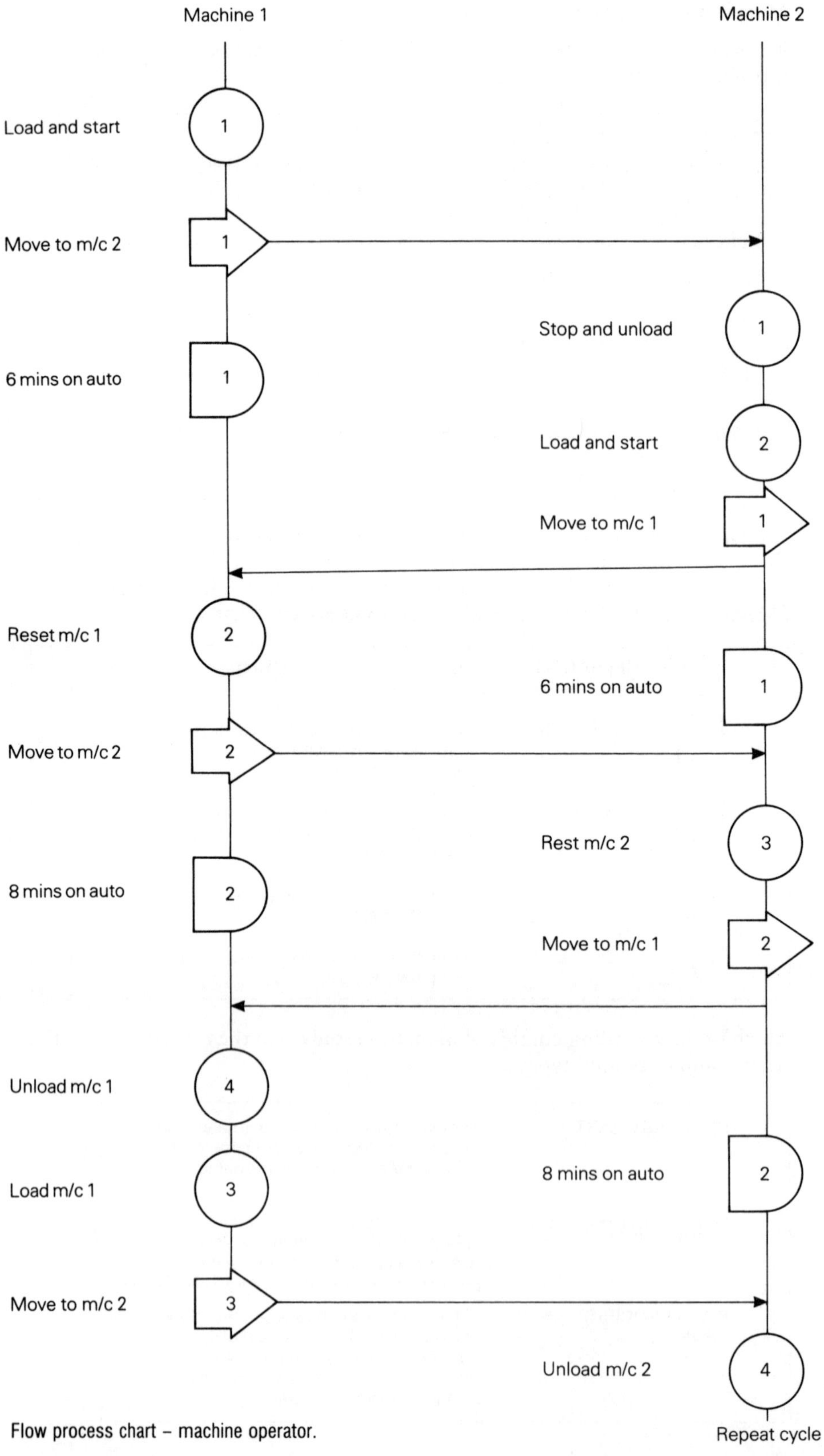

Flow process chart – machine operator.

Other recording methods include:

String diagrams There are situations in which the physical movement of people or procedures is an important factor in the investigation of working methods. Typical examples are stores personnel, hospital staff, supermarket staff and loaders, who normally move about the working environment.

String diagrams are based on a two-dimensional representation of the workplace layout on which the movement of the subject is traced by a thread passed round pins placed at the termination point of each individual movement. Recording over a period of time produces a pattern of movement showing the frequency with which each movement is made.

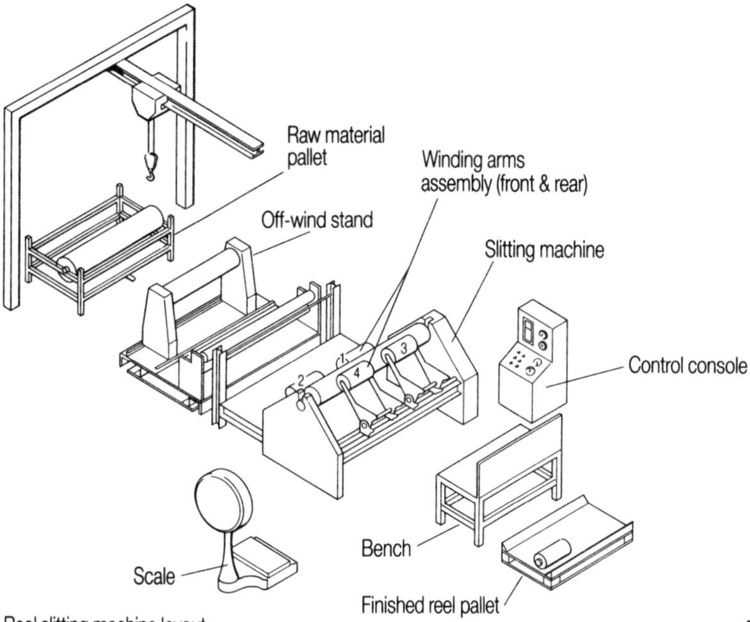

Reel slitting machine layout.

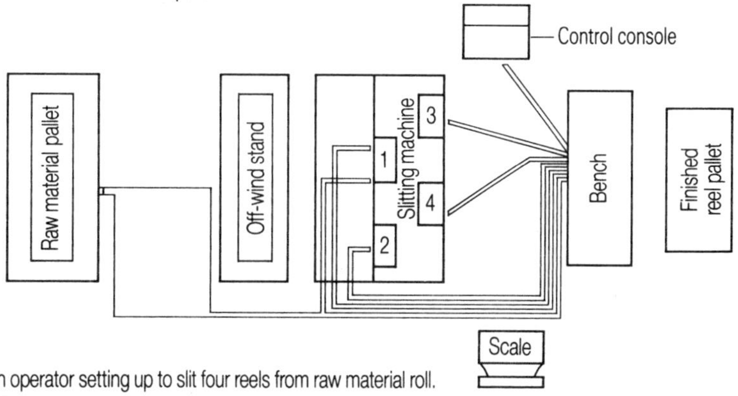

Movement of an operator setting up to slit four reels from raw material roll.

The layout model is to a known scale, so that measuring the thread will determine the distance moved. Our example is in the form of two diagrams: the first shows the layout of a reel slitting machine; the second demonstrates the application of string diagrams to that machine. Where more than one operator or procedure is involved different coloured threads are used.

Advantages of the string diagram:

a Demonstrates to those concerned the benefits to be obtained from a change in working methods,

b Compares the advantages of alternative layouts,
c Traces the movement from one workforce to another,
d Establishes the movements of a team of workers.

Multiple activity charts These are used to examine the activities of more than one factor of production – for example, man and machine interface – on a single chart so that a direct comparison can be made. Charts can be coloured or shaded to identify the different time factors, as shown in our example.

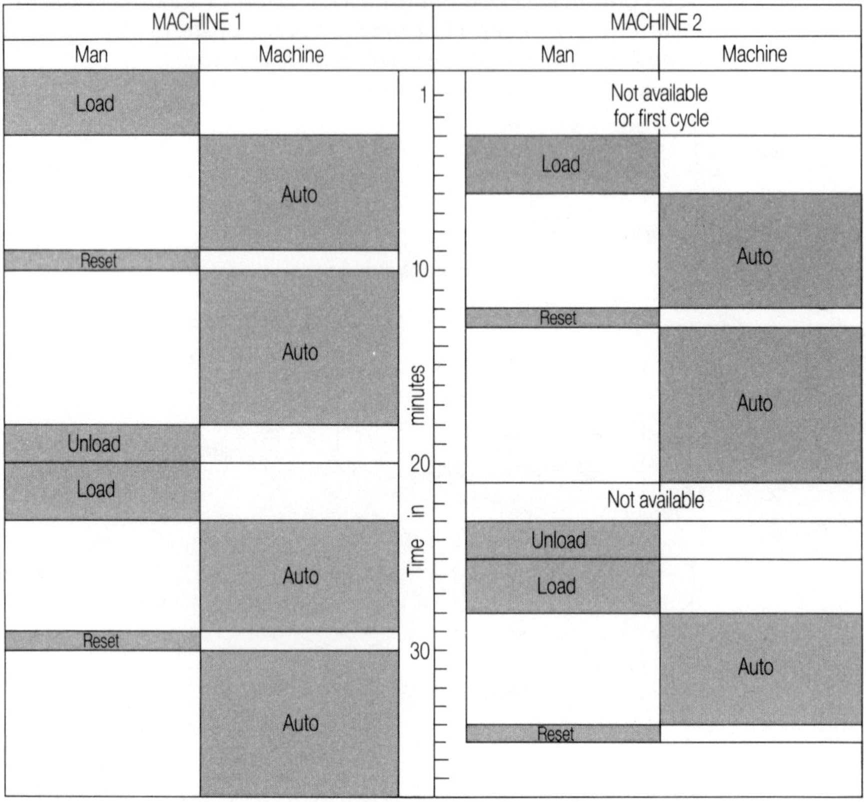

Multiple activity chart.

Multiply activity charts These are used to examine the activities of more than one factor of production – for example, man and machine interface – on a single chart so that a direct comparison can be made. Charts can be coloured or shaded to identify the different time factors, as shown in our example.

There are a number of other sophisticated recording methods, involving the use of photography, time lapse filming, video recording etc. These can be used for long-term observations or to speed up long-term events. An example of the latter is the study of air traffic flow at airports.

Activity 9

A group of workers in a large office have been informed that their working methods are going to be method studied. They are very apprehensive about this, although they have been assured that there will be no redundancies arising out of any change in working methods.

Outline notes for a talk to be given by a senior manager to the work-force in an attempt to allay the fears.

Critical examination

The **questioning technique** is used to examine critically, objectively and impartially, the sequence and nature of the activities which make up a specific task. Flow charts represent the activities, using ASME symbols. The activities fall into two groups:

1 Those in which something is happening to the product in terms of being worked on, moved, or inspected.
2 Those in which the product/procedure is not being worked on because of delay or being in storage.

The activities in Group 1 may be subdivided into three more groups:

a *Make ready operations*: concerned with the preparation of the product or procedure.
b *Do operations*: those which change the shape or condition of the product or procedure.
c *Put away operations*: those in which work is moved aside to storage or to await the next stage in the completion of the overall task.

Since it is only the **do** activities that are productive, the questioning technique is usually applied to the non-productive activities, following a well-established pattern, to examine:

THE	PURPOSE	for which	the activities are undertaken in order to	ELIMINATE
	PLACE	at which		COMBINE
	SEQUENCE	in which		REARRANGE
	PERSON	by whom		OR
	MEANS	by which		SIMPLIFY

Developing the new method Alternatives to the present working methods are devised by the questioning techique which is developed from the simplified statement above to ask:
What should be done?
Where should it be done?
When should it be done?
Who should do it?
How should it be done?

PURPOSE	PERSON
What is done?	**Who** does it?
Why is it done?	Why does **that** person do it?
What else **could** be done?	Who **else** might do it?
What **should** be done?	Who **should** do it?

A form of standard layout similar to that shown below is used for the analysis and development of the method.

EXISTING METHOD		NEW METHOD	
Activity	Method Purpose/place/sequence etc	Alternatives could/should	Proposed method

Critical examination layout.

Work measurement

Work measurement is the application of techniques to the work content of a specific task in order to calculate the time required by a qualified worker to carry it out. To a work study engineer, a qualified worker is any person who is accustomed to the task being measured.

There are a variety of methods for the measurement of work. The best known is probably the use of the stop-watch, and this is also the method which seems to generate the greatest resistance. Being timed adds to the annoyance of being observed while working, and work study must be introduced on a planned basis to dispel some of the fears.

Procedure for taking a time study

1 Record all information concerning the job to be studied and the environment in which it is performed.
2 Draw up a complete description of the working method, broken down into **elements** which can be easily defined.
3 Measure (usually with a stop-watch) and record the **observed time** taken to complete each element of the task.
4 While observing the time taken, **rate** the performance of the operator in comparison with a predetermined 'normal' speed.
5 Convert the observed time to a **normalized time**.
6 Determine the **allowances** to be made over and above the 'normal' time for the operation.
7 Determine the **allowed time** for the operation.

To carry out the procedure outlined, you will need some detailed information about using a stop-watch and some definitions of terms used.

The 'fly back' method This requires a watch fitted with a stop mechanism which allows the second hand to return to the zero position and to continue immediately to time. The observer must be trained to read the watch at the instant the lever is depressed. Element times can be directly recorded, cutting out any need for further calculation. This method is sometimes criticized on the grounds that the small amount of time lost when the second hand returns to zero can be significant over a long period of timing. Also repetitive timing of elements may influence the observer's assessment of the operator's performance and lead to biased rating.

The continuous timing method The watch is allowed to run continuously and the observer records the time elapsed at the end of each element without returning the second hand to zero. This involves calculating each element time when the study is completed.

Elements An element can be described as any part of an operation in which a distinct and definite piece of work, with an identifiable beginning and ending, is carried out. The point at which one element ends and another starts is known as the **break point**.

Observed time As its name suggests, this is the time observed at the conclusion of each element of work. Each element is observed and measured a number of times and an average time is calculated.

Rate A work study engineer requires considerable training to become proficient in rating, the purpose of which is to provide a means of assessing the pace at which an operator is working and comparing it with a standard pace.

The standard pace is known as the **normal performance**, generally accepted in the UK as the speed equivalent to the motions of the limbs when someone walks without a load on a level surface at three miles an hour. This concept is converted into a scale which provides the input for the formula to convert the observed time into the normalized time.

Applying the rating factor Using a scale where 100 represents 'normal' performance, the observer would decide whether the operator is performing less effectively or more effectively than normal.

If less effectively, a rating factor of less than 100 would be applied – say 85 or 90. (It is usual to round up ratings in steps of 5.)
If more effectively, a rating factor of more than 100 is applied – say 110 or 125.

Therefore:	Observed time	×	Rating factor	=	A constant
	2.0 (min)	×	100	=	200
	1.6 min)	×	125	=	200
	0.25 (min)	×	800	=	200

From the above examples, you will see that the observed rating divided by the normal rating is a percentage which can be applied to convert the observed time to the normalized time:

$$\text{Observed time} \times \frac{\text{Rating}}{\text{Normal Rating}} = \text{Normalised time}$$

Activity 10

Using the British Standard 0/100 rating factor, calculate the normalized time for the following observations. Round the calculated normalized time up or down to the nearest 0 or 0.5.

Observed time (mins)	Observed rating	Normalized time
8.0	115	
9.5	100	
11.0	85	
12.0	75	
7.5	125	
10.5	90	
8.5	105	
12.5	75	

Calculating the average normalized time Normalized time must now be converted into the **allowed time.** People at work do not work at a consistent rate of output throughout the working day. There are many reasons for this, the obvious one being fatigue.

Allowances have to be made for working conditions. Extra time is added to the normalized time to ensure that the time allowed to do the job is realistic.

The International Labour Office defines a number of allowances in their publication *Introduction to Work Study*, as follows:
1 *Process allowance* Given to compensate for enforced idleness (which would otherwise cause loss of earning power) on the part of an operative owing to the character of the process or operation with which they are involved.
2 *Rest allowance* An addition to the normal time (usually calculated as a percentage) intended to give the worker an opportunity to recover from the effects of expending energy in the performance of specified work under specified conditions and to allow attention for personal needs.

3 *Special allowances* Given for any activities which are not normally part of the operation cycle but are essential for the satisfactory performance of the work. Such allowances may be permanent or temporary.
4 *Policy allowance* Any allowance given at the discretion of the management over and above allowances given to features inherent in the work under consideration.

Allowed time = Normalized time + Rest allowance + Any other allowances

Activity 11

Given the following allowances:

Rest allowance 10%
Special allowance 5%
Policy allowance 3%

Calculate the allowed time for the average normalized time calculated in the office studied in Activity 9.

Assuming that the allowed time you have calculated represents the allowed time for a complete cycle, calculate the number of cycles which could be completed by an operator in a 7½ hour working day.

If the total allowances were 8 per cent more than they should be, how would this affect the scheduling of work into the work-load?

Organization and methods

Organizations and methods (O and M) is the application of work study techniques to the administrative procedures of an organization.

As the complexity of production methods and the amount of information which has to be processed increases efficient methods make an essential contribution to cost reduction.

The work of the O and M department covers three broad areas: **procedures**, **equipment** and **manpower**. These are further subdivided as shown below:

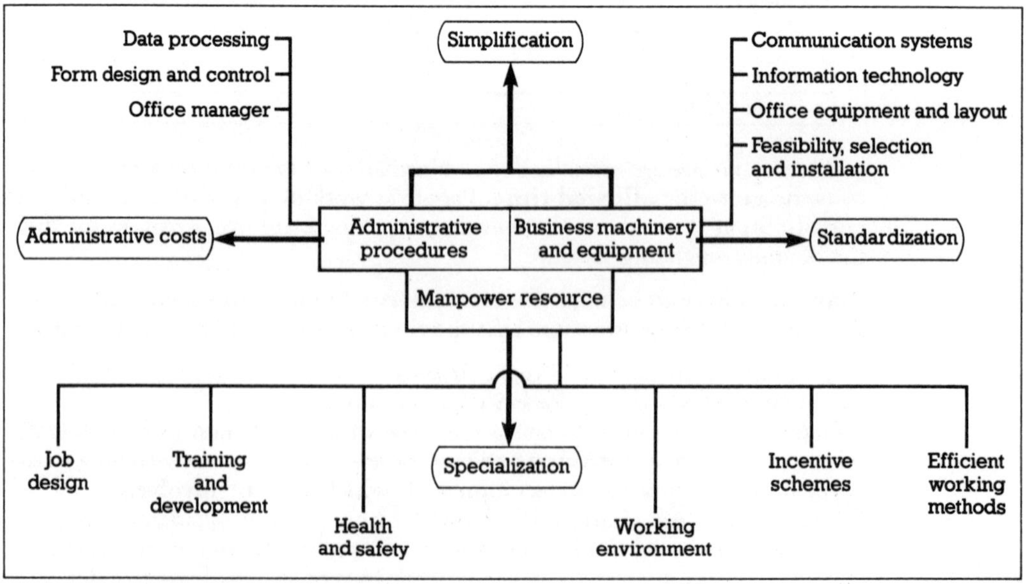

Organization and methods.

Organization and methods may be included in the management services function, which examines the application of market research, corporate planning and data processing.

Method study procedures are the same as in work study, except that there are additions to the charting symbols which enable paperwork procedures to be recorded. See the illustrations.

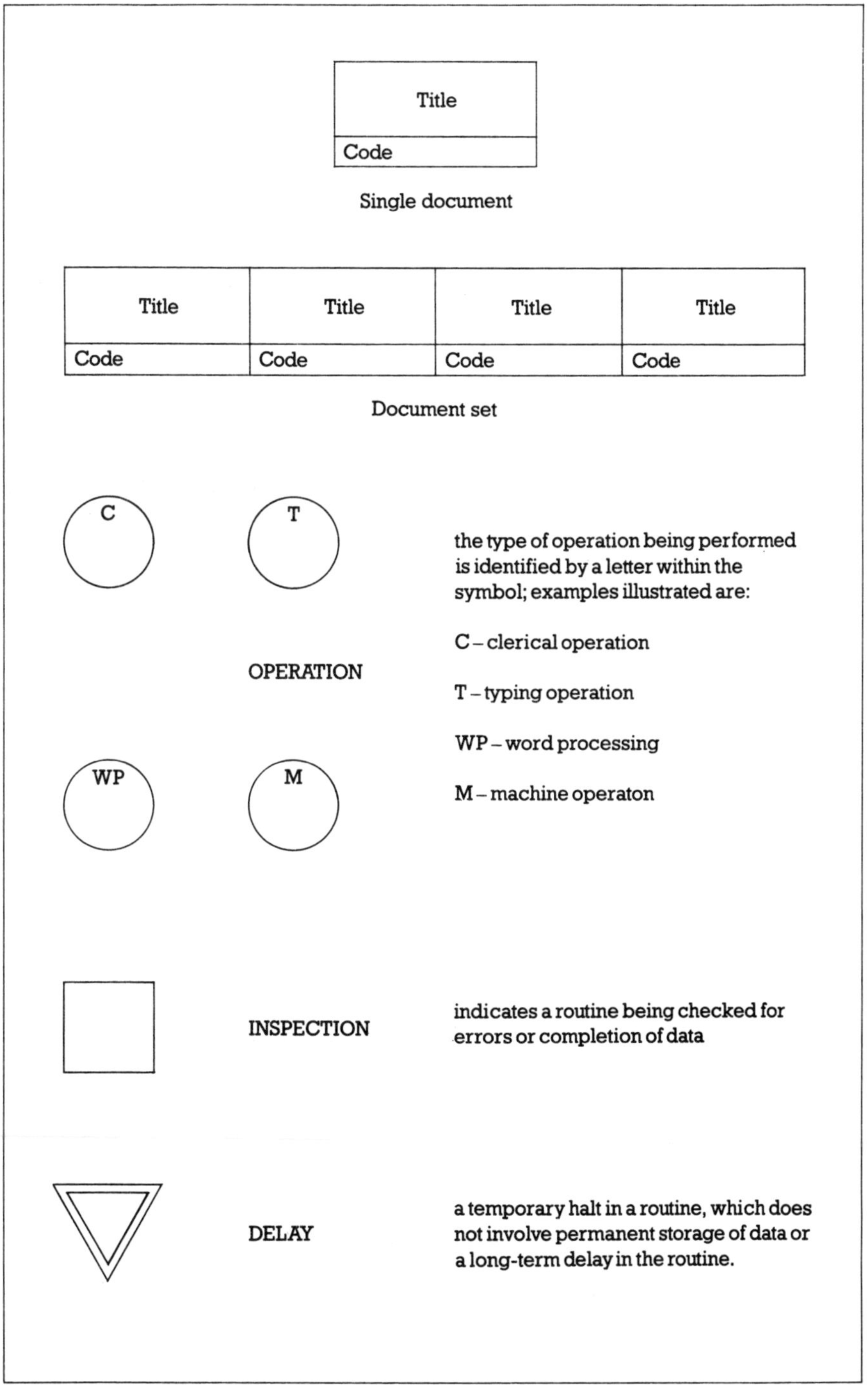

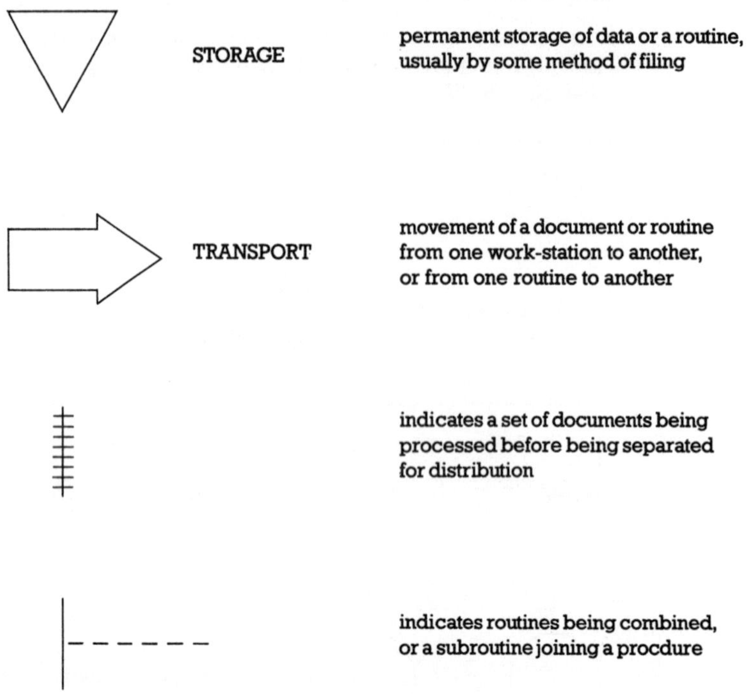
STORAGE
permanent storage of data or a routine, usually by some method of filing
TRANSPORT
movement of a document or routine from one work-station to another, or from one routine to another
indicates a set of documents being processed before being separated for distribution
indicates routines being combined, or a subroutine joining a procdure

O and M charting symbols

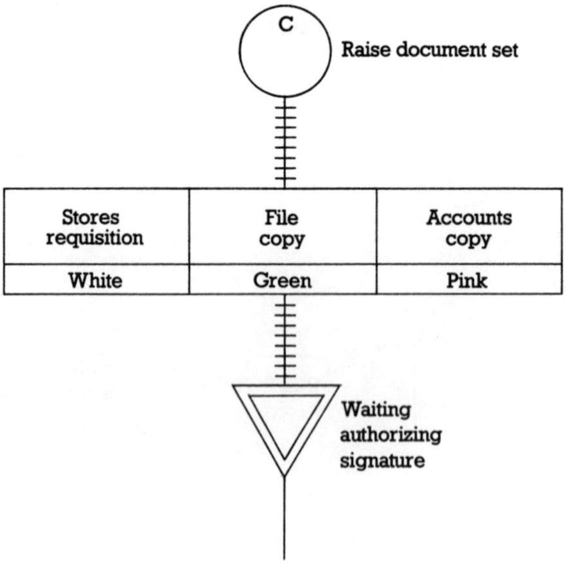
C
Raise document set
Stores requisition
File copy
Accounts copy
White
Green
Pink
Waiting authorizing signature

Section of an O and M chart

Documentation for O and M.

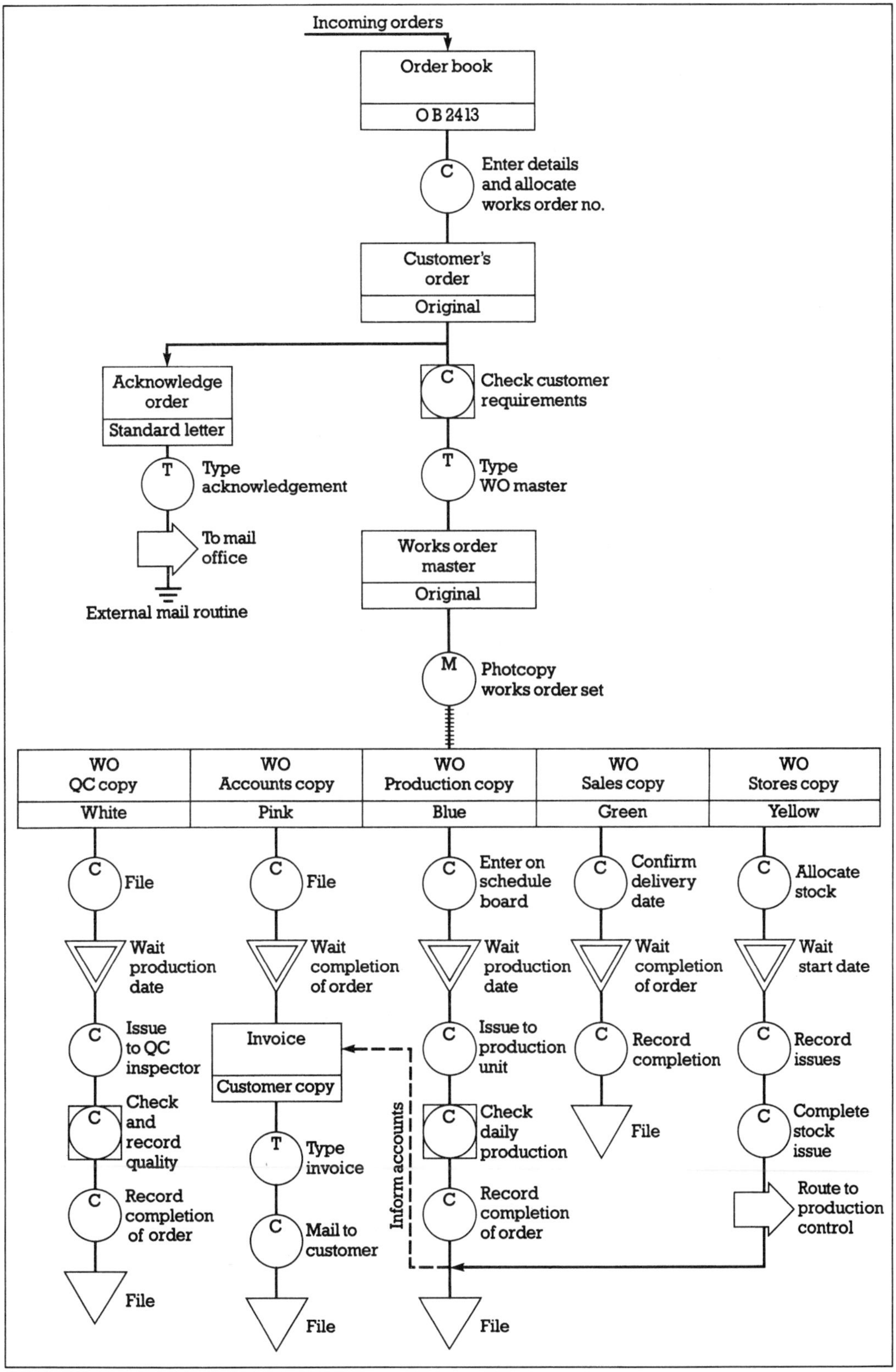

Works order routine.

Objectives of O and M

In common with work study in the production function, the objectives of the O and M department will vary from one organization to another. The following represent the major objectives which should be embodied in the O and M policy:

1 Make all administrative procedures efficient by establishing control over form design and use.
2 Maximize the use of business machinery and information technology available to the organization.
3 Reduce the manpower cost related to the administration of the business.
4 Plan and implement the training of administrative staff.
5 Provide pleasant working conditions for office staff.
6 Promote safe working conditions within the office environment.
7 Establish feedback and control over all the functions which go to make up the organization structure.
8 Carry out work measurement and design incentive schemes to improve the productive output of administration staff.

Clerical work measurement

The stop-watch is not widely used in the office, but it may aid the analysis of a particular procedure or establish times required in setting up an incentive scheme. Timing may also be used as a basis for controlling the output of repetitive routines by setting work targets.

With the increase in the application of information technology, business machines tend to set the pace for output on many routines and reduce the areas where work measurement can be applied. However, when used in conjunction with other techniques such as **activity sampling** or **multiple activity charts**, it may determine whether an operator could work more than one machine or cope with more than one routine simultaneously.

Ergonomics

Ergonomics is a technique you are likely to have heard about without understanding its relevance to people in organizations. It combines a number of disciplines, including psychology, anthropology, anatomy, physiology and engineering, in order to study the individual in the working environment. Its aim is to establish the conditions under which people are able to perform efficiently without detriment to themselves. To do that, the job has to be fitted to the person, taking into account the limitations of the human body. In the past machines have been designed solely on the basis of what they were required to do. As a result, machine operators in the engineering industry have to bend, reach and sway in order to operate standard production lathes and milling machines. These are time-wasting and fatiguing actions.

Fitting the job to the worker

When manned space flights where first undertaken, the size of the payload for a rocket restricted the size of the capsule, in which the astronaut was required to carry out complicated tasks within a life-support environment. In the capsule, the human frame was subjected to tremendous G (gravity) forces during the initial and final stages of the flight.

Some understanding of the significance of G in ability to perform tasks can be gained by considering its effect on the pilot of a light aircraft pulling out of a

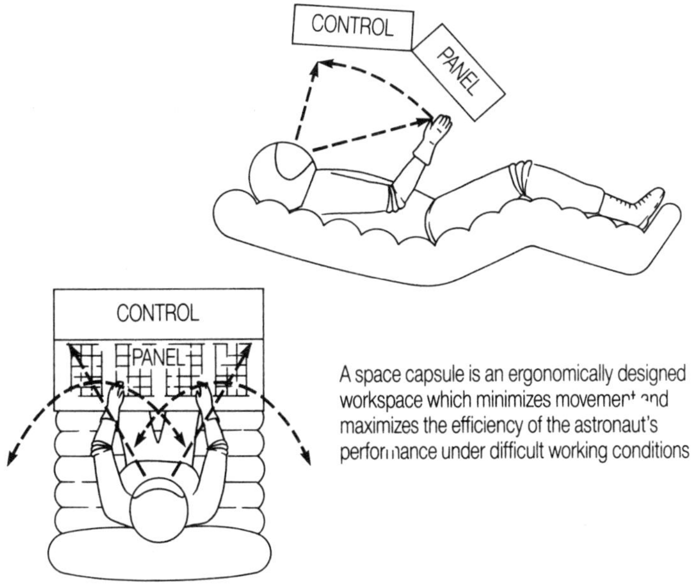

CONTROL
PANEL
CONTROL
PANEL
A space capsule is an ergonomically designed workspace which minimizes movement and maximizes the efficiency of the astronaut's performance under difficult working conditions

An application of ergonomics.

steep dive. The pilot is subjected to 2 to 2.5 G, which means that a 10-stone pilot exerts a pressure of 20 to 25 stone on the seat of the aircraft. This is a modest force compared with what is generated by an accelerating space rocket; that is capable of preventing the heart pumping blood to the brain, causing a blackout.

Applying ergonomics to the design of the capsule resulted in couches being moulded for each astronaut in which they lay prone and supported, as illustrated. To minimize the movements needed to control and fly the mission, the panels where situated above, within easy reach of the pilot. In addition, consideration was given to the total environment. The pilot would not perform at the high level demanded if he was too hot, too cold, unable to see instruments clearly, confused by noise or had difficulty in communicating with the command centre.

This is, of course, an extreme example of a difficult working environment, but the same principle can be applied to any working environment where similar factors have some significance.

One thing the modern office worker shares with the astronaut is the requirement to work with visual displays. No one really knows what the best colour combination is to reduce eye strain in word processor operators, or the long-term effects of working with VDUs.

Activity 12

Look at the illustration of the astronaut, which shows the most efficient arc of vision in relation to the flight control panel to prevent eye fatigue.

Given the task of designing the instrument panel layout, where would you place those instruments which would indicate:
1 immediate danger,
2 normal flight conditions,
3 fuel consumption?
Write a short report justifying your choice.

The human body and work situations

There is no work tool with greater flexibility and adaptability than the human body. In layman's terms, it consists of solid bits joined together by hinged bits and swivel bits. If we treat our human frame with reasonable respect it does not fall apart, but it does protest at misuse by producing pain or fatigue. In some instances the pain can be severe and reduce the quality of life.

We were not designed to sit at desks for long periods, operate machinery in noisy conditions or concentrate for long periods on dials, gauges and flashing lights. All these tasks have been forced on us through the manner in which we produce goods and services.

The effects of these conditions can be minimized if the human frame is provided with the support required to ease the situation. The next illustration shows how the human body can be considered when designing a work-station for a task involving sitting for long periods of time.

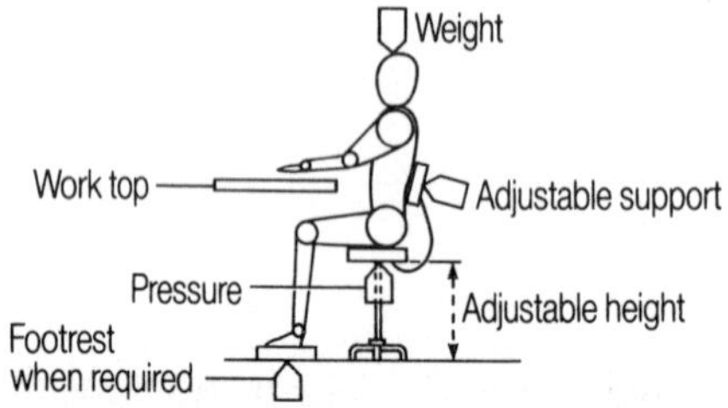

Application of ergonomics to the design of a work-station.

Back problems are the most common industrial ill which plague us. People who sit for most of their working day are particularly prone to back pain, yet much can be done to minimize the risk by providing the correct seating, as illustrated. A seat which is designed to adjust to the many variations in a cross-section of the working population will reduce fatigue and the risk of back problems. However, its purpose will not be achieved if the person sitting on it crosses their legs and places extra weight on one hip!

Ergonomics in the office

Modern office routines are increasingly being carried out at work-stations with electronic equipment rather than at desks for processing paperwork. Workplace layout is an essential factor in aiding the employee to perform at the highest level.

Our diagram shows the layout of an executive work-station, based on the minimum and maximum arm reach of the average administrative worker. Many other factors have to be taken into account. These include environmental factors, which will be considered next.

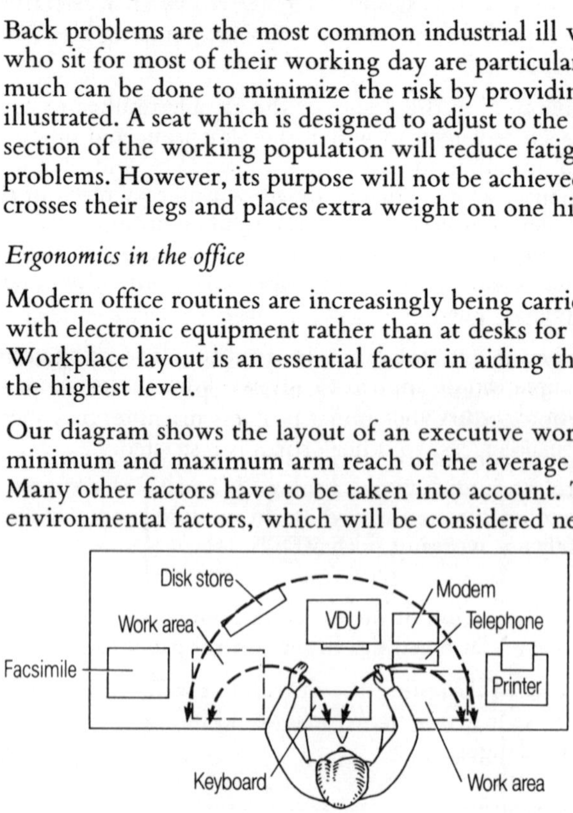

Ergonomics applied to an executive work-station.

Office planning and layout

The objectives in office planning and layout are similar to those in the planning of a production unit and can be summarized as follows:

1 Within the constraints which the design of the building imposes, routines and procedures should move through the layout in the most economic and logical way possible.
2 Environmental conditions should be maintained at a high standard to provide pleasant working conditions.
3 Where possible, arrangements should be made for people to work in small groups, rather than in isolation.
4 Work-station design should prevent individuals from sitting at one task for the whole of the working day.
5 Movement of staff around the working area should be made as easy as possible by providing adequate gangways and by siting work-stations sensibly.
6 Some allowance should be made for changes in routines requiring expansion of the work area or relocation of functions.
7 Legal requirements imposed by the Health and Safety at Work Act 1974 must be observed.
8 Managers and supervisors should be located close to their areas of responsibility and to the personnel they directly control.

These ideals may be impossible to realize in view of the design of the building and the type of work being undertaken. Ultimately, the design of a specific office tends to be a compromise between what is desirable and what is practical.

Types of office layout

Specific purpose or closed office

This is an office in which a number of people are employed on one specific aspect of the business, such as accounts, or in which one person works on a specific task. Where the work undertaken is confidential, this type of layout may be the only one suitable. As the system is closed, it tends to isolate people and procedures and to hinder the flow of work between departments.

Layout of desk and equipment is limited by the position of walls, doors and windows, and communication with other departments may present some difficulties. Photocopiers and similar business machines may have to be duplicated because access to other offices is restricted.

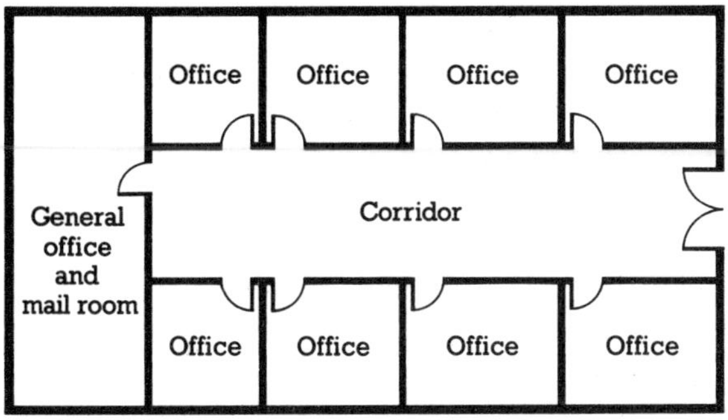

Closed (cellular) office layout.

Open-plan office

A large open space in which the desks are sited in rows gives the office planner and the O and M specialist the opportunity to organize the work flow in the most efficient manner.

The greater degree of flexibility allows reorganization when changes in routines or technology make this desirable. The restrictions imposed by walls and doors are removed, along with the cost of maintaining and decorating these barriers. Corridors between offices are not required, making extra space available for work areas.

Heating and ventilating are easier and more cost effective in large open areas than in individual closed offices. Business machinery and equipment can be located so that joint use can be made of them. Communications are much improved by the absence of walls and partitions between offices.

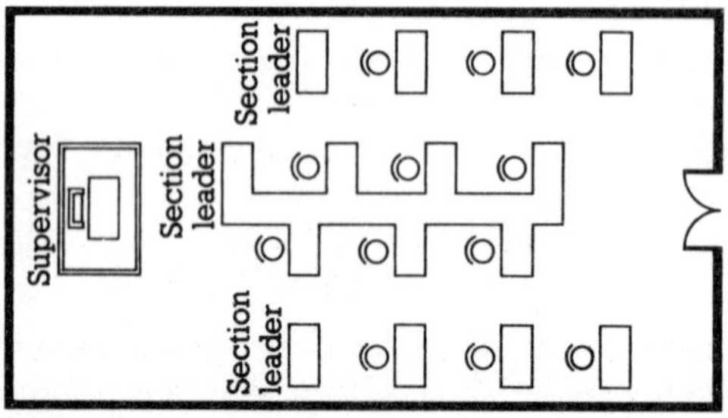

Open-plan office layout.

Against these advantages, the planner has to set the problems of noise from telephones, typewriters and conversation, plus the disadvantages arising from lack of privacy.

Open-plan offices usually have the supervisor in a position where all the staff can be overlooked, often following the American system of placing the supervisor on a raised platform. Setting desks out in rows tends to create a 'factory' atmosphere in the office environment which is disliked by many employees.

Landscaped offices

These are sometimes referred to as **panoramic** offices. They have all the advantages of the open-plan office, but remove the factory atmosphere by grouping working activities in areas subdivided by screens, display boards, banks of filing cabinets, pictures and plants. The result is a cross between the reception area of a large hotel and an airport VIP lounge and provides a pleasant working environment.

Morale and communications are improved when all levels of management and staff work in the same area. Supervision is no longer viewed as overseeing of the work of individuals, but as working as part of the group.

Noise can be significantly reduced by using screens as barriers and a degree of privacy can also be achieved. Landscaped offices have had a marked effect on the design of office furniture and equipment, which now has to look presentable as well as being functional.

In a large organization, it may be advisable to use closed offices as well as open or landscaped offices in order to provide facilities for confidential work, interviewing and large-scale use of business machines.

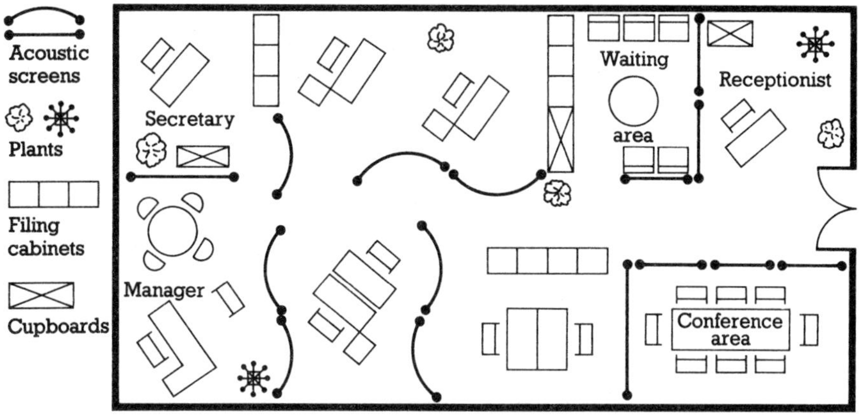

Landscaped office layout.

Ergonomics and office planning

The ideal way to plan any working area is to start by finding out what is required in terms of manpower and equipment. This determines the other requirements such as floor loading (if the office is not on the ground floor), the working space needed, services (such as power and telephones) and the type of ventilation.

Many of the requirements included in the following list are dictated by the Health and Safety at Work Act 1974. Others arise out of O and M techniques.

Flooring Office flooring should, if possible, be of sound-absorbing materials. Floors can be very effective sounding boards and a source of irritating noise. The material selected needs to be easily cleaned and maintained, and non-slip.

Decor Decorative schemes can contribute to morale and working efficiency. Modern offices are decorated in light pastel shades which reflect light but do not produce glare. Minimum use is made of dark colours in the red, blue, green and brown ranges.

Lighting Minimum standards are laid down by the Health and Safety at Work Act, but the quality of light can depend upon the task being performed. As a general rule, natural daylight is the best source. Building design and hours of daylight make this source unreliable, but modern glass technology has done much to improve the use of daylight. Unless the task being performed demands it, pools of intense light are best avoided. Too much light can be as fatiguing as too little.

Heating Where the work being performed is predominantly of a sedentary nature, a temperature which is maintained at 18° centigrade is considered to be ideal. The number of people working within a specified area needs to be taken into consideration: body heat contributes to the warmth in the work area. Heating may involved a trade-off between heating systems and ventilation systems.

Ventilation When the oxygen content falls, ability to perform any task also falls and fatigue soon sets in. Two complete air changes an hour will maintain the required oxygen levels, so any ventilation equipment installed should have this ability. Sophisticated ventilation systems can produce the ideal environment; they take in air and wash, filter and warm it before delivering it to the office.

Noise It has been established that there is a relationship between noise and productivity. Noise causes fatigue and nervous tension, which can have long-term effects on health. This is one of the most difficult problems to solve in office planning. Some progress has been made by using materials which absorb noise rather that transmit it, by the introduction of the muted telephone and the increasing replacement of the typewriter by the word processor.

Not all the noise is generated within the office. Many office buildings are sited on busy main roads or in close proximity to noisy production plants. In extreme cases, an acoustics expert is needed to solve the problem with wall insulation, double glazing, acoustic tiles, etc.

Services Offices need electrical power and telephone services. These require a considerable amount of wiring, which cannot be allowed to trail over floors and desks because of safety implications. Ideally, wiring should be in ducts beneath the floor, providing a grid of safe connection points for equipment.

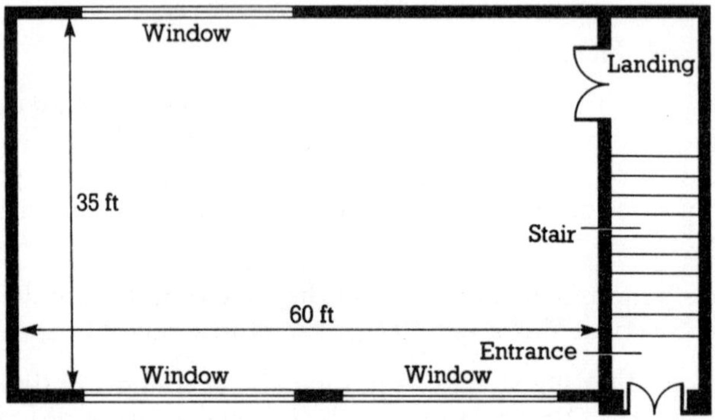

Activity 13

The office space shown in the diagram above represents accommodation made available to a firm of accountants and tax consultants.

The firm is a partnership of two accountants, with two secretaries, four accounts clerks, two typists and one telephonist/receptionist.

During the past five years the partners have built a considerable reputation amongst a number of large organizations. They want the new premises to reflect the professional status of their work and instil confidence in visiting clients.

1 Produce a scale diagram of the office space.
2 Design a layout which will meet the requirements of the two partners.
3 Consult office furniture catalogues and suggest what should be bought.
4 Suggest the office equipment and machinery which should be bought.
5 List the ergonomic factors which have to be taken into account in the design.

Summary

We have described some of the techniques used to maintain control over the production processes. In order to survive in the face of competition, the organization must ensure that the customer is provided with goods/services of right quality, quantity, price. All this has to be achieved whilst maintaining an acceptable profitability.

Human relations aspects related to the application of the techniques have been demonstrated by examples of workplace layouts and the application of Ergonomics.

Skills

Skill	*Activities in which skill is developed*
a Information gathering	4, 6, 7, 8, 16, 17
b Learning and studying	1, 2, 3, 4, 5, 6, 6, 7, 8, 9, 10, 11, 16, 17
c Working with others	1, 2, 9
d Communicating	1, 2, 3, 4, 6, 7, 8, 9, 11, 17
e Design and visual discrimination	1, 4, 5, 7, 16, 17
f Identifying and tackling problems	1, 2, 3, 16, 17
g Numeracy	2, 3, 6, 10, 11
h Information processing	1, 2, 3, 4, 6, 7, 8, 11

Block 7
Purchasing and supply

Introduction

Materials control is an important part of management's function in every type of organization. This block looks at purchasing policy and the related administrative routines. Methods of calculating the right quantity to purchase are considered and the role of the purchasing function in relation to production and stock control is described.

The block covers the communication skills required in day-to-day contacts with suppliers of goods and services.

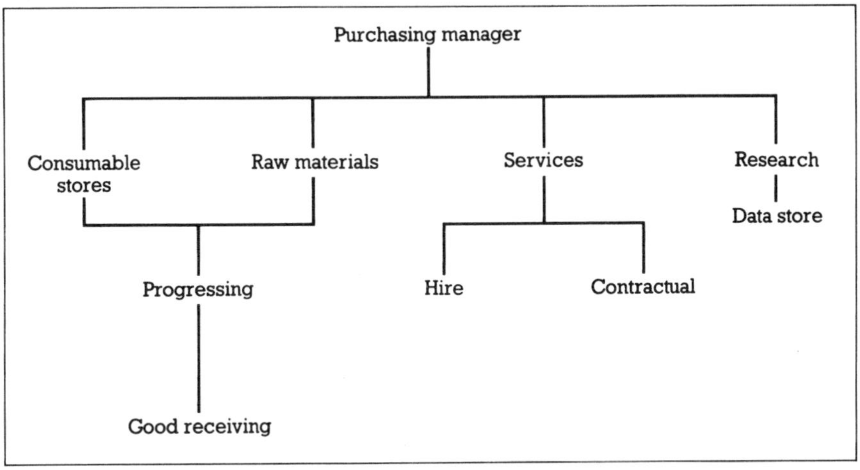

Purchasing structure.

Purchasing

Purchasing is defined as the provision of goods and services required at the right **price**, of the right **quality**, in the right **quantity** and at the right **time** to facilitate the attainment of the company's objectives.

The three main categories of goods ordered by a business organization are:

1 Goods bought for resale or raw materials to be converted into finished products.
2 Materials and services purchased in order to keep the business running on a day-to-day basis; sometimes known as consumable stores, these include stationery, cleaning materials and packaging.
3 Goods designated as assets of the business and intended for long-term use, such as computers, production machinery and transport vehicles.

The purchasing function tends to differ according to the size of the organization and/or the importance of materials control in relation to the cost of production. In determining the relative importance, there are a number of factors:

1 **The degree of competition** involved in the purchase of goods and services. Some goods are in short supply or may be seasonal. Others have market prices which are subject to considerable fluctuation. Purchasing expertise is needed in these situations.

2 **The supply agreements** the company has to enter into. Large organizations tend to buy in bulk and can command certain advantages in the terms of the contract for supply. The purchasing manager of a company ordering in bulk would expect extended credit terms and substantial discounts. Smaller organizations are not able to obtain such favourable terms. Credit terms are likely to be restricted and discounts are likely to be available only if payment for goods is prompt. Research into suppliers giving the most favourable terms is an essential purchasing activity for the small company.

3 **The source of supply**, which may be in the vicinity of the company, elsewhere in the UK, or in another country. Obviously the site of the source has some bearing on the price because of transport costs. Using a source of supply outside the UK may involve problems of continuity of supply.

4 **The extent of 'forward buying' necessary**. Many raw materials have to be purchased well in advance of the production activity, involving forward buying on the relevant commodities market. This type of purchasing is highly specialized. An error of judgement could cost the organization a considerable amount of money.

Examples of this type of commodity are:

coffee

wheat

copper

fuel oil

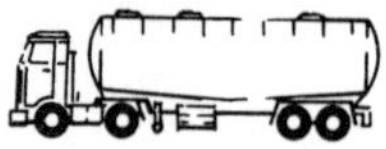

Activity 1

Suggest which of the four factors set out above would apply to the following business activities:

a Canning vegetables.
b Manufacturing cement.
c Purchasing cereals for manufacturing corn flakes.
d Bulk purchase and bottling of fine wines.
e Undertaking office cleaning under contract for a multinational company.

Purchasing policy

The aim of the purchasing policy is to strike a balance between the demand for materials and services and the prevailing market conditions. There is a variety of methods and one or more of the following may be used.

Purchasing for immediate requirements

There is some risk in doing this for raw material supplies if the supplier cannot maintain short lead times. However, if supplies can be guaranteed, use of the method saves storage space. As a general rule, this type of purchasing is restricted to small quantities.

Japanese car manufacturers are now insisting that their suppliers reduce lead times to a matter of hours rather than days or weeks. This is practical only if there is a medium- to long-term purchasing commitment. Components are delivered as they are demanded by the production unit. The advantages are obvious:

1 Considerable reductions in the capital tied up in holding buffer stocks.
2 Saving of space used to hold stocks.
3 Saving in wages related to the storage of stock.
4 Minimum risk of pilfering and obsolesence.

The success of this approach depends entirely on the reliability of the supplier. Where price does not fluctuate, or fluctuation is within acceptable limits, it is reasonable to enter into medium- or long-term agreements with suppliers. Considerable price advantages may be obtained by committing the company to long-term purchases as this enables the supplier to plan production scheduling effectively.

Contract buying

Large quantities of raw material are sometimes required over long periods. A typical example is fuel oil for heating and production processes. Price advantage can be negotiated in return for long-term contractual commitment; future supplies can be purchased at current prices; and delivery can be planned to meet requirements and reduce storage costs.

Speculative buying

A number of companies use raw materials for which the price at the time required is to some extent unpredictable.

Example

A company manufactures confectionery based on chocolate. The main raw material is the cocoa bean, which is subject to climatic conditions and infestation by pests. When the harvest yield is low, the price will rise; when the harvest is good, the price will drop.

If the company has the purchasing expertise to forecast price changes, it can purchase the material before any price increase and gain a competitive advantage or increase its profits.

If the price movement is miscalculated, then the organization could make a considerable loss. Because of the financial risks involved, speculative buying has to be authorized through company policy.

Where large quantities are being purchased, a relatively small movement in price can involve considerable profit or loss:

Cost of material purchased:	£50 000
Price movement of 5p in £:	£ 2 500

If the price movement is up, the company makes £2500 profit.
If the price movement is down, the company makes a £2500 loss.

Activity 2

Identify three raw materials used in industry, apart from oil, which are subject to unpredictable price fluctuation. Make brief notes on the causes of the fluctuation for each of them.

Principal activities of the purchasing function

Research

a The availability of cheaper materials consistent with specifications.
b The availability of alternative materials to those being used at present.
c Developments in the machinery and equipment used by the organization.
d New sources of supply coming into the market.

Standardization

a Material specifications, to ensure consistency of performance.
b Equipment purchased for the organization, to ensure compatibility.

Intelligence

a Examining market prices and trends to determine the bulk-buying strategy.
b Examining the international trading situation to assess the effect on materials purchased by the company.
c Being aware of government economic policies to assess the possible effect on the price, supply, restrictions and taxation of the materials purchased.

Development

a Of efficient purchasing procedures through the application of research, standardization and purchasing intelligence.
b Of liaison between the purchasing function and the other functions in the organization.
c Of good relationships between the company and the organizations which supply it.

Control

a By maintaining adequate records of all transactions within the purchasing function.
b By monitoring the incoming goods and materials for quantity and quality against the order placed.

Commercial

a Selling the scrap materials and redundant plant and equipment at the best possible price.
b Negotiating contracts for supplies, leasing, renting, purchasing plant and equipment.

Centralized purchasing

Many large organizations with numerous departments dispersed over a wide area centralize the purchasing function. One example is Her Majesty's Stationery Office, which caters for the requirements of all government departments for stationery, printing and office machinery.

A number of local authorities have followed the government lead, centralizing their purchasing and relating this function to stores and stock control.

There are a number of advantages:
a allows bulk purchasing with price reductions,
b prevents duplication of ordering and stock holding,
c enables standardization of supplies and equipment,

d records can be kept on data base,
e suppliers more willing to enter into contracts for bulk supplies,
f centralization of stock records,
g purchasing can be budgeted,
h reduction in overhead costs,
i reduction in storage space,
j standardized specifications,
k co-ordination of purchasing and stock inventory.

Activity 3

Obtain a mail order catalogue. List the different types of goods advertised in each section.

Draw a purchasing department organization chart for the mail order company.

Identify two items of stock which would require special purchasing expertise and market knowledge. Give reasons for your choice.

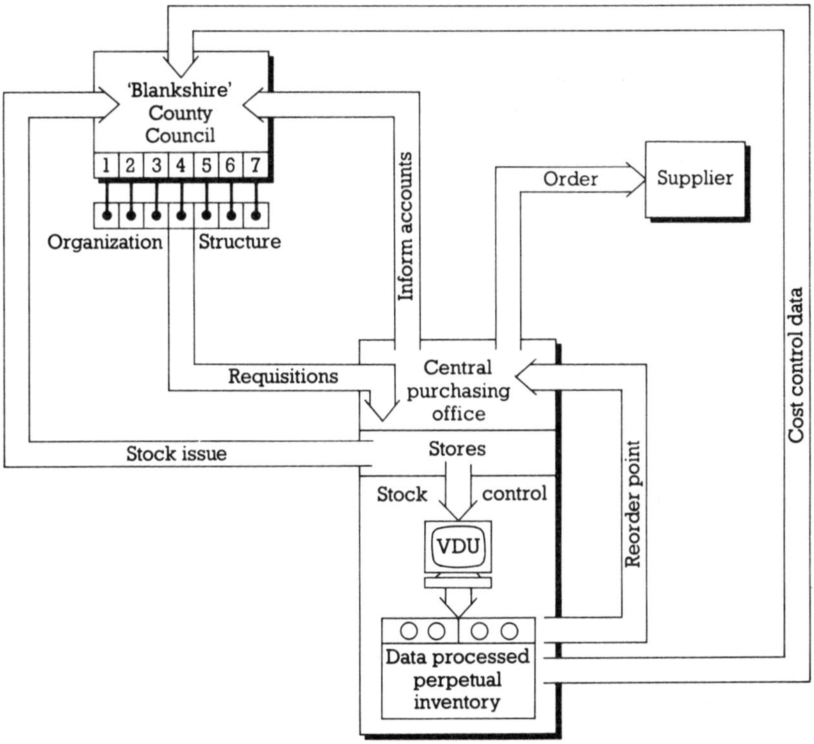

Local authority central purchasing system.

Information about source of supply and prices

The buyer must keep informed about the current situation in the supply field, which is why **purchasing intelligence** is of vital importance. Assuming that the purchasing office has an adequate library of catalogues, trade magazines and advertising matter, this information together with the suppliers' price-lists should give a good guide to sources and prices. Another valuable source of information is the sales representatives who visit the company regularly. They will make sure buyers know about new developments.

Purchasing terminology

Quotation If the buyer is unable to obtain firm information concerning price and terms of business for a certain product, a **letter of inquiry** or **standard inquiry form** is despatched to the supplier, requesting a **quotation**.

Firm offer Made by a supplier who undertakes to supply goods at a certain price and under certain conditions. A **firm offer** is depatched to the buyer, who is expected to respond with an **order** within a short space of time.

Estimate Some goods and services, because of the nature of the work to be done, cannot be presented in catalogues or quoted in price-lists. To obtain a price, the buyer must ask a number of suppliers for an **estimate** for the work to be undertaken. These estimates are then compared and the most favourable one selected.

Tender Similar to an estimate; requested by local authorities and public bodies who want work of a specific nature carried out, eg, the demolition of a large public building. An advertisement is placed in the press inviting interested companies to submit **tenders** by a specified date.

Trade discount A buyer would expect to obtain a **trade discount** on the purchases made for the company. When making bulk purchases, it is assumed that the supplier will be prepared to scale up the amount of discount allowed in relation to the amount ordered, or in return for prompt payment.

Order form When the decision to purchase has been made, the **order** is made out and signed by an executive authorized to commit the company to pay for the goods.

Relationship between purchasing and stock control function

In Block 6, you were introduced to the method of calculating the **reorder point** for a particular item of stock. It was pointed out that there are three key levels of stock: maximum, minimum safe working and zero. These are shown in the 'Saw tooth diagram'.

Maximum stock represents the largest amount that the organization wishes to hold. **Minimum safe working stock** incorporates a **buffer stock** over and above the amount needed to cover the period between ordering and replenishment of stock, plus any calculated amount to cover a delay in delivery or any unscheduled increase in demand.

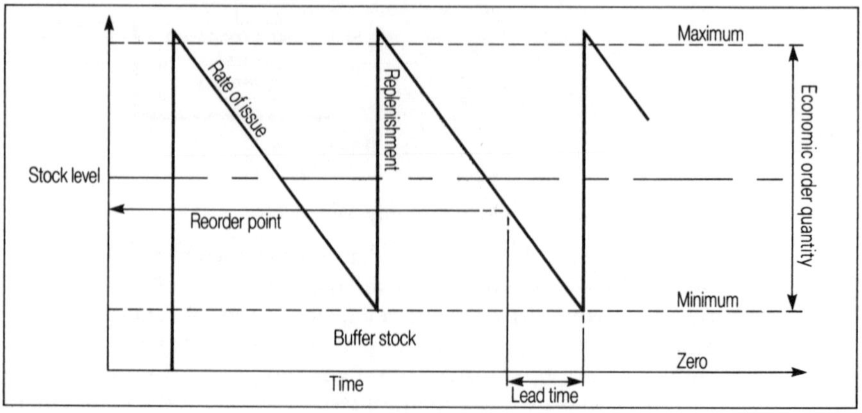

Saw tooth diagram.

Purchasing stock incurs a cost to the organization which the purchasing function will wish to keep as low as possible. These costs depend upon size, the type of materials held and fluctuations in demand. However, the following represent the costs incurred by the majority of organizations:

Cost of obtaining stock
a loss of interest on money spent on stock;
b interest paid on loans to purchase stock;
c administration costs related to the purchase of stock;
d transportation and delivery costs.

Cost of holding stock
a rent, lighting, heating of floor space taken up;
b insurance on valuation of stock;
c wages of stores personnel;
d administration costs related to stock control;
e loss or deterioration of stock.

The cost of obtaining stock may be reduced by purchasing strategies such as bulk purchase or by taking advantage of a fall in price. These advantages may be off-set by the additional cost of holding more stock than is required to meet current demand. Stock purchasing is at its most economic when a balance can be struck between the **cost of purchasing** and the **cost of holding stock.** The graph 'Economic order quantity' illustrates this relationship.

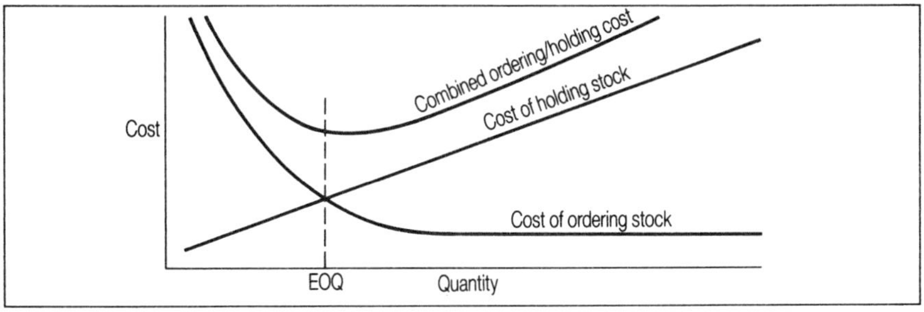

Economic order quantity.

Calculating the economic order quantity

Cost of ordering $\frac{AP}{Q}$ per annum

Where: A = annual expected demand
P = provisioning costs
Q = quantity required each year

Cost of holding $\frac{QIC}{2}$

Where: Q = quantity required each year
I = inventory holding percentage (about 15% to 20%)
C = cost per unit of stock

The cost of holding any item of stock for one year is the sum of the ordering and holding costs.

Lowest combined cost occurs when the cost of ordering equals the cost of holding:

$$\textbf{When } \frac{AP}{Q} = \frac{QIC}{2} \textbf{ or } Q = \sqrt{\frac{2AP}{IC}}$$

Activity 4

The design office and the mail room of a publishing firm were both re-equipped with chairs only last April but already problems are arising:

1 The head of design, Marianne Wills, has a tweed-covered swivel chair which has a longitudinal split in the upholstery of the seat.
2 The receptionist, Carol Baxter, has a swivel typing chair on wheels. The back-rest has collapsed because the thread on the support pin has flattened. She keeps complaining of backache.

Mr Alvin Cuerden, the purchasing manager, intends to complain and asks you to get out the file. You discover that the supplier was Universal Office Equipment, of 12 Sandstock Way, Utkinton UT6 2AB; that Mrs Wills's chair was coded VB 236 and cost £235; and that Carol's typing chair was coded ST 198 and cost £120.

Write a letter of complaint to Universal Office Equipment for Mr Cuerden's signature, stating what you bought and describing the faults. Say that you consider the goods to be unsatisfactory and ask for replacements.

The role of the buyer

Individual buyers in a large organization are responsible to the purchasing Manager for the following:

1 Seeking the most reliable source of raw materials and services. This involves continuous study of the commodity markets to keep informed of the current market prices, trends and delivery times.
2 Researching alternative materials to those already in use which might improve production methods or costs. Obtaining instructions and samples for testing.
3 Standardizing materials and equipment used where this would be an advantage to the organization in terms of cost saving or reduction of stock holding.
4 Developing goodwill between the company and its suppliers' representatives, in order to ensure continuity of supply and to gather purchasing information.
5 Keeping in touch with the organization's stock control situation in order to take advantage of any situation which brings about a buyer's market.
6 Negotiating the best deal when a situation arises which produces a seller's market in order to maintain supplies.
7 Selecting suppliers who will maintain continuity of supply consistent with required quality standards.
8 Raising inquiries and collating the quotations that result in order to select the best source of supply.
9 Progressing and following up the orders placed with the supplier, as laid down within the organization's purchasing policy.
10 Liaising with production and technical management to co-ordinate the buying policy and procedures with all other activities related to company policy.

In fulfilling this role the buyer must be aware that the lowest price may not be a bargain. A low purchase price may have to be paid for by higher scrap rates in production or poor performance of the product. A supplier who undercuts the market in order to gain business may not survive to become a reliable source of supply.

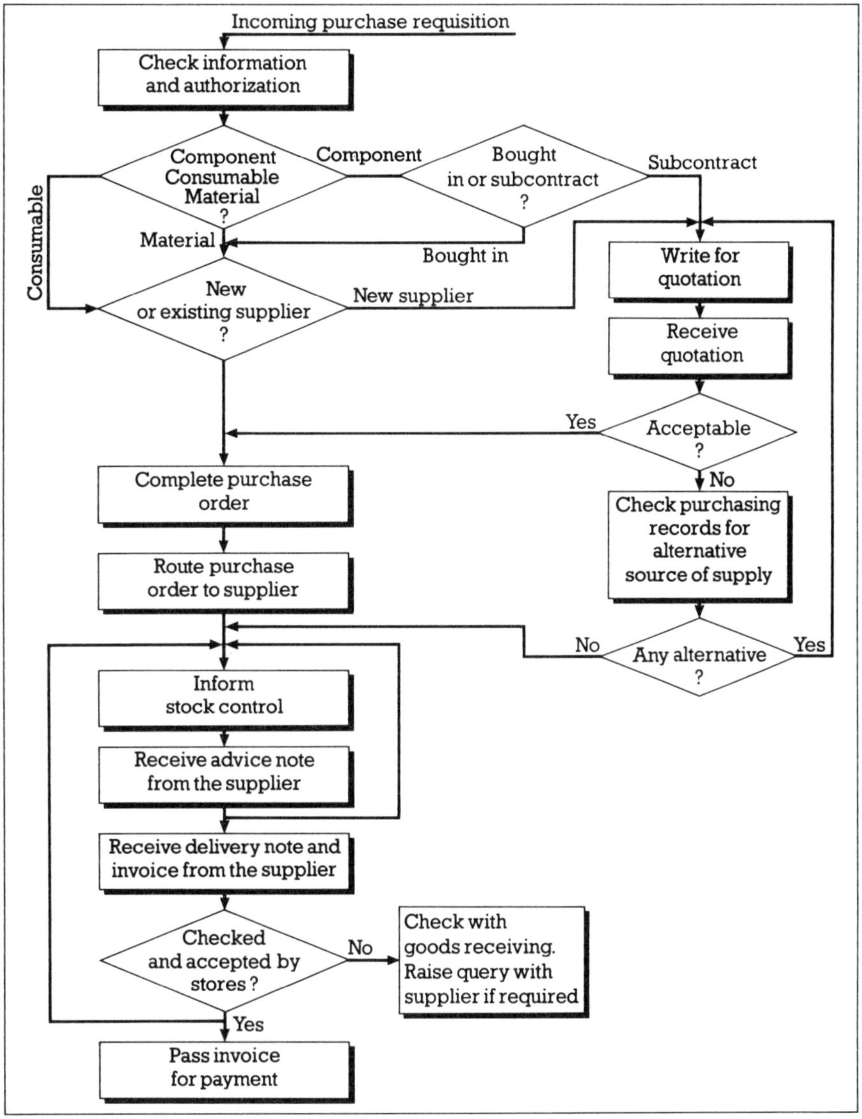

Purchasing routine.

The order form

This document commits the organization to payment for goods and/or services. It must be authorized by someone who has the responsibility for purchasing and is accountable for the money spent.

Order forms should contain the following information:

1 The name and address of the purchasing company.
2 The name and address of the supplying company.
3 Any reference which has to be quoted on documents and correspondence.
4 The price of the goods, including any trade discount and VAT.
5 The quantity ordered and a correct description of the goods.
6 Agreed terms of payment, including any allowance made for early payment.
7 Instructions for delivery: own or contract carrier; carriage paid (by supplier); carriage forward (paid by the purchaser).
8 Authorizing signature.

Activity 5

1 A company receives the following invoice from a supplier:

ABC General Suppliers plc

INVOICE

To:
Plastex Formers Plc
Eastern Road
Hightown Trading Estate
Berkshire

Date:
19th October 19..

Quantity	Material	Price (£)
100 bags. 50 kilo/bag.	Gunge (Grade A).	200.00
10 Pallets. 500 kilo/pallet.	Stixit. B/29.	400.50
	Total	600.50
	VAT (15%)	90.08
		690.58
	Discount (10%)	69.06
	Amount due	621.52

Terms: Discount. 10% in 14 days. 7.5% in 28 days. 5% in 90 days.

a Describe the checks that should be made on receipt of this invoice.
b Suggest a clerical routine which would ensure that the supplier is paid.
c Assuming that the company receives the above quantity of goods every two weeks, calculate the savings to be made over the trading year by prompt payment of the account.

2 The purchasing manager has received three rejection notes from the goods inwards inspection, for deliveries of Gunge from ABC General Suppliers over the past three weeks.

As a buyer in the purchasing department, you see an article in a trade magazine in which a new supplier in the field claims to have developed a new and improved product which will replace Gunge. Draft a letter requesting information.

Following receipt of your letter, the new supplier sends you a price-list which indicates a 15 per cent price advantage for bulk purchases. List the factors which should be taken into consideration before deciding to change to the new source of supply.

3 A letter of complaint has been received from the company supplying the bulk of the consumable goods used by your company. The letter claims that payment is outstanding on a statement submitted four months previous to the date of the letter. The sum involved is £15 000.
a State the procedure which should be followed to deal with this matter.
b Draft a reply to the supplier.
c Identify some of the problems which could arise if this situation is not dealt with promptly.

Activity 6

Extruded Plastic Tube Ltd are about to purchase a microcomputer to process all their accounts data and calculate wages and salaries.

Describe the purchasing activities required to ensure that the most appropriate hardware and software are supplied.

Documentation – receiving goods

Invoice Despatched to the purchaser when the goods have been sent. This document details the quantity despatched and the price, with details of any discounts allowed.

Advice note Required when the supplier does not make regular deliveries. On despatching the goods, the supplier informs the customer of the amount despatched and the form of transport being used. If the goods fail to arrive at the stipulated time, the supplier can make a claim against the transporting organization. The advice note may include the term E & OE (errors and omissions excepted), indicating the seller's right to correct any error or omission on the invoice.

Delivery note Many business organizations deliver goods by using their own transport fleet. A delivery note and duplicate are made out to send with the goods. The driver of the vehicle hands the purchaser the delivery note and obtains a signature to verify delivery. The purchaser retains the duplicate copy; the original copy is kept in the supplier's filing system.

Consignment note Some goods are delivered by an independent public carrier outside the control of the business. The supplier makes out a consignment note with a duplicate. The top copy is passed to the driver of the vehicle when the goods are collected; the duplicate copy is kept by the supplier. The carriers will make out their own delivery note to record that the delivery has been made.

Goods received note Goods delivered to the organization should be checked for quantity and damage. This check is carried out in the goods inwards section. The person checking makes out a goods received note indicating the name of the supplier, the date of delivery and the amount received, and giving a description of the goods. Goods received notes are attached to copies of the delivery note and the advice note before being routed to the purchasing office.

Debit/credit note A debit note is used when the customer has been undercharged for the goods delivered. A credit note is the reverse, being a recognition on the part of the seller that they have overcharged on the invoice. Debit/credit notes are a means of correcting errors arising in invoicing.

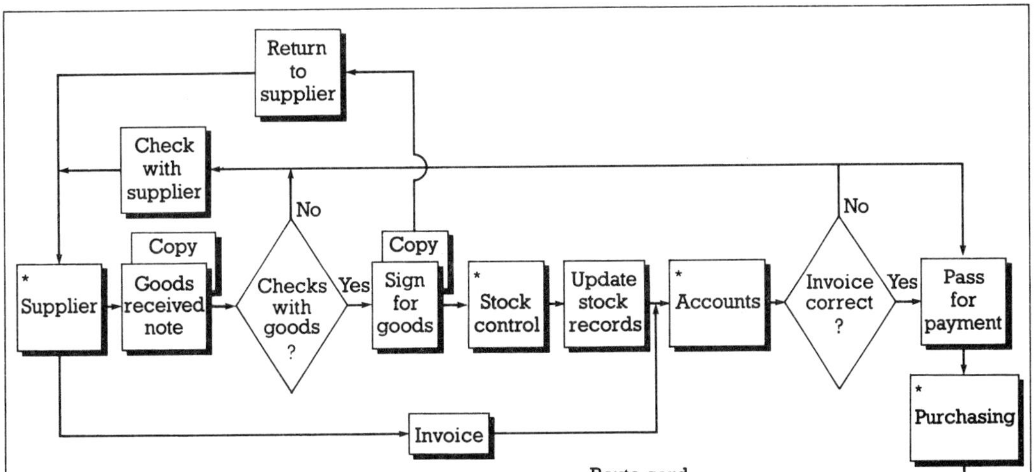

Routine – receiving raw material
1 Date stamp and number GRN in goods inwards
2 Make out route card
3 Attach route card to GRN
4 Place GRN in internal mail for stock control

Route card

Invoice No. 479		
Route to:	Rec	Date
Stock control		
Accounts		
Purchasing		

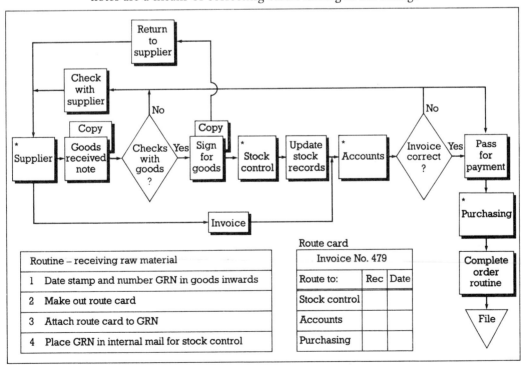

Receiving goods.

Speaking in business

Even in an electronic world, well over half the communication at work is carried out by the spoken word, whether face-to-face in conversations, group discussions or meetings, or over the telephone. The speed and flexibility of verbal exchanges makes many people choose them in preference to the written word whenever the situation is delicate, tricky or obscure. The possibilities of adjusting what you are saying in the light of its reception by the hearer are infinitely greater than when written messages are passed, and the speed at which adjustments can be made greatly surpasses anything a computer can offer.

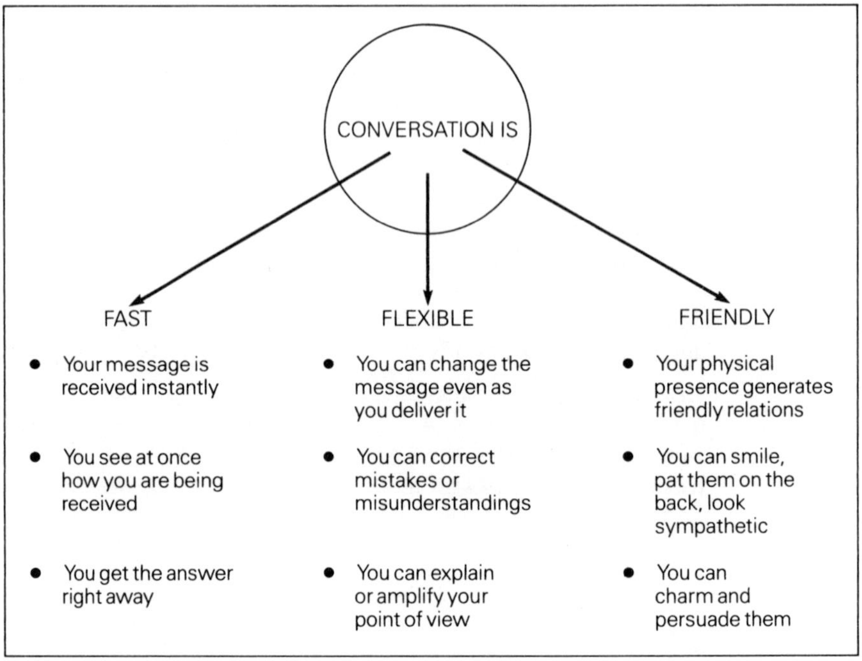

Face-to-face communication

All communication is at least a two-way process. It will involve you in continual switches from being a message sender to being a message receiver.

Getting the message

Unless you are sensitive to the messages coming in to you, you will not be able to make the appropriate responses or to adjust what you are saying to meet the minute-by-minute changes in the climate of your conversation. Many people use the period during which someone else is taking their turn at talking to get their breath back for another onslaught on the person they are talking to rather than to tune in to the atmosphere and temperature of the exchange. The most valuable benefits of a face-to-face exchange are totally lost if you do that. You need to listen actively and sensitively to the words being spoken, and to be receptive to the non-verbal signals in the facial expression, eye movements and gestures of the person who is addressing you. In framing a judgement of what the combination of signals means you learn what your response should be in order to achieve your objectives – or perhaps realize that a quick modification of the objective is called for.

- Give the speaker your total attention
- If possible, move to a position where you can see as well as hear
- Try to reach behind the person's appearance and attend to the words being spoken
- Try to discount accent, grammar and pronunciation
- Get beyond your prejudices and listen to the heart of the message
- Be prepared to adjust your thinking and your intentions, to some extent at least, in the light of what you hear

A checklist of listening skills.

Getting the message over

You will need a certain level of technical competence in speech if you want to be understood. You must at least be audible. Though only the very shy may have difficulty in making themselves heard in a two-handed conversation, most people have to pay some attention to the problem when talking in a group and in a large room.

Audibility Suppose that you play the violin. If you were asked to get up in front of your whole firm and play the instrument, you might feel nervous – but the fiddle wouldn't. When you get up to talk to a room full of people, you are the instrument and this instrument feels nervous. Your breathing may become shallow, your throat constricts, your shoulders hunch and your mouth goes dry. Is it any wonder that you have difficulty in speaking?

Good posture Do not let embarrassment cause you to keep your head lowered so that you are muttering into your chest. You will simply become more embarrassed by the poor performance you hear yourself giving. You need to hold your head up and let your voice float out across the room. Try to stand upright with your weight on both feet so that your chest cavity can get enough air in it to project your voice across the space.

Acoustics The size of the room will largely dictate how many decibels you should generate. Remember that it is almost as bad to shout at your audience as it is to speak so quietly that they cannot hear properly. In either case the audience will switch off in self-defence. If the room has many hard surfaces, you will hear your voice bouncing off them. If the room is well upholstered, carpeted and curtained, your voice will be absorbed by the furnishings. You need to listen to yourself and adjust your volume as appropriate. You may also need to check the clarity of your diction and get rid of woolliness by articulating more carefully.

Accent and dialect Regional accents and dialect are usually acceptable, or at any rate understood, in the region to which they belong. Even so, it may be unwise in some settings to speak with a heavy regional accent if you wish to get a sympathetic hearing.

Outside your region, a regional accent may be something of a handicap, either because it is hard to understand or because of snobbish attitudes. Rightly or wrongly, there is something that constitutes standard or accepted speech; if you ignore this fact you may be conveying more about your loyalty to your region than about the matter in hand. Remember too that there may be a penalty for getting the usage mixed up. Communicators who move freely between speech communities pride themselves on their ability to speak appropriately whatever company they find themselves in.

Pronunciation Pronunciation is rather different from accent and dialect. Accent and dialect are regional variations and may include changes in grammar and vocabulary as well as a particular set of sounds. Pronunciation is a matter of speaking distinctly and conforming with the accepted rules in stressing or emphasizing particular syllables. Whilst slurred speech can never be acceptable, there is controversy about how to pronounce certain words – 'controversy' is one of them – though there is general agreement about 99% of the words in the English language. If you insist on pronouncing 'comment', for instance, with the accent on the second syllable you will be widely regarded as being uneducated, however well educated you may be. And with some words, the meaning actually changes according to the syllable stressed – as in 'convict'.

Delivery No matter how interesting the information you have to convey is, you will rapidly bore your listeners if your delivery is flat. You need to vary the pitch and pace to enliven your delivery and to allow you to draw attention to important sections of your discourse. Pitch is a matter of the rise and fall of your voice, and pace is the speed of speaking – including pauses. A pause is a difficult thing to learn to use; a long pause calls for considerable nerve on the part of a speaker and much sensitivity to the response of the audience. When used expertly, it is very effective in calling attention to key concepts in your exposition.

- Speak clearly and sufficiently loudly
- Give your vocal equipment a chance by trying to relax your muscles
- Adjust your voice to the acoustics of the room
- Use a neutral accent
- Check the pronunciation of words
- Vary the pace and pitch of your delivery

A checklist of speaking skills.

Persuasion

Whether by the spoken or the written word, great efforts are made in business to persuade decision makers and others to follow a particular line of action. Fortunes have been made by offering courses which claim to teach people how to influence others and gain their trust.

The head versus the heart

When you yourself are doing the persuading, you can choose to convince by the sheer logic of your argument, or you can choose a more oblique approach via the feelings, emotions and even the prejudices of your audience.

Sharp practice?

It is quite legitimate to work with the attitudes and expectations of your audience firmly in mind. It is less respectable to use these attitudes to manipulate them into agreeing with you or your policy. We are moving into the field of business morals or ethics here: the dividing line between what is acceptable and what is sharp practice can be a fine one.

Can you believe it?

Few people make a formal study of logic at school, but the climate of the times encourages a sceptical attitude. We have in general been taught to be questioning rather than accepting, especially in matters of advertising and economics.

Does it follow?

In business we must assess carefully whether the conclusions drawn really do follow from the information on which they are based, or whether they are coloured by self-interest, cynicism or even ignorance. We also have to recognize that our own thinking may not always be absolutely rational and objective and that we can delude ourselves as well as be deluded by others.

Does it add up?

Even with something as seemingly concrete as numerical information, the information can be skewed – perhaps literally – by an inaccurately drawn graph with misleading scales, or by the exclusion of figures which would point to a different conclusion.

> Once we are on the look-out for this difference between 'objective' and 'emotional' meanings, we shall notice that words which carry more or less strong suggestions of emotional attitudes are very common and are ordinarily used in the discussion of such controversial questions as those of politics, morals, and religion. This is one reason why such controversies cannot be settled.
> There is a well-known saying that the word 'firm' can be declined as follows: I am *firm*, thou art *obstinate*, he is *pig-headed*. That is a simple illustration of what is meant. 'Firm', 'obstinate', and 'pig-headed' all have the same objective meaning – that is, following one's own course of action and refusing to be influenced by other people's opinions. They have, however, different emotional meanings; 'firm' has an emotional meaning of strong approval, 'obstinate' of mild disapproval, 'pig-headed' of strong disapproval.
>
> Extract from *Straight and Crooked Thinking*, by R.H. Thouless, 1930

Objectivity versus emotion.

Activity 7

The words on the left are approving; those on the right are disapproving. Find words to fill in the gaps.

	Approval	Disapproval
	determined	ruthless
1	vigorous	...
2	...	subversive
3	boyish	...
4	...	fickle
5	ask	...
6	...	antiquated
7	smell	...
8	...	exorbitant
9	loud	...
10	...	premature

Non-verbal communication

Nothing gives away a person's true thoughts and feelings as much as non-verbal signals – also known as body language. People may give information in words, but at the same time they give off further information in their gestures and facial expression and the way they move about. In both verbal and non-verbal communication people may falsify the information by deceit or feigning, but the observer may be alerted to this by discrepancies between the verbal and the non-verbal signals; invariably, more weight is given in such situations to the non-verbal ones.

Other factors are also involved. Stance gives a strong indication of feelings, as does physical position relative to the person addressed. Actual physical contact also tells us something; a forefinger prodding your chest conveys a quite different message from an elbow digging you in the ribs.

Your capacity to interpret these signals, and to tailor your discourse accordingly, is a prime factor in successful face-to-face communication. You probably learnt this skill early in your childhood, though you may remember occasions when you failed to 'read' the parental mood, with unfortunate results. Women are often considered to be superior interpreters of body language – what is known as woman's intuition almost certainly relies on sensitivity to unspoken signals – and perhaps their need to interpret such signals in their infants sharpens this faculty. In a business context, this capacity may make a woman an excellent negotiator.

If you are already in work you will have many opportunities of observing signals, both intentional and unintentional, passing between colleagues. A capacity to interpret signals from customers or clients will enable you to time and pitch your responses to the best advantage.

You need to bear in mind that you give off non-verbal signals yourself and that the person you are speaking to will take these into account along with the message carried by your words. Awareness of this accounts for some people's preference for using the telephone on occasions when they want to hide their motives or otherwise mislead someone.

TO GET ON GOOD TERMS	
DO	DON'T
• Look at the person you are talking to for at least 60 per cent of the time	• Refuse to meet their eye
• Smile at them	• Use a cold and forbidding facial expression
• Have open palms and open-arm positions	• Clench your fists and cross your arms defensively
• Use their name early in the exchange	• Refuse to address them by name
• Show you are following their discourse by giving little nods and supportive noises	• Either interrupt or listen in cold silence
• Be polite if you have to disagree – and say why	• Resort to personal remarks if you disagree
• Own up if you are in the wrong	• Decline to admit to any mistakes
• Touch them lightly if it is possible	• Stay remote and decline the slightest contact

Body language checklist.

Activity 8

If you were able to make a video film of the consensus discussion you had in Activity 24 of Block 3, run it again now.

Make notes on the body language of each person in the film, then as a group discuss your findings.

Discussion

Discussion requires a certain amount of give and take. You must be prepared to listen to the others and to take your turn. If everyone is very voluble, jot down the point you want to make and revert to it when you get a chance to speak. If you don't note it, you are likely to forget it. Arrange your thoughts in your head in a sequence the others will be able to follow, and speak as persuasively as you can. The idea is to convince them that your point of view is right – not to devastate them with sarcasm or abuse. If you are not sensitive to other people's feelings, they will be inhibited from expressing their views and the discussion will be strangled.

The size of the group and the seating arrangements can play a vital role in discussion. Generally speaking, the larger the group the less likely people are to open up. If the subject matter for discussion is not personal, people may be prepared to speak but unable to get a word in. You can have a chairman to give everyone a chance, but that turns it into a meeting – which is somewhat different from a discussion.

If the seating arrangements prevent you from seeing each other's faces, which is likely if the group is large, you are prevented from picking up little visual clues about how people are feeling or how they are receiving you. The smiles, the frowns, the downcast eyes, the pursed lips – all give you valuable information which may be contrary to the message being conveyed in words. It is indications such as these which enable you to adjust your discourse to your audience, and the audience is the major consideration in any kind of communication.

Activity 9

EPTL runs three separate dining-rooms: the works canteen for weekly paid staff, the staff dining-room for the office staff (who are salaried) and the executive refectory for the senior staff.

You have been in the canteen, which is clean but spartan, very noisy, overcrowded and full of smoke. You usually have your lunch in the staff dining-room and have found it adequate. It has self-service, pleasant decor and edible food, but there is often a very long queue so you don't get much time to eat. You have not been in the executive refectory but, like everyone else, you have had a look through the double-glazed windows and can see that it is very comfortable, with carpeted floor, white tablecloths, waitress service, plenty of space and exotic plants.

The eating arrangements at EPTL are typical of many systems of privileges for staff as they move up the ladder. Sometimes even the office furnishings reflect the status of the occupant, eg, no carpet for junior clerks, a runner 1m long for section supervisors and wall-to-wall carpet for the directors.

Discuss as a group what you think of systems of privileges such as these.

Activity 10

MEMO

TO:	Mr J. Sharpe	DATE:	3 October 19..
FROM:	Keith Saville Premises Department	SUBJECT:	Alterations to Works Canteen

We shall be starting repairs to the floor of the Works Canteen on Tuesday next, and would like the Canteen vacated for three days. The kitchen will not be affected.

K.S.

When he gets the above memo, Mr Sharpe asks you to:

1 Write a memo to Mrs Thomas, the canteen supervisor, telling her what is happening. Meals will have to be served in the staff dining-room during the repairs. Tell her that the chairs and tables will be moved out by the premises department after 4 pm on Monday. She will not be best pleased at the news, so strike an amiable and helpful note.
2 Then write a memo to Keith Saville asking for a crew to move the tables and chairs out of the canteen on Monday after 4 pm and back again on Friday afternoon.
3 Next design a poster to go on the door of the canteen on Monday, informing users that meals will be in the staff dining-room for the rest of the week. Tell them where it is, in case they don't know.

Speaking in public

Addressing a large meeting calls for careful preparation, cool nerves and sensitivity to enable you to take full account of the reception your audience is giving you. Later on, we look at technical aspects of voicing a hall, and visual aids.

Never read to them

On no account read your speech: not only will you present the crown of your head – a poor substitute for your face – to your audience but your delivery will be boring and lifeless and you will look extremely amateur. Know your material inside out and then write a sequence of topic headings in capital letters on half a postcard and use that to keep you on course.

Rehearse it

Your talk must appear fresh and impromptu. You will only achieve this by rehearsing beforehand, preferably in front of a full-length mirror. Time your speech so that you have enough material to keep you going but not so much that you have to make cuts whilst you are speaking in order to finish in the allotted time. Watch yourself for mannerisms, both visual and verbal – though they will probably not appear until you are actually performing and under pressure.

Look at them

You will hold your audience's attention best if you look around the room, picking up eyes. Do not transfix one unfortunate listener; allow your gaze to travel freely around. If you cannot bear to do this, you can give an impression of it by letting your eye roam across the back wall just above their heads.

Transfixed!

What style?

Your style should be adjusted to suit the situation and the audience. You may be out to persuade them, shock them, motivate them or amuse them – or to achieve any combination of those aims – and you will need to select your material, vocabulary and presentation accordingly.

The shape of the talk

You must say something interesting to begin with or you will never get your listeners' attention. Limit the number of points you want to make and don't be afraid of repeating yourself, using variations or anecdotes that illustrate your theme. Speech is ephemeral. If a point is missed or misunderstood the audience has no way of recapturing it, so don't cover the ground too fast or go into minute detail.

Happy endings

The ending should be pithy and delivered with enthusiasm and gusto. Never let your voice tail away at this point. According to circumstances, you can finish with a climax or punchline or summarize (very briefly) what you have said before so that the whole train of thought is left fresh in their minds.

It may be worthwhile having your last sentence prepared word for word in your head. Nothing is more dampening than to have a speaker finish with a muttered 'Yes – well, that's it really.'

- Make sure you know what topics you should cover
- Find out what sort of people you will be talking to
- Get all the information together
- Decide on the shape or sequence of your talk
- Prepare brief headings on a card as an *aide-mémoire*
- Decide if you need any visual aids
- Rehearse your talk in front of a long mirror
- Watch out for distracting mannerisms
- Decide what to wear
- Get there in time to check that necessary preparations have been made

Preparing a speech or talk.

Audio-visual aids

Various aids can be used to enliven or illustrate what you are saying, provided that the venue has the technical facilities needed.

You must be slick in operating these aids. Nothing damages your credibility as much as having to struggle with machinery in front of an audience.

Blackboards, whiteboards and flipboards

You may need to practise writing in a vertical plane if you want to use boards. It takes experience to write legibly on a wall or spell accurately, as many graffiti bear witness.

Overhead projectors

This lecturing aid allows you to write on a transparency on a flat, illuminated surface and have what you are writing projected onto a vertical screen. Alternatively, you can prepare transparencies ahead of time, for instance by photocopying onto them.

Slide, sound and slide/sound

Photographic slides to illustrate your speech can be projected onto a screen. If your slides are slotted into a circular carousel you can have a remote control which allows you to stand in front of the audience, and you can use a light-pen as a pointer. You need to check your carousel right through as a missing or upside-down slide can put you off your stroke.

You can play sound cassettes if there is good amplification. Your slide projector could be coupled with a sound cassette which plays a synchronized pre-recorded tape.

Video

Video cassettes can be useful if you have a giant TV screen that everyone can see. Make sure the tape and the video system match.

Film

If you use a film projector, a screen and a relevant film, you are perhaps commenting on a film rather than making a speech. Films tend to be costly to hire or buy and need careful checking for faults or breaks.

Oral reports

Reporting to a senior

In Block 2 we considered how to make a written report. When reporting orally you will not actually use the expressions **terms of reference**, **procedure** etc, but you should give the appropriate information in the right order.

Much reporting is done orally – sometimes backed up by a confirmatory memo or minute – and the oral report calls for skill in face-to-face communication. You should try to present an acceptable appearance; if you do not your report may be discounted for reasons totally unconnected with its content. What is acceptable will, of course, vary and there may be no way of overcoming prejudice in some situations. You can, however, choose a tone of voice which is pleasing to a listener and a style of delivery which will hold his or her attention. Using a brisk voice, be prepared to catch your listener's eye, look interested yourself and watch his or her face to see if you are holding his or her interest. Know your material and be prepared to develop a dialogue, especially in one-to-one reporting.

Reporting to a small group

You may be required to carry out some investigation and report to a meeting of your section or department. This is a somewhat different communication situation. You may feel it is necessary to prepare fairly full notes to work from. You will almost certainly find it awkward to be addressing several people with identifiable opinions – often opposing ones – at the same time. Aim for as informal a tone as you feel you can get away with; this will allow you to deal with each person as an individual, varying your approach according to the signals of agreement or disagreement you receive.

Addressing committee meetings

Organizations often have a committee structure which generates or supports their policy decisions, and junior managers can find themselves representing their section at such meetings. In addition, various trade union, management/staff and social committees may offer you an opportunity to learn committee skills – an opportunity worth taking.

Say something If you become a committee member, you must be prepared to contribute something to the deliberations. Occasionally, a junior manager is so modest and retiring, or so overawed, that he or she sits in silence through meeting after meeting. This is neither helpful nor impressive.

Address the chair A committee has a chairman or chairwoman and you should address your remarks to the chair. Signal that you wish to speak by catching their eye or raising a hand, and wait to speak until they nod at you or call your name to indicate that it is your turn.

Keep calm People can become unbelievably heated in committee, but however strong your feelings are you should never become abusive or argue across the table. The chairman is there to keep things in order. A good chairman will insist on polite usage and will allow all factions to air their views in turn.

Keep alert For a busy committee meeting with a long agenda, you will probably be sent quite a lot of paper in support of the business to be transacted. Such documents are notorious for vanishing from view during the meeting and whilst you are searching for them the committee may move onto the next item. Be alert to the discussion, therefore, even whilst you are engaged with the documents. Backtracking on items already dealt with or entirely missing the item you were sent by your colleagues to discuss will be embarrassing for you and make a very poor impression.

Make yourself heard It is essential that you are audible in committee. Committees reach their decisions by voting and you will never win votes if the members cannot hear your point of view. Many of the skills you can use in public speaking are denied you in committee – time is very limited, the audience is impatient, you are speaking impromptu – but clarity and audibility are available and essential.

Keeping track of the situation.

Don't be bullied Junior members of a committee are sometimes bullied by a more senior and powerful member. If this happens to you, you should ask the chairman to ask that member to stop bullying you. Occasionally the chairman himself will bully you, and you should not stand for this either. The formal structure of a committee makes it possible for you to say, 'I must ask the Chairman to cease bullying me.' You will almost certainly have the sympathy and support of every other committee member.

Learn the rules If you are going to do much committee work you should make yourself familiar with committee procedure by reading books on the subject. In all but the most informal committees, procedure is a minefield. You will never speak effectively if you are having to concentrate on where you are putting your feet.

The problem	You say	What happens
The speaker is being irrelevant, has run over his allotted time or is committing a similar irregularity.	'On a point of order, Mr Chairman ...', then state the problem.	The speaker is interrupted, your point of order is discussed and the chairman gives his decision.
The discussion on a motion has gone on too long already.	'I move the closure.'	If 'the closure' is carried, the chairman must ask the mover to reply to the debate and then put the motion to the meeting. If 'the closure' is lost, the debate continues.
A decision in either direction would create embarrassment or – more commonly – you want to prevent a vote which could go against your interest.	'I move the previous question.'	If 'the previous question' is carried, the original motion is abandoned and the meeting moves on. If it is lost, the mover must reply to the debate and the motion is put.
There is too much trivial discussion and time is being wasted.	'I move next business.'	If 'next business' is carried the motion is abandoned and the meeting moves on. If lost, the discussion on the original motion can continue.
The meeting has lasted too long. You need either a break or to go home.	'I move the meeting stand adjourned ... [for x minutes if you only want a break].'	If 'the adjournment' is carried, the meeting is automatically adjourned for x minutes or is terminated. If 'the adjournment' is lost, the meeting continues.

Let's get on with it.

Committee meetings - secretary's duties

If you become the secretary of a committee, you will be responsible for the efficient running of its business. The chairman will conduct the actual meeting but it will be up to you to see that the members are called to it and given the appropriate documents. The chairman will probably rely heavily on you to keep him on the right lines, know the latest position on everything and keep in mind what the earlier decisions of the committee have been.

"Sir Gawain said he was sorry he had slain the woman. Sir Bors then proposed a resolution opposing the slaying of women, which was passed. A very large knight rode in and challenged the entire company; this was tabled for a twelvemonth. There being no further business, we adjourned."

The Round Table.

Procedure **Command meetings** are not group decision-making bodies. The decisions are made by the manager who called those in his command together to air their views and or hear his. He will make his own procedural rules.
Committee meetings usually arrive at group decisions by vote or group consensus. Members are expected to abide by these decisions thereafter. Committee procedure is broadly the same everywhere but the details and the degree of formality vary.
Councils have their procedure laid down by Act of Parliament and standing orders.
Companies' procedure is regulated by the memorandum and articles of association, which are required by company law.
Social and voluntary clubs have procedures defined in the constitution drawn up when the club was formed.

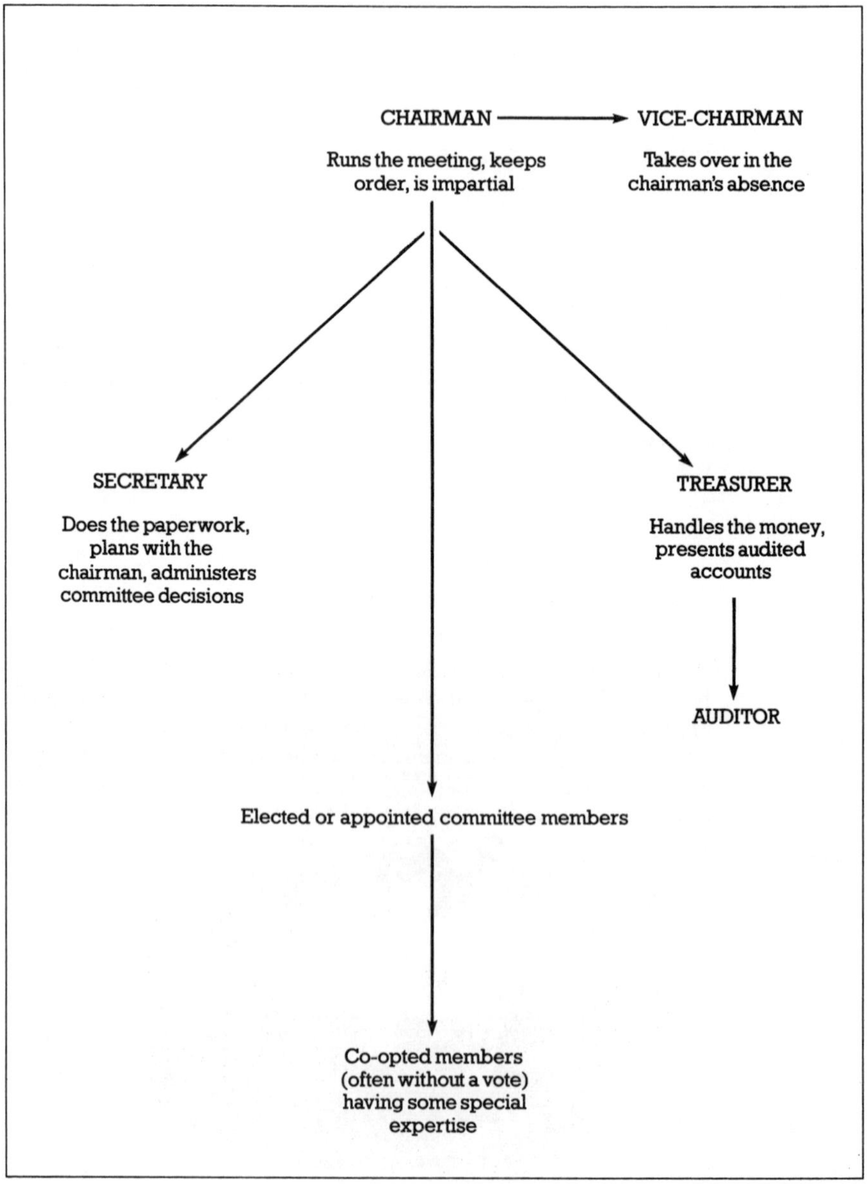

Committee personnel.

NOTICE OF MEETING

Every member must be given notice that a meeting is to be held. The standing orders or constitution will lay down how much notice should be given – often twenty-one days.

SOCIETY OF DENTAL PRACTITIONERS - S E REGION
Tolpuddle Chambers, Lawkland RC3 2LS

187 November 19 _ _

Dear ...

The next meeting of the society will be held in room 14, Tolpuddle Chambers, on 30 November 19 _ _ at 20.00 hours.

I attach a copy of the agenda and look forward to seeing you

Yours sincerely

Margaret Owen (Mrs)
Secretary

AGENDA

The agenda is a list of items to be discussed at the meeting and is usually drawn up by the secretary in consultation with the chairman. The agenda should be circulated to the members along with the **notice of meeting** so that they have time to think about the topics to be discussed.

AGENDA

1 Apologies for absence.

2 Minutes of last meeting.

3 Matters arising.

4 Easter conference.

5 Change in membership rules:
Proposal: The students in their final year should be allowed Associate Membership.
Proposed: J.G. Ware.
Seconded: K. Abernethy.

6 Any other business.

7 Date of next meeting.

Chairman's agenda

A special version of the agenda will be provided for the chairman showing beside each item extra information, such as who is to speak to the item, reminders about previous developments etc.

CHAIRMAN'S AGENDA	NOTES
1 Apologies.	Mr Sangsster is unlikely to be back but he has left the details with Miss Deighton.
2 Minutes of last meeting.	
3 Matters arising.	Item (2) R.F. Fisher has accepted our invitation for the Christmas Celebration Supper Item (4) I have put the question of student members as a separate item below.
4 Easter Conference.	Mary Addleshaw has suggestions for a venue.
5 Change in membership rules. Proposal: That students in their final year should be allowed Associate Membership. Proposed: J G Ware. Seconded: K Abernethy.	The matter of the fee is not touched on by Col. Ware's proposal.
6 Any other business.	
7 Date of next meeting.	

Chairman's agenda

A special version of the agenda will be provided for the chairman showing beside each item extra information, such as who is to speak to the item, reminders about previous difficulties, latest developments etc.

Paperwork for committees.

Agenda items

The agenda format for a meeting will vary according to whether it is an annual general meeting, an extraordinary general meeting, a monthly committee meeting or an *ad hoc* meeting dealing with a one-off matter. For help in deciding on the format and degree of formality, refer to the files of your committee.

ST MARTIN'S CHURCH COUNCIL
meeting on 30 November 19__
AGENDA

1. Apologies for absence.
2. Minutes of the last meeting.
3. Matters arising.
4. Restoration fund.
5. New vestry.
   Proposal:
   That the new vestry be sited at the S.E. corner of the church.
   Proposed: Edward Waite.
   Seconded: Rosemary Pollard.
6. Any other business.
7. Date of next meeting.

Agenda items.

011 Grosvenor Museum

Curator's report (ENCLOSURE 'G')

ENCLOSURE H

012 Hoole Community Centre

(i) Progress report

(ii) Appointment of representatives - City Secretary & Solicitor to report.

013 Customer Service Programme - item included at the request of a member.

014 Grant Aid to Village Halls - City Secretary & Solicitor to report

015 Sports Council Campaign 'What's your Sport?' - City Secretary & Solicitor to report

016 Annual Review of Grants to Local Voluntary Bodies (Mins p. 37) - report of Treasurer

017 Chester Arts '87 - City Secretary & Solicitor to report

018 Exclusion of the Public and Press- To consider passing a resolution under Section 100(A)(4) of the Local Government Act 1972 (as amended by the Access to Information Act 1985) to exclude the public from the meeting for the remaining item on the agenda, because it is likely, in view of the nature of the business to be transacted, that if the public were present there would be disclosure to them of exempt information as described in paragraph 12 in Schedule 12A to the Act.

PART 2 - ITEMS TO BE DEALT WITH IN PRIVATE SESSION

019 Northgate Arena - Flooring - Director of Technical Services to report

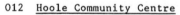

Part of county council agenda.

Drafting motions

For a large formal meeting, proposals will have been submitted in writing ahead of time, duly proposed and seconded.

In smaller meetings, a motion commonly arises out of discussion on the topic. You will have to get it on paper, suitably phrased, and expressed so unambiguously that there can be no doubt about what is being voted on.

Motions are introduced by the word 'that', eg:

'That this committee strongly objects to attempts by the Executive to limit its freedom of expression.'

Proposed: F. Smolenski
Seconded: B. Ducas.

(NB: If a motion is proposed from the chair, no seconder is needed.)

A **proposal** is submitted in writing prior to the meeting, duly signed by the proposer and seconder.

A **motion** is presented or drawn up at the meeting, and needs a proposer and seconder.

A **resolution** is the name given to a proposal or motion that is agreed upon.

Writing the minutes

As the meeting progressed, you will have made notes on the proceedings, noting the names of the proposers and seconders and recording the voting. Now you need to write up a coherent version.

The **minutes** of what took place constitute the written record of the decisions of your committee. They may be referred to in years to come and they must be implemented, unless they are changed by the committee itself. It follows that they must be accurate. They will be circulated or read out at the next committee meeting under the heading 'Minutes of the last meeting'.
When they have been agreed upon and signed by the chairman, they become a legally binding document which could be produced in a court of law.

Minute style The form the minutes take varies from committee to committee. For guidance look at the minute book for your committee. Some committees have **resolution minutes**, ie, only the resolutions are recorded. Other committees have **narrative minutes**, which include a summary of the discussion leading to the resolution (or to a consensus view or general agreement).

Minute styles.

```
                        RESOLUTION MINUTES
Resolved:  That the King's Assembly Rooms to be confirmed as
           the venue for the Easter Conference 19__.
```

```
                        NARRATIVE MINUTES
There was considerable discussion following Mrs Addleshaw's proposal
that the King's Assembly Rooms should be booked for the Easter
Conference 19__. Some members felt that the Palace Conference
Suite was more suitable as its facilities were more modern, whilst
others approved the King's Assembly Rooms for aesthetic reasons.

Mrs. Addleshaw proposed, Mr Peruzza seconded:
'That the King's Assembly Rooms be confirmed as the venue for
the Easter Conference 19__.

The motion was carried nem. con.
```

Minutes of the Association of Dental Practitioners
held on 30 November 19__ in Tolpuddle Chambers, Lawkland,
at 20.00 hours

Present: In the chair Mr Jake Prescott.
Mesdames Addleshaw, Deighton and Smith.
Messrs Abernethy, Ducas, Peruzza, Smolenski and Ware

1 Apologies were received from Miss Jane Pepper and Mr. K. Sangster.

2 Minutes of last meeting. The minutes of the last meeting were read and signed as a correct record.

3 Matters arising. Item 2. The Secretary reported that R.F. Fisher has accepted the invitation to speak at the Christmas Celebration Supper.

4 Easter conference
After some discussion of the relative merits of the King's Assembly Rooms and the Palace Conference Suite as a venue for the Easter conference:
RESOLVED That the King's Assembly Rooms be confirmed as the venue for the Easter conference 19__

5 Change in membership rules
The committee discussed ways of allowing students to join the Association before qualifying.
RESOLVED (1) that students in their final year should be allowed Associate Membership.
(2) that they should pay 60 per cent of the current membership fee.

6 Any other business
There was general agreement that room 14, Tolpuddle Chambers, was too small and the Secretary was asked to book the new committee room for the next meeting.

7 Date of next meeting
The next meeting of the Association was fixed for 17 January 19__ at 20.00 hours.

Signed as a correct record

________________ Date ________

Example of minutes.

Agenda	– a list of items to be discussed at a meeting
Apologies	– list of those who have notified that they cannot attend
AOB	– business raised without notice at the end of the meeting
Minutes	– written record of the proceedings at a meeting
Quorum	– minimum number who must be present for the resolutions of the meeting to be valid
In camera	– in private
Adjourned	– postponed to another occasion
Nominate	– to name a candidate for office/position
Ex officio	– by virtue of office (applied to members)
Co-opted member	– a person invited to attend the committee, not elected
Motion	– a proposal
Resolution	– a motion that has been passed
Amendment	– a proposal to change a motion
Proposer	– person putting forward a motion
Seconder	– another person who wishes the motion to be voted on
Pro	– in favour
Contra	– against
Abstention	– decision not to cast a vote
Carried	– result when more in favour than against
Unanimous	– result when everyone in agreement
Nem. con.	– nobody voted against

Meeting and conference terms.

Activity 11

Prepare a notice of meeting and an agenda for the next meeting of EPTL's management committee, which is to be held in Mr Southgate's office next Monday at 10.00 am. The managing director will take the chair.

Members have already asked for the following items to be discussed:
1 Mr B. Roberts (financial director): this period's budget.
2 Miss B. Milner (personnel): first aid post.
3 Mr Harry Balme (production): bonus scheme.
4 Mr John Hardy (marketing): promotion competition for agricultural tubing.

Divide into groups to form the management committee, composed of the five people mentioned, a secretary and any others you think appropriate, and work through the agenda.
1 The managing director must control the proceedings.
2 The secretary must take the minutes and write them up.
3 The financial director should present a period budget based on the information in the budgetary control statement in Block 9 (see Activity 9), but with a budget of £8300.
4 Personnel should use information in a report from the joint consultative committee referred to in Block 8.
5 Production should propose a scheme to increase productivity amongst hourly paid workers (see wage rates in Activity 1 of Block 9).
6 Marketing should present six competitions designed by the class to promote the agricultural tubing and the committee should select the best one. (See page 147.)

Activity 12

Write the minutes following a meeting of Wicklow Parish Council in the Parish Hall on 1 June at 8.00 pm. Mr J. Jackson was in the chair and there were fifteen members present. Apologies were received from Miss Barnet and Colonel Martlew. The secretary had been in correspondence with County Hall about the bad state of the High Street. The treasurer reported a balance of £306 and that there were outstanding bills for £22.50. A motion that the village should enter for the best-kept village competition was proposed by Mrs Benson, seconded by Mr Parfitt and carried unanimously. A motion that the parish join with the neighbouring parish of Morton to hold a fete on the village green at Morton on 1 August was proposed by Mr Smith, seconded by Mr Todd and carried, 13 pro and 2 contra. Mrs Halstead volunteered to organize the refreshments for this event. During AOB, Mr Griffiths made an impassioned protest against the boys revving up their motor cycles outside the hall on Saturday nights and the secretary was asked to write to Mr Lloyd, the Youth Club leader. The next meeting was fixed for 4 July at 8.00 pm.

Summary

In this Block we have looked at the function of Materials Control in supplying raw materials/components/consumable stores, for the organization. Reference has been made to the work of the Purchasing department and its role in controlling costs.

Related skills of communications between individuals and groups concluded this aspect of administering a business organization.

Skills

Skill	*Activities in which skill is developed*
a Information gathering	3, 4, 9, 10, 11
b Learning and studying	1, 2, 3, 7, 8 11
c Working with others	8, 9, 10, 11
d Communicating	2, 4, 5, 6, 8, 9, 10, 12
e Design and visual discrimination	8, 10
f Identifying and tackling problems	2, 4, 5, 7, 9, 11
g Numeracy	11
h Information processing	1, 3, 4, 5, 6, 8, 11, 12

Block 8
Personnel Aspects

Introduction

The personnel function is a major factor in the consideration of people in organizations.

The block starts with a look at the personnel policy an organization might wish to put into operation. Policy leads onto the consideration of the methods used to recruit staff to meet the organization's objectives.

Training and staff development methods are described, and also the application of financial rewards to motivate the work-force.

The block finishes with an introduction to industrial relations and joint consultation procedures.

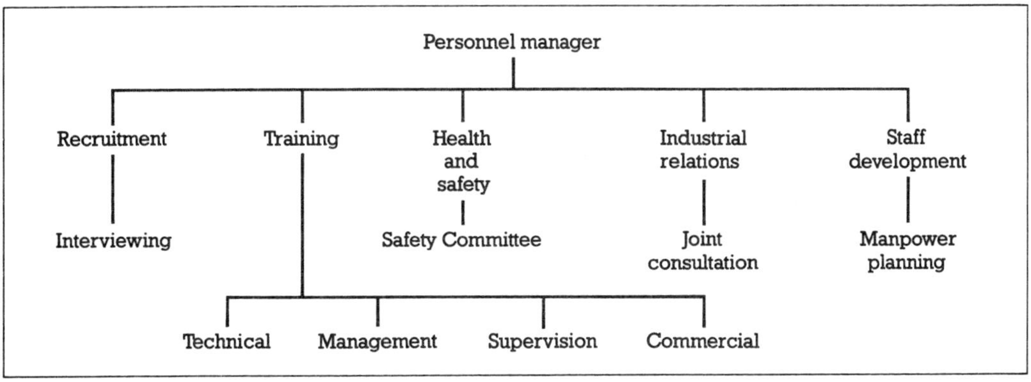

Personnel structure.

Manpower planning

Organizations are similar to other social groups. People come and go and move up and down the structure and some find on occasions that they are no longer required. The environment in which the organization operates is subject to constant change.

A vital part of management's function is to forecast these changes and prepare the organization to meet them. Few organizations remain static: they either expand or contract, which usually leads to significant changes in manpower.

Manpower planning deals with the labour force as a whole rather than as individuals. Its objective is to forecast the future requirements in quantity and quality and the manner in which the manpower resource can be used efficiently. The accuracy with which this can be done depends upon the environment in which the organization exists. Where the market or demand for a product or service is stable, long-term forecasting will be more reliable than where demand is subject to rapid change.

Factors which influence the demand for labour

Increase or decrease in demand for the product or service These can arise out of changes in the economic environment; for example, changes in interest rates, credit facilities, spending power, stability of the UK and other currencies.

Changes in technology The introduction of technology will reduce the demand for unskilled workers in some organizations and replace skilled operators in others. Organizations often require new skills for the operation and maintenance of new technology.

Government intervention in industry and commerce This can alter the conditions of employment or create new jobs and responsibilities. Examples within the past ten years are:
a The Health And Safety At Work Act 1974
b Trade Unions and Labour Relations Act 1974 and 1976
c Employment Protection Act 1975
d Social Securities Pensions Act 1975
e Sex Discrimination Act 1975
f Race Relations Act 1976
g Employment Protection (Consolidation) Act 1978

The cost of labour content in comparison with the cost of other resources This may lead the organization to seek ways of reducing the labour force.

Manpower policy

Consideration has to be given to the following factors:
1 Are the most efficient working methods being used?
2 Is the organization overmanned or undermanned?
3 What skills are required for present and future working methods?
4 What total manpower is required for any proposed change?
5 What plans need to be made to deal with deficit or surplus?

The policy is put into operation by:
1 Recruiting the right quality and quantity of labour.
2 Providing the right type of planned training.
3 Developing the skills and abilities of existing staff.
4 Establishing good labour relations.
5 Providing the right type of working environment.

Forecasting and planning manpower requirements

The organization has to consider:
- Existing skills available and new skills required
- Training and retraining programmes required
- Age structure of existing staff
- Time to complete change

Taking the example of expansion arising out of change in technology:

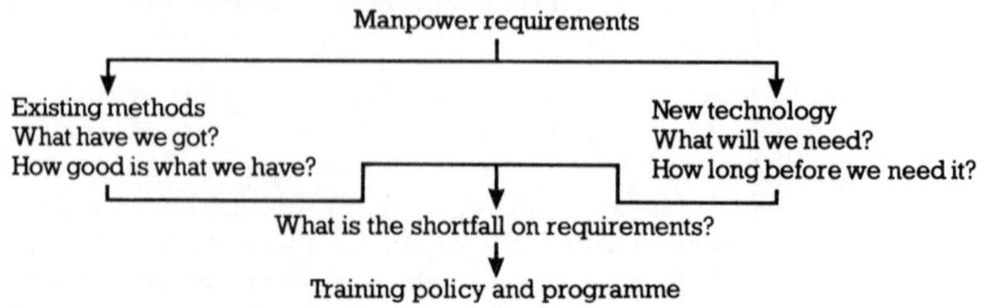

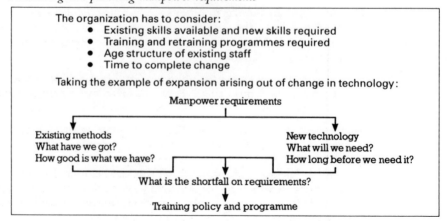

If the organization is going to expand.

The organization has to consider:

- What labour will have to be shed?
- What will be the best method of shedding labour:
  - early retirement?
  - redundancy?
  - natural wastage?
- What redeployment can be put into effect?
- What will be the ultimate labour requirement in all grades of employee?
- How will the redundancy policy be formulated?
- How long before the shedding of labour must be completed?
- What joint consultation will be undertaken?

If the organization is going to contract.

Some advantages of manpower planning

1 Labour recruited in the right number and at the right time for every level of the organization structure.
2 Changes needed in recruitment, training and promotion can be forecast.
3 Planned development of staff can act as a motivator to the work-force.

Some disadvantages of manpower planning

1 It can be costly to administer. Detailed records have to be kept and constantly updated.
2 Where the rate of change in the organization's environment is rapid, accurate forecasting becomes very difficult.
3 The cost involved may not be justified.

Activity 1

A multinational company employs 365 people in the clerical/administrative grade. The breakdown shown in the personnel records is as follows:

Age:	18–20	21–5	26–30	31–5	36–40	41–5	46–50	51–5	56–60	61–5
No of males:	3	5	8	10	19	23	43	50	32	3
No of females:	5	20	38	45	28	15	8	5	3	2

Draw a graph showing the labour profile and explain the likely cause of the difference between male and female numbers.

Suggest a manpower plan to cope with the introduction of information technology.

Personnel

Definition The function which provides a supply of trained and motivated labour capable of performing the duties required for the organization to meet its objectives.

Personnel policy

Personnel policies may differ from organization to organization. For example, the requirements in manpower would be very different in a government research organization and a company supplying contract labour for office cleaning. Policy content, however, should be based on the following activities.

Recruitment Like any other market, the labour market has areas where the supply is available in both quantity and quality, and other areas which are short in both. Constant research into the availability and location of the labour required will be a feature of the policy.

Selection Having identified the source of labour, selection needs to be based on accurate job descriptions and planned interview techniques.

Training Starts with a planned induction of the new employee and continues to train the employee at all levels of his or her career in the company. Planned training is related to staff development. Training may be:
a on-the-job training at the place of work;
b provided by training consultants who specialize in a specific aspect, such as data processing or management training;
c professional training carried out at a college on a day-release basis.

Salary and wages The organization needs a fair and equitable wage/salary structure. This may include payment of bonuses or merit pay incentive schemes. Wage structures may be subject to national agreements entered into by the employers and the trades unions.

Industrial relations The company will enter into agreements on wages and conditions of work with the elected representatives of the work-force. These agreements will be negotiated by agreed joint consultation procedures.

Health and safety The company undertakes to protect its employees within the requirements of the Health and Safety at Work Act 1974.

Recruitment and selection of labour

The basic unit of any organization is the individual employee, who has to carry out an allotted task in the most efficient manner. The planning needed for the selection of the labour force starts with the organization deciding what jobs need to be done and and producing **job descriptions** outlining the duties involved.

Advertising for labour

A number of avenues are open:
Local and national press: this form of advertising is expensive, the local press being less costly than the national.
Trade magazines: used when highly specialized labour is required.
Recruiting agencies: for administrative and clerical staff.
Job centres: for employees up to senior administrative and management staff.

For senior staff, the Professional and Executive Register is updated on a regular basis by the Department of Employment.

The purpose of the advertisement

The aim of the advertisement is to attract the right type of candidate for the job, reducing the time and cost of dealing with applicants; to provide prospective candidates with sufficient information to enable them to assess their qualifications and experience in relation to the post being offered; and to promote the organization as a good employer.

Format for the advertisement

The format depends upon organization policy, which includes the manner in which it wishes to present itself.

An examination of the situations vacant section of a newspaper will reveal a variety of approaches. Whatever the format, the advertisement should aim to give information about the company, the job, the qualifications required, the rewards which can be expected and clear instructions about how application should be made.

Job description	– a broad statement of the purpose, scope, duties and responsibilities of a particular job
Job analysis	– the process of examining a job to identify its component parts and the circumstances in which it is performed. This is a technique to discover the facts in order to describe the tasks to be done and to indicate the qualifications needed. Covers: WHAT the worker does HOW the task is carried out WHY the worker performs the task SKILL involved, such as job knowledge, mental application, dexterity, accuracy and responsibility.
Job specification	– the product of job analysis. A detailed statement of the physical and mental activities involved and, if relevant, of social, physical and environmental aspects. The specification is usually expressed in terms of behaviour: what the worker does, what knowledge is used in doing it, the judgements made and the factors taken into account in making the judgements.
Personnel specification	– an interpretation of the job specification in terms of the kind of person suitable for the job. Characteristics are often set out on the basis of the NIIP seven-point plan.

Steps in the employment procedure.

The National Institute of Industrial Psychology seven-point plan

Devised by Professor Rodger, the plan consists of a number of questions divided into seven categories and making up a list of items which should be considered in interviewing candidates.

The order in which the points are presented is not indicative of the order of importance. The relative importance of points will depend upon the type of work the candidate is being interviewed for.

Division into seven categories is only a matter of convenience. People are not made up of a number of identical qualities. The plan simply provides guidance for assessing a person at a given time, bearing in mind what is known about a specific job at that time.

In common with similar interview plans, the NIPP plan indicates questions to be asked about the candidate rather than questions to be addressed to them.

EXTRUDED PLASTICS TUBE LTD

Require

A CLERICAL ASSISTANT

THE COMPANY

A major manufacturing company in the field of plastics tube extrusion. Our products are used in many engineering applications related to the oil, chemical and waste disposal industries.

THE JOB

Will involve undertaking a wide variety of clerical and administrative duties under the direction of the Administration Manager, but responsible to Department Managers when seconded for specific duties.

THE QUALIFICATIONS

Applicants should have some formal business study training up to the BTEC National Certificate standard.
A G.C.E. O Level in English and mathematics would be an advantage.

THE REWARDS

A good starting salary will be paid. The company operates a bonus scheme for its administrative staff based on a profit sharing scheme.
The job offers a wide variety of experience and provides a good basic training for those seeking early promotion.

Apply in writing to:
The Personnel Manager
Extruded Plastic Tube Ltd
Site 26,
Eastwood Trading Estate
Newtown L26 Z29
Telephone 021-366-9720

THE SEVEN POINT PLAN.

1. PHYSICAL MAKE-UP. What health, strength, stamina, eyesight, hearing, speech, appearance, is required for the job?
2. ATTAINMENTS. What technical knowledge, experience and general level of education is desirable?
3. GENERAL INTELLIGENCE. What level of reasoning and learning ability does the job demand?
4. SPECIAL APTITUDES. What aptitudes such as mechanical skill, dexterity, numeracy, clerical, creative, verbal are required?
5. INTERESTS. Are any general interests likely to be relevant to success or failure in performing the duties involved in the job?
6. DISPOSITION. What are the requirements to get on with people, display initiative, work alone, take responsibility, work under pressure?
7. SPECIAL CIRCUMSTANCES. How will the job effect domestic arrangements. Is relocation of home and family involved, frequent travel in U.K. or abroad, unsocial working hours, shift working, excessive overtime?

Applying for the job

Some organizations will ask the applicant to send for an application form in the first instance. In our examples, EPTL have asked for applications in writing.

On receipt of the written application, EPTL will send an application form to those people it wishes to interview for the present vacancy or consider for employment in the future. A **job description** which outlines the duties and responsibilities in greater detail than in the advertisement will accompany the application form.

Activity 2

1 Using the job specification provided as a guide, write a letter of application to EPTL.
2 Survey the situations vacant columns in local and national dailies and select:
a advertisements which you consider to be lacking in information about job content and qualifications;
b advertisements which you consider would attract the type of applicant wanted.
3 EPTL are not very satisfied with their present application form (see below). Make a list of the improvements which could be made in order to allow applicants to give more information about themselves.

APPLICATION FOR EMPLOYMENT

For the position of:

Surname

Christian names

Address	Date of Birth
	Nationality
	Marital status
Tel	No. of children

Full-time education			Part-time education		
School	From	To	College	From	To
Certificates gained			Qualifications gained		

Previous employment

Employer's name and address	From	To

Note
Please type or use black pen

Signed ....

Date ....

Application for employment.

Job applications

Hiding your light under a bushel

Neither an application form nor a letter of application will get you a job. What they can do is get you an interview. It follows that your application will have to have a special quality if it is to get your name on the short list of those who will be seen. Undue modesty is a luxury you cannot afford in the circumstances. A careful analysis of the advertisement and job specification will allow you to decide what qualities and skills are required, and if you have them you should certainly say so. A certain amount of tact is required so that you do not sound unbearably conceited, but in a job application you are effectively selling a commodity – yourself.

Presentation

Needless to say, for most jobs the prospective employer will instantly discard messy, ungrammatical or badly spelled applications. There will be plenty of others to choose from.

Application forms

Firms that ask you to fill in an application form relieve you of the stress of writing a suitable letter. However, if the job is a fairly senior one, an application form is likely to have a large blank space which invites you to say why you are specially interested in the post or why you feel you are a particularly suitable candidate.

Letter of application and curriculum vitae

A letter of application should not be too long. The details of your education and experience should be listed on a separate sheet known as a **curriculum vitae** or résumé, preferably typed or word processed and very carefully laid out. The letter of application should be handwritten; even these days many messages in business are written by hand and employers like to know you can write legibly. Take the opportunity to amplify and emphasize those features of your life with special relevance to the post, without going into detail. You must aim to project your personality so that the prospective employer gets some idea of you as a person, a unique individual who may be just the person he is looking for. On the curriculum vitae you should list the examinations you have passed, with the grades you achieved. Some firms want to know about every examination you have ever taken, whether you passed or not, but if this is not specifically asked the ones you passed will suffice. It is dishonest and very unwise to claim qualifications you do not possess. Your claims are likely to be checked and a fake claim will lose you the job and possibly get your name on a blacklist.

References

It is usual to give the names of two referees; generally one who has known you a long time and who will speak for your good character and one who knows you in a school or job context and can say what a good worker you are. Your character referee should not be a relative and, if possible, should hold some position in the community such as a clergyman, youth leader or doctor. You should ask your referees for permission to use their names in advance of sending in the application. It will help your referees to write a suitable reference if you let them know what kind of job you are applying for and what qualities are expected or required.

CURRICULUM VITAE

NAME:	JANE CARTER
ADDRESS:	7 MILL LANE, HARDWICK, YORKS HK2 4FT
TEL:	57423
DATE OF BIRTH;	6 September 19__
EDUCATION:	Kilgannon High Hardwick 19__ to 19__
	Exams: GCSE English C
	Maths B
	History C
	General Science B
	French D
	Hardwick College Church Land Hardwick 19__ to 19__
	BTEC Diploma Business Studies
	GCSE French - Grade B
WORK EXPERIENCE:	Trumans Supermarket Dingle Road TOLTON
	Shelf filler, evenings 19__
	Check-out, summer holiday 19__
	Assistant to wine-buyer, summer 19__
OTHER QUALIFICATIONS:	Full clean driving licence
	St John Preliminary First Aid Certificate
REFERENCES:	1. Mrs Catherine Hyde JP 27 Poplar Grove Hardwick Tel: 51262
	2. Mr John Truman 43 Green Lane Tolton Tel: 28585

Letter of application.

7 Mill Lane
Hardwick
Yorks
HK2 4FT

1 JUNE 19__

The Personnel Officer
Seager, Dee and Co. Ltd
Bank Buildings
TOLTON
HK6 2BS

Dear Sir,

I should like to apply for the post of trainee in the Import Department which you advertised this week in the 'Hardwick Herald'.

I have had an interest in wines for a number of years, especially French wines, and have had two wine-tasting holidays, one in the Bordeaux district and one in the Loire.

I am just completing a two year course in Business Studies and expect a good result. I have also continued my French Studies and have 'O' level, grade B as well as a reasonable conversational standard.

My summer job at Trumans gave me an opportunity to work in the wines and spirits sections where I took a special interest in table wines.

I would very much like the opportunity to combine my knowledge of wine with my training in business techniques and could assure you of my enthusiasm and dedication.

I shall be leaving college at the end of the month and could start immediately thereafter.

I attach my curriculum vitae and would be pleased to attend an interview at any time convenient to you.

Yours faithfully

Jane Carter

JANE CARTER (MISS)

Activity 3

Read the following letter from Jamie Reynolds and answer the questions below on one side of A4.

a In your opinion, would it have been better for Jamie to have typed the letter? Give your reasons.

b Is 'The Manager' the most suitable person to address such a letter to or is there some specialist to deal with it? How could you find out the situation in a firm you were interested in applying to?

c What do you you think of the timing of the application, ie, dated October?

d If you received this letter, what would you still want to know about Jamie?

e Has Jamie made any mistakes in the layout of the letter?

5, Green Street,
Top Moss.
Renwick
MC 3Y 2 JW

10th October 19__

The Manager,
E.P.T Ltd.,
Eastwood Trading Estate,
NEWTOWN
L26 Z29

Dear Sir,

I am writing to ask if you are likely to have any vacancies for office staff in the near future.

I left school in July and have 4 'O' levels and RSA Communication in Business Stage One. I am particularly interested in figure work and can use a calculator (all functions).

I am available for an interview at any time and look forward to hearing from you.

Yours sincerely

Jamie Reynolds.

Selection interviews – employer's standpoint

Most people interviewing candidates for the first time are almost as nervous as the candidate and need to prepare as carefully.

Plan your strategy

You should decide ahead of time what you want to find out. On the whole, candidates who feel relatively comfortable at an interview will be able to display their abilities better and give a clearer picture of themselves. There are jobs, however, where an ability to tolerate stress, think quickly or respond to personal factors will be a requirement; for this reason it is sometimes quite legitimate to put some pressure on candidates.

Pressure

The pressure can come from the way the seating is arranged or the number of people on the interviewing panel or the nature of the questions. Exactly the same factors need to be taken into consideration if you are trying to make things easy for the candidates.

Questions

Plan your questions in advance and phrase them so that the candidate has an opportunity to develop a theme or idea when replying. Make sure that you do not do much talking yourself, except to convey basic facts that the candidate needs to know about the organization and the job. Don't ask questions that leave the candidate to guess what answer you are expecting.

Three ways not to interview.

Most interviewers ask the candidate if they have any questions they would like to ask before the interview ends.

Selection interviews – employee's standpoint

We have provided guidelines for you to follow when you are the candidate in the form of an illustration, 'Being interviewed'.

Getting Ready

- Plan to look right for the job
- Look up what you said in your letter/form
- Check the information they have supplied
- Find out something about the organization yourself
- Work out what else you want to know

On the Day

- Be there in good time
- Try to develop a conversation with the interviewer(s)
- Make sure they know how good you are
- Don't ask for information they have already supplied
- Have at least one question about future prospects ready

Being interviewed.

Patterns of employment

We have been looking at the process of applying for jobs in the early 1990s. There is no doubt that patterns of employment and types of work will be very different by the time you are well established in your working life.

Full employment of the available work-force five days a week for a fifty-year working life is not likely to be seen again – unless some catastrophe wipes out half the adult population. It is likely that in future people will work intermittently or part-time or for part of their lives only. To those who have been in full-time employment since the day they left school, this seems an idyllic prospect; to those who have not been able to get a start in the world of work, it seems like a betrayal of hopes and ambitions.

Already there are signs of profound changes in the way jobs are offered. Few 16-year-olds now get work. They are excluded from the employment market on the grounds of lack of experience and are sent on government schemes which provide them with a little income and an introduction to working life. Although the official retiring age for men is 65 years, increasing numbers choose to retire earlier. The age span of the work-force is thus shrinking. Swings in the birth-rate cause successive governments to vary employment policy – usually on an *ad hoc* basis.

There is an increasing tendency for organizations to farm out sections of their operation to subcontractors. For instance, people working in the school meals service are often now employed by a contractor rather than by the county education authority. Subcontractors may be composed of some of the people who have left full-time paid employment. In doing subcontract work, they will still be paid for their skills but not via the payroll.

The electronic age makes its contribution to changes in employment by allowing much that was previously done in offices and other workplaces to be done at home and sent out down wires or via satellites.

Because of the shrinking opportunities for having 'proper jobs', society will perhaps change so that people are 'placed' by what they are like rather than by what they do or have. The question of money is crucial, however. There seems no doubt that either there will be an ever-increasing divide between the 'haves' in employment and the 'have nots' without work, or there will be a levelling-out of incomes all round with the employed ones accepting responsibility for the increasing numbers the country does not need as workers. There is only so much money to go round. The question is, how is it to be distributed?

Activity 4

In discussion, attempt to make outline plans for a just society by 1999. How likely is it that such a society will develop?

Interviewing

The work undertaken by the personnel department includes interviewing those employed at all levels of the organization. As indicated below, there are various types of interview. Each requires the interviewer to have specific skills.

Selection

Obtaining the most suitable candidates for specified jobs within the organization.

Assessment and appraisal

Checking actual performance against planned performance. Identifying training needs. Identifying whether weakness in the employee is due to the individual or the organization.

Discipline

Identifying the offence. Identifying the person responsible; obtaining the evidence. Preventing a repetition of the offence. Applying sanctions.

Fact finding

Collecting facts. Sorting fact from opinion and long-held beliefs. Listening to those who know the facts. Recording for future reference.

Exit

Interviewing those who have decided to leave the organization in order to establish the reason.

The purpose of any interview is to gain or impart information and/or knowledge. The interview can be considered to be a learning situation for at least one of the participants, with knowledge increasing as time passes.

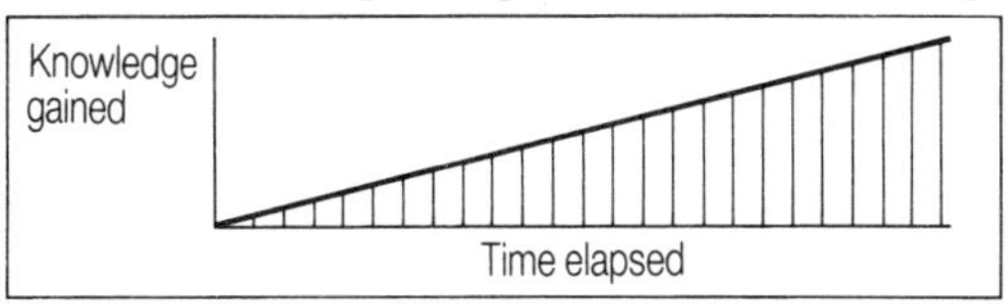

Unfortunately, this ideal is not always achieved. For any activity to be successful, it has to be planned. Those who are going to do any interviewing need to have their objectives clear before the interview starts. For many interview situations this can be difficult. However, when interviewing to select employees, the management can establish objectives by drawing up detailed job specifications and applying skilled interview techniques.

Interview technique

Interviewing is a skill gained through experience and training. Those who are required to conduct interviews have to be trained to be objective so that they do not become emotionally involved. The ability to 'stand outside' the interview situation – the best position for unbiased observation – requires considerable practice.

Planning

The interviewer must have the purpose of the interview clearly in mind.
1 What kind of information is being given or sought?
2 What objectives need to be achieved?

Considering the person to be interviewed

1 What is known about the individual's personality?
2 Does the interviewer have any personal reactions to the interviewee?

Having all the relevant information available beforehand

For a selection interview this would be:
1 the candidate's letter of application,
2 the application form,
3 the job specification.

Activity 5

1 Assume that you are going to interview a fellow student in order to find out about their life style, hobbies and interests. Draw up a list of questions you would wish to put to them.
2 The personnel manager is about to interview an employee who is to be disciplined for consistant poor time-keeping. Suggest the information the personnel manager should take to the interview.

Conducting the interview

There are a number of things to bear in mind to make the interview go well. First, make sure that the environment in which it will be conducted is suitable. Next, observe the following guidelines:
1 Allow sufficient time to conduct the interview.
2 Avoid being interrupted during the interview.
3 Help the person being interviewed to relax as far as the situation will allow.
4 At the beginning of the interview state clearly its purpose and objectives.
5 Ask open-ended questions requiring a more expansive answer than 'Yes' or 'No'.
6 Listen! Talk only to clarify a point or to encourage the person being interviewed.
7 Keep any emotional questions for the closing moments of the interview; they may put up a barrier to communication.
8 End the interview on a positive note.
9 Review objectives to see if they have been achieved.

Note taking/recording during interviews

This should be done as discreetly as possible. Do not interrupt the flow of the interview or make the interviewee feel insecure by pausing to write things down. Writing copious notes during the interview wastes time, but the interviewer may wish to recall the interview later when reviewing the situation or making a selection between a number of applicants for a specific job.

Interview records, similar to the example given below, provide a means of recall. The interview record must not be seen as a score card; it is simply a means of recalling impressions gained during the interview.

Interview record.

INTERVIEW RECORD

Position:

Interviewer: Candidate: Date:

		a	b	c	d
SKILLS	- Typewriting - Word processing - Layout - Tabulation				
KNOWLEDGE	- Telephone duties - Filing systems - Office equipment - General office duties				
EDUCATION	- General - Technical				
DISPOSITION	- Confidence - Communication - Presentation				
CIRCUMSTANCES	- Location - Mobility - Constraints				
GENERAL IMPRESSION					

GENERAL COMMENTS

Training

A company training officer has the following responsibilities:
a Identifying the training needs in the company.
b Planning the training programme, which is based on the identified need.
c Raising the level of efficiency.
d Boosting morale.
e Providing a succession of qualified staff.

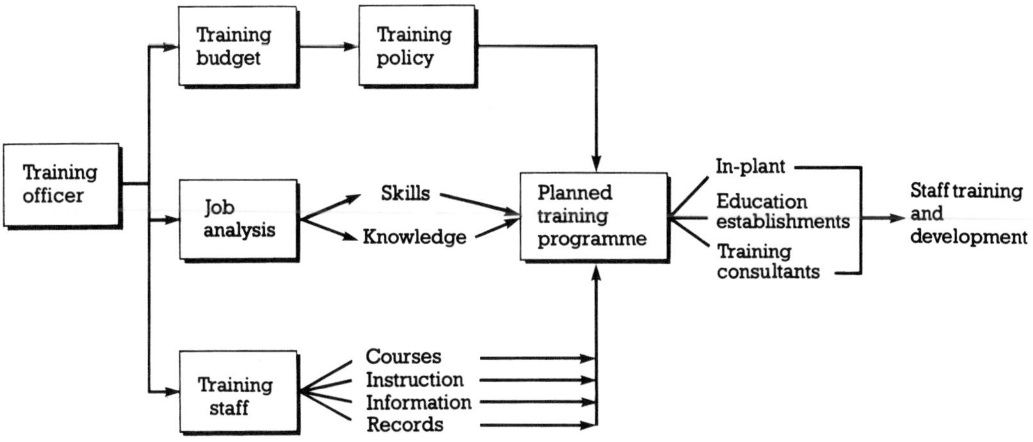

Responsibilities of a training officer.

Planned induction training

Every new employee requires a period of training to familiarize him or her with his or her working environment. Planned training has three main objectives:

1 Economic To enable the new employee to attain an acceptable standard of performance in the minimum space of time possible. Acceptable standards are related to the expected return on the wage/salary rate paid to the employee.

2 Social To allow the new employee to fit in to the new working environment and the working group. This encourages the employee to identify with the organization and its objectives.

3 Safety During the initial days of employment, the new employee is vulnerable to any hazards which may exist; they must be informed about them.

Justifying the cost of planned induction

If no induction training is available, any new employees will be left to their own devices and will have to learn the job as best they can. Inevitably, this means that the rate of training will be spasmodic. Progression will follow a pattern in which something is learnt and a period of time will then pass before further information is picked up. The following diagram illustrates the learning–progress–plateau advance of the do-it-yourself training method.

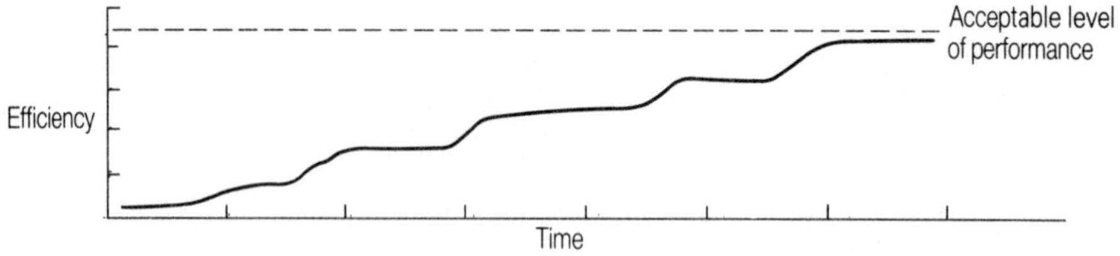

The graph shows that some time will elapse before the organization gets an adequate return on the wages or salary paid to the employee. In addition, the organization may have a demotivated employee at the end of the progression.

Activity 6

You have been allowed one complete day to carry out the induction of new students at your college at the beginning of the first term.

List the activities you consider essential to familiarize the student with the college and the work they will be doing. Arrange the list in the order in which you would wish the student to assimilate the information.

Where the induction training is carried out on a planned basis, the progress of the employee can be predicted. The plateaux in the progress curve which featured in the unplanned training are substantially reduced.

In the majority of jobs, a great deal of information can be given during the early stage of employment, accelerating the progress of trainees and giving them confidence. A graph comparing unplanned and planned induction training would look something like this:

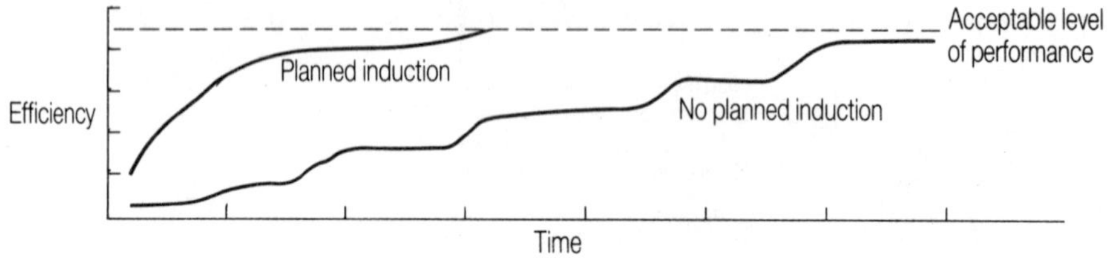

How long should induction training take?

This depends entirely upon the grade of employee concerned. A process worker who will be engaged on a simple, repetitive task may complete induction within one day. A senior executive may have an induction scheme which spreads over several weeks; for example, it would take some time for a sales manager in a new job to absorb the product knowledge and get to know the customers.

Day 1	Employee met at pre-arranged location. Documentation completed and employee entered on company books. Company rule book issued. Contract of employment signed. Introduction to company products given. Conducted tour of the works and offices made. Safety rules and fire drill explained. Introduction to place of work and supervisor.
Day 2	Introduction to office routines related to the work of a clerical assistant. Instruction in the use of the office equipment. The organization structure and names of the management team presented. Supervised training practice undertaken.

Outline of an induction scheme for a clerical assistant.

Activity 7

Expand the above outline of an induction scheme to produce a detailed induction scheme for a new clerical assistant at EPTL.

Types of training a company might undertake

Apprenticeship training This may be subdivided as follows:

a **Graduate apprentice** Graduate who receives training for one or two years which will enable him or her to specialize in one particular aspect of the organization's activities, such as marketing, accounts, design or production.

b **Student apprentice** Recruit with one or more relevant A-levels. Training eventually take up an executive post. An alternative scheme is to provide the trainee with a variety of experience in a number of departments before deciding which one will provide career development.

c **Craft apprentice** School leaver, recruited to complete a three-year course of training and education to prepare him or her for a career in a skilled trade.

Supervisory training Designed to train existing and potential supervisors. Courses are carried out 'in plant' by the company training officers or at an educational establishment which is attended part-time.

Management training Designed to broaden the manager's appreciation of the management techniques available, give an update on company policy and products, and develop skills related to decision making and human relations.

Commercial training Provides office and administrative staff with the training needed to develop their skills and enable them to assimilate new procedures and techniques.

Operative training Training for machine operating and production processes which are specifically required by the organization.

Training documentation

a **Work books** Kept by apprentices; covering the instruction given at each stage of the apprenticeship period. Examined on a regular basis by the training officer to assess the progress being made.

b **Training record** A form designed to show the progressive training during the career of the employee, including information about educational background, courses undertaken, qualifications gained and transfers from one department to another.

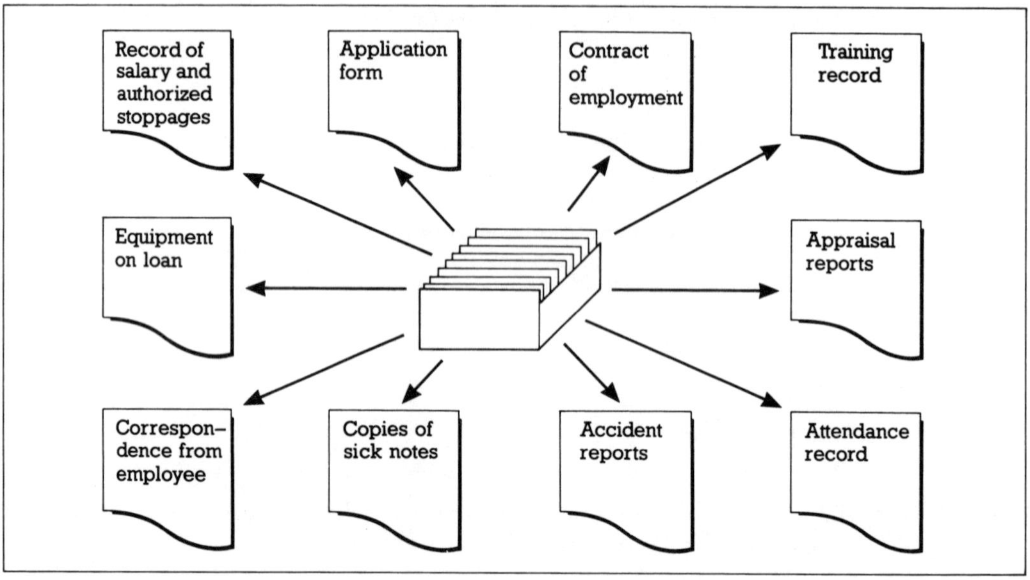

Employee personnel file.

Name Address		Change of address
Department	Job title	National Insurance No.

Education	From To	Qualifications

EMPLOYMENT HISTORY						
From	To	Position held	Department	Salary	Per	Reason for change

Employee record.

Staff development

Manpower is the most expensive resource of any organization. The personnel department is responsible for developing and improving the contribution made by each employee.

In order to assess improvement some yardstick is essential, and for human resources, it is provided by the **job specification**, which details the skills, knowledge and personal attributes required to perform the task. The personnel officer will have made every effort to select the best candidate to match the job specification. A perfect match is unlikely; the job specification describes the ideal candidate. Each employee will have strengths and weaknesses which affect his or her performance in the job.

Staff development aims by planned training and experience to build on the strengths each individual has and to reduce the weaknesses. Strengths and weaknesses of individual employees are identified by **constant assessment** of performance by the immediate supervisor, and by **appraisal interviews** between the employee and the immediate supervisor conducted on a regular six- or twelve-monthly basis.

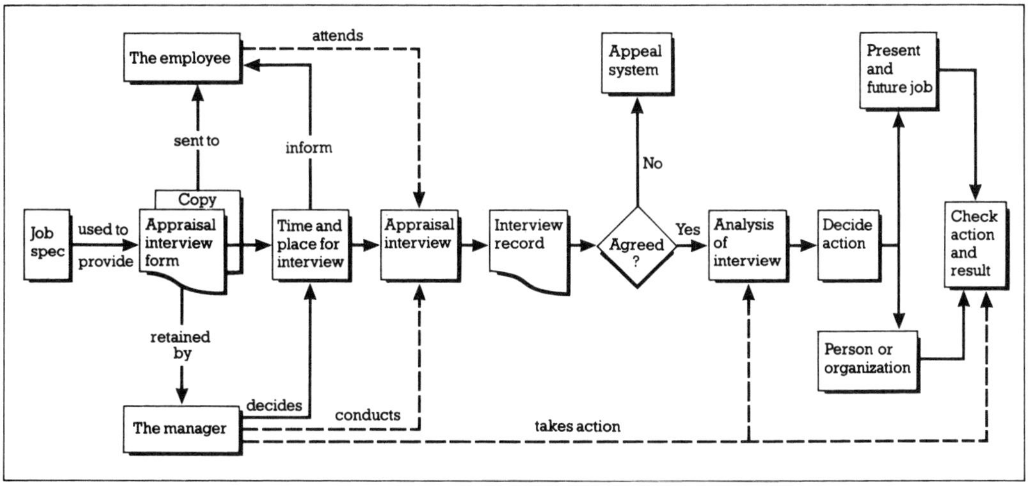

Staff appraisal system.

Staff appraisal

Who is appraised?

Most organizations confine appraisal to supervisory and management grades, plus any other grade making a significant contribution to the future success of the business.

What does appraisal achieve?

1 It identifies the training needs by examining the strengths and weaknesses. All jobs change over a period of time – new techniques and new procedures are introduced, requiring new skills. Responsibilities can change without the knowledge of the employee.
2 It identifies the potential for promotion within each employee. This enables the organization to plan to fill gaps which might occur in the organization.

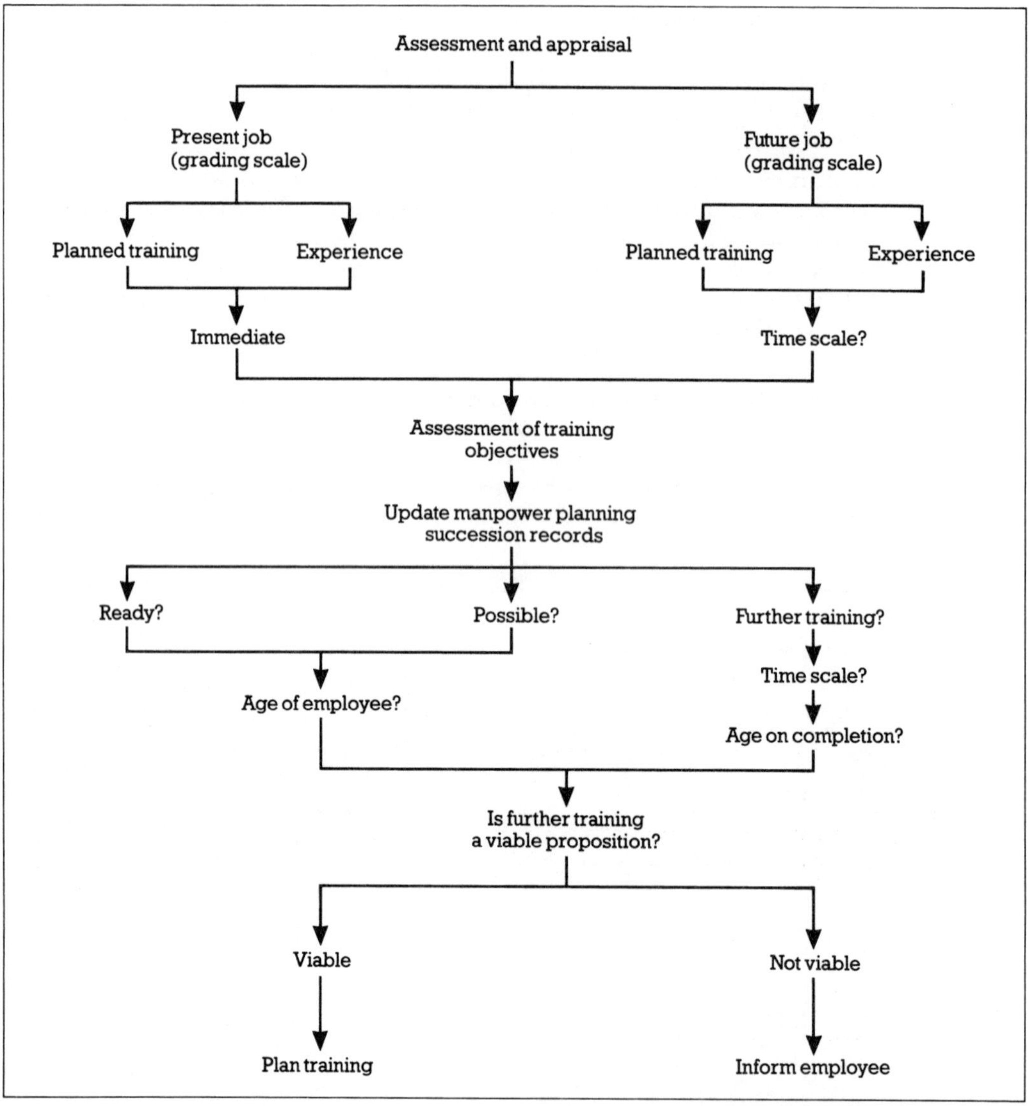

Planning for the present and future.

3 It motivates the employee. Appraisal interviews encourage and motivate the individual by recognizing attributes, offering assistance with weaknesses and improving communications between manager and managed.

Activity 8

When you are in business you gain access to an amazing amount of information about your customers and clients – and about the people you work with. You work at EPTL and find out a number of things about people you know outside work. Discuss in groups how you would handle the following situations. Afterwards write about your views, explaining what factors affected your thinking.

1 Your father's brother, the black sheep of the family whom your father disapproves of, is an undischarged bankrupt with a serious drinking problem. You discover that he is just about to land a lucrative

subcontract with EPTL and know that it is vital to enable a large contract to be met. Will you say anything to those concerned at EPTL?

2 Your mother has a friend of whom she is deeply envious. She and her family have three superb cars, a pool, a holiday home in Marbella and a flashy and expensive social life. Your mother often criticizes your father for not being able to provide all these things. You discover that the friend's husband owes EPTL over £90 000 and has been refused further credit. Will you tell your mother? Your father?

3 The husband of your former headmistress, a terrifying lady who gave everyone you knew at school a bad time, has an executive post at EPTL. You discover that he is having a heavy affair with a girl working on the VDUs. Will you pass this interesting information on to your old school friends?

Wage and salary administration

Objectives

1 To attract the right calibre of labour at all levels of the organization to meet its objectives.
2 To provide incentives which will reward those who contribute most to the organization and keep them working for it on a long-term basis.
3 To introduce systems of payment and reward which can be easily understood at all levels of the organization structure.

Rates of pay

In many instances, the base rate of pay for a specific trade or job is set by national agreement between employers and unions. Over and above these rates, employers may reward their employees as an incentive to improve output, or as a result of bargaining with union representatives about conditions of service and employment.

Methods of payment

The choice of a pay system must depend upon type of work undertaken, the conditions of employment and many other factors, including the bargaining power of the unions involved. There are many incentive schemes used in industry and commerce. In this book we shall look at the schemes most widely used for hourly paid workers.

Flat rate system

The employee receives an agreed amount for each hour of the basic working week. Hourly rates are determined by periodic bargaining between the employer and the employees' representatives. The total amount earned in any one week is based on the number of hours worked and is not related in any way to output.

Employees may have to 'clock on' to provide proof of the number of hours worked. Pay is deducted for late arrival and early departure.

Payment by results (PBR)

A system of payment widely used in manufacturing, particularly in engineering. Using this system, the employee is rewarded according to the number of units of work produced, or to the time taken to complete a specified amount of work. Units of work are calculated by using work study techniques to establish a base rate. An employee exceeding the base rate is rewarded with extra pay on an agreed scale negotiated by management and the union.

When correctly applied, PBR can provide management with high output and give the work-force high earnings. On the other hand, recording individual output may involve an administrative cost, and the quality of the work done may suffer as a result of the worker attempting to maximize earnings.

Measured day work

Earnings through PBR can fluctuate from week to week because of work not being available, poor quality of materials, machine breakdown, and so on. Measured day work is design to level out earnings so that the employee has an assured income each week. The system is based on the establishment by work study of a number of different levels of performance for each job. Once the employee has reached a specific level and sustained it for an agreed time, they are paid at the rate for that level on the agreed scale. Employees are expected to progress through the grades as their efficiency improves with time and experience.

Measured day work was popular with management and unions in the 1970s, but there are some problems associated with it. Once the employee has attained top grade of pay, the only way to ensure that the agreed standard of performance is maintained is to provide some form of supervision or control system which involves recording the output. Disputes can arise when the management does not accept a claim by an employee that he or she has reached a certain level of performance.

Piece work

This system of payment, based on paying a stipulated amount of money for each finished unit (piece) completed, has fallen into disuse in manufacturing.

It was a major cause of industrial dispute and involved considerable clerical and administrative work. Times allowed for each unit are calculated by **rate fixing**, a method whereby a rate fixer watches a number of units being produced while recording the time taken with a stop-watch. The number completed is then divided into the time taken, establishing the time for each unit.

Time recorded on stop watch	20 minutes
Number of units completed	15 piece parts
Time allowed per unit	$\frac{20}{15} = 1.33$ minutes

Piece work has been abused by both management and employees over the years, but the method of payment is still used by some organizations employing out-workers who undertake work in their own homes. There is a long tradition of using this method of payment for out-workers: the system came into being when weaving was a cottage industry, each weaver being paid for each piece of cloth woven.

Activity 9

1 What method of payment would you recommend for the following occupations?

A bus driver	A production line operator in a car factory
A clerical worker	A hospital nurse.

2 A company engaged in high precision engineering for the nuclear power industry is considering paying its skilled work-force on a piece work basis. List the problems you can foresee if this method is adopted.

Salaries

Payment by salary differs from payment by wage in that the amount paid is calculated on a monthly or yearly period. Salaried employees receive payment regardless of output and may enjoy certain privileges, such as being paid in full when off sick.

Rates of pay are usually linked to a grading system with different rates for each grade. Within each grade, there may be subdivisions which allow for salary increases for a number of years. These **incremental scales** are widely used by local government and Civil Service establishments.

Progression through the grades is determined by the salaries policy of the organization. In some, the employee advances automatically through the scale on attaining a required age. Others are based on a system of **job evaluation**, progression being determined by the type of work being undertaken, or being left to the discretion of individual managers.

Activity 10

A bank has a salary grading scheme for its clerical staff which provides annual automatic regrading of employees from their eighteenth birthday.

The Incremental Scale is as follows:

Grade	A.1.	B.1.	C.1.	D.1.
	A.2.	B.2.	C.2.	D.2.
	A.3.	B.3.	C.3.	D.3.
	A.4.	B.4.	C.4.	D.4.
	A.5.	B.5.	C.5.	D.5.

Progression is from A.1 to D.5, at which point the employee will be earning the top salary in the highest grade.

Write a report assessing whether this grading system is likely to be effective in providing an incentive to the individual employee. Identify some of the problems the scheme could present to the management.

Industrial relations

People in organizations are a cross-section of society and therefore have a variety of aims and objectives. Some conflict of interests is inevitable and it manifests itself in the form of industrial conflict.

A look at the objectives of management and managed shows how much they differ.

Aims and objectives of the work-force

1 To maximize return on the sale of their skill and expertise.
2 To have security of employment.
3 To have some control over matters which affect their working lifes.
4 To have safe and pleasant working conditions.

Aims and objectives of the management

1 To minimize the cost of labour.
2 To maximize the productivity of the business.
3 To maximize the profit margin in the interests of the investors.

Where there is a constant source of conflict, it pays to have some established procedure for negotiation. For a large proportion of the working population, the trade union movement is seen as the best way of meeting aims and aspirations.

British trade unions formalize the aims of the work-force into:

1 the distribution of wealth on an equitable basis, in the form of wages, bonuses and other benefits which can be related to cash;
2 worker contribution, through **joint consultation** between worker representatives and the management;
3 **security of employment,** without fear of redundancy or short-time working.

Trade union membership is not restricted to skilled tradesmen and production workers. White-collar and administrative workers also have unions.

Activity 11

1 Discuss with other members of the class the extent to which you think the trade union movement has been successful in meeting its objectives.
2 List the reasons why a white-collar worker should consider becoming a member of a trade union. Bear in mind the growth in technology in the office.

Management negotiates with the union members through an elected representative authorized to act on behalf of the members. These representatives are usually called **shop stewards**, although some unions prefer different titles.

The role of the union representative

An unpaid official of the union, the representative is elected by union members in the department or place of work. Duties are carried out on a part-time basis and the management usually pays for time spent on union business.

In the industrial relations field, the representative provide a service to the management in the following ways:

a providing a recognized line of communication between the management and the work-force;
b bringing a knowledge of processes and practices to the negotiation of any agreements between management and employees;
c conducting the majority of the negotiations and agreements between management and the unions along amicable lines: most agreements entered into are honoured by both sides.

The role of the personnel department in industrial relations is to provide the management team with advice and guidance, to devise procedures for negotiations to be agreed by both the management and the unions and to draw up agreements on rates of pay and conditions of service.

Activity 12

The management of a company have circulated to all employees the following memorandum:

FROM: The General Manager **TO:** All Employees

It has come to the notice of the management that there is a considerable abuse of the time allowed at the end of the morning and evening working sessions for washing and clocking out.

This abuse coupled with the increase in bad time-keeping, is costing the company a significant loss of production and increasing the costs.

An existing agreement between the management and union representatives allows each employee five minutes at the end of each working session to wash and clock out. In future, any employees leaving the place of work before the allowed time will have one hour's pay deducted for every offence.

The management are determined to put a stop to the bad time-keeping practices which now appear to be widespread. As from today's date any employee the management consider to be a continous offender, will be suspended from work without pay for a period of one working week.

1 Assuming you are all union representatives, discuss the action you should take in this situation.
2 Following the discussion, each prepare a statement to submit to the management, outlining the union's point of view.

Trade union organization

Not all trade unions are organized in the same way. An outline of the general guidelines along which most unions are structured follows.

1 *The individual member*

The basic unit of the union organization is the individual member, who pays a **union due** to the organization in order to fund its activities.

2 *The union representative*

Elected by secret ballot on the shop floor to represent the union members in negotiations with the management. The representatives are not paid by the union; most are given time off to conduct union business and are paid by the company for that time.

The representative's role varies with the type of industry or commercial enterprise, but the following list summarizes the range of duties which might be undertaken:

a recruiting new members;
b checking that union dues have been paid;
c negotiating with management on conditions of employment, disputes and matters related to health, safety and welfare;
d representing union members who are involved in disciplinary procedures;
e communicating union policy to members and the management;
f attending the union's branch meetings;
g Attending training courses run by the union and the TUC.

The representative or shop steward is the only contact most union members have with the union organization. The result is that in some industries this gives the shop steward considerable power and influence in negotiating conditions of service.

3 *The union branch*

Members are allocated to a union branch which discusses local disputes and problems, promotes the activities of the union, and provides a communication link between the branch members and the union's head office.

Members are expected to attend branch meetings, but very few do. Average attendance is estimated to be 2% to 5% of total membership.

4 *District committee*

In order to maintain control and establish efficient communications, unions operating on a national basis divide the UK into districts. District committees are formed from members elected from branches in the district. The secretary of the district committee is a full-time paid official of the union, usually known as the **district secretary**. This official may be called upon by the shop steward to negotiate with senior management where a dispute has deadlock. The main business of the district committee is to ensure that union policy is implemented.

5 *National headquarters*

At the head office the general secretary and national executive council carry out the national policy of the union which has been established at the annual conference.

Headquarter's staff includes specialists in welfare, trade union law, economics and politics, and professional negotiators. Their function is to maintain contact with the membership and represent the union to government, the CBI and other bodies.

Free collective bargaining

This is a procedure for resolving conflict arising out of different goals, values and distribution of resources. A **bargain** is a form of agreement reached between employers and a group of employees through recognized representatives or a staff association. Agreements are entered into on the understanding that all parties will honour the conditions imposed.

Typical areas where management is willing to enter into collective agreements are:
a wage rates,
b hours of work,
c holiday entitlement,
d training.

The degree to which management or unions meet their objectives depends upon factors such as the strength of the unions concerned, the unit cost of labour, the level of employment in the industry and the extent of competition outside the UK.

Sanctions the unions can apply in collective bargaining
1 **Working to rule** – in many industries the rules laid down for the work-force are complicated and following them strictly makes activities take a great deal of time. By working to rule, workers can virtually bring things to a standstill, the advantage to them being that they continue to be paid as they have not withdrawn their labour. Transport industries are particularly prone to this form of action.
2 **Random strike action** – withdrawing labour for short periods of time, with either the whole work-force stopping work or individual departments stopping. This type of action can cause a lot of disruption, but the labour force does not lose much pay.
3 **Blacking work** – Where the type of work being done or the technology

used is in dispute, union members can be instructed not to deal with it until some agreement is reached with the management.

4 **Official strike action** – total withdrawal of labour with the backing of the union organization. Union members may be paid strike pay from union funds.

5 **Picketing the place of work** – Union members stand outside their place of work and try to persuade others to support their cause by not entering or refusing to deliver goods. Those who picket have a right to do so providing they do not cause obstruction. Picketing has been much in the news in recent years because of the increase in mass picketing and resulting violence.

Types of unions in the UK

Craft unions Originally these were exclusively for skilled craft workers, each craft having its own union. Examples today are unions for skilled engineering and electrical trades. Amalgamation has led to unions covering a number of crafts with membership opened up to semiskilled and unskilled workers.

Craft unions can exert considerable pressure on management in a bargaining situation as by withdrawing the labour of a few skilled men they can close an industry down.

General unions Open to all grades of workers, regardless of the industry they work in. These unions have considerable power in manufacturing industries.

Bargaining power can stem from the type of work done. For instance, refuse collectors can quickly develop an unpleasant situation by withdrawing labour.

White-collar unions For non-manual workers. Some will recruit workers from jobs and professions regardless of the industry they are engaged in; others cater for workers in a specific activity or profession. Examples are the National Association of Local Government Officers (NALGO) and the National Union of Teachers (NUT).

White-collar unions are the growth area of the trades union movement. This is because of the growth of administrative procedures and the introduction of information technology, two developments which threaten the security of employment previously enjoyed by white-collar workers.

Trade Union Congress

Most unions are affiliated to the TUC, which represents the UK union movement to government and employers. The executive body of the TUC is the general council, elected at the annual congress which meets to discuss common policies. It is attended by delegates from the affiliated unions, who may be union members delegated by their branch or full-time paid union officials.

Congress considers items tabled for discussion by affiliated unions and the annual report of the general council. In carrying out the policy formulated by the resolutions made at congress, the TUC acts as a pressure group on behalf of the unions, attempting to influence employers and government policies.

Activity 13

Compile a list of at least ten of the unions representing workers in the UK and divide them into the three categories described above.

Write a letter to the TUC requesting educational material describing their activities.

Employers' associations

These associations are formed within specific industries to counterbalance organized labour. They decide on common policies in areas such as conditions of employment and minimum rates of pay.

Associations advise members on the conduct of industrial relations within their industry. Employers can ask an association official to represent their case to trade union officials in disputes which have reached local conference stage in the negotiating procedure. Many associations recognize the importance of good industrial relations and conduct research into this field.

Confederation of British Industry (CBI)

Initially founded by an amalgamation of the National Association of British Manufacturers, the Federation of British Industries and the Employers Federation. Membership now consists of employers' associations, individual companies, banking and insurance organizations and public companies.

The CBI has a similar role to that of the TUC. It represents the interests of the business community, acting as an adviser and spokesman. It claims to be non-political, but it is inevitably involved in the defence of free enterprise.

The organization is governed by a council of members and an elected director general who controls the activities of the various departments.

Advisory, Conciliation and Arbitration Service (ACAS)

Set up under the Employment Act 1975, ACAS is a corporate body, which gives it some independence from government control.

It consists of:

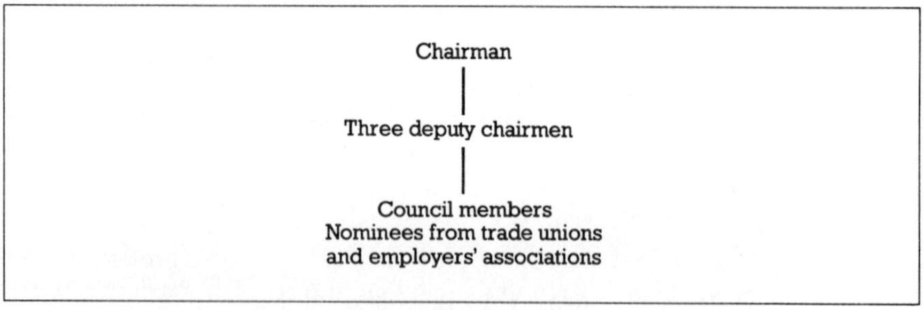

ACAS is empowered to:

a provide a conciliation service and appoint skilled negotiators, who may be officers of the service or independent.

b provide an arbitration service, with a single arbitractor or a board of arbitration.

Conciliation

When employers and unions are in dispute and negotiations have reached stalemate, they may seek a solution by discussing their problems with a neutral third party. This third party can be a conciliation officer, who will attempt to establish areas of common ground for a settlement on the basis of compromise. The conciliation officer's role is purely advisory: a solution cannot be forced on either party.

Arbitration

On occasion both parties in a dispute feel that their case is so strong that there is no ground for discussion or compromise. In this situation they may decide to go to arbitration. Both parties agree to be bound by the decision of the arbitrator. It is therefore essential that the arbitrator, or those making up the arbitration board, has the confidence of both sides.

Activity 14

ACAS provides a number of services apart from conciliation and arbitration; some of these are related to collective bargaining in industry.

Carry out library research on ACAS and draw up a summary of these other services.

Participation in decision making

The distinction between participation in decision making and joint consultation is not always clear. Participation can take various forms ranging from full participation to some degree of consultation.

Participation

Exists when the members of a decision-making group have equal executive powers to influence the direction and control of the enterprise.

Consultation

A formalized system of communication between employers and employees in which the employers take into consideration the views and attitudes of the work-force. Employees are restricted to influencing decision making by persuasion or by the negotiating 'muscle' of organized labour. In many organizations this gives employees a considerable influence on management decision making, equivalent to executive power.

Suggestion schemes

Many organizations are aware that their employees may develop ideas about the way in which the working procedures and environment could be improved. These ideas can be a source of improving efficiency and reducing costs. They can be tapped by giving employees an opportunity to make their ideas known through a suggestion scheme.

Organizations adopt a scheme which best suits them, but the general rule is to provide a way for employees to put ideas forward and a system of rewards for ideas which are put into practice or which stimulate a change in working methods. A committee is appointed to monitor the schemes and to arrange for any professional or skilled assistance which might be needed to promote the suggestions.

Joint consultation

One solution to the problem of the conflict of interests between the objectives of management and managed is a system of joint consultation. This provides a means of discussing matters which management wishes to retain the right to control but which it is willing to consult the work-force about before a final decision is made. Management may also see joint consultation as a valuable method of communication which reduces some of the problems associated with more formal lines of communication.

Committees set up for joint consultation are discussion groups rather than decision-making bodies.

Works committee and staff associations

These committees are set up by management, who draw up a constitution for the conduct of meetings and **terms of reference.**

Terms of reference will depend on the policy of the individual organization and the strength of the organized labour within the organization. In general, the agenda is confined to matters broadly concerned with productivity, a typical example being suggestion schemes.

Committee constitutions usually follow the principle of equal membership of both management and work-force. Management will expect to delegate the specialists they feel will meet the objectives of the committee – such as the chief engineer and the personnel manager – whilst the employee membership will be elected by shop-floor ballot.

Committee membership may be divided into subcommittees to deal with specific aspects. This can result in a committee structure similar to the following:

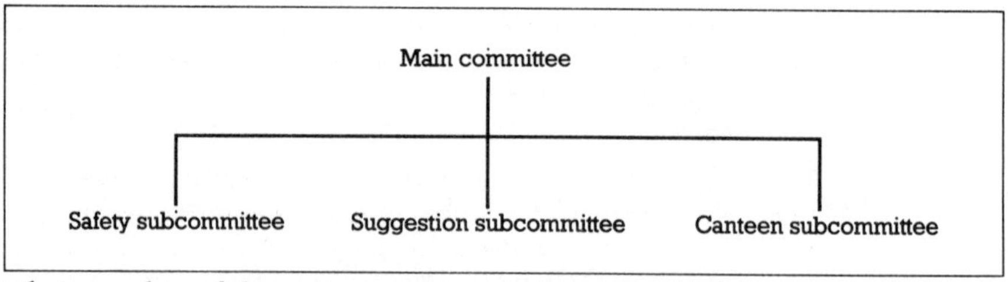

Chairmanship of the main committee is determined by the constitution. A senior manager may be the permanent chairman, or the chair may be allocated to the management and works representatives in alternate years. Subcommittee chairmen are elected by the members of that sub-committee. In order to encourage a free exchange of views, all committee members are usually considered to have equal rank while the committee is meeting.

Committees are normally scheduled to meet once a month on a specified day so that those taking part can be made available to attend. An agenda is circulated by the secretary; this tends to be something of a formality as the matters discussed usually follow a regular pattern. The minutes of the main committee meetings and the subcommittee meetings are pinned on the organization's notice-boards.

The first stage in setting up a joint consultation procedure is to establish what objectives and limitations are wanted and to incorporate these into a **joint consultation plan**. Objectives and limitations will vary from organization to organization. An example is shown on the next page.

Worker directors

The ultimate participation in decision making is involvement in formulating the policy of the organization.

Britain, like all member states of the European Economic Community, is subject to the fifth directive draft on the subject of worker participation.

The objectives of the plan are

1 To encourage contact and co-operation between all personnel, management and the board of directors.
2 To promote the awareness of the company's need to develop its productive capacity and service to the community.
3 To improve the working environment.
4 To endeavour, by discussion, to examine recurring differences arising between management and employees.
5 To investigate the cause of accidents and promote safe working practices.
6 To examine methods of encouraging less waste of the organisation's resources.

Limitation of objectives

1 The joint consultation committee will not discuss any matter which is covered by existing agreements between management and the recognized union representatives, in particular, agreements relating to wages, bonuses and conditions of service.
2 The constitution of the joint consultation committee will be based on the understanding that it is a means for round-table discussion and consideration of proposals and suggestions, and is aimed at maintaining good relations between all grades of employees.
3 The joint consultation committee will operate primarily as an advisory body and will not have executive power to reverse or modify any decision or instruction given by the management.

Joint consultation committee plan.

Arising out of this, the government set up the Bullock committee to examine how to extend industrial democracy to include participation by the trades union movement. The Bullock committee reported in 1977. Among its proposals was that legislation should provide for employees or organizations with over 2000 full-time staff to vote for independent unions to appoint representatives to the board of directors. This was seen as a logical step towards improving industrial democracy.

The *formula for composition of the board* was as follows: equal membership of employee representatives and those nominated by the shareholders, plus three to five independent directors chosen by both the other parties and holding the balance of power.

Neither British management nor the trades union movement received the report with enthusiasm.

1 Management tended to fear that their right to manage would be under attack in the board room, with decision making limited by the degree of consultation which might arise. A further concern was that union appointees could be untrained and unskilled in management techniques.
2 Trades unions took the view that worker directors could become involved in negotiations outside the aims and objectives which trades unions exists to represent. Fears were expressed that worker directors might become 'institutionalized' into adopting management's approach to policy making.

Those who favour worker directors point out the advantages of having at board level advice from people with shop-floor experience, plus the fact that representation at board level would be a motivating factor to the work-force.

European examples

Germany – supervisory boards with one-third of the membership elected by employees, having the power to veto major decisions.

Netherlands – worker representatives on supervisory boards with powers to veto certain appointments in the organization.

Activity 15

Identify two major organizations in the UK which have worker directors and describe the method used for electing them to this office.

Productivity bargaining

A **productivity deal** is an agreement in which the work-force agrees to changes in working practices in return for improved benefits and increased earnings. Management in a number of industries have seen the productivity deal as a way of getting rid of what they consider to be restrictive practices.

When they enter into a productivity deal, each side will have formulated a plan which determines the bargaining points they are prepared to negotiate. As it is rare for both sides to get what they want, there is an element of trading off to arrive at a compromise. It is essential that each side settles feeling that they have a fair deal; otherwise the deal will cause resentment and frustration.

Productivity bargaining increases the role of the shop steward as the deals are usually plant or locally based. Stewards have the detailed knowledge needed to understand the significance of bargaining points. Their role in this has been recognized by the TUC, which has set up training schemes for stewards in productivity bargaining techniques.

A well-known example of a productivity bargain is the agreement made at the Esso oil refinery at Fawley. In return for a substantial wage increase the unions concerned agreed to:

a substantially reduce demarcation barriers;
b eliminate the employment of mates for skilled craftsmen;
c reduce overtime working considerably;
d accept a run-down work-force by natural wastage;
e accept efficient redeployment of the labour force.

Activity 16

1 Write down the advantages of a productivity deal to the organization described below.
2 Identify the bargaining points that management might put forward and what they might expect to achieve if a successful deal were concluded.

Company profile

a An old-established company in its field.
b Originally a private limited company, it became a public limited company in 1978.
c Currently employs 1400 people, 70 per cent of whom are shift workers.
d Orders have been steadily declining over the past five years in the face of competition which has the edge on price and quality.

Product profile

a The company manufactures sheet glass for the building trade and DIY retail outlets. Market research indicates a buoyant market from which the company could sustain 75 per cent to 80 per cent plant activity if it could recapture its share of this potential.
b 65 per cent activity would provide a reasonable profit margin, allow a dividend to be paid to the shareholders and provide investment capital. Average plant activity over the past twelve months has been around 50 per cent.

Labour profile

a Mainly semi-skilled and unskilled workers with a support staff of skilled tradesmen who provide maintenance services.

b Lines of demarcation are strictly adhered to in the production units, the most stringent observers being the craft tradesmen.
c Personnel are moved from one department to another only after negotiations with the union representatives.
d A number of departments are overmanned as a result of agreements made with the unions when new machinery was installed.
e Time-keeping is poor and absenteeism is well above average.

Background information
The company has a complex wages and bonus payment system dating back to the time before it went public. Wages and salaries have always been below the average paid for similar work in the area, but earnings have been high because of the amount of overtime working.

Supervision and middle management are demoralized. They constantly complain about the lack of sanctions to apply to frequent offenders against the discipline code and about the time they have to spend dealing with matters raised by the shop stewards.

Activity 17

You are suddenly designated office worker's representative at EPTL, and you are sent to the meeting of the joint consultative committee in the board room.

The consultative committee is intended to give an opportunity for workers to influence decisions to do with improving the efficiency and smooth running of the organization. In some companies worker participation in management extends to ownership of the assets and profit sharing, but at EPTL the only financial matters the committee discusses are the setting of bonus levels. Some companies use such a committee to hammer out wages, promotion and career prospects, but at EPTL those areas are left to Personnel.

Consultative committees call for considerable trust between management and workers. The management must believe that the workers do have valuable opinions to offer and should not simply let them speak and then ignore them. The workers must be able to take a broad view of the whole organization and not simply pursue the interests of their own section or colleagues.

You find yourself in quite exalted company when you get to the meeting. There is only one other person anywhere near your age, Alison Reynolds, whom you met on the induction course. The chairman is the managing director himself, Mr Southgate, and the secretary is the company secretary, Bryn Roberts. The quality control inspector, John Hind, and Vikki Hadow, the administrative manager from production, are there too.

The chairman's eye falls on you. He tells you he would like you to produce a draft report of the proceedings. A final report will be issued in due course in the form of the monthly broadsheet sent to every member of staff to inform them of the decisions reached by the consultative committee.

Produce a draft headed 'Joint Consultative Committee Broadsheet' giving details of the decisions you reached. Write a memo to the managing director, enclosing it for his approval. (Although you would not normally communicate with him by memo, on this occasion he has asked you to send him your draft, so a memo is satisfactory.)

JOINT CONSULTATIVE COMITTEE

2 o'clock. Board Room. Thursday.

Mr Southgate.
Mr Roberts.
Vikki Hadow.
John Hird.
Me.
Alison Reynolds.

Teabreaks. Supervisors complain workers always back 5 minutes late. Mr Roberts reckons 37 working hours lost every week. Vikki – the queues are too long – not enough canteen staff. John – stagger the breaks.

For a trial period – starting next Monday

10.30 to 10.45 and 3.30 to 3.45 OPERATORS.
10.45 to 11.00 and 3.15 to 3.30 TECHNICIANS.

First Aid Post. Someone had been in on Tuesday and slept there. Left paper cups cigarette ends and crisp bags all over the floor. Previous week all crepe bandages pinched. Scissors always disappear overnight. Vikki said we should have a nurse. Can't afford it. Mr S. – keep it locked. Key to be held by named person in each section. Volunteer key holders wanted. Me to organize.

Production Target. We have reached target 3 months running. M.D. is delighted. congratulates all staff. Keep up the good work.
Finally settled on bonus of 5 per cent. Mr Roberts will produce new figures next meeting. New target set then. This 5 per cent in next pay packet. With luck!

Parties of Visitors. Vikki said when parties of students were being shown round there are lots of wolf whistles and and remarks. Embarrassing. Mr Southgate is disgusted. Remind everyone to treat all visitors courteously. Reputation of company is at stake.

Safety Shoes. New issue of safety shoes now available from Stores. Mr Roberts – everyone must wear them on shop floor. Remind them. Company will not be responsible for accidents if these shoes are not worn.

Notes taken at joint consultative committee

Remember that your work will be brought to the attention of everyone in the organization.

You should use a dignified but not pompous tone. Choose a vocabulary that will neither insult the intelligence of the staff nor mystify them.

The notes you took are, of course, chatty and informal and will need translating into a more formal style ready for printing. Most of the discussion should be omitted. The detail (eg, the crisp bags etc) should be replaced by a term that covers the total situation. Words like 'pinched' need changing. It would be inappropriate to express doubt about the 5 per cent bonus being paid on time. In short, suit your style to the situation and the audience.

Activity 18

One of the matters raised at the joint consultative committee meeting was that of safety shoes.

Write a notice for display in the canteen informing workers that new safety shoes will be available at three specified times next week. Old shoes must be handed back in exchange.

Remind workers that these shoes must be worn on the shop floor.

Health and safety at work

In 1974, the Health and Safety at Work Act was passed by parliament. It covers all people at work (except domestic servants in private employment), including those in educational establishments engaged in further and higher education. It also covers members of the general public when affected by the work of others.

Duties laid down by the Act

Employees must taken reasonable care to avoid injury to themselves or to others, and must co-operate with employers and others to meet the statutory requirements of the Act.

Employers
1 Must maintain safe plant, safe working conditions and safe premises and provide adequate training and supervision in safety matters.
2 Must prepare a written safety policy which is made known to all employees.
3 Must conduct the business in such a way that the health and safety of persons employed, or of members of the general public, are not put at risk.
4 Employers who manufacture or supply articles for use at a place of work must ensure that they are safe when properly used.
5 Must recognize safety representatives appointed by recognized trade unions.
6 Must set up a safety committee if more than two safety representatives require it.

Enforcing the Act Health and Safety inspectors appointed under the Act have considerable powers. These include the power:
a to enter any premises in which work is being carried out under conditions which make them subject to the Act;
b to interview and take statements from employees;
c to issue a **prohibition order** requiring the employer to stop any process which is dangerous to an employee or others;
d to issue an **improvement order**, requiring a potential hazard to be remedied within a specified time;
e to seize and destroy any substances which might be a danger or might cause serious injury;
f to prosecute offenders in a court of law.

Selection of safety representatives Independent trades unions which are recognized by the management have the right to appoint safety representatives from the employees. The election of safety representatives usually follows the union's balloting procedures.

Function of the safety representative As laid down in a regulation to the 1974 Act:
1 Investigation of potential hazards, carrying out periodic safety surveys of the working areas.
2 Investigation of complaints made by those they represent regarding potential hazards or unsafe practices.
3 Making representation to the management on matters arising out of complaints made by the employees or matters arising out of an investigation.
4 Consulting with and receiving information from inspectors of the Health and Safety Executive.
5 Attending meetings of the safety committee where one exists in the company.

Function of the safety committee

1 Ensure that the safety policy is implemented.
2 Receive reports from safety representatives.
3 Investigate accident statistics.
4 Prepare and carry out safety campaigns.
5 Circulate information received from bodies such as the Royal Society for the Prevention of Accidents (RoSPA).
6 Issue an annual report to the management.
7 Promote safety training.
8 Keep a register of all accidents reported in the company.
9 Check the safety regulations related to the installation of new equipment or working methods.

The safety policy Has the objective of ensuring, as far as is reasonably possible, that the employees of the company work in a safe environment. Individual organizations tend to word their policies in a manner which best suits the product or methods of working, but the following items are often included.

The company will:

a thoroughly investigate all accidents reported with the aim of trying to prevent them happening again;
b conduct a continuous review of accident prevention methods and update procedures when processes or materials used change;
c carefully select new employees to eliminate the problems related to those employees not physically or mentally suited to a particular job;
d train all employees in safe working practices and provide the necessary clothing and equipment for protection;
e encourage safety campaigns and promotions instigated by the safety committee;
f provide adequate first aid and medical facilities, as required under the Act.

Activity 19

A company had intended to use the following accident report form as a standard document for all accidents occurring in the works.

At present, the accident report form is only in draft. The personnel department has yet to issue instructions for its use.

Since the form was drafted, the safety committee has suggested that the accident statistics should be broken down into the following categories.

Male:	Under 21	Cause of accident:	Falls
	Over 21		Lifting
Female:	Under 21		Machines
	Over 21		Hand tools
			Miscellaneous

1 Devise a method of recording accidents which would enable the statistics the safety committee wants to be extracted, and make any other modifications to the design of the form you feel are necessary.
2 Using a block flow diagram, prepare instructions for using the modified form, starting with:

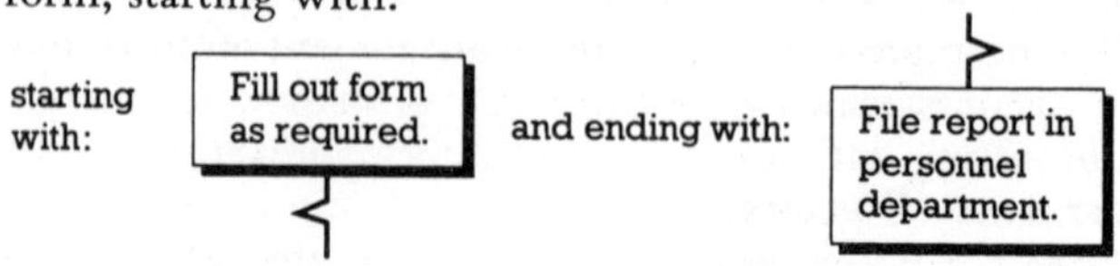
starting with:
Fill out form as required.
and ending with:
File report in personnel department.

and ending with:

ACCIDENT REPORT
On completion, forward to the Personnel Department.

Name:............... Clock No:....... Department:.............
Date Accident Occurred:..............

Cause of Accident:

Injury Sustained:

Witnesses:

Time:........Normal Hours? (Y/N).......Overtime? (Y/N)........
First Aid Given? (Y/N)....Did Employee Attend Hospital? (Y/N)...

Any Other Employee Involved?	Any Person Other Than Employee?
Name:......................	Name:........................
Department:................	Company:.....................
Clock No:..................	Home Address:.................
	....
How Involved:	How Involved:

Signature....................

Accidents at work
Every year in the UK about 1000 people are killed in accidents at work and approximately three million working days are lost through accidents. Many of the accidents occur to people under the age of 21. A disabling injury sustained when young can have a long-lasting effect on the quality of life.

Major causes of accidents at work

Falls People fall from improperly used ladders and chairs, fall down stairs and trip over obstacles left in walkways.

Lifting Where working methods include lifting weights, adequate training must be given in the correct procedures. Heavy weights can be safely handled if the prescribed methods are used, yet a severe injury can result from lifting a relatively light load in the wrong way.

Falls and lifting incorrectly often result in back injuries, a major cause of lost time in industry.

Using machinery Accidents related to the use of machinery can often be traced back to two causes. The primary cause of machine accidents is summed up in the old saying, 'Familiarity breeds contempt.' Taking a short cut in a working method or ignoring a safety procedure has cost many an individual dearly. The other major cause is ignorance. Operatives who are not properly trained, or people who operate equipment without being authorized to do so, are likely to find themselves in trouble. People who cannot see a machine or piece of mechanical equipment without yielding to the temptation to fiddle with it are a menace to themselves and others.

Using hand tools Hand tools cover a wide range of devices which help the employee in carrying out the work task. Accidents are caused by poor maintenance and misuse. A knife is an ideal tool for cutting, but when used to prize the lid off a tin of paint it can break and cause an injury.

Horse play There is nothing wrong with having a sense of fun as long as it does not result in the injury or death of another person. Horse play often results in misuse of equipment and services. A common cause of serious accidents in industry is the misuse of compressed air in incidents intended to be 'a bit of fun'.

A particular danger is the increased use of chemicals which are flammable or corrosive. These have to be handled correctly at all times.

No working environment can be considered safe. After all, a number of people are killed every year by accidents which occur in their own homes.

The office might be considered to be a reasonably safe working area, but severe injuries have resulted from pencils sharpened at both ends, electrically powered office equipment and corrosive and flammable fluids used in reprographic equipment. Hands are often crushed in filing cabinet drawers.

Activity 20

John Black is in the third year of his apprenticeship as a skilled carpenter and joiner with a large building company.

He has been doing very well with his practical training, and the company has been receiving good reports from the college where he is attending day-release classes.

The building firm is currently involved in a contract to repair fire damage to the roof of a large country house owned by the National Trust. Work was on schedule until two joiners employed on the job went off sick with influenza and a joiner from the workshop was transferred to the site to replace them. The workshop foreman asked John Black to assist the joiner at the site in order to give John some roof work experience.

Two days after being transferred to the site, John had a fall and was taken to hospital, where he is being detained.

ACCIDENT REPORT

Employee: John Black **Department:** Joinery Workshop

Witness to Accident: Andrew Browning **Department:** Joinery Workshop

Was The Employee Engaged On Normal Job At Time Of Accident? **YES/~~NO~~**

STATEMENT Andrew Browning and the apprentice John Black were engaged on the replacement of roof joists. Access to the working area was obtained by steel scaffolding erected by the company's own scaffolders. The roofing joists were being lifted by means of a rope and pulley and stacked on the scaffold prior to being used in the repair work.

Browning became concerned about the weight stacked close to the repair area and instructed Black to find another suitable area. When moving along the scaffolding to find a new stacking point, Black was tripped by an unsecured scaffold board and fell twelve feet, striking a steel scaffold pole as he did so.

First Aid was rendered and Black was not moved until the ambulance staff were in attendance and he was taken to hospital.

Signed: David Harvey
(Site Foreman)

Date: March 19--.

Details from note from John Black's father to the managing director:

> I was asked to see the Consultant Surgeon at the hospital today. He informs
> me that John has a serious back injury and will not be able to lift
> anything heavy or take part in any sporting activities for the rest
> of his life.
>
> I will keep you informed of any further developments.

Discuss with the rest of the class the circumstances which led up to this accident. Also consider the likely effects on John's social life and future employment.

Fire Precautions Act 1971

This Act covers the requirements relating to the layout of buildings, the equipment contained within them, planned escape routes and fire-fighting equipment and training in their use.

A fire certificate is required where more than twenty people are employed. Issue of the certificate is subject to all the requirements being met.

Attached to the certificate must be a plan showing:
a the use made of the building,
b location of the fire escapes,
c location of the fire-fighting appliances,
d location and type of fire-warning equipment.

Other requirements:
a escape routes must be kept clear of obstruction,
b fire-fighting equipment must be regularly serviced and maintained,
c employees must be trained in fire procedures,
d regular and recorded fire drills must be held.

Finally, the procedure to be followed in case of fire must be clearly displayed in every work area. An example is shown below.

```
                     FIRE DRILL

On hearing the fire bell:

                 Close all doors and windows
                 Switch off all electrical appliances
                 Proceed to the assembly point indicated below
                 Report to the assembly point supervisor

     DO NOT      Re-enter the building for any purpose until
                 given permission by the assembly point
                 supervisor

                 Use lifts as a means of escape

                 Attempt to fight the fire unless specifically
                 trained to do so.

Assembly point:

                    MAIN CAR PARK
```

Activity 21

1 Survey the fire-fighting equipment in your college or place of work. List the types of extinguisher provided and record the dates when they were last tested.
2 Make a tracing of the layout of the EPTL factory (see Block 1) and plan suitable fire escape routes for the factory and the offices.
3 Research the various types of fire-fighting equipment. Recommend the most suitable types for the following places: a hotel kitchen, an estate agent's offices, a printing firm's premises.

First aid

The Health and Safety at work Act requires the employer to provide first aid boxes according to the number of people employed. Three categories are specified:

a less than 10 employees,
b more than 10 but less than 50 employees,
c more than 50 employees.

One box is the minimum requirement for up to 150 employees. The contents of the box are specified under the Act; they depend on the number of employees. There are five categories: 1–5, 6–10, 11–50, 51–100 and 101–50. Dressings contained in the boxes must be maintained at the level laid down by the Act and must conform to standards specified by the British Pharmaceutical Codex.

The Health and Safety Executive recommend that the first aid box should be placed so that injured workers can get treatment as soon as possible. In practice, first aid boxes are placed where they are required to meet the safety standards of the company and this invariably means that the positioning is better than the Health and Safety Executive's recommendation.

Activity 22

1 Research the information on health and safety in your library. Write a report outlining the requirements relating to trained first aiders.
2 Design a system suitable for a company employing over 150 people which will ensure that the first aid boxes are restocked after first aid has been given to anyone.

Activity 23

To: You Subject: Safety in the Office

From: Brenda Milner Date: Yesterday

H.M. Inspector of Factories was not best pleased with our safety standards in the offices when he came last week. I have noticed one or two things whilst I have been going round myself recently - it is time we tightened up before something happens.

1. I often see drawers standing open in filing cabinets. I caught my shoulder on one last month - I still have the bruise. If they open too many the cabinet could tip over.
2. The fire doors were propped open upstairs last Tuesday. What was the point of all the expense of having them installed?
3. I saw a tiny girl staggering across the office with a typewriter the other day. They shouldn't attempt to lift things beyond their capabilities.
4. Somebody sprained his ankle going downstairs carrying a huge pile of files he could not see over. This is ridiculous; he should make 2 trips or send for a messenger.
5. People should bury the points of pins securing documents or they should use a stapler, though that has been known to cause injuries too.

6. I wish everyone would stop smoking - I shall get round to doing something about that soon. Meanwhile they must take care - even metal bins are full of scrap paper. Stub them out in the ashtrays.

7. All this electrical equipment we now have results in trailing wires. We have ample sockets; they should keep the equipment close to the outlet.

8. We seem to have some high-spirited youngsters on the payroll at the moment. There's too much skylarking about. I saw one lad firing staples at another. And I was nearly felled when a girl galloped down the corridor the other day. We must put a stop to it.

Send a memo to all office managers about this, will you, saying I am extremely concerned and expect action. A list of do's and don'ts is what's wanted. If I've forgotten anything, you put it in.

B.M.

You will find literature in your college library about safety in the office. Write the list and the memo Miss Milner has asked for and send them to the typing pool supervisor, together with a distribution list. Ask for it to be treated as urgent and sent out this week.

Summary

In this block we have looked at the many activities of the personnel department, starting with its duty to recruit suitable staff. The system of drawing up a specification of the experience and qualities required and for advertising for applicants was looked at. Applications and interviews were discussed, first from the candidate's point of view and then from the employer's. Personnel's continuing responsibility to train and develop the staff's potential and to appraise their performance was considered. The need to arrive at equitable pay agreements led to a consideration of industrial relations and trade unions. Finally, we looked at the onus on personnel to consider the health and safety of all employees.

Skills

Skill	*Activities in which skill is developed*
a Information gathering	2, 5, 13, 14, 15, 16
b Learning and studying	2, 4, 6, 11, 3, 14, 15, 16, 18, 22
c Working with others	4, 5, 11, 18, 20
d Communicating	1, 2, 3, 4, 6, 7, 9, 10, 11, 12, 14, 15, 16, 18, 19, 20, 21, 22
e Design and visual discrimination	1, 2, 3, 4, 5, 7, 8, 9, 10, 12, 16, 20
f Identifying and tackling problems	1, 2, 3, 4, 5, 7, 8, 9, 10, 12, 20
g Numeracy	
h Processing information	2, 5, 6, 12, 13, 22

Block 9
Financial Aspects

Introduction

Employing the work-force and providing other resources used in the organization involves a cost to the business.

This block is no substitute for an accounting course, but it does draw your attention to the need to maintain control over costs and cash flow. Resources of manpower, materials and machines are considered in monetary terms through the application of budgeting principles. A practical approach is taken, involving you in a budgetary control exercise which gives you the chance to practise your numeracy skills.

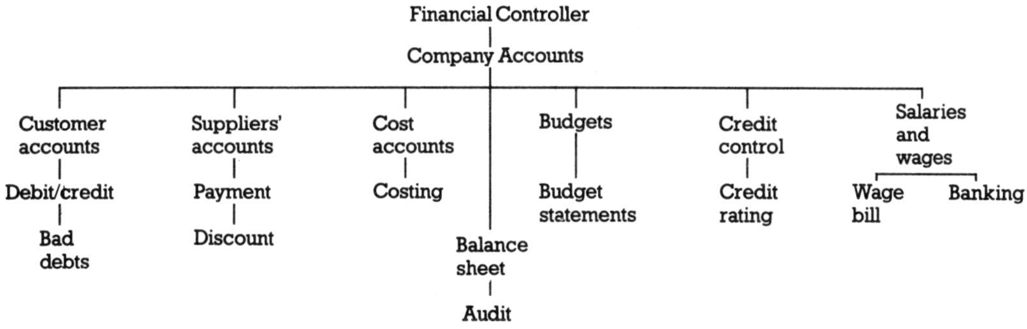

Financial structure.

Finance department

Definition The finance department is the function of the business which ensures that the cash resources of the organization are subjected to careful control. Cash resources in any organization are finite; the amount available to conduct the business depends on:
1 control over expenditure on resources,
2 control over credit extended to customers.

A major activity of the finance department is the monitoring of the flow of cash IN from the sale of goods and services and OUT to pay wages, taxes, suppliers and investors.

When cash out exceeds cash in the business is in danger of failing. Financial control techniques are used to forecast and prevent the **cash flow** situation from getting out of hand.

Cash in any organization can exist in a number of forms:
1 Money
2 Assets
3 Stocks
4 Outstanding debts.

In the following diagram, 'Examples of cash flow', you can compare the situation in a family with that in a business organization.

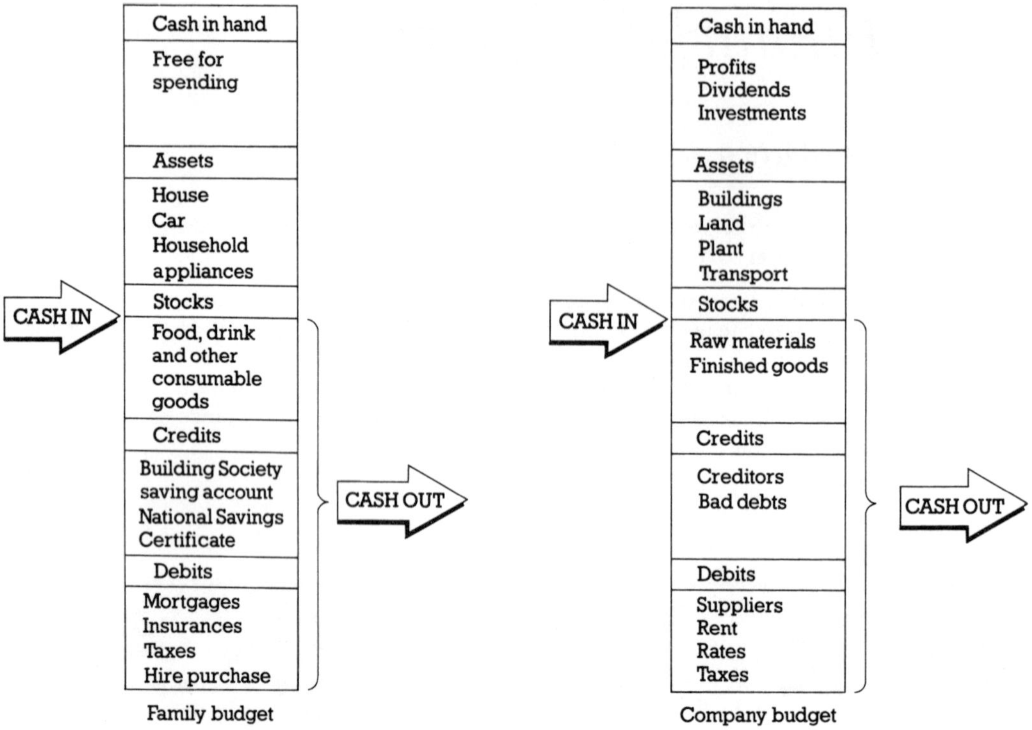

Examples of cash flow.

A detailed consideration of financial and costing techniques is given in another unit of the course. This book looks at activities related to customer accounts, wage payments and budgetary control.

Customer accounts

Business transactions are not conducted in the same way as a purchase in a shop, where the money is paid at the point of sale. Contracts for the sale of goods to other organizations are subject to a period of credit before the account is settled. There is more about this in Block 7.

This means that the supplier has committed cash in the form of wages, materials and overheads. These remain as assets of the business but are not available in cash form. The business is unable to make use of the assets until the customer pays for the goods or services provided.

Costing

A **cost** is the value of the resources used in the production or other activity being costed.

Cost = Usage × Cost per unit

Unit cost A **unit of production** to which costs can be allocated. Units of production can be expressed in many terms, for example, batches, contracts, gallons, tonnes. Alternatively, **units of service**, such as kilowatt hours, therms of gas, miles of transportation.

Cost centres A part of the organization that can be clearly defined as a separate entity to which costs can be applied. Each organization defines cost centres to suit its objectives. They can be single machines, groups of machines, individual workers, groups of workers, departments or types of work being done.

Example

A cost centre at EPTL – extruder in production shop.

	£ per annum
Depreciation	3 000.00
Maintenance	800.00
Power	1 000.00
Rent, rates, heat, light	400.00
	5 200.00
Output per annum	10 000 metres
Cost per unit	5 200.00 / 10 000

= £ 0.52 per metre

Data required for standard costing:
The number employed in each cost centre
Standard hourly/weekly rate of pay
Standard processing times on machines
Calculated use of resources

Established by work measurement

A cost centre at EPTL – extruder in production shop.

Classification of costs

Direct costs – those which can be established as directly used in the production process.
Indirect costs – those not directly attributable to production, but necessary for production.
Administration – costs incurred in providing support functions such as sales, distribution, office services.

Direct labour Direct materials Direct expenses	= Prime costs	= Total cost
Indirect factory labour Indirect factory materials Indirect factory expenses Administration expenses Sales/distribution expenses	= Factory costs	

Activity 1

From the information supplied below and in the illustration, 'Package film production unit':

1 Establish clearly identifiable cost centres.
2 List those factors which could be attributed to the cost of administration.
3 List those factors which could be considered as fixed costs.

Annual rent:	£ 30 000
Annual rates:	£ 12 000
Annual insurance:	£ 6 000

Wage/salary costs	
General manager:	£ 18 000
Production manager:	£ 15 000
Production controller:	£ 14 000
Personnel manager:	£ 14 000
Sales staff:	£ 40 000
Purchasing staff:	£ 25 000
Accounts staff:	£ 20 000
Quality control staff:	£ 15 000
Stock control staff:	£ 15 000
Maintenance staff:	£ 24 000
Stores staff:	£ 20 000
Supervisory staff:	£ 48 000
Hourly paid work-force:	£120 000

Package film production unit.

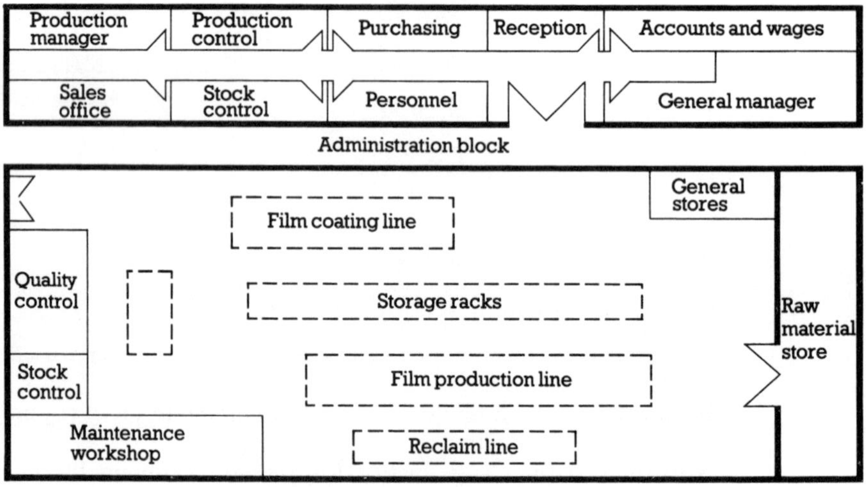

Cost control

There are four main components of working capital:

1 Stock The costs associated with stock are:
a the **opportunity cost** incurred by tying up capital in stock;
b the **cost of holding** stock, comprising reorder costs and cost of maintaining the storage area.

Stock-holding policies have also to take into account the discounts which can be obtained from bulk purchase and the advantage of buying before price increases.

2 Work in progress Work may have to be completed in batches, with some form of delay before each batch proceeds to the next stage. Work stored in an uncompleted state is categorized as **work in progress** (WIP).

Stock and **work in progress** are often the major components of a company's working capital. The greater the level of these two components, the smaller the amount of capital available to the organization to meet current expenses.

3 Debtor control Debts are a problem at the best of times. When credit is tight and liquidity low, they represent a real danger. Prevention is better than cure. Organizations should carry out credit investigations through agencies which specialize in this area.

Some companies play on the reluctance of suppliers to press for money and risk loss of future business. They may respond to gentle pressure in the form of a polite reminder. Those who do not may not be worth having as a customer; the organization should take the appropriate action to get the money owed.

4 Cash budgeting Having cash available on demand, known as liquid assets, is a safeguard to the business. Any increase in the demand for expenditure or in debts could reduce liquidity to the point where the company has to obtain a bank overdraft. This situation is known as **overtrading** and can lead to a company going out of business.

Cash budgeting six or twelve months ahead will enable cash requirements to be anticipated and expenditure to be tuned to keep the liquidity position viable and any overdraft to a minimum.

Advantages of costing

a Effective cost control over all departments and activities.
b Increased efficiency in production.
c The activities of each section of the business can be analysed to reveal its profitability.

Activity 2

Draft a standard letter to be used by a firm selling building supplies to remind customers that their account is overdue for payment.

Activity 3

EPTL need to make changes in their record-keeping. You are allocated the task outlined in the following memo.

MEMO

FROM: K. S. Shaw DATE: Yesterday
TO: You SUBJECT: Receipts and payments

Starting next month, we shall have to make a monthly return of receipts and payments.

Please design a form to show:

a total payments made to suppliers
b invoices received from suppliers but not yet settled
c moneys received but unpaid after 7 days, 14 days, 21 days and 1 month
e bad debts.

Specify 'Correct to the nearest penny'.

Add a box at the bottom to show the petty cash a) paid out and b) still in hand.

K.S.S.

Activity 4

EPTL want to improve their cash flow. They have decided to offer a 5 per cent discount to all customers who settle their bills within seven days.

a Write a circular letter to go to all customers telling them about this offer. It would be wise not to mention the cash flow – say how much you value their custom and make the discount sound like a reward.
b Send your letter to reprographics with a memo asking for a run of 500 copies as soon as possible.

The organization's financial function must keep a close watch on the following aspects of cash flow:

1 Who owes the organization money?
2 How much money is involved?
3 When is payment due?
4 Is payment now overdue?

Activity 5

Examine the end of year financial situation outlined below and:
a state the likely outcome if the situation is allowed to continue;
b propose a solution which could rectify the situation.

End of year invoiced sales	1 450 000	1 450 000
Outstanding Debts – 6 months credit	350 000	
Outstanding long-term Bad Debts	70 000	
Wages and salaries	350 000	
Overheads	45 000	
Stock of raw materials	220 000	
Stock of finished goods (unsold)	180 000	
Taxes due for payment	175 000	
Creditors due for payment	92 000	
	1 482 000	1 482 000
		– 32 000

Control of cash flow – customer accounts

When the organization has made a delivery to the customer, an **invoice** is despatched informing the purchasing organization of:
a the amount delivered,
b price to be paid,
c credit terms agreed.
A copy of this document is routed to the financial department, which enters the details into the **customer account.**
On the due date, the finanical department sends the customer a **statement** which details the deliveries invoiced, the amount due and the date by which the account should be paid.

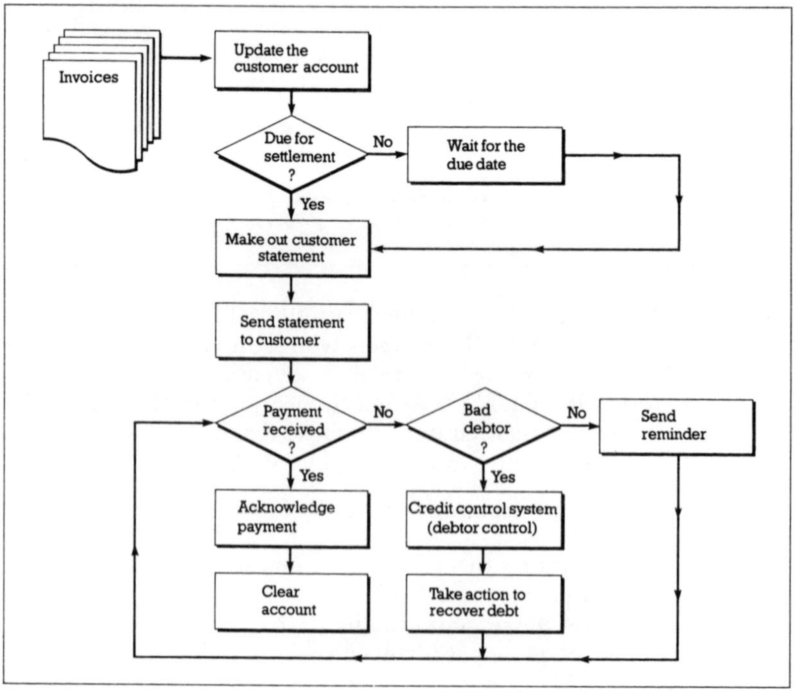

Customer accounts procedure.

Credit control

Sales policies often include the practice of giving the customer some form of discount and a period of credit.

Discounts are related to the amount purchased. Credit terms are related to the **credit-worthiness** of individual customers – the company's financial advisers decide on the amount of credit which can be extended without risk. Credit control allocates a **credit rating** to each customer and this determines the conditions of sale.

All organizations have a number of customers who incur **bad debts**. Some of these debts will never be recovered because the customer has gone out of business. This represents a loss of income to the business which efficient credit control can minimize. Other debts will be recovered in due course when the customer has been pressured to settle the account.

Poor credit control can lead to the organization having to borrow from its bank in order to meet commitments which could be covered by money owed to it.

Petty cash

A number of items and services purchased by the organization involve trivial amounts of cash and do not justify the cost of a full purchasing routine. A quantity of cash under the control of a **cashier** is kept on the premises to provide payment for these **petty cash** items.

Petty cash book A record is kept of the payments made and receipts are obtained for the purchases. Where a receipt is not obtainable, a **petty cash voucher** signed by the person receiving the cash and authorized by a responsible member of the management will serve as a record of cash issues.

Examples of petty cash expenditure are travelling expenses, cost of entertaining customers and individual items of stationery.

Activity 6

Make petty cash book entries and show the balance for the following payments:

Received cash from accounts department	£100.00
Receipt for purchase of two calculators for sales office	£ 24.00
Petty cash voucher – train fare for purchasing officer's visit to supplier	£ 3.75
Receipt for lunch, crown hotel – Mr Hicks, senior buyer of EG & T plc	£ 28.50

The basic principle of the petty cash system is that there is written proof of every item of expenditure. Petty cash books are audited on a regular basis by the accounts department to check that there are no discrepancies.

Budgetary control

Budgetary control is a plan based on the forecast activity of the organization and on the allocation of costs and expenses in relation to the objectives set as a result of the forecast.

The procedure for introducing budgetary control is related to the specific needs of the organization. A basic principle of any system is that controllable costs can be traced to the manager or supervisor of the department concerned.

To determine where control can be established
Fixed costs: those costs which have to be met regardless of the productive activity of the organization; examples: rent, rates, insurance, administration.
Variable costs: those costs which vary with the degree of productive activity of the organization; examples: manpower, materials, machine time.

Interaction between these two variables can be demonstrated with a **break-even chart**, which indicates the point at which the total cost of carrying out a specific operation is equal to some forecast return on sales or income.

Fixed cost + Variable costs = Production cost
Production cost + Profit = Selling price

The significance of the above relationships can be shown by considering the result of an increase in variable costs, which would increase production costs. This would leave the organization with the alternatives of increasing selling price or reducing profit margin.

Fixed costs are only fixed in relationship to the organization, not to the unit of production. Therefore, the amount produced will have an effect on the fixed cost per unit.

Example
Fixed cost £10 000 pa
Output per annum 1000 units
Fixed cost per unit £10 00

If the forecast output drops from 1000 to 500 units:
Fixed cost £10 000 pa
Output per annum 500 units
Fixed cost per unit £20

Activity 7

The production department of a manufacturing company has an annual fixed cost of £150 000. The sales forecast for the coming twelve months is estimated to be in the following range:
a 10 000 units
b 8 000 units
c 7 000 units.
Working to the nearest decimal point, calculate the unit fixed cost for each level of productive output.

Break-even chart

Break-even charts are a graphical representation of the relationships discussed above, using the co-ordinates of costs, revenue and output.

Charts are constructed as shown in the next diagram. For Stage 1, the first line of the graph to be entered is the **fixed cost**. Since this cost is fixed regardless of productive output, the line will be parallel with the output co-ordinate.

Constructing a break-even chart.

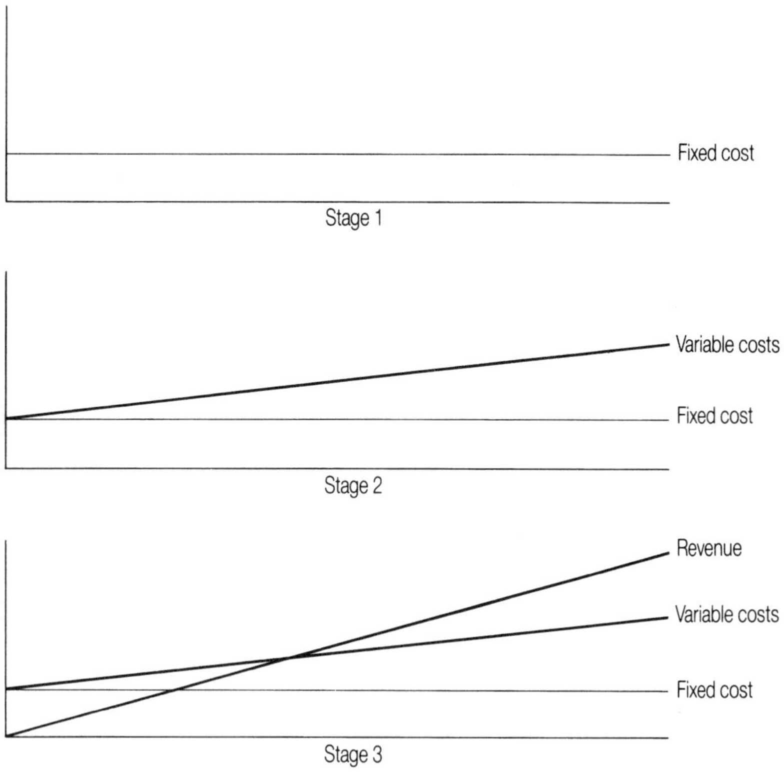

The second stage is to include the **variable costs**. Production cost is fixed cost plus variable costs; hence the variable costs must start from the fixed cost line.

The third stage is to enter the **revenue** accrued from the sale of the product.

Where the three lines on the graph intersect, the fixed and variable cost are equal to the revenue accrued. At this point, the organization will neither make a profit nor a loss: this is the break-even point.

Break-even chart.

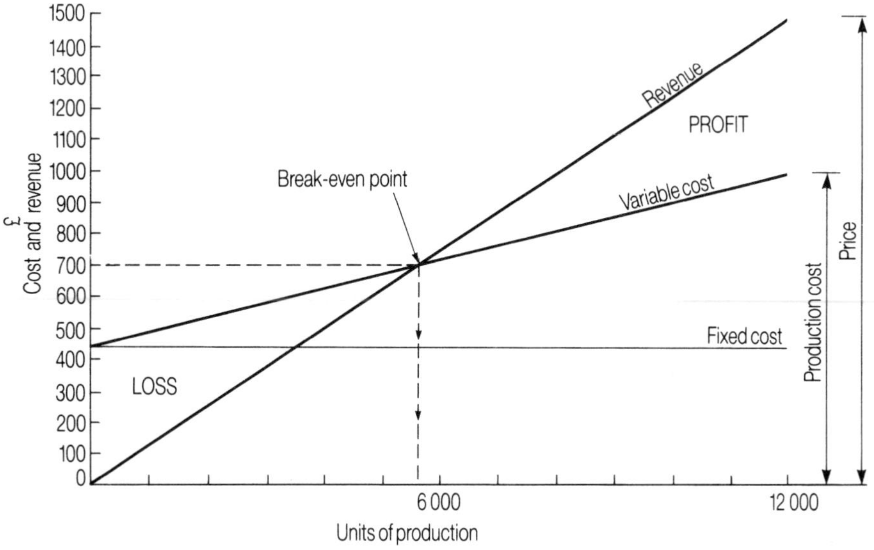

Activity 8

1 Construct a break-even chart from the following data:

Costs and revenue co-ordinate	£0 to £15 000
Units produced co-ordinate	0 to 12 000 units
Fixed cost	£450
Variable costs	£0 to £900
Revenue	£0 to £12 500

2 Calculate the units of production required to break even on cost of production.
3 Calculate the approximate change in the break-even point in the event of the units produced falling from 12 000 to 10 000.

Established the fixed cost Total fixed costs for the whole organization have to be apportioned to each department. This subdivision divides the organization up into **cost centres**, which, as we have seen, are based on departments, products or functions. Fixed costs can then be allocated to each cost centre on the basis of:

a demands made on the services provided, such as personnel, accounts, stock control, engineering;
b demands for services, such as electricity, gas, water;
c utilization of sales and administrative functions;
d calculated proportion of rent, rates and insurance absorbed in maintaining the department.

This ensures that each department bears its share of the total fixed costs. Some departments will make bigger demands for a service that others. Taking the cost of heating as an example, it would make sense to allocate a greater proportion of the heating to the cost centres covering the greatest area. Bear this point in mind when you complete the next activity.

Activity 9

EPTL are considering introducing a budgetary control system. Using the factory plan provided in Block 1, suggest how the organization could be subdivided into cost centres.

The annual rent paid by EPTL is £15 000. Assuming that this will be allocated on the basis of the demand made, apportion the fixed cost of annual rent to the production shop (to nearest £).

Establishing the variable costs The organization can start from one of two points. It can produce a **sales forecast** for the number of units of sales anticipated for the next twelve months. Alternatively it can calculate the number of units which must be sold in order to make the commitment of resources a viable proposition.

Having forecast the unit output, individual departmental managers estimate the **total variable costs** involved in meeting the forecast demand.

Example

EPTL have established the production shop as a cost centre. The forecast sales of tube has been calculated at x thousand metres of saleable product.

If variable costs for the department are manpower, machine time and materials, total variable cost is the total of:

a cost of the manpower required to produce x thousand metres
b cost of the machine time to produce x thousand metres
c cost of materials to produce x thousand metres.

Budget period Budgetary control is an application of the control loop, with feedback checking the planned activity against actual performance. Control depends upon regular feedback so that effective corrective action can be taken in good time if needed.

In order to establish this control, the **budget year** is divided into a number of **budget periods**. At the end of each budget period, the manager responsible for the cost centre will receive a **budget statement** similar to that shown in the diagram, 'Bugetary control statement', showing the **budgeted** use of resources, the **actual** use of resources and the **deviation** from the planned usage.

Activity 10

Examine the budget statement shown in the diagram and list the information the statement is providing for the manager of the cost centre.

Budget Period: ---------- Department: -----------

Fixed cost	£	Variable costs	Budgeted	Actual	Variance Plus	Variance Minus	Plus	Minus
Rent	300	Manpower	3000	3000	–	–	50	–
Rates	220	Materials	2000	2800	800	–	800	30
Lighting	200	Machines	2000	2100	100	–	100	–
Heating	180	Overtime	75	100	25	–	25	–
Administration	160							
	1060		7075	8000			975	30

Budgetary control statement.

The master budget This consists of all the subsidiary budgets, such as the sales budget, production budget and capital expenditure budget, for the established cost centres. It is the responsibility of the budget controller in the financial department.

Activity 11

We shall now look at EPTL's product planning and budgetary control.

Using the following forms for calculating the weight per metre length of extruded tube and time to complete orders, complete the following. (Round up all calculations to the nearest whole number.)

Calculating weight per metre

Type OD	Type ID	Radius outside	Radius inside	Volume cm^3 $\pi \times 100\,(0R^2 - 1R^2)$	Volume per metre	Weight per metre in grammes Volume × Density	= Weight	Weight in kilos per metre
20	18	10	9	314.2 (100 − 81)	314.2 × 19	5969.8 × 1.5	8954.7	8.96
15	13	7.5	6.5	" (56.25 − 42.25)	" × 14	4398.8 × 1.5	6598.2	6.60
10	8	5	4	" (25 − 16)	" × 9	2827.8 × 1.5	4241.7	4.30
				" (−)	" ×	× 1.5		

Calculating time to complete an order

Type	Kilos: Weight per metre	Kilos: Output per shift	Metres per shift	Metres per day	Required production	Time in days – Production ÷ Output
20/18	8.96	582	65	195	2000	2000 ÷ 195 = 10
15/13	6.6	490	74	222	5000	5000 ÷ 222 = 23
10/8	4.30	800	186	558	10 000	10 000 ÷ 558 = 18
15/12						÷ =

1 Calculate the weight per metre of the 15/12 tube.

2 Calculate the weight of material required for each of the following orders (ignore the scrap factor for this exercise).
a 2000 metres of 20/18
b 5000 metres of 15/13
c 10 000 metres of 10/8
d 2000 metres of 15/12

3 Use the information given in the example showing output per extruder towards the beginning of this block, and calculate the number of shifts you would have to schedule for each individual order in 2 above.

4 Note the following information:

Wage cost per hour for each extruder	£3.50
Machine costs per hour	£2.50
Total fixed costs for the production unit	£4.00 per hour

Prepare a simple budget statement for one week's production on the extruder producing the 10/8 order.

Wage payment

A large proportion of the working population in the UK is paid on an hourly basis. An agreed amount is paid for each hour the employee works. Some system of recording the time spent by the employee at the place of work is needed. See the example of a clock card.

Amounts paid for the working hour and the methods by which the rates are calculated are determined through bargaining between management and the employees' representatives. There may be some form of bonus or merit pay included in the rate; on the other hand, these payments may be calculated on a separate basis.

Example of clock card.

CLOCK CARD					
Name	W. JOHNSON	No			127
Dept	STORES	Week ending			7.9.19__
DAY	IN	OUT	IN	OUT	HOURS
MON	8.0	1.0	2.0	5.0	8.0
TUES	8.0	12.55	2.0	5.0	8.0
WED	7.55	1.0	1.55	5.02	8.0
THURS	8.0	1.02	1.59	5.0	8.0
FRI	8.0	1.0	2.0	5.0	8.0
SAT	9.0	1.0			4.0
SUN					
			TOTAL HOURS		
Ord. time 40	Overtime 4.0		O/time addition		6.0
			HOURS PAID		46.0
Rate £2.50	Gross wage		£		
Employee's sig.:					
Supervisor's sig.:					

Payment of wages is an activity which demands the utmost care. Nothing will upset the employee more than a mistake in a wage packet which means they are underpaid. Management will also want to be sure that they are not paying someone for hours not worked.

Data must be collected on a weekly basis for each employee in order to calculate the wage; for example:

Number of hourse worked
Agreed hourly rate
Bonus performance

Number of hours worked at standard rate
Number of hours worked at overtime rate

Standard rate is paid for the agreed working week. Payment for overtime or continuous shift working attracts a higher rate of pay as an incentive for working extra or unsocial hours.

Activity 12

A company employs its hourly paid workers on an agreed five-day working week of forty hours. Hours above forty are paid at the following enhanced rates negotiated with the union representatives:

Up to two hours' overtime in normal working week	Plus one-third base rate
Over two hours' overtime in normal working week	Plus one-half base rate
Saturdays: first two hours worked	Plus one-half base rate
Saturdays: after first two hours worked	Double base rate
Sundays: for all hours worked	Double base rate

Calculate the total earnings for an employee on a base rate of £3.00 per hour who worked:

1 A full working week: 8.00 am to 6.00 pm each day.
2 Overtime: 6.00 pm to 8.00 pm Tuesday, 6.00 pm to 7.00 pm Thursday.
3 Overtime: 9.00 am to 11.00 pm Saturday.

If you are already employed, one of the first lessons you will have learned about pay is that you do not get it all. A number of deductions are made by the employer before wages are paid. Some of these deductions are made to comply with the employment law; examples are income tax and National Health Insurance contributions. Other deductions may be made if the employee agrees: examples are contributions to a charity, contributory pension schemes and repayment of loans made by the company.

plus	Wages at base rate Hours paid at overtime rate Bonus earnings
	--------------
Gross wages:	
	--------------
less	PAYE National Insurance Red Cross contribution Pension scheme
	--------------
Net wages:	

The payroll

In order to pay the wages to the employees, the wages section must know the total amount of cash to be drawn from the bank to make up the wage packets.

A **master payroll** is made up which shows the earnings of each employee and the required deductions for each working week. The amount to be drawn from the bank will be the total net earnings of all the hourly paid employees, not the gross total earnings.

Employers will need to keep detailed records of payments made to employees in a form such as that shown in the example of a payroll sheet.

Payroll and wage payment calculations are essentially a 'number crunching' exercise. They lend themselves to electronic data processing, with the computer recording the times worked, calculating the pay, making the necessary deductions, updating the payroll and printing out the pay slips.

PAYROLL

WAGES: w.e........... Tax week no.: ....

Clock no.	Name	Hours			Rate	Gross wages		Deductions				Net wages	
		Ord	O/T	Total		£	p	Tax	NI	Pens.	Other	£	p
										Total			

Example of layout of master payroll.

PAYROLL Week no. ....
DEPARTMENT: ....

Clock no.	Name	Hours	Rate	Gross this week	Gross pay to date	Tax-free pay	Total taxable pay to date	Tax due to date	Tax due this week	Refund of tax	Nat. Ins. ded.	Other deductions	Total deductions	Net pay	Employers' Nat. Ins.	Total Nat. Ins.

Payroll sheet.

Activity 13

You are employed as a clerical assistant in the wages section of a new company which will start production in one months time. The hourly paid employees will record the time attended by clocking in on a clock card. Wages will be paid at the place of work during working hours.

Suggest a scheme which will give the company proof that each employee has received the pay due and provides for the recorded return to the cashier of any wage packets not paid.

Activity 14

EPTL has a hardship fund (made up of contributions from both management and unions) to assist employees who are in financial difficulties.

The hardship committee is chaired by the financial director and consists of representatives from accounts, production and personnel and yourself.

The fund currently stands at £2326. No further income is expected for seven months. Two applications for help are before the committee today. Divide the class into small groups, each acting as the committee. Decide what money you will allocate, if any.

Different committees will probably reach different decisions. In a session combining the groups, consider what factors affected your thinking.

Name: Dai Rees

Department: Stores

Length of service: 5 years

Mr Rees worked well and efficiently for the first nine months. His work deteriorated after Christmas and in March he took 2 months' sick leave for 'nervous debility'.

In August of that year he applied to the Fund for £100 to get his electricity re-connected. At this time it emerged that he was an alcoholic who had started drinking again during the Christmas festivities. His foreman reported that Mr Rees was taking liquid lunches and was not sharp in the afternoons. The Fund Committee awarded him £50 and extracted a promise that he would seek medical help at once.

In November of the following year Mr Rees again went sick for two months with 'nervous debility' during which time he was actually drying-out at a private clinic. When he returned to work he asked us for £180 for electricity and rent arrears which had mounted up whilst he was in hospital. His foreman reported that Mr Rees was sober and working hard. The Fund awarded him £150.

After 18 months Mr Rees made a further application for £130 to pay his gas bill. It appeared that his wife had left him two months earlier and he had resumed drinking. His foreman reported poor attendance and shoddy work. Personnel took the view that his problems would diminish now his wife had gone and recommended payment on condition he took further treatment. The Fund awarded £80.

Mr Rees has now applied for £120 for rent arrears. It appears that six months ago he acquired a common-law wife who is a very extravagant shopper. He is working well and apparently dry. Personnel take the view that if we help him now we may prevent his going back to drinking.

Application 1.

```
Name:               Julius Carrington

Department:         Computers

Length of service:  18 months

Mr Carrington is head of the computer department, a brilliant
young man who is invaluable to the company.

He is asking for help with an outstanding bill for £8000 for
school fees for his two sons at Winchester, a prestigious
public school.


Mr Carrington has got into difficulties because of the illness
of his wife, who is in hospital with a bone marrow disease.
Mrs Carrington formerly earned a great deal as a dress
designer.  They have mortgage repayments of over £1000 a month
to meet and the very considerable expense of running their
large executive residence.  Mr Carrington is having to pay a
housekeeper in the absence of his wife.  Although they had a
good income from joint earnings, they have no capital.
```

Application 2.

Case study – the country club

Introduction

An American company who are successfully established in the hotel and leisure industry in the USA are interested in extending their activities in Europe and the UK. A head office has been set up in Manchester to centralize administration, personnel, wages and salaries for the group activity in the UK. Already a number of hotels in England and Scotland have been purchased. These operate as independent units within the policy set by the parent company.

An opportunity has arisen to purchase a large manor house and 150 acres of park land in a well-known tourist area. Included in the site are a trout stream and access to a stretch of lakeside with mooring rights. The lake consists of some 20 acres of water on which sailing small craft is permitted. Fishing and boating rights are included in the sale of the propety.

The company has sent a team of experts to assess the potential of the property before making a bid to purchase. This assessment has now been completed and a preliminary report has been sent to the board at head office. A summary of their conclusions is outlined below:

Summary of design team report

The property is a manor house which has been in the hands of one family for several generations. It has come on to the market following the death of the owner in order to discharge death duties on the estate and other outstanding debts.

Preliminary negotiations with the agents and vendor indicate an acceptance price in the range of £750 000 to £1 000 000 if a quick sale could be

guaranteed. Suitably converted, the property would provide the following facilities:
1 a restaurant to seat 80 people,
2 28 double bedrooms and 7 single bedrooms for guests,
3 living accommodation for 15 staff,
4 a residents' lounge,
5 a functions room for 150 guests,
6 a lounge bar accommodating 100 people,
7 a conference suite for 50 people.

This would involve carrying out some modifications to the structure of the building, the general fabric of which is in good condition and well maintained. None of the proposed modifications would endanger the structure or alter the character of the building.

Further capital investment could provide:
1 a site for 20 luxury mobile homes for self-catering or time share holidays;
2 a site shop for the mobile home park;
3 a riding school;
4 a complex containing a swimming pool, sauna, gymnasium, four squash courts and two hard courts for tennis.

An artist's impression of the building and a site plan plus an indication of the initial costs are attached.

Summary of sports and entertainment team report

The property is situated in an agricultural area of natural beauty with no significant industrial or commercial activity within a radius of ten miles. It is not an isolated spot; a motorway is ten to fifteen minutes drive away. Popular tourist areas of mountains and seaside resorts are within one hour's drive.

A local village of some 700 inhabitants would provide the full-time and part-time staff required to run the country sport pursuits. Unemployment in the area is in the order of 24 per cent. Local inhabitants have to travel up to fifteen miles to obtain work.

The property could be developed to provide holiday facilities for the middle-class range of UK, European and US holiday-makers. Time sharing, residential and self-catering holidays could all be considered in order to make the most of the potential accommodation.

Market research indicates the need for a conference centre in the area. As the site is within thirty miles of three major industrial conurbations, it is ideally situated to meet this demand. There is also a shortage of good hotel accommodation in the area. Lack of competition has resulted in mediocre standards of service for tariffs around £45–60 per person for bed and breakfast, with à la carte dinners at £25–40

Leisure is a growing industry in the UK and this could be exploited in a number of ways to ensure all-year-round use. The sports and hotel facilities could be used as a country club; initial market research has indicated that this would attract substantial membership (500 in the first 12 months) from a catchment area of up to 30 miles radius. Similar clubs in the UK have annual fees of around £350 per member.

A site shop would be a profitable asset. The village shops are not open for seven days a week, nor do they have the opening hours that could be covered by our staff.

Summary of personnel team report

Initial estimates for the first year of operation are as follows:

Division of labour	Related Activities	Staff
Health	Gymnasium Swimming pool Sauna	8
Sport	Fishing Swimming Squash Riding	8
Hotel	Catering Restaurant Conferences Holidays Entertainment	20
Mobile homes	Hiring Site shop Site maintenance	6
Administration	Staff Marketing Purchasing Customer accounts Legal aspects Security	12
Maintenance	Building fabric Services Grounds and gardens Lake and fisheries Equipment	12
		66

The majority of the labour force could be recruited locally. A small number are currently employed as gardeners and domestic servants. Employing local labour will reduce some of the problems related to working the unsocial hours necessary in the hotel and catering industry.

A review of the local rates of pay indicates that our rates for comparable jobs would be attractive to the potential labour market.

Training facilities for the hotel, catering and leisure industry are not good. Trainees on day-release courses would have to travel thirty miles to the nearest college. This disadvantage is offset to some extent by the fact that the college has a good reputation in the industry and would ensure that our trainees met our standards.

Specialist skills in entertainment, catering, hotel management and maintenance are in short supply in the area and staff would have to be recruited on a national basis until we were able to develop and train our own employees. Staff recruited from major cities for supervisory and management posts would have no difficulty in obtaining reasonably priced property in the area.

As employment in the area is largely agricultural, with much of the work of a casual nature, labour is not highly unionized or militant. Our policy of joint consultation, our negotiation procedures and attractive conditions of service should achieve the good management/worker relationship we have elsewhere in the UK.

In view of the nature of the enterprise, requiring the interaction of a number of differing managment skills, it is suggested that a matrix structure similar to that shown in the attached diagram would provide the most efficient type of organization.

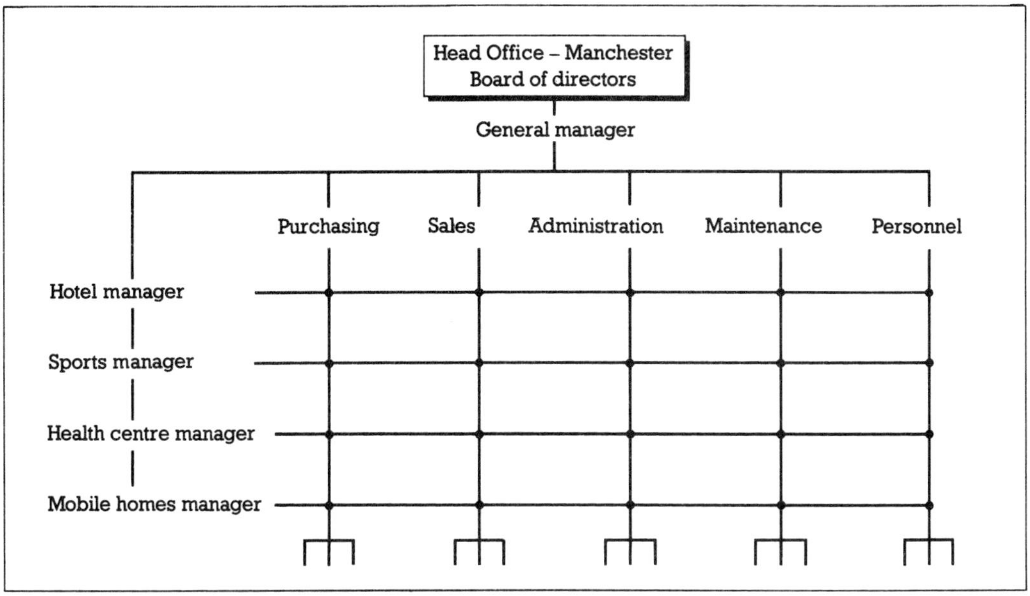

Organization structure – proposed country club.

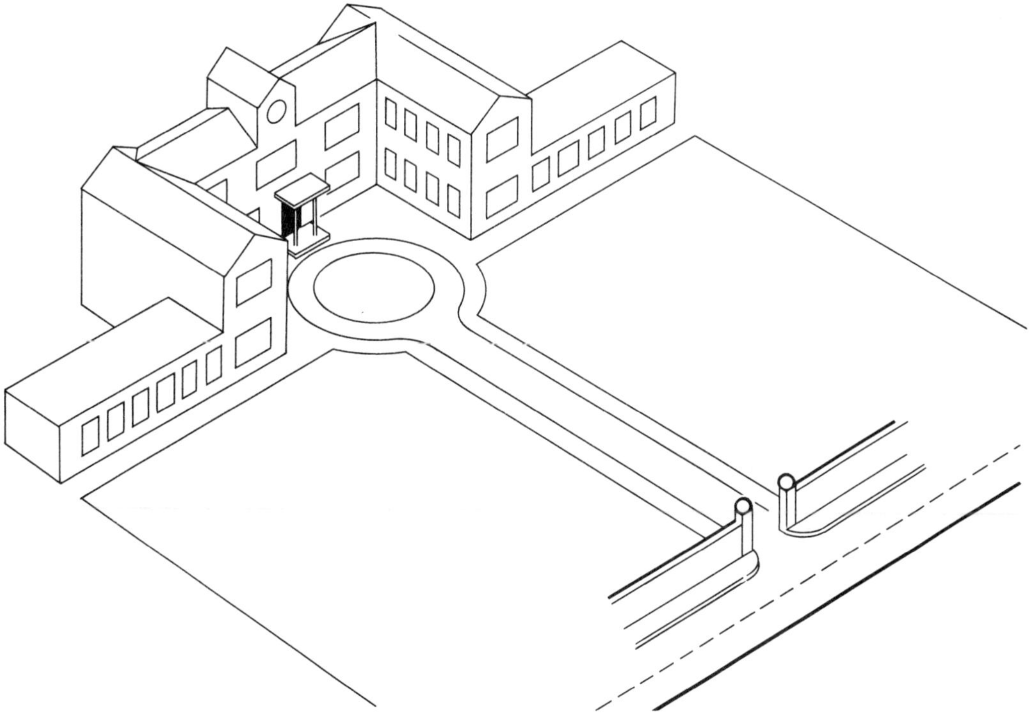

General view of building.

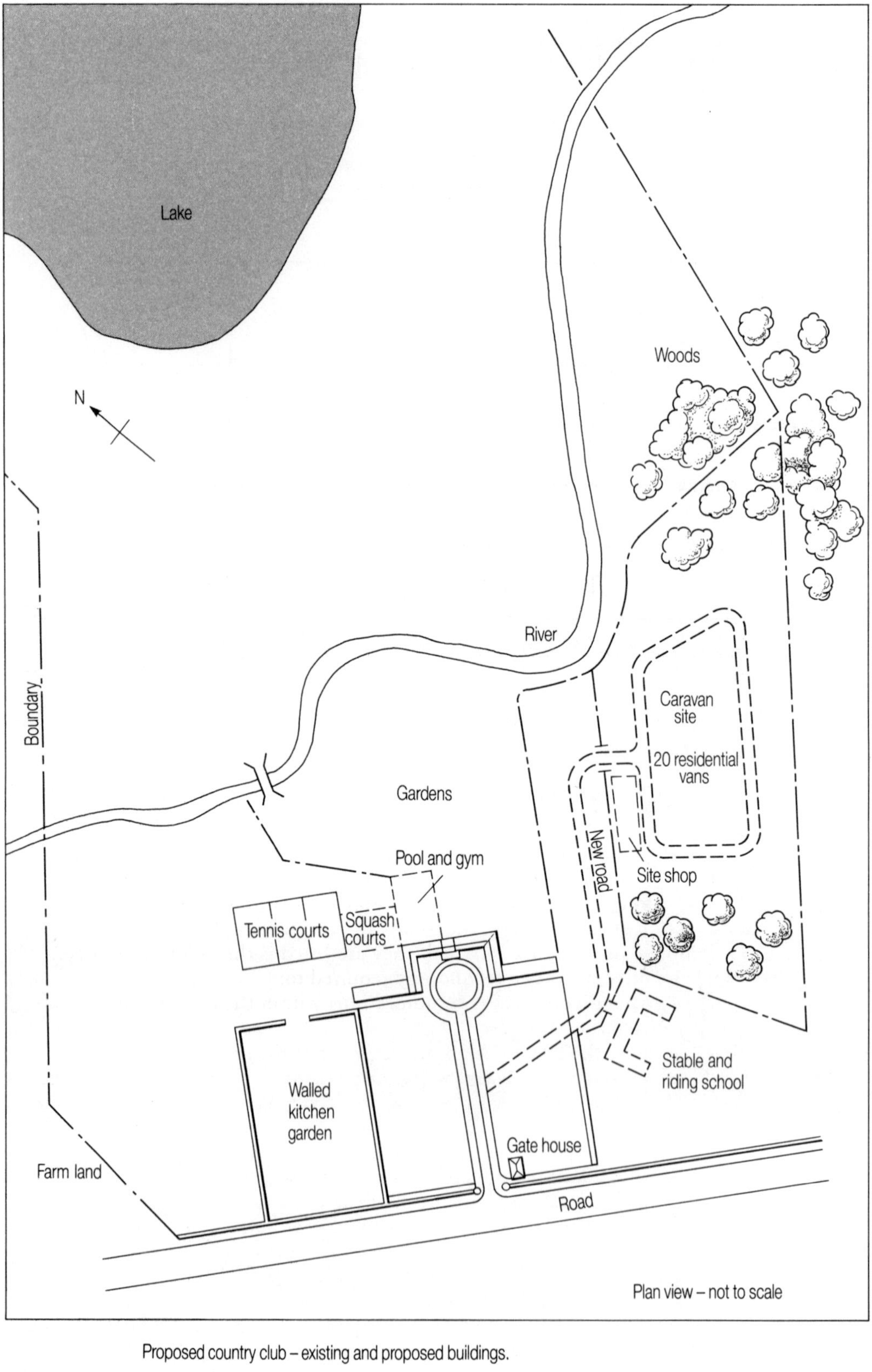

Proposed country club – existing and proposed buildings.

Projected costs.

These costs are preliminary estimates obtained from local contractors and the relevant departments in the organization. Every effort has been made to ensure that they are as accurate as possible, given the restrictions imposed by the time available to prepare this report. Past experience has shown that such estimates are accurate within the limits of plus or minus 10 per cent.

	£	
Manor house building		
Modification and renovation	600 000	
Furnishing and equipment	300 000	
		900 000
Riding stable		
Prepare site	2 000	
Buildings	5 000	
Equipment	1 000	
Stock	2 000	
		10 000
Swimming pool		
Prepare site	1 000	
Build pool	18 000	
Building fabric	15 000	
Filtration and heating equipment	4 000	
		38 000
Sauna		
Building fabric	2 000	
Equipment	1 000	
		3 000
Gymnasium		
Building fabric	18 000	
Equipment	4 000	
		22 000
Mobile home site		
Site preparation	4 000	
Purchase of vans	200 000	
Supply services	6 000	
Build shop	5 500	
		215 500
		1 188 500

Tennis courts
Two hard courts installed three years ago are in good condition

Final activity

On the basis of the initial report, the US board of directors have decided that the country club venture is a viable proposition. As a trainee in the company, you have been given the opportunity to be involved in the next planning stage. You have the following tasks to complete. (You should not assume that the order in which they are listed is the order of priority.)

1. Identify the office technology required to:
   a maintain efficient communications within the country club organization;
   b allow the country club management to maintain contact with its customers and suppliers, the UK head office and the US head office.
   You will need to show evidence of having surveyed current literature and trade magazines in the course of coming to a decision about what equipment would be most suitable.
2. Suggest a number of computer packages which could be purchased to aid administration and control of the country club.
3. Identify those areas of the country club which could be established as cost centres and list the fixed costs which could be allocated.
4. Describe the role of central and local purchasing in a business enterprise such as a country club.
5. Name the local authority departments which will have to be contacted during the planning stage of the project.

6 Outline a procedure for recruiting cleaning staff for the hotel.
7 Draw a preliminary classical organization chart for the hotel and catering staff.
8 Describe the problems which can arise out of having to co-ordinate the activities of a number of specialist managers and administrators in a matrix structure.
9 Draw up a job specification for one of the management posts shown on the matrix structure chart, and outline how the post would be advertised.
10 List the contents of a mail shot to advertise the facilities provided by the country club and produce an O and M flow chart for collating and mailing the information.
11 Suggest ways in which work study techniques discussed in this book could aid the management of the country club.
12 Plan an official opening day for 150 guests, including a VIP, and use a critical path diagram to plan the event.
13 Investigate the pros and cons of franchising activities such as the mobile home shop and the riding school.
14 Research the legal requirements of the fire regulations for this type of commercial operation.
15 Obtain information about the wage rate paid to the type of work-force required by this type of operation and estimate the weekly wage bill.
16 Briefly explain the financial problems which could arise out of inefficient stock control systems.
17 Find out what role the local Job Centre might play in the recruitment and training of staff.
18 State briefly why you consider the policy of staff development, indicated in the personnel team report, to be better than recruiting from outside sources.

Summary

Emphasised the role of cost control as an aid to preventing cash flow inbalance endangering the stability of the organization.
The working relationship between the Financial function and other department functions has been illustrated. Particular attention was drawn to the technique of Budgetary Control and the department's responsibility for the administration of wages and salaries.

Skills

Skill	*Activities in which skill is developed*
a Information gathering	1, 15
b Learning and studying	1, 5, 15
c Working with others	14, 15
d Communicating	1, 2, 4, 5, 6, 9, 10, 11, 12, 13, 14, 15,
e Design and visual discrimination	8, 13, 15
f Identifying and tackling problems	1, 5, 7, 9, 11, 12, 13, 14, 15
g Numeracy	1, 4, 5, 6, 7, 8, 9, 10, 11, 12, 15
h Information processing	2, 6, 8, 10, 11, 12, 15

Index